Van —
What a joy to serve
with you on The ECCU board!
Here is my long awaited book.
I hope you and Maxine
enjoy it.
Thanks for being my
good friend!

A
History of
Christian School
Education

A
History of
Christian School
Education

Volume One

by

Paul A. Kienel

ASSOCIATION OF CHRISTIAN SCHOOLS INTERNATIONAL

Copyright © 1998
The Association of Christian Schools International
PO Box 35097
Colorado Springs, CO 80935-3509

Subject Heading: **Religious Education – History**

Library of Congress Card Catalog Number: 98-74291

Library of Congress Cataloging-in-Publication Data

Kienel, Paul A., 1933-
  A History of Christian School Education/Paul A. Kienel
  Selected bibliography p. 379
  Includes Index
  ISBN 1-58331-019-3

Scripture taken from the New King James Version. Copyright © 1982 by Thomas Nelson, Inc. Used by permission. All rights reserved.

Printed in the United States of America

The paper used in this publication meets the minimum requirements of the American National Standard for Permanence of Paper for Printed Library Materials Z39.48, 1984.

This book is dedicated to my wife, Annie.
She has been my tireless companion
in the research and development
of this volume.
This work would not have seen the
light of day without her.
Thank you Annie. I love you!

Statements of Support
(Continued from back cover)

This distinguished study features fresh research, excellent scholarship, and a clear historical perspective. Facts and truth are the basis of this refreshing, instructive work. It is highly recommended for those who desire to know the drama and impact of the Christian school movement. *To God Be the Glory, Great Things He Hath Done.*

Byrle Kynerd, Ph.D., Superintendent
Briarwood Christian School
Birmingham, Alabama

Carefully researched and meticulously documented, Paul Kienel's *A History of Christian School Education* is a true scholarly benchmark. Paul and Annie Kienel made a year-long foray into both American and European libraries. Their findings collate previously unknown data, discern prevailing tides of religious educational thought, and humanize such giants as Luther, Calvin, and Knox.

Not only is the historical accuracy impeccable, but the content is riveting—it alternately chills the bones and elicits a hallelujah—while Kienel's warm style keeps the reader turning pages.

Virginia Kirley Leih, Ph.D., Author and English Faculty (retired)
St. Cloud State University
St. Cloud, Minnesota

It is imperative that we know and understand the roots of the high calling to which God has called us—educating children in God's truth. Paul Kienel masterfully traces the hand of God from Rome to the Reformation, giving the reader a factual but fascinating account of the development of Christian school education. This book is a must for all teachers who desire to know the riches of their "high calling in Christ Jesus."

Debbie Schindler, Administrator
Snohomish County Christian School
Mountlake Terrace, Washington

Paul A. Kienel has produced a rare book. Rare because the history of Christian schools has never been told, because it is scholarly history written and illustrated for educators and not just for scholars, and because its specific story is woven into the exciting and fascinating history of the Church.

Jack Layman, Ph.D., Professor of Educational History and Philosophy
Columbia International University
Columbia, South Carolina

Contents

Acknowledgements xi

Introduction xiii

1. The Dawn of Christian School Education 1

2. An Overview of Greek, Roman, and Jewish Education....................9
   The Diverse Educational Patterns of Greece
   The Transition from Private to State-Run Education in Rome
   Lessons from Early Jewish Education

3. The Great Transition Period 35
   The End of Pagan Education and the Rise of Christian School Education
   The Fall of the Roman Empire
   The Formation of the Catholic Church and the Emergence of the Persecuted
      Evangelical Church

4. Birth of a Religious Empire 55
   Theological and Administrative Patterns of the Catholic Church
   Forms of Education in the Religious Empire
   Stamping Out the Opposition

5. Education in the Late Middle Ages 85
   Educational Implications of the Crusades and the "Black Death"
   The Liberalization of Ecclesiastical Education
   The Rise of Catholic Universities

6. Decline of the Religious Empire...117
   Understanding Papal Power
   The Eve of the Reformation
   Reformation Martyrs

7. Martin Luther, the Great Education Reformer...........................153
   Martin Luther, the "David" Who Took On "Goliath"
   Dramatic Changes Caused by the Reformation
   Luther as the Education Reformer

8. What Luther Believed About Education 185
   How Luther's Educational Background Influenced His Views on Education
   Luther's Ideas on Education
   Lessons from Luther's Shortcomings

9. John Calvin and John Knox—the Great Church School
   Educators 211
   The Historic Setting of Calvin and Knox
   A Comparison Between the Calvin and Knox Schools
   What Calvin and Knox Wrote About Christian School Education

10. The Lesser Reformers as Educators 243
    Their Place in History
    Their Achievements in Christian School Education
    A Critique of Their Educational Philosophy

11. The Appearance and Disappearance of the Protestant
    Schools of France 265
    The Events Leading to the "Death to the Heretics" Campaign
    The Huguenots and Their Commitment to Christian School Education
    The Extirpation of All Protestant Schools in France

12. Christian Schools and the Counter-Reformation 299
    The Political and Ecclesiastical Objectives of the Counter-Reformation
    *The Forms of Christian School Education That Flourished in the Counter-
       Reformation*
    Lessons Learned

13. English Education During the Reigns of Henry VIII and
    His Children 331
    Four British Royals Who Changed the Course of English History
    The Shifting Educational Pattern of English Schools
    The Menacing Climate of Conformity

14. Just Who Were the Pilgrims and Puritans? 357
    *The Hostile Political and Ecclesiastical Environment Faced by England's
       Evangelical Believers*
    The Puritans and Pilgrims Compared
    The Pilgrims and Puritans—Catalysts for Change

Selected bibliography 379

Index 383

Acknowledgments

Martin Luther said, "I will continue to polish the truth and make it shine." There has been a great effort to ensure the accuracy of the information in this volume. I am particularly grateful to the dedicated editorial team of eleven members who carefully analyzed each chapter as it was written. I gratefully acknowledge the following individuals:

Dr. Sharon Berry	Dr. Derek Keenan
Dr. Paul Brown	Dr. Byrle Kynerd
Dr. Eugene Fadel	Dr. Jack Layman
Dr. Kenneth Gangel	Dr. Virginia Leih
Dr. John Holmes	Debbie Schindler
Mary Lee Kay	

Four staff members at ACSI headquarters deserve special recognition for their part in this project: art director Julia Evans, graphic artists Matthew Garmany and Paula Ricchi, and technical editor Mary Endres. I am also grateful for the strong administrative support of ACSI's president Dr. Ken Smitherman and vice president of operations Tom Scott. Dr. Derek Keenan, ACSI's vice president of academic affairs, has provided excellent editorial oversight and generous words of encouragement.

The members of the ACSI Executive Board have my profound gratitude for responding so favorably to my progress reports given at each of their meetings.

Two individuals from outside agencies were particularly helpful; namely, Loren Muehlius of Global Mapping International, who produced the custom maps for this volume, and researcher Cecil R. Price of Christian Information Ministries International, who found numerous texts that would not have been available to me without his assistance.

I am especially thankful to the numerous individuals and corporations that contributed funds to offset the cost of research and production of these volumes. We gratefully acknowledge the following:

Braaksma-Himmelman Construction	Paul H. Johnson, Inc.
Evangelical Christian Credit Union	Dr. James Dobson
Church Mutual Insurance Co.	IntegraColor, Inc.
Virginia Leih	Dr. Paul Brown
Gary Hess	Russell B. Sands
Sam Rosen	Debbie Schindler
Gene Yergensen	John & Wanda Summers

In preparation for this project, my wife, Annie, and I spent a full year gathering vital research materials from twenty-three libraries in the United States and nine European countries. We gratefully acknowledge the following libraries and their gracious personnel who were so willing to assist us:

United States
The Library of Congress, Washington, DC
The National Library of Education, Washington, DC
Gutman Library, Harvard University, Cambridge, MA
New England Historic Genealogical Society, Boston, MA
Massachusetts Historical Society Boston, MA
Virginia Theological Seminary Library Alexandria, VA
Dallas Theological Seminary Library Dallas, TX

Germany
Lutherhalle Library, Wittenberg

France
Bibliotheque Nationale, Paris
American Library, Nancy
The Protestant Research Library, Strasbourg

Ireland
Union College Seminary Library, Belfast

England
Bodleian Library, Oxford University
The University Library, Cambridge
The Huguenot Library, London University
The Evangelical Library, London

Scotland
Centre for Theological Study and Research, Edinburgh
New College Library, Edinburgh

Switzerland
Musée Historique de la Reformation, Geneva
University of Geneva Library

Holland
The Free University Library, Amsterdam

Belgium
Zaventem Library (Operation Mobilization)

Italy
Biblioteca-Archivio, The Vatican, Rome

Introduction

To our knowledge this is the first attempt at a complete chronological history of Christian school education. Many of the facts, therefore, in this first volume of a two-volume work will be 'headline news' to a majority of Christian school educators serving in schools around the world. I, for one, was surprised and amazed to learn that Christian school education was prominent among the early church Christians in Rome and in other cities in the Roman Empire. I was equally amazed with the findings of a turn-of-the-century historian, Adolf Harnack, who reported that "the regular method of attack in bringing the new religion into any community for the first time was through the [Christian] school."

As you read your way through this volume, you will discover as I did that Christian school education was much larger in the past than ever I dreamed it was and that we have, as a movement of Christian educators, spiritual ancestors whose exploits and heroic deeds demand our utmost reverence and gratitude. I must confess that I wept numerous times as I read and wrote about the catacomb dwellers in Rome and their school for martyrs and those amazing Waldensian Christians who for centuries provided clandestine Christian schools for their children in the rocks and caves of the Italian Alps. I was deeply moved as I wrote about John Huss, president of Prague University, who defied medieval Catholic authorities by publishing the Bible in the language of his fellow Bohemians and was burned at the stake for doing so. Until my research uncovered it, I was unaware that John Huss and his followers established hundreds of Christian schools in his homeland a hundred years before the Great Reformation in 1517. You would weep as I did when I saw Belgium's memorial to William Tyndale, who was choked and burned at the stake for translating the Bible into the English language.

I learned that the great church reformers—Martin Luther, John Calvin, John Knox, Ulrich Zwingli, and others—gave as much energy to establishing Christian schools as they gave to reforming the church. To them Christian school education and church reform were inseparable allies. Neither, they believed, could succeed without the other.

In preparation for this volume I read all or a part of 236 books and journals from twenty-three libraries in ten countries. In so doing, one quickly learns that historians write from a particular bias. I found that even Protestant historians and theologians wrote, often with eloquence, about Huss, Luther, Zwingli, Calvin, and Knox, and with remarkable historical dexterity never once mentioned the thousands of Christian schools they and their successors established as an inseparable part of their mission and ministry.

I have attempted to format the book to make it useful as a teaching tool. As a former classroom teacher, I know the usefulness of subheads and divisions within the chapters. Therefore, except for chapter 1, each chapter has three divisions with ample subheads.

Rather than giving facts of history in isolation, I have attempted to present the history of Christian school education as a connected narrative. As the historical scenes change throughout the volume, I have provided what I believe to be a suitable background of civil and ecclesiastical information to bring about greater clarity and understanding. Covering vast periods of time as I have in this work, I acknowledge that a large part of the Christian school education field remains untilled. We will leave it to future researchers and writers to reap the greater harvest of information that still abounds.

I have, as you may have, friends, relatives, and acquaintances who are of the Roman Catholic faith. Because this volume includes disturbing historical facts about the Catholic Church during the Middle Ages, I want to make clear that it is not meant as a reflection on the Catholic Church today. To its credit, the Catholic Church has changed its mind about many of its medieval practices—such as including the Bible on their Index of Forbidden Books, their grim policy of death to "heretics," and their thousand-year ban on all forms of education except ecclesiastical education, a policy that left the general population of western Europe ninety percent illiterate. It is my understanding that the Catholic Church is in the process of apologizing to the world for some of its past deeds in what the Vatican calls a "purification of memory." I will let you judge whether or not this is an adequate gesture, but it is indeed an encouraging sign.

In spite of my efforts to present you with a carefully documented work, I can hardly hope to have avoided all mistakes in interpretation of historical facts. I readily acknowledge the potential for error, and in a future edition I will gladly correct any and all errors brought to my attention.

Volume 2 of this work will begin with early American education and conclude with the modern day Christian school movement which includes, of course, the history of the Association of Christian Schools International. My advance reading and research for volume 2 reveals that American education, including almost all forms of public education, was surprisingly Christian in character up through the turn of the twentieth century. It is only in recent decades that one could characterize America's tax-supported schools as "religiously neutral" or non-Christian.

This book ends with the Pilgrims and Puritans sailing to America in 1620 and 1630 respectively. Volume 2 of this work will begin with the fascinating history of those courageous Christian believers who brought to this country the rich heritage handed down to them by their spiritual ancestors, beginning with the first-century Christians in Rome. I conclude with the insightful words of the pastor of the Pilgrims, John Robinson, who said, "There is no creature so perfect in wisdom and knowledge but may learn something for the time present—and to come—by times past." I couldn't agree more.

P.A.K.

xvi

The Dawn of Christian School Education

As Jesus spoke to a crowd at the Temple in Jerusalem, he prophesied that the historic city of Jerusalem would be totally destroyed, including the magnificent Temple itself. He said, "The days will come in which not one stone shall be left upon another."[1] Christ's prophecy was carried out in two stages. In A.D. 70 Roman Emperor Vespasian sent his son Titus and a substantial military force to Jerusalem. After a seven-month siege the city was destroyed,[2] but not at the level of destruction described in Christ's prophecy. In A.D. 132, however, under Emperor Hadrian, Jerusalem was totally demolished and plowed over. To further humiliate the Jews, the Romans built a pagan temple to Jupiter Capitolinus on the former Temple site and forced the Jews to pay an annual tax for its upkeep.[3]

The destruction of Jerusalem and the Temple brought about the great dispersion of Jewish Christian believers throughout the vast Roman Empire and the spread of the Gospel of Christ throughout the then-known world. And, as we will see, it also thrust the Christians into a pagan environment that forced them to establish Christian schools for their children. J.W.C. Wand says, "The importance of the dispersion [of the Christian Jews] for the spread of Christianity can hardly be exaggerated."[4] Historian Will Durant describes the zeal of the early church Christians:

> Nearly every convert, with the ardor of a revolutionary, made himself an office of propaganda. The roads, rivers, and coasts, the trade routes and facilities of the Empire largely determined the lines of the Church's growth. . . . "Men proclaim," said Tertullian, "that the state is beset with us. Every age, condition, and rank is coming over to us. We are only of yesterday, but already we fill the world."[5]

The popular saying "we already fill the world," referred to by North African scholar Tertullian, is an overstatement, but the growth of the early church and the enthusiasm of the first Christians were phenomenal. Speaking of those early believers, historian Pierre Marique writes:

The Church had begun in an obscure corner of the Roman Empire, as a small community of a few hundred followers of Christ, "an outcast sect of an outcast race"; at the end of the first century Christian communities were to be found in practically every province of the Empire, and by the beginning of the fourth it was evident that the Church was to be the society of the future.[6]

Thousands of Jewish and Gentile Christians immigrated to the pagan city of Rome. That city was so pagan that Petronius, a Roman governor and poet, said, "Our country is so full of divinities that it is much easier to find a god than a man."[7] The Romans had a god for every phase of Roman life. Among the hundreds of Roman gods were these:

Jupiter   - god of thunder and lightning (chief among Roman gods)
Neptune - god of the seas and rivers
Juno   - goddess of women and marriage
Mercury - god of merchants and thieves[8]
Apollo   - god of sunlight, music, and poetry
Volcanus- god of destructive fire[9]

The chief purpose of Roman religion was to gain the approval of the multiple deities so as to: (1) avert calamity, (2) read the future, (3) understand the universe, and (4) obtain personal assistance. Interestingly, Roman gods neither offered a standard for personal morality nor required acceptance of a belief statement or creed.[10] As Paul Monroe says, "The religions of the ancients had little influence on morality."[11]

Imagine the dilemma of Jewish and Gentile Christians suddenly immersed in the hostile, pagan world of Rome. Imagine the dilemma of Christian parents living in Rome with school-age children. What about their education? The Jewish Christians, especially, had been accustomed to Judaism's elementary

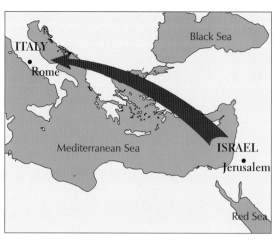

Figure 1. In A.D. 70 many first century Christians migrated from Jerusalem to Rome, a distance of approximately 1,400 miles.

schools, which met in the homes of teachers or in a synagogue. These Jewish schools had constituted a compulsory system of learning since 75 B.C. The common name for one of these schools was "The House of the Book," and indeed the books of the Old Testament Scriptures were the only texts.[12]

Figure 2. A sketch of a coin struck by the Romans commemo-rating the capture of Jerusalem. It was sent throughout the vast Roman Empire, from Mesopotamia to England, to remind the Empire's con-stituents of the folly of revolt.

The Gentile Christians living in Rome were also ill at ease with the Roman schools. In his classic work *The History of Education*, Elwood P. Cubberley wrote:

> In fact the early Christians felt but little need for the type of intellectu-al education provided by the Roman schools, and the character of the educated society about them, as they saw it, did not make them wish for the so-called pagan learning.[13]

Speaking of the early church parents living in Rome, professor of education Elmer Wilds says:

> They were bitterly opposed to the subjects taught in the pagan schools, and blamed pagan culture for the vices and corruption of pagan soci-ety. To them its literature was full of impurities; its art depicted immoralities and was associated with immoral religions; its philosophy undermined and destroyed Christian faith, because it led to trusting one's own wisdom. . . . the pagan school was the enemy of the church, and its curriculum was to be despised by all true believers. . . . Physical training, literature, art, science, rhetoric, human philosophy—all were eliminated from early Christian education; and subjects quite foreign to the later pagan schools, moral and religious training, took their place.[14]

Since Rome's pagan schools offered no moral instruction, the early Christians, in their house schools, focused on Levitical law, which con-cerned agricultural regulations and civil laws having to do with marriage and divorce. They studied other biblical laws related to health and human purity. Instruction included basic arithmetic, reading, and music built around the Psalms.[15] As we will discover, this form of instruction contrast-ed dramatically with Roman education. French historian M. Boissier wrote:

All the schools were pagan. Not only were all the ceremonies of the official faith . . . celebrated at regular intervals in the schools, but the children were taught reading out of books saturated with the old mythology. There the Christian child made his first acquaintance with the deities of Olympus. He ran the danger of imbibing ideas entirely contrary to those which he had received at home. The fables he had learned to detest in his own home were explained, elucidated, and held up to his admiration every day by his masters. Was it right to put him thus into two schools of thought?[16]

For most early church Christians the choice was obvious. They would form their own schools. Nearly two thousand years later, Christian parents around the world are faced with the same dilemma—with one important difference. Paganism in non-Christian schools today is far less obvious than it was in Rome in A.D. 100.

As the first-, second-, and third-century church continued its explosive growth, its ever-widening circle contained more and more people of influence including great scholars—men such as Ignatius of

Figure 3. The "Arch of Titus" in Rome, as it appears today, was built in celebration of the destruction of Jerusalem and the confiscation of billions of dollars in gold taken from the Jewish Temple in A.D. 70. This imposing arch is within sight of the famous Roman Colosseum, where thousands of Christians died for their faith.

Antioch, Justin Martyr of Carthage, Tertullian of Carthage, Augustine of Hippo, Origen of Alexandria, and Polycarp of Smyrna. These were among the finest minds in the Roman Empire and played a major role in solidifying the early church. William Barclay claims:

It is well to remind ourselves of the at first astonishing fact that there was no better educated group of men in the Roman Empire than the

Christian apologists. There is scarcely one of them who could not have had a scintillating career in secular life, and there were many of them who actually had such a career.[17]

These early Christian scholars often spoke out against Christian involvement with pagan teaching and pagan literature. Tertullian wrote:

What indeed has Athens to do with Jerusalem? What concord is there between the Academy and the Church? What between heretics and Christians? Our instruction comes from "the porch of Solomon," who had himself taught that "the Lord should be sought in simplicity of heart." Away with all attempts to produce a mottled Christianity of Stoic, Platonic, and dialectic composition! We want no curious disputation after possessing Christ Jesus, no inquisition after enjoying the gospel! With our faith, we desire no further belief.[18]

Like others, Jerome, an early church biblical scholar, wrote negatively about Roman literature. He asked, "How can Horace go with the Psalter, Vergil with the gospels, Cicero with the apostles?"[19] The early church sentiment toward pagan literature is clearly expressed in the Constitutions of the Holy Apostles:

VI. Abstain from all heathen books. For what hast thou to do with such foreign discourses, or laws, or false prophets, which subvert the faith of the unstable? For what defect dost thou find in the law of God, that thou shouldst have recourse to those heathenish fables? For if thou has a mind to read history, thou hast the books of the Kings; if books of wisdom or poetry, thou hast those of the prophets, of Job, and Proverbs, in which thou wilt find greater depth of sagacity than in all the heathen poets and sophisters because these are the words of the Lord, the only wise God. Do thou, therefore, utterly abstain from all strange and diabolical books.[20]

During the first 250 years the early church believers had no special buildings either for church or school.[21] Worship and educational activities took place in private homes much as they had in the old city of Jerusalem. Frank Gaebelein says:

It is evident that Christian education, though not carried on in separate schools, went on in the first-century church, which, without its unremitting faithfulness in proclaiming the Gospel and teaching the Word, would not have grown. [22]

Given the persecution of early church Christians and the uncertainty of their lives, the children of these families represented hope for the future. Those with roots in Jewish tradition believed that children were the most important people in their community. One Jewish leader said, "The world exists only by the breath of school children."[23] Jewish historian Flavius Josephus, born A.D. 37, wrote: "Our ground is good, and we work it to the utmost, but our chief ambition is for the education of our children."[24] It is not surprising, therefore, that these Jews, now Christian Jews, and other Christians in the Roman Empire were committed to Christian education.

Lewis Sherrill says that parents in the early church were admonished by New Testament teaching to provide Christian education for their children:

> When stable Christian churches begin to appear outside of Palestine, we hear almost immediately of the responsibility of Christian parents to their children. . . .
>
> About the end of the first century there were several references from various parts of the church, urging upon parents certain aspects of their duty toward their own children, and stressing the importance of their education. The implication plainly is that as soon as Christian communities began to be stable congregations into which children were born, it was recognized that children should have Christian teaching.[25]

Did Christian schools exist among the first-century Christians? Yes, they did. They may not have had the same academic patterns as Christian schools today. Their teaching and learning styles were different, but they had the same objective—to provide an education and training program for children and young people that would not offend Christ and their Christian family traditions. Literacy historian Harvey Graff writes:

> Increasingly, Christian opposition grew to the worldly, pagan culture of the Graeco-Roman world. On one hand, distinctly Christian schools began to develop; on the other, many Christians withdrew from Roman schools.
>
> A new tradition, of Christian schooling, dates from these early centuries after the birth of Christ. . . . In part, it was the tradition of *lectio divinia*: the centrality of reading the Holy Scriptures, reflecting that aspect of Christianity's origins that stressed the Word as written and building on the Greek and Roman achievements in alphabetic literacy and in its popular dissemination. At the heart of this impulse was the inseparable connection of schooling with morality, which constitutes a major legacy.[26]

That "major legacy" continues to this day only because of the ultimate sacrifice of countless martyrs who gave their lives that "schooling with morality" would still be available to us nineteen hundred years later and, hopefully, to generations of children and young people to come. We who believe in Bible-centered morality in education are profoundly indebted to the first-century Christians. Monroe writes, "The early Church enforced a moral education that was entirely new in the history of the world as well as in the history of education."[27]

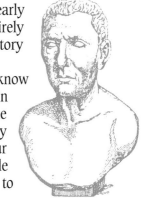

Cicero, Rome's foremost thinker, said, "Not to know what took place before you were born is to remain forever a child."[28] Over the few decades in which the modern Christian school movement has existed, many Christian school educators have been unaware that our work and our mission is a continuation of a noble legacy that spans nearly two millennia and goes back to those courageous first-century Christians. Now, however, we know that our Christian schools have roots that parallel the history of the body of Christ and predate denominations, mission boards, and

Figure 4. Cicero (106–43 B.C.) was Rome's foremost thinker.

Sunday schools. We know that Christian school education is the second oldest form of continuous education in the Western world, second only to Jewish schools.

We will return to the early church Christians and the distress and distraction of the "Great Persecution Period" to their lives and to the education and training of their children. We must now give our attention to an overview of Greek, Roman, and Jewish education. Almost every form of Western education has roots that go back to those ingenious pioneers of basic literacy and learning in the Greek, Roman, and Jewish worlds.

Endnotes - Chapter One

1 Luke 21:6. Christ's prophecy regarding the destruction of the city proper is found in Luke 21:20-24.

2 J.W.C. Wand, *A History of the Early Church to A.D. 500* (London: Methuen & Co. LTD, 1937), p. 13.

3 James Moffatt, *The First Five Centuries of the Church* (London: Univ. of London Press, 1938), p. 4.

4 Wand, p. 7.

5 Will Durant, *Caesar and Christ* (New York: Simon and Schuster, 1944), pp. 600-601. Durant's quote of Tertullian is found in Apol., XXXVII, p. 4.

6 Pierre J. Marique, *History of Christian Education*, vol. 2 (New York: Fordham University Press, 1926), p. 1. The quote "an outcast sect of an outcast race" is attributed to G.B. Adams, *Civilization During the Middle Ages*, p. 39.

7 Quoted in a footnote by Ellwood P. Cubberley, *The History of Education* (Boston: Houghton Mifflin Company, 1920), p. 82.

8 Edwin Yamauchi, "The Religion of the Romans," *Introduction to the History of Christianity*, Tim Dowley, ed. (Minneapolis: Fortress Press, 1995), p. 74.

9 H.J.R. "Roman Religion," *Encyclopaedia Britannica*, vol. 19 (Chicago: London: Toronto, William Benton, Publisher, 1929-1961), pp. 459-460.

[10] W.E.H. Lecky, *History of European Morals,* chap. 4, quoted in Ellwood P. Cubberley, *The History of Education,* p. 82. Also see L.E. Elliott Binns, *The Beginnings of Western Christendom* (London: Lutterworth Press) Lutterworth Library, vol. 29, pp. 42-43.

[11] Paul Monroe, *A Textbook in the History of Education* (New York: AMS Press, 1970, first published in 1905), p. 226.

[12] Frank E. Gaebelein, "Christian Education," *The New International Dictionary of the Christian Church,* J.D. Douglas, General Editor (Grand Rapids, Michigan: Zondervan Publishing House, 1974), p. 330.

[13] Cubberley, p. 93.

[14] Elmer Harrison Wilds, *The Foundations of Modern Education* (New York: Rinehart and Co. Inc., 1936, 1971), p. 160.

[15] C.B. Eavey, *History of Christian Education* (Chicago: Moody Press, 1964), pp. 55-56. Also see Linus Brockertt, *History and Progress of Education* (New York: Barnes and Burr, 1860), p. 59.

[16] M. Boissier, *La Fin du Paganisme,* vol. 1, p. 200. Quoted in Cubberley, p. 93.

[17] William Barclay, *Educational Ideals in the Ancient World* (Grand Rapids, Michigan: Baker Book House, 1974), p. 210. Quoted in Kenneth O. Gangel and Warren S. Benson, *Christian Education: Its History and Philosophy* (Chicago: Moody Press, 1983), p. 85.

[18] *Tertullian Against Hermogenes.* Quoted in Gangel and Benson, p. 85.

[19] Gaebelein, p. 331.

[20] The Apostolic Constitutions VI quoted in Ellwood P. Cubberley, *Readings in the History of Education* (Boston: Houghton Mifflin Company, 1920), p. 54, no. 41. This is a collection of sources and readings to illustrate the development of educational practice, theory, and organization.

[21] Michael A. Smith, "Spreading The Good News," *Introduction to the History of Christianity,* p. 81.

[22] Gaebelein, p. 331.

[23] Cited in Barkley; quoted in Gangel and Benson, p. 86.

[24] *Josephus Against Apion,* 1. 12.; quoted in Gangel and Benson, p. 86.

[25] Lewis Joseph Sherrill, *The Rise of Christian Education* (New York: The Macmillan Co., 1944), pp. 158-159.

[26] Henry J. Graff, *The Legacies of Literacy* (Bloomington and Indianapolis: Indiana University Press, 1987), p. 30.

[27] Monroe, p. 226.

[28] John Briggs, "God, Time and History," *Introduction to the History of Christianity* (Minneapolis: Fortress Press, 1995), p. 14.

Illustration Sources

Figure 1   *Map* - Global Mapping International, Colorado Springs, CO.

Figure 2   *Coin* - Used by permission of Thomas Nelson Publishers, Inc.

Figure 3   *Arch of Titus* - Photo by Author (PBA).

Figure 4   *Cicero* - M. Tullius, included in Ellwood P. Cubberley, *Readings in the History of Education* (Boston: Houghton Mifflin Company, 1920), p. 37.

CHAPTER

2

700 B.C.—TIME PERIOD—A.D.300

An Overview of Greek, Roman, and Jewish Education

In this brief overview of Greek, Roman, and Jewish education, you will discover that the objective of each educational program clearly dictated its patterns of teaching and learning. Each program's objectives were shaped by religion, political structures, economic conditions, family traditions, community culture, and to some degree by political leaders.

The Greeks, aside from their preoccupation with their gods and their integration of multiple deities into the curriculum, followed patterns of pedagogy, especially in Athens, that are seen in nearly every form of education today. The three divisions of chapter 2 are:

1. *The Diverse Educational Patterns of Greece*
2. *The Transition from Private to State-Run Education in Rome*
3. *Lessons from Early Jewish Education*

As a preamble to this study, it is essential to understand the great importance of the Greek alphabet and the Greek language. Literacy historian Harvey Graff claims the Greek alphabet was invented in the mid-seventh century before Christ. He agrees with those who say, "This is the alphabet that conquered the world." He explains:

> **The Greek alphabet, the first in the West to allow**

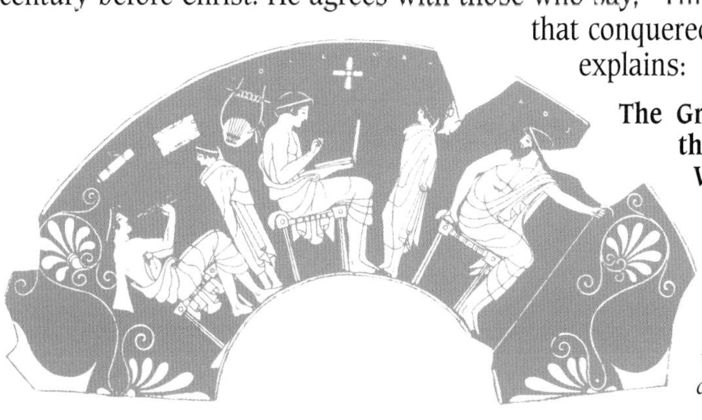

Figure 1. Athenian grammar and music school scene from a vase painting, sixth century B.C.

full literacy, was created only after ca. 700 B.C.E., and only in Greece; several hundred years were required for it to lead to literacy in a mode recognizable to us. The Greek alphabet reduced syllables to acoustic components, distinguishing vowels from consonants and, thus, creating an efficient reading instrument. Only then was the transition from restricted, elite literacy to full, popular literacy possible.[1]

In time, the Greek language became the cross-cultural, universal language of choice for all people, east and west in the Mediterranean world. Consequently, it was an inspired choice that led early church fathers to select Greek as the language for the Old and New Testaments.[2] That important choice greatly facilitated the rapid dissemination of the Gospel throughout the Roman Empire.

1. The Diverse Educational Patterns of Greece

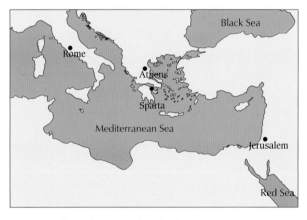

Figure 2. The educational patterns established by Sparta, Athens, Rome, and Jerusalem have shaped almost every form of education in the Western world.

Greece is located east of the long boot of Italy, separated from it by a hundred miles of the Ionian Sea. Most of the Greek Islands surrounding the mainland of Greece are on its east side, like jewels nestled in the Aegean Sea. Greece, of course, is the birthplace of democracy. Theirs was a direct form of democracy, not a representative government, and not all their city-states participated. While formally it was a government "by the people," it was not government by *all* the people. Women and slaves were not participants. It was a "for men only" government. Slaves were held in low regard, and as H.G. Good points out, they had no political rights:

> In Sparta and Athens . . . the slaves were far more numerous than the citizens. Some of them were owned by the state; and their lot, under this public exploitation, was much worse than that of the privately owned and, especially, the domestic slaves. None of them had any

political rights; and they usually received no education, although, because they could be used as writers and as merchants, there were exceptions to this rule. But they were after all slaves, and slavery corrupts both the master and the slave.[3]

We will limit our study to the Grecian city-states of Sparta and Athens. The contrast between the two will become immediately apparent.

SPARTA

The phrase "spartan conditions" evokes images of a lifestyle that is austere, simple, strict—lacking luxuries of any kind. It is with good reason that the phrase "spartan conditions" is often used to describe such a lifestyle. In nearby Athens, the aim of education was to prepare boys for public life as citizen-statesmen, but the purpose of a Spartan education was to prepare young men for military service and to subordinate all males to the state. Education in Sparta was strictly a function of government and existed only to serve the state's interest. When a man reached age thirty, his marriage was arranged by the Spartan government, and all children born to him were considered property of the state. A child's mother was a "state nurse," and her duty was to raise the "state's child" in a manner approved by the state.[4]

Plutarch, a Greek who lived in Rome as a diplomat (A.D. 46–120), wrote the following about Spartan education in a description of the "glorious work" of Sparta's foremost lawgiver, Lycurgus:

> It was not left to the father to rear what children he pleased, but he was obliged to carry the child to a place called *Lesche,* to be examined by the most ancient men of the tribe, who were assembled there. If it [the child] was strong and well proportioned, they gave orders for its education, and assigned it to one of the nine thousand shares of land; but if it was weakly and deformed, they ordered it to be thrown into the place called Apothetae, which is a deep cavern near the mountain Taygetus; concluding that its life could be no advantage either to itself or to the public, since nature had not given it at first any strength or goodness of constitution. [5]

The purpose of Spartan "schooling" was to prepare students not for personal independence and the ability to make a living, but rather for a life of service to the state:

> Its aim was to rear a nation physically invincible, capable of enduring hunger, thirst, torture, or even death without flinching; a people unequaled in military skill, and with absolute devotion to the state.[6]

Student discipline was harsh in Sparta, as indeed it was in Athens and Rome—but in Sparta it was more extreme. Aristotle was critical of Sparta's educational system, saying the discipline was "brutal."[7] Professor Wilds agrees:

> Discipline was most severe and cruel. Corporal punishment was used both for moral delinquencies and for mental inattention and lack of alertness. Every grown citizen was expected to punish any boy caught in the act of violating one of the rules of proper conduct, and fear of public disapproval was used as a strong motivating influence. Emulation and rivalry also were used extensively as means of stimulating learning.[8]

The pressure to demonstrate courage and endurance was so intense that boys volunteered to participate in the annual flogging contest that took place at the altar of the goddess Artemis Orthia. The beatings and scourgings were so severe that many boys died. There seemed, however, to be no lack of volunteers.[9] The winner, the boy who was flogged the longest without expiring, was greatly honored.

With reference to Spartan education, Plutarch said, "As for learning they had just what was absolutely necessary."[10] Basic literacy however—reading, writing, and arithmetic—was not regarded by Spartan "educators" as "absolutely necessary." Education historian Eby writes:

> The lack of intellectual training was the dark side of Spartan culture. Spartans had no interest in letters and taught neither reading nor writing. Happily, these primary arts were not wholly forbidden, and some learned them privately. It is quite certain, however, that very few of the citizens were ever able to read. The bare elements of mental arithmetic were acquired, but even for this they had little use. . . . Spartan education produced not a single artist, not a philosopher, not a dramatist, in fact not a single man of genius, nor indeed any outstanding contribution to higher civilization. Sparta was the ideal realization of primitive communism, and of the effective education of the military state.[11]

Spartan boys were trained to listen intently to the war stories of the old soldiers and repeat them back succinctly and precisely. Their short, pithy answers were known as "laconic wit."[12] One of the better known writers of Greek history, K.J. Freeman, wrote about a Spartan's short "laconic" responses:

> Long speaking and lengthy meditation he regarded with contempt, for he preferred deeds to words and thoughts, and the essence of a situation could always be expressed in a single sentence. This Spartan conception of citizenship fixed the aim of Spartan education. Daily

hardships, endless physical training, perpetual tests of pluck and endurance, were the lot of the Spartan boy. He did not learn to read or write or count; he was trained to speak only in single words or in the shortest of sentences, for what need had a Spartan of letters or of chattering? His imagination had also to be subordinated to the national ideal: his dances, his songs, his very deities, were all military.[13]

Spartan teenage boys were taught to sing songs in praise of manly virtue, war songs, and to chant the laws of the state. Twenty-year-old supervisors of the boys, called *Irens*, would spontaneously put questions to them such as: "What conduct deserves the best honor? Who is the best man in the city?" and "What do you think of this or that action?" If the answers were not concise and well formulated, the *Irens* would punish the boys by biting their thumbs.[14]

This narrowly focused Spartan "education" continued for seven hundred years with little change. Plutarch wrote:

> The citizens were for centuries obedient, frugal and self-denying. Like bees, they acted with one impulse for the public good. . . . They were possessed with a thirst for honour, an enthusiasm bordering upon insanity, and had not a wish but for their country.[15]

The "schools" of Sparta stood in direct contrast to the schools of Athens just two hundred miles away.

ATHENS

The city-state of Attica, best known for its capital, Athens, is smaller than the state of Rhode Island. In its most prosperous years it boasted a population of 200,000 inhabitants, including 70,000 slaves. The city-state was blessed economically with rich silver mines worked, of course, with slave labor. The citizens of Sparta, Athens, and Rome were all addicted to a life of ease made possible by slaves captured in the course of many wars.

Our Athens study will focus on the fifth and fourth centuries B.C. It was a prosperous period called the Golden Age of Greece, when Athens became the intellectual, cultural, and political capital of the world.[16]

Education in Athens, as in its neighboring cities, was limited to boys. Girls were trained at home by their mothers in how to manage a household. The goal of education was to make male citizens fit for full participation in their form of government, which was a direct democracy. The following passage is an excellent description of Athenian democracy:

> The citizens gave their attention solely to conducting the affairs of state, and to war. There was civil equality among them, and they filled most offices by lot. The government was, therefore, not a representative

democracy as we practice democracy today. But it was a direct democracy in that every citizen took part on an equal footing in the conduct of government, a circumstance that contributed greatly to the stimulation of social intelligence. In addition to attending public assembly, every citizen served on the jury, acted as a judge, and fought as a soldier. Moreover, he could hold any of the various offices from the most petty to the most exalted. Consequently, he had to be free from obligations at all times in order that he might give his undivided attention to the affairs of state.[17]

The Western tradition of preparing an educated citizenry to perpetuate democracy or "government by the people" clearly has its roots in Athenian ideals.

Formal education in Athens began at age seven. Families that could afford slaves had a *pedagogue,* or male slave, whose daily responsibilities included accompanying the boys in the family to school and punishing them if they were involved in any misconduct. The following is a description of a student's pedagogue:

> The pedagogue was an educational agent peculiar to the Athenians. He awoke the boy from sleep, got him ready and accompanied him to and from school. In families where there were several boys, he attended all. He carried the boy's tablet, lyre, and other school apparatus. He made him study his lessons, and helped him recall what he had learned. Another function was that of correcting his pronunciation and insisting upon proper habits of articulation, for the Athenian was meticulous about correct speech. In harmony with the Greek view of education as

Figure 3. The Parthenon in Athens (temple to the goddess Athena) is one of the architectural wonders of the world. It was the epicenter of Greek paganism.

supervision, the pedagogue followed the boy and never let him get out of his sight. Freeman suggests that he was, "a mixture of nurse, footman, chaperon, and tutor."[18]

PRIVATE EDUCATION

All schools in Athens, unlike those in Sparta, were tuition-funded private schools. The boys would typically attend three different elementary schools at three different locations—all the more reason for the pedagogue! Each school was specialized and ungraded. The first school of the day was "the letters school" for reading, writing, and basic arithmetic. The second school was "the music school" where students studied lyric poetry and learned how to play the seven-stringed lyre. The third school was "the gymnastic school" or *palaestra.* The typical school day was from daybreak to sundown.[19]

Figure 4. Plato (429-348 B.C.), was a friend and student of Socrates. (Bust of Plato, Vatican Museums, Vatican State.)

The curriculum was more complex than it may at first appear. Perhaps the best authority on education in Athens is the famous Greek philosopher Plato (429-348 B.C.), founder of the Academy, the world's first university. The following is an extract from his dialogue *The Protagoras:*

> Education and admonition commence in the first years of childhood and last to the very end of life. Mother and nurse and father and tutor are quarreling about the improvement of the child as soon as ever he is able to understand them; he cannot say or do anything without their setting forth to him that this is just and that is unjust; this is honourable, that is dishonourable; this is holy, that is unholy; do this and abstain from that. And if he obeys, well and good; if not, he is straightened by threats and blows, like a piece of warped wood. At a later stage they send him to teachers, and enjoin them to see to his manners even more than to his reading and music; and the teachers do as they are desired. And when the boy has learned his letters and is beginning to understand what is written, as before he understood only what was spoken, they put into his hands the works of great poets, which he reads at school; in these are contained many

admonitions, and many tales, and praises, and encomia of ancient famous men, which he is required to learn by heart, in order that he may imitate or emulate them and desire to become like them.[20]

As Plato noted, Athenian parents sent a son to school "to see to his manners even more than his reading and music." According to Eby and Arrowood, the aim of education was this:

> . . . to produce a young man who would be charming in person and graceful in manners, a beautiful soul in a beautiful body, though as yet they scarcely distinguished the soul from the body. To them the beautiful and the good were identical. . . . Through their system of physical training they aimed to produce beautiful figure, artistic posture, whether standing or seated, and graceful movement. In walking the streets, on entering a room where older men are seated, and in every activity and relation, behavior must be refined and appropriate. The highly sensitive Athenians were offended by every act that was inartistic, clumsy, or awkward. The boy or youth remained much of the time in a statuesque position. If seated, he must not cross his legs, for such a posture was fitting only for slaves. When walking in the streets, one hand must be kept hidden under his mantle. By many such rules the youth was habituated to well-ordered behavior.[21]

Clearly, Athenian education had as much to do with the body as with the mind. Athenians were also concerned about character training, at least character training as defined by Athenian standards. Freeman writes:

> The training of character was before all things the object of Hellenic (classic Greek) education; it was this which the Hellenic parents particularly demanded of the schoolmaster. So strongly did they believe that virtue could be taught, that they held the teacher responsible for any subsequent misbehavior of his pupils.[22]

Intelligent and gifted as they were, Athenians were not even close to biblical standards of personal morality. Historian S.S. Laurie declares they were "light-minded and frivolous, easily swayed hither and thither, vain, . . . shallow, . . . talkative, untruthful, scheming, and pleasure-loving, with a strong tendency to licentiousness."[23] On the same theme Eby and Arrowood write: "The Athenians were vain, shallow and temperamental, and incapable of a deep sense of obligation to any supreme moral law."[24]

A student's "proper behavior," at least "proper" in the classic Greek tradition, was closely monitored and supervised by the family pedagogue and the school teacher, both of whom were accountable to the parents for a youngster's deportment in public places and did not hesitate to flog or otherwise punish a boy if necessary. Student punishment in Athens was severe, though not on the scale of punishment in Sparta. The eminent British historian Arthur Leach describes a Greek mother who obviously does not have the luxury of a man-servant pedagogue to give oversight to her wayward son:

> A mother takes her boy to the grammar school and asks the school-master to give him a good flogging. He has stripped the very roof off her house by his losses, gambling at odd-and-even and knucklebones, while his writing-tablet lies neglected in a corner, and he says his repetition at the rate of a word a minute. The master, nothing loth, brings out his leather strap. The boy is hoisted on the back of another, with two others to hold his hands and legs, and the strap is applied till the boy is "as mottled as a water-snake," while the mother still cries, "give it him, give it him," and threatens him with gag and fetters. We can hardly imagine the Athenian boy of the age of Pericles and Socrates being thus flogged into the service of the Muses and threatened with the treatment of a slave. But this method became the usual one.[25]

At the urging of Plato, the academic level of secondary education was elevated beyond "body beautiful," music, and art, which had been the early Athenian pattern for adolescent boys. Plato advocated more advanced studies in math and science, which required teachers with a higher level of training. It is assumed that Plato's university, The Academy, was the principal teacher training institution.

The age level of Athenian secondary students was thirteen through sixteen. Only a few were given the advantage of a continuing education. Secondary teachers, referred to as masters, were private, independent instructors who were paid by student fees. Their range of subjects included technical grammar, exposition and criticism of the poets, rationalizing the myths concerning the Greek gods, rhetoric, composition, voice culture, geometry, arithmetic, shorthand, horsemanship, and military tactics.

ORIGIN OF THE SEVEN LIBERAL ARTS

The Academy of Plato and the Lyceum of Aristotle constituted the principal sources of higher education in Athens. Together they forged a circle of knowledge that later became known as the Seven Liberal Arts, namely, grammar, rhetoric, dialectic, arithmetic, geometry, astronomy, and music as science.[26]

Thomas Davidson summarizes Greek education as follows:

> The entire period was one of great intellectual activity, with probably a higher average of intellectual attainment than has ever been reached by any people, certainly a period unsurpassed in its intellectual products.

The mental vigor of the entire people was stimulated, their intellectual horizons were broadened, and the content of their thought was much enriched.[27]

HISTORIC FIGURES

Greek education produced numerous historic figures whose achievements are copiously studied to this day. A few of the better known are:

PERICLES   (490–429 B.C.) Statesman — Pericles was the ruler of Athens during the construction of the Parthenon, a pagan temple to the goddess Athena. He promoted Athenian democracy and made special provisions for the poor to see Greek plays and to hold public office. It is said that he held friend and foe "spellbound" with his eloquence.

SOCRATES   (469–399 B.C.) Philosopher — Socrates' wide range of interests included metaphysics, logic, aesthetics, ethics, meteorology, botany, zoology, geology, and medicine. A great intellectual though he was, he did not leave a legacy of written material. Others wrote for him. His lectures disturbed civic leaders because he raised a "climate of doubt" about established theories and certain Greek mythologies. He was forced to drink deadly hemlock following his condemnation by the Athenian city fathers, who believed he was corrupting the city's youth.

Figure 5. Socrates (470–399 B.C.)

PLATO   (429–348 B.C.) Philosopher and Educator—Plato was the founder of The Academy, the world's first university, and the author of *The Republic*, Plato's dream of the ideal state. He was a student and friend of Socrates.

ARISTOTLE (384–322 B.C.) Philosopher—A student of Plato. He founded a school for scholars called a Lyceum in Athens and served as personal tutor to the future Alexander the Great.

MENANDER (343–291 B.C.) Poet Menander's poetry made Athenian life known throughout the civilized world. He was the chief poet of the "Greek New Comedy."

EUCLID (Circa 350–250 B.C., exact birth and death dates unknown) A mathematician, Euclid was a major figure in the world of geometry. He is best known for his work *The Elements* in thirteen volumes. He studied at Plato's Academy in Athens.[28]

Figure 6. Aristotle (384–322 B.C.) is known for the seven divisions of liberal arts, grammar, rhetoric, logic (trivium) and arithmetic, geometry, astronomy, and music (quadrivium). (Bust of Mercury, believed to be Aristotle, Vatican Museums, Vatican State.)

A PUBLIC DUTY

From age sixteen to eighteen, a boy of Athens came under state supervision in a premilitary program at the public gymnasium. His two instructors were a state drillmaster, called a *paidotribe,* and a state moral censor, called the *sophronist.* When he had completed his two years of rigorous military training, he spent the next two years in full-time military service, usually as a guard on a frontier post.[29] Prior to his military service he took a pledge known as the Ephebic Oath:

> I will never bring reproach upon my hallowed arms, nor will I desert the comrade at whose side I stand, but I will defend our altars and our hearths, single-handed or supported by many. My native land I will not leave a diminished heritage but greater and better than when I received it. I will obey whoever is in authority and submit to the established laws and all others which the people shall harmoniously enact. If anyone tries to overthrow the constitution or disobeys it, I will not permit him, but will come to its defense single-handed or with the support of all. I will honor the religion of my fathers. Let the gods be my witnesses, Agraulus, Euyalius, Ares, Zeus, Thallo, Auxo, Hegemone.[30]

At the age of twenty the young, well-educated Athenian became a citizen of Athens and took his place among the civil leaders of the community as a privileged free man. As previously mentioned, the women and slaves of Athens were not so privileged.

In 359 B.C. the Macedonians gained control of the Greek city-states, including Athens.[31] Later, in 86 B.C. the city was taken by Roman general Sulla, and suddenly Athens became a part of the Roman Empire. We will see, however, that many of the educational patterns of the Athenians were quickly adopted by their conquerors.

> Almost invariably the conquest of one people by another has resulted in the imposition of the culture of the stronger upon the weaker. But in the conquest of central Greece by the Macedonians and the Romans, precisely the opposite effect took place. By virtue of its superior culture, conquered Greece was enabled to impose its ideals, its language, and its institutions upon all the known world.[32]

2. The Transition from Private to State-Run Education in Rome

The city of Rome lies on the Tiber River, seventeen miles inland from the central west coast of the Italian peninsula. A transition from Athens to Rome is well described by Davidson:

> Passing from Athens to Rome is as passing from poetry to prose, from an artists' picnic to a business house; from a people seeking to make the present beautiful and to enjoy it rationally and nobly, to a people that subordinates present enjoyment to future gain; from a people that lives by reason to a people that lives by authority.[33]

What Rome lacked in Grecian finesse it made up in skills of administration and the practice of law. The great Parthenon in Athens notwithstanding, Rome far exceeded Greece in architecture and engineering. While Greece impacted the world through its language and literature, Rome conquered the world through its organizational skills and its military might.

Our survey of Roman education will cover the period beginning 100 B.C. through A.D. 300. It should be noted that the midpoint of this period and a few years beyond was the zenith of Roman education.[34] It will be evident from the outset that Rome drew basic educational and training concepts from the traditions of both Sparta and Athens. Dr. Wilds documents a gradual shift from the emphasis on personal virtues characteristic of early Roman education to an emphasis on value-free education during the declining years of the Roman Empire.

> Early Roman education was distinctly a training for practical life. Its aim was the development of the good citizen, the good soldier, the good worker . . . the man possessed of all the virtues essential for the exercise of his rights and the discharge of his duties and obligations. The virtues chiefly prized and inculcated were piety, obedience, manliness, courage, bravery, industry, honesty, prudence, earnestness, sobriety, dignity, fortitude, and gravity. . . .The aim of later Roman education was mainly . . . intellectual development, language ability and success in public speaking and debate. . . .[35]

As mentioned in chapter 1, Roman education from 100 B.C. to A.D. 300 and beyond was woefully short on moral purity, honesty, and other fundamental virtues essential to a civil society. Therefore, it is not surprising that the new immigrant Christians found the Roman lifestyle awash in gross immorality, dishonesty, theft, and human cruelty. British historian Binns describes why the shift in values occurred:

> Education had largely lost its ideals. In the best period of Roman life, instruction had been begun and continued in the home under the eyes of the parent, and there had been a full recognition of the importance of moral influences and an austere environment. The basis was largely legal; Cicero learnt the Twelve Tables as a boy. But the growth of Greek influences, with their emphasis upon rhetoric, had an unfortunate effect and tended to make education superficial and purely literary. The pupil was only fifteen when he went to the school of Rhetoric, the great aim of which was to produce orators and men of the world. There he learned that form was more significant than matter, or even than truth: that the chief concern of the orator was to make a good impression and to serve the interests of his party or client.[36]

The law of the Twelve Tables was at the center of early Roman education much the same as the Bible is the moral foundation for Christian school education. The major emphasis of the Twelve Tables was the various aspects of civil law such as judicial proceedings, inheritance laws, property rights, and marriage laws prohibiting intermarriage of the two classes of Roman citizens. The most startling feature of the Twelve Tables was Table Four, which reads:

TABLE IV. The Rights of a Father.

1. Provisions as to the immediate destruction of monstrous and deformed children.
2. Relating to the control of a father over his children, the right being given him, during their whole life, to scourge them, imprison, keep rustic labor in chains, or sell or slay, even though they may hold high office.

3. Three consecutive sales of a son by a father finally releases him from his father's control.[37]

What a contrast Table Four is to words of the Apostle Paul, "Fathers, do not provoke your children to wrath, but bring them up in the training and admonition of the Lord."[38] A father's rights as practiced in early Rome understandably would not be acceptable in the current climate of human rights.

A DECLINE IN ROME'S MORAL LAW

The excessiveness of such Roman laws set the stage for a pendulum swing to a more permissive environment. Even a revered Roman senator such as Marcus Cato the Elder, later called "Cato the Censor,"[39] could not hold this transition in check. Cato was concerned about the great influx of educational ideas pouring in from Greece. He said, "Believe me, the Greeks are a good-for-nothing and unimprovable race. If they disseminate their literature among us, it will destroy everything."[40] Cato had good reason to be concerned about Greek education. In the years just prior to the capture of Greece by the Romans, Greek education had lost its moral teeth. Moral instruction had all but vanished. Historian Eby says, "The moral rottenness of their civilization is beyond description."[41] Although Cato pushed two laws through the Roman senate to impede Greek influence, his laws did little to stem the tide of moral decline throughout the Roman Empire, which by this time encompassed all countries of the then-known world.[42]

A new unstructured style of education came to Rome by way of newly vanquished Greeks involuntarily migrating to Rome as slaves for the upper-class Roman families. Many Greek slaves became tutors or *custos,* the Roman equivalent of Greek pedagogues, for the children of Rome's upper class. Thus, gradually, the ideas of Greek education drifted into Rome's broad system of private education. Much to the consternation of Roman senator Cato, Greek instructors, slaves though they were, "poured into Rome" to serve as elementary and secondary teachers.[43] Paul Monroe writes, "Never before, perhaps never at any time, has one people attempted to appropriate so thoroughly the intellectual life of another."[44] Obviously, "captive Greece led captive her rude conqueror."[45]

Rome's aforementioned organizational ability led to the development of a widespread system of private schools.

> Schools were private institutions in this period. . . . The Roman genius for organization produced a degree of uniformity which permits us to call this the first organized system of schools with three clearly marked out levels, the elementary, secondary, and higher. In Greece, the organization of secondary education was vague and indefinite; and the university

was a chance and customary grouping of students and professors. At Rome the institutions were more clearly outlined. Elementary education began about the age of seven under the *ludi magister*, the master of the play school, who taught boys reading, writing. . . .[46]

QUINTILIAN

The Roman idea of elementary education as a "play school" springs from the educational philosophy of Rome's foremost education thinker, Marcus Fabius Quintilian (A.D. 35–96). In his retirement Quintilian wrote his best known work, *De Institutio Oratoria* (on the education of the Orator).[47] While true to the Roman emphasis on oratory, Quintilian had extremely different ideas about elementary education. Given the harsh educational methods often employed by traditional Greek and Roman educators, Quintilian's ideas were radical indeed. Later they would be particularly appealing to the liberal minds of the Renaissance period. Freeman Butts writes, ". . .when the *Institutio* was rediscovered during the Renaissance, it became virtually the educational bible for generations of humanist educators."[48] H.G. Good says that during the Renaissance, "Quintilian was read more than any other ancient educational writer."[49]

Quintilian's innovative ideas included the following:

1. Rewards should be given for positive behavior instead of corporal punishment for bad behavior. Children should be "won for learning" rather than forced to learn out of fear of flogging, which had long been the pattern of Greek and Roman education.
2. Reading and writing skills should be introduced to three-year-olds within the context of games and songs.
3. Educational toys such as large ivory letters and wax tablets should be used.
4. Study should be balanced with play.
5. Contrary to Roman practice, school need not begin at dawn.[50]

The idea that education could be mixed with play, even at Rome's lowest level of instruction, was contrary to all that had been practiced in the combined history of Greece and Rome. Merging study with play was like mixing oil and water to the Romans, as well as to their Grecian slave teachers and tutors. The most shocking element of Quintilian's list, however, was his concept of rewarding students for positive behavior and exacting no physical consequences for bad behavior. In the minds of Greek and Roman educators, teaching and flogging with a leather strap went hand in hand at every level of learning. This harsh approach was the principal means of developing a disciplined mind. Simply complaining about the system did not change it. It had seemingly worked for centuries. Still, no less than Aurelius Augustine complained bitterly about the harshness of his early education:

> What miseries and mockeries I experienced when obedience to my teachers was set before me as proper to my boyhood, that I might get on in this world and distinguish myself in the science of speech, which should bring me honour among men and deceitful riches. After that, I was put to school to get learning, of which (worthless as I was) I knew not what use there was; and yet, if slow to learn, I was flogged.[51]

Wilds provides a further description of Roman elementary education:

> At the elementary level, the methods were those of memorizing and imitation. Material was meager. The pupils sat upon the floor or upon stones and rested their tablets on their knees. School hours were long, lasting from sunrise until sunset; but there was no school in summer, and holidays were numerous. The pupils were taught the names and order of the letters of the alphabet without learning anything in regard to their shape. All the possible combinations of syllables were then learned by rote. Next, writing and reading were taught by means of exercises dictated by the teacher. Pronunciation, enunciation, and intelligent expression received special attention. Writing was taught by copying and tracing on a wax tablet with the stylus, as in Greece. Counting was done on the fingers, with pebbles, or with the abacus. Discipline was severe; the rod and the lash were used frequently.[52]

Gradually Quintilian's educational ideas took root, but a pendulum reaction began that did not have a positive effect on Roman education. Excesses in one direction, then as now, often bring about excesses in the opposite direction.

Quintilian's more practical contributions came at the upper levels of education. First, however, we must review in more detail the three levels of Roman education. These included the schools of literature, grammar, and rhetoric. Professor Wilds describes them as follows:

> For the elementary level, they developed the "school of the litterator" (the school of the teacher of letters). This was the outgrowth and successor of the earlier *ludus* and was attended by both boys and girls from the age of seven to ten. For the secondary level, they developed the "school of the grammaticus" (the school of the teacher of grammar), for boys only, from ten to sixteen. This school existed in two types: (1) the Greek grammar school for the study of Greek grammar and literature, and (2) the Latin grammar school for the study of Latin grammar and literature. The Roman boy attended both, but Quintilian

advocated that he should go to the Greek school first and afterwards attend the Latin school. For the higher level there was developed the "school of the rhetor" (the school of the teacher of rhetoric), providing a course of two or three years for boys from the age of sixteen on.[53]

BILINGUAL EDUCATION

Because Roman educators integrated Greek culture and Greek academics with their own, it became necessary to offer, for the first time in history, bilingual education.[54] Consequently, Roman students were required to attend a Greek grammar school as well as a Roman or Latin grammar school. In order for Roman students to succeed in the upper-level rhetoric schools, they had to prove their proficiency in two languages and be conversant with the literature of both Greece and Rome. Speaking of Rome's dual-language grammar schools, Wilds writes:

> From imperial Roman times to the present nearly every European people has gone through the experience in which their vernacular had to struggle against Latin for pride of place in secondary education. And the idea spread around the world: the first secondary schools among English-speaking peoples in the American colonies were Latin grammar schools. The belief that someone else's language is better than one's own for educative purposes has had a long tradition.[55]

In Rome's dual-language grammar schools, instructors drilled their students in sentence diagramming, parts of speech, and syntax, with endless exercises in composition and poetry writing.

In addition to language studies, Quintilian advocated a variety of other subjects such as music, moral maxims, correct speech, astronomy, philosophy, and geometry to broaden the curriculum and to break up the monotony of the long school day. He also advocated the systematized study of one subject at a time. The idea of grade-level instruction did not occur to Quintilian, but he did suggest adjusting the curriculum to fit the individual ability of each boy.[56] Math computation was not well developed in Roman education mainly because Roman numerals are difficult to comprehend in a complex math problem. Can you imagine a long division or multiplication problem using Roman numerals?

The highest level of learning in Quintilian's Roman oratorical educational system was the school of rhetoric. Students sixteen and above concentrated on the preparation and delivery of speeches. The purpose, of course, was to prepare young men for their future roles in the executive, legislative, or judicial branch of Roman government. In his "cult of eloquence"[57] as H.G. Good calls it, Quintilian strongly emphasized style, delivery, and voice

Figure 7. Reading a manuscript.

modulation. He believed that memory was "the chief symptom of ability."[58] Therefore, students in rhetoric school committed to memory long passages of the great poets of the past: Cicero, Homer, and other Roman and Greek literary giants.

As previously stated, early Roman education was private. French historian Harrent says, "As a matter of settled policy in ancient Rome, parents controlled the education of their children."[59] The quality of private education in Rome was sustained for centuries by free-market competition among teachers and the academic reputation of individual schools. For example, Cicero, Rome's consummate literary artist, complained because as a youngster, he was unable to enroll in the school where a notable rhetoric teacher, Lucius Gallus, taught:

> As great numbers flocked to his school, so that all who were most devoted to study were eager to take lessons from him, it was a great trouble to me that I was not allowed to do so.[60]

FROM PRIVATE TO PUBLIC SCHOOLS

Public schools gradually came into existence in the latter centuries of the Roman Empire. H.G. Good claims, "The Roman schools had reached their highest point of development by A.D. 100."[61] Imperial patronage of schooling began slowly with a public library and museum. Then began the practice of endowing "chairs" out of the public treasury for secondary teachers of Latin, Greek, and rhetoric. Interest from government loans to Italian farmers was used to pay for secondary education throughout the empire. This new public funding program began with Emperor Antonius Pius:

> Antonius Pius (r. 138–161) decreed that salaries be paid to rhetoricians and philosophers. . . . Salaries were thus paid by the public from about A.D. 150. This regulation applied to all provinces. As to the number of instructors to be supported at public expense, Antonius stipulated: Small cities may have 5 physicians, 3 sophists, and 3 grammarians; Larger cities 7 physicians, 4 sophists, and 4 grammarians; Capital cities 10 physicians, 5 sophists, and 5 grammarians. These numbers could not be exceeded.[62]

As in numerous government programs throughout history, the numbers were exceeded many times over. As Roman education became more centralized and bureaucratic, it quickly suffered from stagnation. As professor of education Edgar Knight says:

> The bureaucratic character of the imperial government was soon reflected in the stagnation of education. The spirit of education changed. Lack of political freedom made [education] empty and superficial.[63]

Rome's new public schools, however, spread throughout the empire, and private schools were ultimately outlawed. Scottish historian William Boyd says, "The intervention of the emperors began with friendly patronage, and ended by bringing education under the control of the state."[64] Thankfully, as we will learn in chapter 3, an amazing turnaround occurred in the fifth century, when Rome's pagan schools were outlawed.

3. Lessons from Early Jewish Education

More wars have been fought for the possession of Jerusalem than for any other city on earth. To this day, Jerusalem is one of the most visited places in the world. The focus of this study is on Jewish education in Jerusalem, 75 B.C. to A.D. 70. It is well known that, for the most part, the Jews in Jerusalem did not accept Jesus Christ as their Messiah. They were, however, fully devoted to the teachings of the Old Testament and highly motivated by biblical passages such as these:

> For I have known him, in order that he may command his children and his household after him, that they keep the way of the Lord, to do righteousness and justice, that the Lord may bring to Abraham what He has spoken to him (Genesis 18:19).

> Hear, O Israel: The Lord our God, the Lord is one! You shall love the Lord your God with all your heart, with all your soul, and with all your might. And these words which I command you today shall be in your heart; you shall teach them diligently to your children, and shall talk about them when you sit in your house, when you walk by the way, when you lie down, and when you rise up. You shall bind them as a sign on your hand, and they shall be as frontlets between your eyes. You shall write them on the doorposts of your house and on your gates (Deuteronomy 6:4–9).

With the exception of Samuel's "school of the prophets," which was not a school for children, there is no mention of "school" in the Old

Testament.[65] There is no question, however, that the Jewish people were committed to the education and training of their children. Note the following by Frederick Eby and Charles Arrowood:

> No mention of a school, as such, is anywhere found in the Old Testament. The Hebrew language, however, was rich in words that have to do with instruction; at least thirty-four root words imply the idea of teaching, and the words *teach* and *teacher* were frequently used.[66]

At the time of our study there were 480 synagogues in Jerusalem.[67] The principal use of the Jewish synagogue was worship on Saturday, the Sabbath for adults and children. Clarence Benson writes, "The regular Sabbath service of worship in the synagogue included afternoon Bible study for old and young, with an intermission between the morning and afternoon sessions for dinner."[68] Included in every synagogue complex was a school building called a *Beth Hassepher.* Lewis Sherrill provides the following description:

> The elementary school was called *Beth Hassepher,* that is, the House of the Book, for its purpose was the teaching of "the Book," which means the Scriptures, the written Torah. Commonly this Beth Hassepher was housed in the synagogue. It became the custom to build a room next to the synagogue, for educational use. It was expected that each synagogue should have its schools.[69]

The Jews were the first to establish a church-supported religious school system complete with compulsory attendance laws for citizens of all classes. The Old Testament was their only textbook. The system was founded in 75 B.C. by Simon ben Shetach. "He was a brother of Queen Salome, who encouraged his efforts."[70] Dr. Swift writes:

> The synagogue was the earliest, the most widespread and the most enduring of all the educational institutions after the [Babylonian] exile. It was the first institution to offer systematic instruction to both sexes. It was the parent of the scribe college and the elementary school. Out of it arose the movement which resulted in universal education.[71]

The genesis of the Jewish schools sprang from the Jews' seventy years of exile in Babylon, which began in 586 B.C. While in exile, the Jews could not offer sacrifices at the great Temple in Jerusalem. Therefore, they built synagogues, which were designed not for traditional sacrifices but for biblical instruction and for prayer. When the Jews returned from exile, hundreds of synagogues were constructed throughout Palestine. They served the Jewish community in three ways: centers of worship, schools, and local law courts.[72] The fact that the synagogues were local was very important to the preservation of Jewish life, including Jewish education. Increasingly, Jewish leaders were demanding a higher level of learning than most fathers could provide for their sons. Their long tradition of home instruction was not adequate. Lewis Sherrill says:

> One may suppose that too many fathers were negligent in their duty which Judaism was coming to stress so greatly, that of formally teaching the Torah. They [Jewish leaders] had been holding fathers responsible for a task which fathers could not accomplish with any large degree of effectiveness. The authorities in Judaism therefore began to enlarge the circle of parenthood, taking teachers into that revered precinct. In time it came to be held that the honor due a teacher is even greater than that due to a father, comparable to that which one owes to God.[73]

The inefficiency of early home instruction brought about the need for elementary education. A Jewish high priest, Joshua ben Gamala, organized a system of school districts in Israel and established that children should begin school at the age of six or seven.[74] Eby and Arrowood describe the Jewish elementary schools:

> All authorities agree that the elementary school, called Beth-sepher (house of the book), was either in the synagogue itself or in an adjoining room. In these elementary schools boys from six to ten years of age were taught by a scribe assisted by the *hazzan,* or by the *hazzan* himself. This official was the attendant of the synagogue. The textbook was the Pentateuch, beginning with the creation story. The chief task, however, was the memorizing of the Levitical Deuteronomic law. Reading, writing, and arithmetic were taught. Arithmetic was necessary in calculating the tithe and in transacting business. Some knowledge of chronology would also be generally necessary for calculating the Sabbath and the time of the annual feasts.[75]

The Jews, like the Greeks and the Romans, depended heavily on classroom memorization. Girls as well as boys were required to know Jewish law or the law of Yahweh.[76] Also, like the Greeks and the Romans, Jewish schools started early each day. Dr. Sherrill writes:

> School began about sunrise, with a session in the morning and another in the late afternoon. Nothing indicates that there were any vacations, and there was a saying that children must not be kept from going to school, not even for the building of the Temple. School was not suspended even on the Sabbath, though there were restrictions as to what might be done in teaching on that day. A new passage might not

be studied for the first time on the Sabbath, but it was permitted to "make a first revision on the Sabbath," which appears to mean that mistakes in learning the passage might be corrected.[77]

It is little wonder that 2 Timothy 3:15 reads: "And that from childhood you have known the Holy Scriptures. . . ." A study of Jewish education also clarifies another passage, in which Jesus said, "A disciple [student] is not above his teacher, but everyone who is perfectly trained will be like his teacher" (Luke 6:40). It was the objective of every student in a Jewish school to become exactly like his or her teacher. A Jewish student acquired from his teacher not only knowledge but every other characteristic, including hand gestures and voice inflection. Christian schoolteachers today might like the Jewish ruling that read: "All manner of service that a slave must render to his master, a student must render to his teacher, except that of loosening his shoe."[78] The idea was that a student revered a teacher so much that he felt unworthy to loosen his shoe, like John the Baptist when he said of Jesus, "There comes One after me who is mightier than I, whose sandle strap I am not worthy to stoop down and loose" (Mark 1:7).

It appears that only boys advanced to a secondary school at age ten. The secondary school curriculum featured the memorization of more Jewish laws—those having to do with agriculture, feasts, festivals, marriage and divorce, civil and criminal law, animal sacrifices at the temple, and laws of purity and impurity. Advanced students continued in the rabbinical school at age fifteen.[79] The course of study was rigorous:

> The number of boys must have grown smaller at each step in the educational "ladder"; for it was said that a thousand boys go to the school house to learn to read the Scripture and only a hundred go out of it; a hundred go on to study the Mishnah and only ten go further; ten go to the study of the Talmud and only one of them completes it.[80]

It is impossible to overstate the respect the Jewish people had for education and for the teaching profession. Note the following Jewish sayings:

1. "What does God do in the fourth hour? He teaches little children."[81]
2. "The world exists only by the breath of school children."[82]
3. "Respect your teacher as you would God."[83]
4. "The teacher precedes the father; the wise man, the king."[84]
5. "If one's teacher and one's father are in captivity, one must ransom his teacher first."[85]

In Jerusalem a teacher was second in social standing only to a rabbinical scholar. Teachers at any age level had status among the highest levels of society. Such was the reverence for Jewish educators, and such was the respect by the Jews for education. In Israel, sending children to school was more than a duty. It was the focus of national pride. Lewis Sherrill says:

> The true protectors of the people were regarded as being, not the political leaders, but those who instructed the youth. . . . The school was held in highest regard as a symbol of all that education meant to the Jew.[86]

Historians Eby and Arrowood say it best:

> Hebrew education is unlike any other whatsoever in that it made God the beginning. . . . It began with the abstract and unseen, and not with the seen and the concrete; with obedience to law and reverence for God, and not in the acquisition of the arts of reading and writing. Truth was deduced from this divine, original principle, and not learned by induction. Jewish education was spiritual and therefore it stood in direct contradiction to the empirical and naturalistic systems of other peoples. The fact that it has outlasted every system whatsoever makes it the most successful educational experiment ever staged in the history of civilization.[87]

German historian Dittes agrees: "If ever a people has demonstrated the power of education, it is the Hebrew people."[88] But all was not perfect in Jerusalem. Secular and temple taxes required approximately 35 percent of family income. The greater Jewish community bemoaned the fact that "enormous sums of gold controlled by the priesthood lay idle in the Temple,"[89] and the priests showed little apparent compassion for the poor. On the contrary, religious leaders grew increasingly arrogant, adding more and more man-made "religious law" to every detail of Jewish life. In response, they were regarded with growing distrust and contempt.

The prevalence of this attitude is reflected in the opening pages of the New Testament. Given their intimate knowledge of the Scriptures and the many Old Testament prophecies of a coming Messiah, the Jewish religious leaders should have recognized Christ as the Savior He was and championed His acceptance among the people. Instead they saw Him as a threat to their base of authority and openly rejected Him. They assumed that Christ's humiliating crucifixion was the end of Him, though it was actually the beginning of God's eternal plan of redemption for all people.[90]

Clearly, the educational patterns of the Greeks, Romans, and Jews laid the foundation for education for the next two thousand years. Modern educators have championed many an educational innovation, but none have exceeded the creativity or literacy level of those early pioneers.

Now we return to Rome for one of history's most dramatic transition periods.

Endnotes - Chapter Two

[1] Harvey J. Graff, *The Legacies of Literacy* (Bloomington and Indianapolis: Indiana University Press, 1987), pp. 20-21.

[2] Frederick Eby and Charles Flinn Arrowood, *The History and Philosophy of Education Ancient and Medieval* (New York: Prentice-Hall, Inc. 1940), p. 467.

[3] H.G. Good, *A History of Western Education* (New York, The Macmillan Company, 1960), p. 19.

[4] Ibid., p. 21. Also see Eby and Arrowood, pp. 202-204.

[5] Plutarch's Lives, Lycurgus; selected passages, included in Ellwood P. Cubberley's valuable collection of *Readings in the History of Education* (Boston: Houghton Mifflin Company, 1920), pp. 2-3.

[6] Elmer Harrison Wilds, *The Foundations of Modern Education* (New York: Rinehart and Co. Inc., 1957), p. 87.

[7] Good, p. 36.

[8] Wilds, p. 91.

[9] Eby and Arrowood, p. 207.

[10] Plutarch in Cubberley, p. 3.

[11] Eby and Arrowood, p. 211.

[12] James Reed and Ronnie Prevost, *A History of Christian Education* (Nashville: Broadman and Holman Publishers, 1993), p. 26.

[13] K.J. Freeman, *The Schools of Hellas* (London: 1907), pp. 275-279. Quoted in Cubberley, pp. 7-8.

[14] Eby and Arrowood, p. 215.

[15] Plutarch, quoted in Eby and Arrowood, p. 216.

[16] Eby and Arrowood, p. 219.

[17] Ibid., p. 220.

[18] Ibid., pp. 235-236. Eby quotes Freeman, p. 66.

[19] Good, pp. 24-25.

[20] Plato, *The Protagoras;* selected. Quoted in Cubberley, pp. 4-5.

[21] Eby and Arrowood, pp. 228-229.

[22] H.T. Freeman, *The Schools of Hellas* (London, 1907), p. 81. Quoted in Henry H. Sweets, *The Church and Education* (Richmond: Presbyterian Committee of Education, 1939), pp. 16-17.

[23] S.S. Laurie, *Historical Survey of Pre-Christian Education* (New York: Longmans, Green & Co. 1895), p. 217.

[24] Eby and Arrowood, p. 223.

[25] Arthur F. Leach, *The Schools of Medieval England* (London: Methuen and Co. Ltd., 1916), p. 14.

[26] Good, pp. 38-39.

[27] Thomas Davidson, *Education of the Greeks,* p. 30, quoted in Wilds, p. 104.

[28] A compilation of data from the following: R. Freeman Butts, *The Education of the West* (New York: McGraw-Hill Book Co., 1973), p. 100; *New International Dictionary of the Christian Church,* p. 68; Thomas L. Heath, *The Thirteen Books of Euclid's Elements* (New York: Dover Publications Inc., 1956), vol. I, pp. 1-6; and *Encyclopaedia Britannica* (1961 edition).

[29] Wilds, p. 95.

[30] G.W. Botsford and E.G. Sibler, *Hellenic Civilization* (New York: Columbia University Press, 1915), pp. 478-479.

31 Merrill F. Unger, *The New Unger's Bible Handbook* (Chicago: Moody Press, 1984), p. 353.

32 Eby and Arrowood, p. 467.

33 Thomas Davidson, *A History of Education,* p. 106, quoted in Wilds, p. 118.

34 Good, p. 49.

35 Wilds, pp. 121,122, and 131.

36 L.E. Elliot Binns, *The Beginnings of Western Civilization* (London: Lutterworth Press) p. 43.

37 Cubberley, p. 25.

38 Ephesians 6:4.

39 Reed and Prevost, p. 38.

40 Quoted by Pliny, *Natural History, XXIX,* 7,14. Pliny was the Roman governor of Bithynia. Quoted in Wilds, pp. 130-131.

41 Eby and Arrowood, p. 513.

42 Cubberley, p. 33.

43 Good, p. 47. Also see Eby and Arrowood, p. 534.

44 Paul Monroe, *A Textbook in the History of Education* (New York: The Macmillan Co.), p. 197. Quoted in Wilds, p. 132.

45 Eby and Arrowood, p. 522 and Wilds, p. 131. None of the authors provide the original source for this often quoted line.

46 Good, p. 46

47 Reed and Prevost, p. 41.

48 Butts, p. 127

49 Good, p. 55.

50 Leach, pp. 15-16.

51 Augustine, iv, l6, quoted in William Boyd, *The History of Western Education* (London: Adam and Charles Black, 1921), p. 76.

52 Wilds, p. 137.

53 Ibid., pp. 133-134.

54 Good, p. 50.

55 Wilds, p. 119.

56 Eby and Arrowood, pp. 159-161.

57 Good, p. 55.

58 Quintilian, *Institutes of Oratory,* Bk. 1, c. 3, and 1, quoted in Eby and Arrowood, p. 559.

59 A. Harrent, *Les Ecoles d' Antioche* (Paris: Thorin et Fils, 1898), pp. 47-49

60 Cicero, Suetonius, *On Rhetoricians,* c.2, quoted in Eby and Arrowood, p. 539.

61 Good, p. 46.

62 Eby and Arrowood, p. 499.

63 Edgar W. Knight, *Twenty Centuries of Education* (Boston: Ginn and Company, 1940), p. 82.

64 Boyd, p. 78.

65 Samuel G. Kahn, *A Short History of Education* (Jerusalem: Yesodot Publishers, 1960), p. 116.

66 Frederick Eby and Charles Flinn Arrowood, *The History and Philosophy of Education Ancient and Medieval* (New York: Prentice Hall, 1940), p. 140.

67 Clarence H. Benson, *A Popular History of Christian Education* (Chicago: Moody Press, 1943), p. 27. Note: I am presuming that the zenith of Jewish education occurred during the 75 B.C. - A.D. 70 period. This was the period of compulsory education of Jewish children. Also see Linus Bockett, *History and Progress of Education* (New York: A.S. Barnes & Burr, 1860), p. 58.

68 Ibid.

[69] Lewis Joseph Sherrill, *The Rise of Christian Education* (New York: The Macmillan Company, 1944), p. 55.

[70] Eby and Arrowood, p. 143.

[71] Fletcher H. Swift, *Education in Ancient Israel* (Chicago: The Open Court Publishing Company, 1919), p. 90. Quoted in Eby and Arrowood, p. 141. Also see Sherrill, p. 53. Sherrill adds that Shetach was a Pharisee, president of the Sanhedrin, and was known as "The Restorer of the Law." His brother-in-law was King Alexander Janneus, who ruled from 103 to 76 B.C.

[72] John D. Davis, *Davis Dictionary of the Bible* (Nashville: Royal Publishers, Inc., 1973), p. 792.

[73] Sherrill, pp. 54-55. Sherrill cites Baba Mezia II, 11; Aboth IV, 12.

[74] Baba Bathra 21a. Quoted in Sherrill, p. 54.

[75] Eby and Arrowood, p. 146.

[76] Ibid., p. 147.

[77] Sherrill, p. 60. Sherrill cites Shabath 119b and Nedarim 37a.

[78] Ibid., p. 69. Sherrill quotes Kethuboth 96a; cf.

[79] James E. Reed and Ronnie Prevost, *A History of Christian Education* (Nashville: Broadman and Holman Publishers, 1993), p. 50.

[80] Sherrill, p. 61. Sherrill cites Midrash Leviticus Rabba II.

[81] Eby and Arrowood, p. 156.

[82] Resh Lakish, cited in Barkley, quoted in Gangel and Benson, p. 86.

[83] Eby and Arrowood, p. 156.

[84] Ibid.

[85] Baba Mezia II, 11. Quoted in Sherrill, p. 69.

[86] Ibid., pp. 68-69.

[87] Eby and Arrowood, p. 157.

[88] H.M. Liepziger, The Education of the Jews (New York: T. Laurie, 1890), p. 187. Quoted in Sherrill, p. 157.

[89] Sherrill, p. 75.

[90] Isaiah 53, John 3:16.

Illustration Sources

Figure 1   *Grecian Vase* - Berlin Museum (A. Kulix) pictured in A. F. Leach, *The Schools of Medieval England* (London: Methuen & Co. Ltd., 1916), p. 16.

Figure 2   *Map* - ACSI.

Figure 3   *Parthenon* - Mary D. Sheldon, *Studies in Greek and Roman History* (Boston: D. C. Heath & Co., 1887), p. 88.

Figure 4   *Plato* - Alinari/Art Resource, New York, NY.

Figure 5   *Socrates* - Ellwood P. Cubberley, *Readings in the History of Education* (Boston: Houghton Mifflin Co., 1920), p. 15.

Figure 6   *Aristotle* - Alinari/Art Resource, New York, NY.

Figure 7   *Reading Manuscript* - Cubberley, p. 32.

The Great Transition Period

The changes that took place in Rome between A.D. 300 and 600 impacted Western civilization, and to a lesser degree Eastern civilization, for the next one thousand years. The three primary changes were:

1. *The End of Pagan Education and the Rise of Christian School Education*
2. *The Fall of the Roman Empire*
3. *The Formation of the Catholic Church and the Emergence of the Persecuted Evangelical Church*

1. The End of Pagan Education and the Rise of Christian School Education

Figure 1. These symbols were etched by Christians in Rome's Catacombs.

We begin with the end of pagan education. Pagan education never really ends, of course, but it ceased to be the official philosophy of public education for the Roman Empire. Its final chapter came at the hand of Roman Emperor Justinian, ruling from Constantinople in A.D. 529. Justinian simply decreed that pagan schools were illegal. One hundred thirty-eight years before that, Emperor Theodosius had outlawed all pagan worship. This, too, was an amazing development! Ellwood Cubberley describes these two historic events:

In 391 the Emperor Theodosius forbade all pagan worship, thus making the victory of Christianity complete. In less than four centuries from the birth of its founder the Christian faith had won control of the great Empire in which it originated. In 529 the Emperor Justinian ordered the closing of all pagan schools and the University of Athens, which had remained the center of pagan thought until the success of Christianity closed its doors. The victory was now complete.[1]

The demise of Rome's public schools is an important piece of the larger picture of why the Roman Empire began unraveling. In A.D. 476 the barbarous Teutons, from what is now Germany and Eastern Europe, invaded Rome and were suddenly in control of the western portion of the Roman Empire.[2] This produced a blending of German and Roman emperors that accelerated confusion in an empire already in turmoil. When Emperor Justinian finally closed the schools, pagan education had already lost much of its credibility. H.G. Good says, "The edict of Justinian (A.D. 529) closing pagan schools was hardly needed because most of these institutions had already disappeared."[3]

Rome's public schools failed for a variety of reasons. Among them was the ever-growing irritation of heavy taxation upon Roman citizens, who no longer regarded their schools as "the passport to wealth and power."[4] This led to a general reduction in educational expenditures from the imperial treasury for teacher salaries and school facilities.[5] In the latter years of the empire, "three quarters or more of the population were illiterate."[6] Jerome Carcopino paints the following gloomy picture of Rome's public schools:

> On the whole we are compelled to admit that at the most glorious period of the empire the schools entirely failed. . . . They undermined instead of strengthened the children's morals; they mishandled the children's bodies instead of developing them; and if they succeeded in furnishing their minds with a certain amount of information, they were not calculated to perform any loftier or nobler task. The pupils left school with the heavy luggage of a few practical and commonplace notions laboriously acquired and of so little value that in the fourth century Vegetius could not take for granted that new recruits for the army would be literate enough to keep the books of their corps. Instead of happy memories, serious and fruitful ideas, any sort of intellectual curiosity vital to later life, school children carried away the gloomy recollection of years wasted in senseless, stumbling repetitions punctuated by savage punishments. Popular education then in Rome was a failure. [7]

MARTYR'S SCHOOL

Before we look at the rise of Christian schools, it is important to review the hostile environment the early Christians faced. As Roman emperors became more and more dictatorial and assumed the status of gods, Christians throughout the empire became the objects of imperial

Figure 2. The Roman Colosseum as it appears today. There early church Christians died because they refused to worship Rome's emperors.

scorn—scorn because most Christians refused to capitulate on emperor worship and the worship of Rome's pagan deities. Over a period of 249 years (A.D. 64–313), there were ten Roman emperors who inflicted horrendous persecution on Christians: Nero, Domitian, Trajan, Marcus Aurelius, Septimus Severus, Maximinus the Thracian, Decius, Valerian, Diocletian, and Galerius.[8] As Lewis Sherrill says:

> There were periods of peace, but for approximately two hundred and fifty years no Christian knew when he might have to choose whether he would do honor to the person of the Emperor as divine and thus deny the Lord whose sovereignty he had taken upon himself, or whether he would refuse to meet the state's requirements and thus incur the charge of treason to the Empire. The common penalty for the latter was death. Many weakened under pressure and lapsed from their

Christian faith, but from Nero to Galerius a great company of men and women either chose death or had it thrust upon them, with the result that beheading, burning, crucifixion, being thrown into the amphitheater, exile, or forced labor, was known everywhere as the possible price of being a believer in Christ.[9]

Because martyrdom was a real possibility for every Christian, some early church Christians actually trained in what might be called a martyr's school. Note this description by H.D.M. Spense-Jones:

> It was not a haphazard temporary piece of work, this "training for martyrdom," but as we shall see a veritable "school," a protracted education for an awful, for a not improbable contingency. At the end of the second and through the third century it was evidently a recognized and important Christian agency.[10]

Spense-Jones says the martyr's school even had training manuals, which stressed the following:

1. How to answer judges when brought into a Roman court.
2. How to focus on heaven and the eternal reward of being a martyr for Christ.
3. How to rehearse the heroism of earlier martyrs.
4. How to prepare the body through physical exercise to endure public flogging, all forms of torture, long periods in prison and even death by hanging, crucifixion, sword, fire, and possibly by the fangs and claws of beasts in the Roman Colosseum before forty-five thousand spectators.
5. How to prepare heart and mind through memorization of such Scriptures as, "Therefore whosoever confesses me before men, him will I also confess before my Father who is in heaven" (Matt. 10:32) and "Blessed are those who are persecuted for righteousness' sake, for theirs is the kingdom of heaven" (Matt. 5:10). [11]

Prospective martyrs were comforted by the words of Tertullian, a great writer and Christian leader of the time:

> You are about to pass through a noble struggle in which the living God acts the part of Superintendent, in which the Holy Ghost is your trainer, in which the prize is an eternal crown of angelic essence. . . . Therefore, your Master, Jesus Christ. . . has anointed you with his spirit, and led you from a condition more pleasant in itself, and imposed on you a harder treatment [as a course of discipline] that your strength may be greater. [12]

Prospective martyrs were inspired by such heroes of the faith as Justin Martyr, who said as he was being led to the Colosseum in Rome:

I give injunctions to all men that I am dying willingly for God's sake, if you do not hinder it. I beseech you, be not an unseasonable kindness to me. Suffer me to be eaten by the beasts . . . I long for the beasts that are prepared for me . . . so I may attain to Jesus Christ![13]

Will Durant pays the following tribute to the persecuted Christians and to Christ:

There is no greater drama in human record than the sight of . . . Christians, scorned or oppressed by a succession of emperors, bearing all trials with a fierce tenacity, multiplying quietly, building order while their enemies generated chaos, fighting the sword with the Word, brutality with hope, and at last defeating the strongest state that history has known. Caesar and Christ had met in the arena, and Christ had won.[14]

Figure 3. There were 587 miles of underground tunnels in Rome's Catacombs like the one above. The Catacombs provided a safe haven for Christians.

As persecution intensified, Christians and Jews hid in sandstone quarries located outside the walls of Rome. These quarries were greatly expanded into enormous underground communities called Catacombs. The remains of the Catacombs were discovered in the sixteenth century. Excavation begun in the 1950s has revealed much about the courageous inhabitants who lived, worshiped, and died in the Catacombs of Rome. One archaeological report reveals the following:

About six million persons are buried in sixty Catacombs, fifty-four of which are Christian, and six Jewish. Each of these has a rather obscure entrance, from which a stairway leads down to subterranean tunnels and galleries which, branching off at right angles one to another, create a network of tunnels and streets, with here and there a chapel. Some have as many as four levels, each connected by a stairway. On each of these levels is an immense maze of narrow tunnels—so many that if all the tunneled streets in all the Catacombs were placed end to end they would extend 587 miles.[15]

It is very possible there were underground Christian schools in the Catacombs. We know underground churches existed where Christians sang and worshiped together. We know that children lived there with their parents.[16] Given the commitment to basic literacy of the early Christians, it is highly probable that Christian school education occurred in the underground world of the Catacombs. Whatever formal and informal education took place there, the students and their families experienced the continual interruption of their normal life patterns, through the sorrow of losing family members and the terror of being discovered by Roman authorities. It is difficult to comprehend the life those courageous Christians led.

There were, of course, varying degrees of commitment among the early church Christians. Many cooperated with the Romans. For example, Roman officials often required all citizens to appear in town squares for a test of loyalty to the emperor in which they publicly burned a pinch of incense in his honor. Many Christians complied.[17] A few Christians even purchased bogus certificates on the black market supposedly certifying to the commissioners of sacrifice that they had poured the drink offerings and tasted the sacrifices to the pagan gods.[18] Additionally, as much as Christians despised Rome's pagan school system, some enrolled their children in its free public schools. This was especially true at the elementary level even though a growing number of public school teachers who had become Christians subsequently lost their teacher's license and were no longer permitted to teach.[19] However, the mainstream of Christians, many of whom lived in the Catacombs, were wary of Rome's public system. H.G. Good writes, "The ideas of Christian home and pagan school not only were different, but violently contradicted each other."[20] Boyd says that Christians up through the fourth century held a "distrust of pagan learning and the same inability to conceive of any practical alternative."[21]

Early church leaders such as John Chrysostom, an eloquent spokesman for the Christian community, were totally committed to Christian education for children. Chrysostom likened the soul of a child to a city that should be governed with great care: "The mind of a child is therefore a city, a city newly built and furnished, a city full of new inhabitants, and as yet wholly unexperienced. 'Tis an easie matter to instruct and model such!"[22]

THE CHRISTIAN SCHOOL—
A KEY TO THE GROWTH OF THE EARLY CHURCH

There is no question that the growth of the early church was greatly accelerated through Christian school education. Historian Clarence Benson cites Celsus, a pagan critic of Christians, who asserted that "Christianity was propagated most successfully among the young children."[23] Benson quotes Baron Bunsen, who says, "The apostolic church made the school the connecting link between herself and the world."[24] A significant statement regarding the impact of Christian schools on the remarkable expansion of the Christian community in the Roman Empire is provided by historians Eby and Arrowood:

> The modern world has not sufficiently recognized the profound role played by teaching in the triumph of Christianity over pagan civilization. Attention has naturally centered upon the Church to the detriment of its indispensable ally, the school. Teaching was in no way subsidiary to the method of preaching, but of equal dignity and of more abiding effectiveness. Through their schools Jewish rabbis had dominated the life and religion of the Jewish people. The Greek civilization, too, had been . . . interwoven with the schools of rhetoric and philosophy. It was, therefore, not at all strange that Christian propaganda was obliged to employ the lowly method of instruction and exposition in addition to enthusiastic preaching. The regular method of attack in bringing the new religion into any community for the first time was through the [Christian] school.[25]

CHRISTIAN SCHOOL EDUCATION REPLACED PAGAN EDUCATION

As the body of believers grew dramatically throughout the Roman Empire, Christian school education began to be widely respected. Benson writes:

> As the Christian church grew and came to have a larger place in the political control of towns and communities, the Bible became a part of the curriculum of the schools. When Gregory entered upon his work in Armenia, at the beginning of the fourth century, he adopted a compulsory system of Christian schools for the children in every city there. "It would seem," says H. Clay Trumbull, "that at that period, as also earlier, there were public schools for the training of both heathen and Christian children in the knowledge of the Scriptures, in Mesopotamia, Cappadocia, Egypt, and elsewhere." In all of these Christian schools, as in the earlier Jewish educational institutions, it was the Bible text itself which was the primary subject of study and teaching.[26]

At the turn of the fourth century, the empire's pagan educational system had lost much of its momentum. In fact, some of Rome's public schools became Christian schools![27] Little is known of these schools other than the fact that they existed. The imperial decrees set by previous emperors curbing private schools and private school teachers had been rescinded.

Even more amazing was the Christian conversion of Emperor Constantine, "The Augustus of Rome," who in A.D. 312 accepted Jesus Christ as his Savior. Freeman, in a burst of eloquence, describes Constantine's conversion:

> The miracle of miracles, greater than dried-up seas and cloven rocks, greater than the dead rising again to life, was when the Augustus on his throne, Pontiff of the gods of Rome, himself a god to the subjects of Rome, bent himself to become the worshiper of a crucified provincial of his Empire.[28]

Some historians question the sincerity of Constantine's conversion, suggesting that it was politically motivated. There is room for this sort of speculation concerning his early years, but there is strong evidence that as he grew older his devotion to Christ was sincere.[29]

Before Constantine came to power, Emperor Galerius, in A.D. 311, had issued a general edict of toleration for all Christians in the Roman Empire. That edict came only eight years after he had issued an edict of open persecution of all Christians.[30] One year after his conversion to Christ, Constantine did what no other Roman Emperor had done. Knight describes the momentous event:

> In 313 Constantine issued the famous Edict of Milan, which recognized and legalized Christianity. By this act Christianity was greatly strengthened in the Roman Empire, for Christians were now favored over the followers of other religions.[31]

This event and other tide-turning developments of the early years of the fourth century changed not only the Roman Empire but also the balance of the world's history. Ironically, however, the fact that Christianity was now the Emperor-approved religion of the empire would prove detrimental to the early church and to Christian school education. In reference to Christianity becoming the official religion of Rome, Dr. Wilds says:

> This was a fine thing for the growth of the church organization, but it is an open question whether it was equally favorable to the continuation of the early emphasis upon Christlike living on the part of the whole membership of the church.[32]

We will explore this important issue later in this chapter. Now, however, we must review some of the forces that brought about the fall of Rome and her great empire.

Figure 4. The Arch of Constantine in Rome is adjacent to the Roman Colosseum. In A.D. 313 Emperor Constantine legalized Christianity. The close proximity of the Arch to the Colosseum is symbolic of the great transition period. In the Colosseum Christians were thrown to wild beasts. A few feet away the Arch of Constantine stands in stark contrast as a monument to complete religious freedom for Christian believers.

2. The Fall of the Roman Empire

An analysis of why Rome fell is a meaningful study and has significance for Christian school educators. The citizens of Rome in A.D. 100 probably believed that their empire was the greatest in the world and would last forever. It was, indeed, powerful. Rome's armies dominated the Western world and large portions of the East. The city of Rome was rich and filled with great treasures—spoils from her many conquered lands. The male citizens of Rome were well educated. As previously mentioned, in A.D. 100 Rome's school system had reached its zenith, and it had served its citizens well. Rome had a highly organized system of government. These were all reasons to believe that the Roman Empire would be a substantial permanent power throughout the world.

Rome was founded in the fifth century B.C. and lasted until the fifth century after Christ. Her empire spread from Britannia and Hispania in the West to Mesopotamia in the East.[33] The population of the Roman Empire at the time Constantine came to power was sixty to eighty million people.[34] Like the "unsinkable" *Titanic* that went down in 1912 on her maiden voyage, the great and powerful Roman Empire seemed invincible. Historians generally agree that A.D. 476 is the year of its fall. In that year the German General Odoacer deposed Emperor Romulus Augustus[35] after a series of invasions and battles that Knight describes as follows:

> About 337 the Roman Empire began to be invaded by barbarians. The Visigoths crossed the Danube in 376, Alaric besieged and plundered Rome in 410, the Vandals invaded Africa in 429, the Saxons invaded England two decades later, Attila the Hun invaded Gaul in 451, when the battle of Châlons, one of the fiercest struggles in history, was fought. And in 476 the [Roman] Empire in the West came to an end.[36]

The seat of the empire's waning power was moved to Constantinople, the city founded by Constantine. The great imperial base of power in Rome was gone.[37]

But the causes of the fall of Rome were internal as much as external. Will Durant writes, "A great civilization is not conquered from without until it has destroyed itself within."[38] The fall of Rome was not a single event but a three-hundred-year process of gradual decline. As Durant says, "Some nations have not lasted as long as Rome fell."[39]

A partial list of causes for the Roman Empire's fall is as follows:

Figure 5. This is a characterization of a "barbarian" warrior who invaded Rome in A.D. 476.

1. All classes of people enjoyed too much leisure and idleness. The cruel practice of slavery proved disastrous. As Wilds explains:

    > The superabundance of slaves made it unnecessary for the citizen to work; he could be supplied in his idleness with the most luxurious shelter, clothing, food, and amusements. The people had fallen more and more into vicious customs and habits, following the example set by the upper classes. "Bread and circuses" were the only things demanded by the common people. Divorce became frequent, and common to all strata of society; infanticide and child exposure were practiced by all classes. Disgusting wantonness in private life, public ceremonies of the most immoral type [and] bloody gladiatorial shows.[40]

2. School teachers were corrupt. The decadent lifestyle of schoolmasters became a serious liability to Rome's public schools.

3. Educational standards declined. Mayer says, "The decline of Rome can be ascribed to its system of education almost as much as to any other cause."[42] You will recall from the previous chapter that during Rome's early centuries of private education, the principles of the Twelve Tables and family values were strongly emphasized in their private school curriculums. These principles and values were greatly de-emphasized in Rome's public schools. During the transition from private to public schools, there was a devastating academic shift from broad intellectual training to a narrowly focused vocational training, from an emphasis on personal literacy skills to a civic education through which the student became a skilled orator. This turned out to be a highly inappropriate educational objective for the general population.

4. Roman emperors became despotic. Emperor Octavian in 27 B.C. assumed the title of Dominus, the Latin word for "lord" or "god." From then on succeeding emperors became increasingly dictatorial, and the Roman senate was left with declining authority.[43] The empire lost its representative form of government.[44] Rome's "god-like" emperors often heard words of adoration like these:

> Thou, our father, it befits to look down from the very summit of the empire to the common world and, with a sign of your heavenly head, to decree the fates of human affairs, to grant the auspices to those who prepare campaigns, to establish the laws that govern treaties of peace. . . . Our Lord. . . has restored the human race, extended the Roman rule and dominance, and founded eternal security. . . . [45]

The life of a Roman emperor, however, was anything but secure. In a span of thirty-five years, thirty-seven men were proclaimed emperor, most of whom were assassinated by officers in the Roman army.[46] But while they lived, they lived well. Durant describes the lifestyle of the youthful emperor Elagabalus:

> The water in his swimming pools was perfumed with essence of roses; the fixtures in his bathrooms were of onyx or gold; his food had to be of costly rarities; his dress was studded with jewelry from crown to shoes; and gossip said that he never wore the same rings twice. When he traveled, 600 chariots were needed to carry his baggage.[47]

5. Bureaucracy and taxation became burdensome. As the Roman government became more and more centralized in the power of

the emperor, bureaucracies and taxes mushroomed. Gangel and Benson put it well:

> A very critical problem in the fall of Rome was that too many noncontributory members of society had to be fed by too few productive workers. The army and the bureaucracy had increased in size substantially.[48]

There was also the irksome practice of tax exemptions for a privileged few. As the empire declined, independent farmers who owned small farms were assimilated into large farm conglomerates owned by rich nobles who, because of influence and position, paid no taxes.[49] This pattern set the stage for the brutal class system of serfs and nobles that was characteristic of the grim Dark Ages to follow.

6. Rome's leaders made decisions based on astrology. Roman citizens had long held a fascination with hundreds of household gods, such as Vesta, spirit of the hearth, and Penates, spirit guardian of the storeroom.[50] As mentioned in chapter 1, Governor Petronius claimed there were more gods than people in Rome. As things became more desperate in Rome's declining years, emperors turned to astrology. Macmullen says:

> From the latter of the two periods we have more lucky stones and amulets, more treatises on spells, horoscopes, and enchantments, more charges of hexing and laws against it, more mumbo jumbo in what passed for philosophy, more appeal for aid from demons, more miracles credited by the "more educated."[51]

To this list could be added many more reasons why Rome fell—the corruption of courts, a serious imbalance of trade, the decline of the army, depopulation, and the devastating loss of an educated class of statesmen to counter the radical ideas of power that obsessed emperors. As Gangel says, "By the fifth century the empire might not have been worth saving."[52] There are obvious lessons for present-day societies in the fall of the Roman Empire, not the least of which is that a nation is at risk when fundamental learning and godly principles are ignored.

3. The Formation of the Catholic Church and the Emergence of the Persecuted Evangelical Church

As we shift our focus to the formation of the Catholic Church, it is important to understand a very significant political shift in the Roman Empire.

"Constantine the Great" not only changed the course of history by declaring Christianity the "official religion" of the Empire; he also moved the seat of Roman power to Constantinople in Turkey, leading some to refer to Constantinople as the "New Rome." This move provided a basis for the "Greek East" to consider itself equal to the "Latin West."[53] These significant political and ecclesiastical changes established what historians refer to as the "imperial church period"—a period that laid the foundation for the formation of the Roman Catholic Church. An entry in *Unger's Bible Handbook* reads:

> The imperial church of the 4th and 5th century became a different institution from the pilgrim church of the first three centuries.[54]

Constantine was not the founder of the Catholic Church, but there is little doubt that his imperial decrees inadvertently accelerated its development. If history had gone as Constantine planned, the Roman Catholic Church of today would be referred to as the Constantinople Catholic Church. Note the following explanation for Constantine's removal of the capital from Rome:

> In 326 Constantine determined to remove the seat of empire from Rome to the East, and before the close of the year the foundation-stone of Constantinople was laid. It is probable that this step was connected with Constantine's decision to make Christianity the official religion of the empire. Rome was naturally the stronghold of paganism, to which the great majority of the senate clung with fervent devotion. Constantine did not wish to do open violence to this sentiment, and therefore resolved to found a new capital for the new empire of his creation. He announced that the site had been revealed to him in a dream. The ceremony of inauguration was performed by Christian ecclesiastics on May 11, 330, when the city was dedicated to the Blessed Virgin.[55]

Over time, however, the seat of the imperial Catholic Church drifted back to Rome. Catholic historian Robert Sencourt refers to the city of Rome as "the legacy which the Roman Empire bequeathed to the Catholic Church, when the emperors left Rome to the popes, and went themselves to . . . Constantinople.[56]

Anyone who doubts the imperial nature of the imperial church should read the following edict of Emperor Theodosius II in A.D. 438:

> We desire that all those who are under the sway of our clemency shall adhere to that religion which, according to his own testimony, coming down even to our own day, the blessed apostle Peter delivered to the Romans. . . .

We ordain that the name of Catholic Christians shall apply to all those who obey this present law. All others we judge to be mad and demented; we declare them guilty of the infamy of holding heretical doctrine; their assemblies shall not receive the name of churches. They shall first suffer the wrath of God, then the punishment which in accordance with divine judgment we shall inflict. [57]

Within five years of the Catholic emperor's decree, seven early church bishops were executed on charges of heresy.[58] It is interesting that Emperor Constantine ended the persecution of Christians by pagans but inadvertently set in motion the formation of the imperial Catholic Church, which killed those who refused to become Catholic Christians. The threat to early church Christians shifted from Roman pagans to Roman Catholics.

It was during this imperial period that the future Roman Catholic Church gained its initial wealth. In A.D. 312, fourteen years before he laid the foundation stone for Constantinople, Constantine began construction on what would become St. Peter's Basilica on Vatican hill in Rome. Macmullen describes its construction:

Construction began in 312 or 313 and ended in 320. When complete, the cathedral measured 250 by 180 feet, with a height of 100 feet. Down its length ran two pairs of aisles split by rows of twenty-two columns.

The nave was flanked by two lines of fifteen columns and ended in an apse holding an enthroned statue of Christ and four angels, of purest silver, with jewels for eyes. Big enough to contain several thousand people, the cathedral was grand enough to overwhelm them, too. Gold sheathed the apse; columns were of rare green, red, and yellow marbles; gold glittered again high above on the beams, and from no less than seven solid altars; mosaics lined the underside of the intercolumnar arches. Across the sanctuary stretched a silver screen. When light failed from the windows, six silver candlesticks and one hundred and fifteen candelabras could be lit.

In the same papal complex stood a baptistry of incredible luxury, lined throughout with porphyry and containing, among other costly objects, a solid silver font, a solid gold candelabra of 52 pounds on a gold platter, itself on a porphyry column; and sculptured silver statues of such figures as Christ and St. John, with weights specified: 170 pounds, 80, 125.

Over St. Peter's tomb Constantine erected another basilica, later in his reign (beginning 324–330). Because of the importance of the site, provisions had to be made for extraordinary crowds. A part of the Vatican hill was carved away and transported as fill to a lower part to form a terrace. Such a campaign of construction, surrounding the city with a circle of jewels like a tiara, had not been seen within men's memories.[59]

In his zeal to further establish his imperial Christianity, Constantine built numerous cathedrals and basilicas. In addition, he endowed them with property. Macmullen says, "Some of the crown lands now coming into Constantine's possession he promptly reassigned as further endowments to St. Paul's, St. Peter's, and to other Roman basilicas."[60] It was also during this imperial church period that Constantine established the pattern of exempting church properties and church leaders from taxation. Church leaders were also exempted from military service and other municipal duties.[61]

Constantine, though well intentioned, attempted to unify the growing body of believers into one church over which he would preside. It was Constantine who called church leaders together from throughout his empire to formulate the Nicene Creed[62] and to accelerate church unification. The domineering patterns of Roman imperialism soon became evident in the manner of spiritual conversions. The apostle John had said, "Whosoever desires, let him take the water of life freely" (Revelation 22:17), but the idea that conversion to Christ is an act of individual choice was a foreign concept to Roman emperors. For example, Constantine declared on October 28 of A.D. 312 that his army was "officially Christian."[63] It is obvious that little individual choice or personal faith was reflected in that declaration!

As the Roman Catholic Church emerged from the ashes of the fallen Roman Empire, it was evident it had assimilated many characteristics of Roman paganism. Will Durant states:

[The Catholic Church adopted] . . . the stole and other vestments of pagan priests, the use of incense and holy water in purifications, the burning of candles and an everlasting light before the altar, the worship of the saints, the architecture of the basilica, the law of Rome as a basis for canon law, the title of Pontifex Maximus for the Supreme Pontiff, and, in the fourth century, the Latin language as the noble and enduring vehicle of Catholic ritual. The Roman gift was above all a vast framework of government, which, as secular authority failed, became the structure of ecclesiastical rule. Soon the bishops, rather than the Roman prefects, would be the source of order and the seat of power in the cities; the metropolitans, or archbishops, would support, if not supplant, the provincial governors; and the synod of bishops would succeed the provincial assembly. The Roman Church followed in the footsteps of the Roman state; it conquered the provinces, beautified the capital, and established discipline and unity from frontier to frontier. Rome died in giving birth to the [Roman Catholic] Church. . . . [64]

Exactly when was the Roman Catholic Church formed? And who founded it? Catholic Church leaders and Catholic historians claim that Christ founded their church when He declared to the Apostle Peter, "You are Peter; and on this rock I will build my church."[65] They assume "my church" is the Roman Catholic Church. They also assume that Peter was the first pope and that Peter lives again in each successive pope. The official Catholic list of popes gives the supposed "apostolic succession" as Peter, Linus, Cletus, Clement, and on to the present pope in Rome.[66]

Nowhere in Scripture is Peter referred to as a pope, nor was he designated as "Chief of the Apostles," nor does the Bible suggest that he was ever in Rome. Yet Catholic historian H.H. Milman implies all three:

Pagan Rome had been the head of the heathen world; the empire of her divine religion was to transcend that of her worldly dominion. Her victories had subdued the earth and the sea, but she was to rule still more widely than she had by her wars, through the peaceful triumphs of her faith. It was because Rome was the capital of the world that the Chief of the Apostles was chosen to be her teacher, in order that from the head of the world the light of truth might be revealed over all the earth. [67]

Protestant historian Boettner suggests that there is no biblical evidence that Peter was ever in Rome; nor is there any archaeological evidence:

Exhaustive research by archaeologists has been made down through the centuries to find some inscription in the Catacombs and other ruins of ancient places in Rome that would indicate that Peter at least visited Rome. But the only things found which gave any promise at all were some bones of uncertain origin. L.H. Lehmann, who was educated for the priesthood at the University for the Propagation of the Faith, in Rome, tells us of a lecture by a noted Roman archaeologist, Professor Marucchi, given before his class, in which he said that no shred of evidence of Peter's having been in the Eternal City had ever been unearthed, and of another archaeologist, Di Rossi, who declared that for forty years his greatest ambition had been to unearth in Rome some inscription which would verify the papal claim that the apostle Peter was actually in Rome, but that he was forced to admit that he had given up hope of success in his search. He had the promise of handsome rewards by the church if he succeeded.[68]

The idea that the Apostle Peter, whose ministry was to the Jews, would perform in the manner of a pope is contrary to what we read of him in the New Testament. Boettner agrees:

Peter refused to accept homage from men—as when Cornelius the Roman centurion fell down at his feet and would have worshiped him, Peter protested quickly and said, "Stand up; I myself also am a man" (Acts 10:25, 26). Yet the popes not only accept, but demand, such homage, even to the extent that men, including even the highest cardinals, prostrate themselves on the floor before a newly elected pope or when making ordination vows before him and kiss his foot.[69]

If Christ was referring to the greater body of believers rather than the Roman Catholic Church when He said "my church" and if Peter was not the first pope—who founded the Catholic Church and when? The initial purpose of the early church fathers coming together was to find common ground on statements of faith and creeds. There is no question there were numerous factions and even heresies in the early churches. Many examples occur in the New Testament of the apostles correcting the errors in the various apostolic church bodies. After the last apostle died, these errors multiplied. Durant says:

> About 187 Irenaeus listed twenty varieties of Christianity; about 384 Epiphanius counted eighty. At every point foreign ideas were creeping into Christian belief, and Christian believers were deserting to novel sects. The Church felt that its experimental youth was ending, its maturity was near; it must now define its terms and proclaim the conditions of its membership. Three difficult steps were necessary: the formation of a Scriptural canon, the determination of doctrine, and the organization of authority.[70]

Some claim the Catholic Church "developed its distinguishing characteristics between A.D. 160 and 190."[71] Others suggest that the Catholic Church became the Catholic Church when it "absorbed all other forms of government, and became virtually the State."[72] This occurred in A.D. 590 under Pope Gregory. You will recall the earlier statement by Unger: "The imperial church of the fourth and fifth centuries became a different institution from the pilgrim church of the first three centuries."[73] Power and wealth are difficult to manage. Constantine, well intentioned as he may have been, corrupted the meekness of a large segment of the early church. That corrupted segment became the imperial Roman Catholic Church. Note the following observation of Eby and Arrowood:

> With the growth of the Church in numbers and in wealth, its organization lost its primitive simplicity and democracy. The clergy became a class apart, with powers and privileges to which the laity were not admitted. Gradually the laity lost the power of electing the bishops. The Church was not, as yet, divided, and as the privileges and ranks of the

clergy developed, the Bishops of Alexandria, Antioch, Constantinople, Jerusalem, and Rome came to be recognized as pre-eminent. Rome, alone of these cities, belonged to the Latin part of the Church, and it enjoyed the prestige of its ancient imperial dignity.[74]

With the full force of the imperial state behind it, the newly empowered church began to press its advantage in a variety of ways, not the least of which was to suppress all forms of opposition. Latourette says, "With the aid of the state it rooted out all opposing faiths except Judaism."[75] That is a bit overstated, of course, because the old Roman paganism and several elements of the evangelical Christian community survived even the best efforts of the Catholic Church to stamp them out.[76]

"Stamping out the opposition" becomes a major theme of the next segment of history known as the Dark Ages, the first part of the medieval period. We will learn in chapter 4 that the torch of the true Gospel of Christ flickered at times but never went out as it was passed from generation to generation. In those dark years, the church was often under severe persecution from Catholic leaders who drove evangelical Christians into hiding. We will also learn that these courageous Christians, in the midst of it all, provided Christian school education for their children.

Endnotes—Chapter Three

[1] Ellwood P. Cubberley, *The History of Education* (Boston: Houghton Mifflin Company, 1920), p. 91.

[2] Edgar W. Knight, *Twenty Centuries of Education* (Boston: Ginn and Company, 1940), p. 88.

[3] H.G. Good, *A History of Western Education* (New York: The Macmillan Company, 1960), p. 63.

[4] William Boyd, *The History of Western Education* (London: Adam and Charles Black, 1950), p. 96.

[5] Ibid., p. 88.

[6] Ramsay Macmullen, *Christianizing the Roman Empire* (New Haven: Yale University Press, 1928), p. 21.

[7] Jerome Carcopino, *Daily Life in Ancient Rome: The People and the City at the Height of the Empire*, Henry T. Rowell, ed. (New Haven: Yale University Press, 1940), pp. 106–107.

[8] Kenneth Scott Latourette, *The First Five Centuries* (New York: Harper and Brothers Publishers, 1937), p. 136.

[9] Lewis Joseph Sherrill, *The Rise of Christian Education* (New York: The Macmillan Company, 1944), pp. 172–173.

[10] H.D.M. Spense-Jones, *The Early Christians at Rome* (London: Methuen and Company, Ltd., 1911), p. 200; quoted and cited in Frederick Eby and Charles Flinn Arrowood, *The History and Philosophy of Education Ancient and Medieval* (New York: Prentice-Hall, Inc., 1940), pp. 633–634.

[11] Ibid.

[12] Tertullian, *"Ad Martyras" The Writings of Tertullian,* vol. I (Edinburgh: T. and T. Clark, 1869), quoted in Eby and Arrowood, p. 634.

[13] Will Durant, *Caesar and Christ* (New York: Simon and Schuster, 1944), p. 611.

[14] Ibid., p. 652.

[15] *Archaeological Supplement to The Thompson Chain-Reference Bible, NIV* (Indianapolis: The B.B. Kirkbride Bible Company, Inc., 1990), p. 4430.

[16] Ibid.

[17] Ibid.

[18] Latourette, p. 149. Also see Ellwood P. Cubberley, *Readings in the History of Education* (Boston: Houghton Mifflin Company, 1920), p. 48. Cubberley includes the wording of an actual certificate to the commissioners of sacrifice dating back to A.D. 250.

[19] Eby and Arrowood, p. 563.

[20] Good, p. 62.

[21] Boyd, p. 88.

[22] John Chrysostom, quoted in *The Writings of John Evelyn*, published by William Upcott (London: Harvy Colburn, 1825), p. 116.

[23] Benson, p. 46.

[24] Baron Bunsen, *Hippolytus and His Age*, quoted in Benson, p. 47.

[25] Eby and Arrowood, p. 605. Also see Adolf Harnack, *The Mission and Expansion of Christianity in the First Three Centuries* (New York: GP Putnam and Sons, 1908), pp. 333–368, 443–444. Translated by James Moffatt. Second enlarged and revised edition.

[26] Benson, p. 43.

[27] Good, p. 62.

[28] E.A. Freeman, *Periods of European History*, p. 67. Quoted in Cubberley (see footnote,), p. 91.

[29] Ramsay Macmullen, *Constantine* (London: Groom Helm, 1969), p. 164. Note: Read Constantine's prayer.

[30] Knight, p. 90.

[31] Ibid.

[32] Elmer Harrison Wilds, *The Foundations of Modern Education* (New York: Rinehart and Company, Inc., 1936), p. 157.

[33] *Encyclopaedia Britannica*, vol. 19 (Chicago: William Benton, Publisher, 1961), p. 391.

[34] Macmullen, *Constantine*, p. 169.

[35] Wilds, p. 167.

[36] Knight, p. 73.

[37] Wilds, p. 167.

[38] Durant, p. 665.

[39] Ibid.

[40] Wilds, p. 158.

[41] James E. Reed and Ronnie Prevost, *A History of Christian Education* (Nashville: Broadman & Holman, 1993), p. 43.

[42] Frederick Mayer, *A History of Educational Thought* (Columbus: Charles E. Merrill Books, Inc., 1960), p. 113.

[43] Durant, p. 668.

[44] Eby and Arrowood, p. 543.

[45] Macmullen, *Constantine*, pp. 15 and 91.

[46] Durant, p. 628.

[47] Ibid., p. 624.

[48] Kenneth O. Gangel and Warren Benson, *Christian Education: Its History and Philosophy* (Chicago: Moody Press, 1983), p. 98.

[49] Eby and Arrowood, p. 576.

[50] Ibid., p. 525.

[51] Macmullen, *Constantine*, p. 7.

[52] Gangel and Benson, p. 98.

[53] George Giacumakus, Jr., *"Constantinople"* in *The New International Dictionary of the Christian Church*, J.D. Douglas, ed. (Grand Rapids: Zondervan, 1974), p. 256.

[54] Merrill F. Unger, *The New Unger's Bible Handbook* (Chicago: Moody Press, 1984), p. 692.

[55] *Encyclopaedia Britannica*, vol. 6 (Chicago: William Benton Publisher, 1961), p. 300.

[56] Robert Sencourt, *The Genius of the Vatican* (London: Jonathan Cape Ltd., 1935), p. 22.

[57] Knight, p. 91. Also see Cubberley, p. 51 and Wilds, p. 173.

[58] Sherrill, p. 174.

[59] Macmullen, *Constantine*, pp. 116–117.

[60] Ibid., p. 161.

[61] Ibid.

[62] Ibid. pp. 174–175.

[63] Macmullen, *Christianizing the Roman Empire*, p. 45.

[64] Durant, pp. 618–619.

[65] Matthew 16:18.

[66] A selection from the writings of the fathers from St. Clement of Rome to St. Athanasius, *The Early Christian Fathers*, ed. and trans. by Henry Bettenson (London: Oxford University Press, 1969), p. 2.

[67] H.H. Milman, *History of Latin Christianity*, 1867, vol. I, p. 228, quoted in E.O. James, *In the Fullness of Time* (London: Society for Promoting Christian Knowledge, New York: The MacMillan Company, 1935), p. 161.

[68] Loraine Boettner, *Roman Catholicism* (Philadelphia: The Presbyterian and Reformed Publishing Company, 1962), p. 113.

[69] Ibid., pp. 118–119.

[70] Durant, p. 616.

[71] Williston Walker, *A History of the Christian Church* (Edinburgh: T. and T. Clark, 1918), p. 57.

[72] Cubberley, *History of Education*, p. 92. Also see Benson, p. 50.

[73] See footnote 62.

[74] Eby and Arrowood, p. 656.

[75] Latourette, *The First Five Centuries*, p. 367.

[76] Thomas M. Lindsay, *A History of the Reformation* (Edinburgh, T. and T. Clark, 1906), Preface IX.

Illustration Sources

Figure 1   *Inscription*—Photo by author (PBA).

Figure 2   *Colosseum*—PBA.

Figure 3   *Catacombs*—PBA.

Figure 4   *Arch of Constantine*—PBA.

Figure 5   *Barbarian soldier*—Helen Pierson, History of Germany (New York: George Routledge Sons, 1884), p.1.

590 —TIME PERIOD—1054

Birth of a Religious Empire

TIME LINE				
30	325	590	1054	1517
Early Church	Imperial Church	Middle Ages or Catholic Era	The Great Schism	Modern Era

The Middle Ages, or the Catholic era, extended over a 927-year period from Pope Gregory in 590 to Martin Luther in 1517. Others adjust the dates for a variety of reasons, but these are the approximate dates of the often grim but colorful Middle Ages, also known as the medieval period. This chapter will focus on the first part of the medieval period, known as the Dark Ages. Historians generally agree that the darkest period of this era extended from 600 to 850.[1] The Dark Ages, however, went well beyond the latter date to the division of the Catholic Church (the Great Schism) between Rome and Constantinople in 1054.[2]

The trail of historical information is not well lighted during the Dark Ages, especially as it relates to evangelical Christians and their Christian schools. The three divisions of chapter 4 are:

1. Theological and Administrative Patterns of the Catholic Church
2. Forms of Education in the Religious Empire
3. Stamping Out the Opposition

1. Theological and Administrative Patterns of the Catholic Church

The medieval period in western Europe was the era of "One World—One Faith—One Church—for a thousand years."[3] Before we trace the events of this period, it will help our understanding to review several theological patterns that guided the Catholic Church in this Catholic era and beyond. Most of these patterns, if not all, will appear to many modern Catholics, to most Protestants, and to others to be laced with serious errors. It should be noted that after 1517 similar errors were also made by Reformation Protestants, and we will look at those later.

It is important to remember that many of the early Catholic leaders were former pagans in Rome. Unfortunately, instead of the spirit of Christ, Catholic policies often reflected the spirit of ancient Imperial Rome. This was, indeed, the case in the Catholic position on heretics.

HERETICS

You will recall the imperial edict of 438, in which Emperor Theodosius II established the name "Catholic Christians" and said, in effect, that all those in his empire who did not convert to Catholicism would be considered "mad and demented" and guilty of "holding heretical doctrine." He then put forth the following threat, which was typical of pagan Rome: "They shall first suffer the wrath of God, then the punishment which in accordance with divine judgment we shall inflict."[4]

St. Thomas Aquinas, "the greatest philosopher and theologian of the medieval church,"[5] wrote the following:

> I reply that heretics must be considered from two points of view, namely, as regards the heretic himself, and secondly, as regards the Church. As for the heretics themselves, there is their sin for which they deserve not only to be separated from the Church by excommunication, but to be sent out of the world by death. It is, indeed, a much more serious offense to corrupt the faith, upon which depends the life of the soul, than to falsify coin, by means of which the temporal life is sustained. Hence, if counterfeiters and other malefactors are justly hurried to death by secular rulers, much the more may those who are convicted of heresy not only be excommunicated but justly put to a speedy death. But on the side of the Church, there is mercy looking for the conversion of the erring. She does not therefore condemn immediately, but only after a first and second admonition, as the Apostle teaches. Should the heretic still prove stubborn, the Church, no longer hoping for his conversion, shall provide for the safety of others by separating him from herself by a sentence of excommunication. She further relinquishes him to the secular judgment to be put out of the world by death. Jerome also says (on the passage in Galatians v.—"a little leaven"), and it is stated in 24. qu. 3, cap. 16, "Foul flesh must be cut away, and mangy sheep must be kept from the fold lest the whole house be burned, the whole mass corrupted, the whole body be destroyed."[6]

A later Jesuit statement on heretics is even more narrowly defined and gives no room for those who "repent":

> The Catholic Church has the right and the duty to kill heretics, because it is by fire and sword that heresy can be extirpated. Mere excommunication is derided by heretics. If they are imprisoned or exiled they corrupt others. The only source is to put them to death. *Repentance cannot be allowed to save them,* just as Repentance is not allowed to save civil criminals; for the highest good of the Church is the Unity of Faith, and this cannot be preserved unless heretics are put to death.[7]

Regrettably, multiplied thousands died during the Middle Ages because of the Catholic policy on heretics.

SALE OF INDULGENCES

Contrary to Romans 5:1, the Catholic Church established that access to God for salvation and forgiveness of sin was through a mediator in the person of a Catholic priest or higher church official. While this is still practiced by Catholics today, during the medieval period the church established a policy of selling forgiveness of sins and remission of part or all of a person's time in purgatory. These "indulgences," as they were called, were actually sold to Catholic parishioners. Indulgences were marketed on a sliding scale depending on the magnitude of the sin. Sometimes they were even sold in advance, before the sins were committed. The practice escalated into a churchwide fund-raising campaign to rebuild St. Peter's Basilica in Rome. In a later period Thomas Gascoigne, Chancellor of Oxford University, said:

> Sinners say nowadays: "I care not how many evils I do in God's sight, for I can easily get plenary remission of all guilt and penalty by an absolution and indulgence granted me by the pope, whose written grant I have bought for four or six pence, or have won as a stake for a game of tennis. . . .[8]

As we will learn, the bizarre nature of this practice helped to ignite the Reformation in 1517.

LEARNING FOR COMMON PEOPLE SUPPRESSED

The vast majority of those in Roman Catholicism's empire were illiterate. Some estimate that the European population was ninety percent illiterate during most of the Middle Ages.[9] There appears to have been an elitist attitude among Catholic officials regarding basic learning for common people. According to historian Cubberley, the prevailing sentiment of the Catholic Church was that "it was not important that more than a few be educated."[10]   Sociology professor Blackmar explains the Catholic attitude toward education:

> The attitude of the Christian church toward learning in the Middle Ages was entirely arbitrary. It had become thoroughly institutionalized and was not in sympathy with the changes that were taking place outside of its own policy. It assumed an attitude of hostility to everything that tended toward the development of free and independent thought outside the dictates of the authorities of the church.[11]

One Catholic priest wrote, "It would be preferable if the peasantry were not able to read and write, for then they would be unable to read heretical books."[12]   Later, after the Reformation was under way, a Catholic bishop in Austria suggested the abolition of all rural schools. This, he believed, would deprive young citizens of the opportunity for basic literacy and thereby "dry up the fountain of poisonous heresy."[13]   Professor Melton says:

> The Catholic Church and the Hapsburg dynasty, obviously, could not entirely dispense with the written word. No matter how remote the parish, someone was needed to read royal decrees and ecclesiastical directives, as a parish priest from Riegersburg (Styria) pointed out in 1752. Although he favored abolishing parish schools, he recommended that at least one pupil from each village learn to read and write so that "the inhabitants of a village don't have to run far and wide to find someone who can read a printed ordinance."[14]

In Scotland, the Catholic paranoia over literacy for common people is clearly seen in this statement by Andrew Miller: "The greatest care was taken to prevent even catechisms, composed and approved by the clergy, from coming into the hands of the laity. . . . Learning was branded as the parent of heresy."[15]   Clearly, Catholic leaders were more concerned about eliminating heretics than providing education. Clarence Benson says, "Instead of advocating education, the popes were busy hunting and murdering the Waldensian believers."[16]

BIBLE READING DECLARED A CRIME PUNISHABLE BY DEATH
A Catholic policy of the medieval period that is difficult for an evangelical mind to comprehend was the ban on reading the Bible. Contrary to the command of Isaiah 34:16, "Seek ye out the book of the Lord, and read," the Catholic authorities at two councils placed a ban on Bible reading for Catholic laity. At the Council of Valencia, Spain, in 1229, the Bible was placed on "The Index of Forbidden Books" with the following decree:

> We prohibit the permitting of the laity to have the books of the Old and New Testament, unless any one should wish, from a feeling of devotion, to have a psalter or breviary for divine service, or the hours of the blessed Mary. But we strictly forbid them to have the above-mentioned books in the vulgar tongue.[17]

Early in the sixteenth century the Catholic Church still strongly enforced this rule. As Cubberley writes:

> Very severe measures were enacted to prevent the spread of the contagion of heresy. All Protestant literature was forbidden circulation in Catholic lands. The printing-press, as a disseminator of heresy, was placed under strict license. Certain books were ordered burned. Perhaps the most extreme and ruthless measure was the prohibition, under penalty of death, of the reading of the Bible. That this harsh act was carried out the record of martyrs shows. As one example may be mentioned the sister of the Flemish artist Matsys and her husband, he being decapitated and she buried alive in the square fronting the cathedral at Louvain, in 1543, for having been caught reading the sacred Book.[18]

Well after the Reformation, at the Council of Trent, Catholic leaders softened the rule by stating that mature members of the laity could read the Bible in the common language provided that it had been translated by Catholic authors and that the readers had written permission. The first sentence of the famous Trent decree reads:

> In as much as it is manifest, from experience, that if the Holy Bible, translated into the vulgar tongue, be indiscriminately allowed to everyone, the temerity of men will cause more evil than good to arise from it.[19]

The troubling portion of that statement is the idea that reading the Bible "will cause more evil than good." This, of course, is incomprehensible to evangelical Christians. The list of disturbing Catholic patterns and policies during the medieval period could go on to include the excessive accumulation of church wealth, the enormous political power of the church, and the immoral and opulent living standards of Catholic officials. The following statement provides a hint of the problem. Catholic Bishop William Durand of Mende wrote to the Council of Vienna in 1311:

> The whole Church might be reformed if the Church of Rome would begin by removing evil examples from herself . . . by which men are scandalized, and the whole people, as it were, infected. . . . For in all lands . . . the Church of Rome is in ill repute, and all cry and publish it abroad that within her bosom all men, from the greatest even unto the least, have set their hearts upon covetousness. . . . That the whole

Christian folk take from the clergy pernicious examples of gluttony is clear and notorious, since the clergy feast more luxuriously . . . than princes and kings.[20]

2. Forms of Education in the Religious Empire

We now move to the educational history of the early medieval period, and in so doing we will shift the spotlight from the Romans to the Germans. First, though, we need to understand the political background of this period. You will recall that the Germans conquered Rome in three successive waves, the last occurring in A.D. 476 at the hands of German general Odoacer.[21] Professor Wilds provides the best description of the Teutonic tribes in Central Europe:

> The Teutonic peoples were inherently as capable as the Greeks and the Italians; but in their geographical location in Europe they had fewer means of learning the arts and institutions of higher civilization. They therefore remained barbarians for a much longer time, but they were, however, far from being primitive savages. . . . The morals of marriage and of the family were pure among them; they respected womanhood more than the later Greeks and Romans. Their sense of personal dignity would not permit these early Teutonic peoples, like the Spartans and early Romans, to yield their liberty to the iron discipline of a state, to make themselves an unthinking part of a social machine. It was the purity of the Teutonic family life and the free, dignified spirit of Teutonic individualism, later directed by Christian principles, which eventually gave to the modern world a distinguishing superiority over the ancient world.[22]

Recall too that at the defeat of the western portion of the Roman Empire in A.D. 476, the seat of power was moved from Rome to Constantinople. When the youthful Emperor Romulus Augustus, the last western emperor, was deposed by General Odoacer, the relocation of the Roman throne became necessary. Wilds describes the transition:

> When this young lad was removed from his throne, and the imperial ornaments of the Caesars were sent to Constantinople in token of the supposed reunion of the Empire under one head, the collapse of the western part of the great Roman Empire of Caesar and Trajan was complete. For, although there was as yet no similar collapse of the Empire in the East, nevertheless the Germans henceforth controlled all the West and were to work out the destiny of Europe.[23]

The eastern portion of the empire, known as the Byzantine Empire, continued until 1453, when the Islamic Turks captured Constantinople,[24] the city originally dedicated in 326 to the Virgin Mary by Emperor Constantine. For all practical purposes, this left Rome and the vast adjacent lands to its sole heir, the emerging Catholic Church, referred to by historians as "the grave of the deceased Roman Empire."[25] From this imposing capital city, the Catholic Church built a large religious empire that included the Holy Roman Empire, which encompassed the kingdoms of Germany, Bohemia, Burgundy, Italy, and the Papal States surrounding Rome. In addition to the Holy Roman Empire, Catholicism's larger religious empire included France, Spain, and England.

THE ORIGIN OF THE HOLY ROMAN EMPIRE

The Holy Roman Empire, a supranational kingdom, was founded in 800 by Pope Leo III and the great German warrior Charlemagne. On Christmas day of that year, in Rome, Pope Leo III crowned Charlemagne with a crown bearing Caesar's diamond. He was the first Catholic emperor to serve under papal authority. Pope Leo said as he crowned Charlemagne, "To Charles, Augustus, crowned of God, great and peace-making emperor of the Romans, may God give life and victory."[26]

The question arises, Why would a Roman pontiff, "the vicar of Christ,"

Figure 1. The Holy Roman Empire was a blending of Teutonic Germany with Latin Italy into a single religious and political entity under the ultimate authority of the Roman pope.

regarded as "God almighty on earth," sovereign over earthly kings, be willing to crown a German king as emperor of the Holy Roman Empire? The answer may well lie in the fact that Pope Leo III had been accused, rightly or wrongly, of adultery and perjury[27] by relatives of Pope Hadrian, his predecessor.[28] Pope Leo had been brutally assaulted in the streets of Rome and had escaped to hide in a local Catholic monastery. Convinced of Pope Leo's innocence, Charlemagne convened a synod of Catholic archbishops, bishops, and counts for "the most important trial conducted in Rome in centuries."[29] The synod ultimately determined that the pope should be his own judge and issued the following statement:

We do not dare to judge the Apostolic See which is the head of all the churches of God. For all of us are judged by it and its vicar; it however is judged by nobody as it is the custom from ancient times. But as the highest pontiff will have decided we shall obey canonically."[30]

Pope Leo III declared his own innocence on December 23, 800,[31] and two days later he crowned Charlemagne emperor of the Holy Roman Empire in

Figure 2. Charlemagne, a German warrior king, was crowned as the first emperor of the Holy Roman Empire on Christmas day, A.D. 800, by Pope Leo III at St. Peter's Basilica in Rome.

St. Peter's Basilica, where the historic trial had taken place.[32] It was the beginning of a brand-new era. Regrettably, it would not be a pleasant one.

Charlemagne's imperial capital in Germany was Aachen, forty-four miles southwest of Cologne. Twenty-eight future emperors of the Holy Roman Empire would be crowned in that city. Aachen became the satellite nerve center of the Holy Roman Empire.[33]

CATHOLIC EXPANSION

The Catholic Era produced an interesting blend of culture and dogma now deeply embedded in the fabric of European history. While it was indeed a period of "intellectual stagnation"[34] as philosopher Robert Cooke describes it, it was also a time of amazing administrative leadership on the part of numerous popes in Rome and on the part of Rome's emperors in the Holy Roman Empire. Popes Leo I (440–461) and Gregory the Great (590–604) were among the primary organizers of Catholic expansion. Pope Gregory, like Leo, would not hesitate to use coercion to bring about conversions to the Catholic faith. Historian Lewis Sherrill writes:

> On learning that peasants in a certain district were still unconverted, he wrote the bishop that such a man should be "loaded with so great a burden of payment that by the very pain of the exaction he will be compelled to hasten to the right way."[35]

Latourette says, "By the end of the fifth century scarcely an important city in the land was without a bishop."[36] Catholicism's emerging administrative pattern and her ecclesiastical hierarchy of pope, cardinals, archbishops, bishops, priests, and monks—plus its civil emperors, such as Charlemagne, and its nobles—all combined to build a formidable empire. It seems the leaders of the emerging Roman Catholic Church retained many of the organizational skills so characteristic of their ancestors in the old Roman Empire. Richard Todd agrees:

> In many ways the Roman church had taken on the shape of the Roman world in which it had grown to maturity. The most obvious example of this is the way in which the church's organization followed the pattern of the imperial administration. Each city was entitled to a bishop and each province to an archbishop. Within the bishop's diocese, the hierarchy of officers was virtually the same as that of the Roman civil administration. Church canon law was modeled on Roman law. At first it contained only decrees of church councils, but eventually included papal decretals, which paralleled imperial edicts.[37]

In a very real sense the Catholic Church sprang from the ashes of the dying Roman Empire.

ENGLAND

Much of the now defunct Roman Empire in the West was, in effect, "repossessed" by the Roman Catholic Church. Pope Gregory, the first pope of the medieval period, championed the idea of "converting by coercion" the lands formally conquered by the Roman emperors. During his fourteen-year tenure, Gregory greatly expanded Catholic territories, including England. Speaking of Pope Gregory in this regard, Eby and Arrowood write:

His most notable missionary achievement [was] the sending of St. Augustine to England in 596. The winning of the Saxons and subsequently of all Britain to the Roman Church is a well-known story.[38]

Noted British historian A.F. Leach describes the coming of Catholicism to England:

When, at the end of the sixth century, Christianity [Catholicism] came to England, it came, not from the Celtic Britons, nor even from the neighbouring and kindred Franks, but "bret hot from Rome," a direct importation from Italy.[39]

Pope Gregory had commissioned Augustine to set up "sees" or "bishoprics" in London and York. In those years London, a small trading center, was referred to as "that monstrous anthill on the plain."[40] It was not the ants of London, however, that diverted Augustine from establishing his first bishopric there. Rather it was Bertha, the wife of King Ethelbert of Kent, who met and welcomed Augustine and his party on their way to London. After their meeting she persuaded her husband to become a Catholic. He then invited Augustine to settle in his capital of Canterbury, fifty miles east of London.[41] It is likely that the enthusiasm and cooperation of King Ethelbert were augmented through a papal gift presented by Augustine. It is not known when the tradition of the "Golden Rose," a pure gold gift of the pope to foreign monarchs, began, but it became a major expansionist tool and friendly persuader for the Vatican. A book describing the royal gifts of Scotland explains the political impact of the pope's famous gift of the "Golden Rose":

The exchange of gifts was an important and integral part of political life in the Middle Ages. Any papal gift to a European monarch had immense prestige and religious significance. One such gift was the Golden Rose.

This was in the form of a cluster of roses mounted on a stem attached to a pedestal base. Flowers and leaves were of pure gold. The largest flower was set with a precious stone of reddish hue, such as an amethyst, and also had a receptacle for balsam and musk to give fragrance to the rose. The Golden Rose conveyed a spiritual message and was a symbol of papal esteem for the recipient. . . . This was a singular honour to the sovereign of a small realm beyond the mainland of Europe.[42]

Other papal gifts included solid gold scepters and swords fashioned by the highly talented goldsmiths in Rome. Such gifts had a powerful impact on monarchs with small kingdoms.

ECCLESIASTICAL EDUCATION IN ENGLAND

Within a year of Augustine's arrival, King Ethelbert was baptized into the Catholic Church and immediately provided Archbishop Augustine with property for a cathedral. A.F. Leach says, "He endowed the archbishop and his see,"[43] meaning that the king gave Augustine not only adequate grounds for a cathedral complex but also substantial income-producing properties to fund his base of operation, including a cathedral school.

A typical pattern of the Catholic Church was to establish a school along with its cathedrals and churches. The primary purpose of the schools was to prepare young men to serve as priests. This practice put growing pressure on the emerging church because of the dismal illiteracy among Catholic priests on mainland Europe. Eavey says:

> Even the education of the clergy, during some three centuries prior to Charlemagne, was very much neglected. By the beginning of the seventh century education was largely in the hands of bishops, priests, and monks, many of whom were themselves illiterate. . . . many of the clergy did not understand the meaning of the services they conducted and the prayers they recited.[44]

The two oldest schools in England today, the King's School of Canterbury and King's School of Rochester (both now Anglican), date from the Catholic Era. Leach describes the founding of the King's School, Canterbury:

> It may be safely asserted then, that in this year, 598, as an adjunct to Christ Church Cathedral, or rather as part of it, and under the tuition of himself and the clerks who came with him and whom Ethelbert endowed, Augustine established the Grammar School which still flourishes under the name of the King's School, not from its original founder, Ethelbert, but from its re-founder, Henry VIII.[45]

The King's School Rochester, located halfway between Canterbury and London, was founded in 604 by Justin, the Catholic Bishop of Rochester, as a part of the St. Andrew Cathedral complex. Both of these schools, and all other Catholic schools and churches, were "refounded" in the dramatic transition from Catholicism to Protestantism during the Reformation in the 1500s.

A third important school in English antiquity is the song school at St. Peter's Cathedral in York.[46] Most cathedrals had at least two schools, a song school, or elementary school, and a grammar school that in reality was a secondary school.

ENGLAND'S CATHEDRAL SCHOOLS,
PIONEERS IN LIBERAL ARTS

Clearly, the educational patterns of the English Catholic Church were decidedly different from those in continental Europe. Perhaps it can be said that, when it came to education, Archbishop Augustine and the other cathedral bishops in England practiced the philosophy of the ancient Chinese proverb, "The Emperor lives over the hill." Pope Gregory and succeeding popes of the Dark Ages were strongly opposed to cathedral schools' offering academic subjects. In a letter in 595, Pope Gregory admonished his bishop in Vienne (now Vienna, Austria) with these words: "It has come to our knowledge that your brotherhood teaches grammar to certain persons." He then refers to the practice as a "crime."[47] As previously stated, the Catholic Church was not a champion of basic literacy and learning for common people nor of the wide distribution of the Bible. Even though ninety percent of Europe's population was illiterate,[48] the Catholic Church did nothing to advance learning unless it pertained to future clergy. As church historian Sherrill says, "The [Catholic] Church did not interest itself in teaching children."[49] It was interested only in what H.I. Marrow called "ecclesiastical education,"[50] which was narrowly focused on Catholic theology and canon law.

In England, however, while the Catholic Church did not offer education for the general population, it did offer elementary and secondary education to those destined for church service and for "a few families of the upper class."[51] English cathedral schools followed the academic designations of the Seven Liberal Arts developed centuries before by Aristotle in ancient Greece: grammar, dialectic (logic), rhetoric (oratory), arithmetic, music, geometry, and astronomy—a course of study regarded by the pope in Rome as pagan learning. In addition to the "pagan" liberal arts of Aristotle, the cathedral schools and the monastery schools of England added an eighth category—Catholic theology.[52]

In 705 Egbert became the archbishop of the cathedral in York and founded a grammar school in addition to the cathedral's existing song school. Archbishop Egbert served as the first teacher in the school, followed by Albert in 750. Albert's most famous pupil was Alcuin, who later became schoolmaster of the York Cathedral School and in 782 was chosen by Emperor Charlemagne to head his palace school in Aachen, Germany.[53] It was Alcuin who introduced the Seven Liberal Arts to mainland Europe.

Alcuin provides an interesting description of an eighth-century cathedral school curriculum taught by his predecessor, Albert:

Figure 3. The site of one of England's schools of antiquity, the Catholic song school at St. Peter's Cathedral in York. Alcuin, the famous schoolmaster at this school, broke the academic barrier of the Middle Ages when he introduced Aristotle's liberal arts curriculum at Charlemagne's palace school in Aachen, Germany.

There he (Albert) moistened thirsty hearts with divers streams of teaching and varied dews of study; busily giving to some the arts of the science of grammar *(grammaticae rationis artes),* pouring into others the streams of the tongues of orators; these he polished on the whet-stone of law, those he taught to sing in Æonian chant, making others play on the flute of Castaly, and run with the lyre over the hills of Parnassus. But others, the said master made to know the harmony of heaven and the sun, the labours of the moon, the five belts of the sky, the seven planets, the laws of the fixed stars, their rising and setting, the movements of the air and the sun, the earth's quake, the nature of men, cattle, birds, and beasts, the different kinds of number and various (geometrical) figures: and he gave sure return to the festival of Easter; above all, revealing the mysteries of holy writ, for he opened the abysses of the old and rude law.[54]

It appears that, in the cathedral school, one teacher taught all subjects. A.F. Leach explains:

The one master taught all the subjects of learning, not only the trivium, grammar, rhetoric, and logic; and the quadrivium, arithmetic, geometry, music, and astronomy; but the subjects of the higher faculties, law, and "above all" divinity. He therefore performed the functions afterwards separated by division of labour between the Grammar Schoolmaster [and] the Song Schoolmaster.[55]

IRELAND

Before we follow Alcuin, the great English schoolmaster, to the imperial courts of Charlemagne in Aachen, Germany, we must focus our attention on the pre-Catholic era of Ireland. While Southern Ireland is currently the most Catholic republic in the world, that has not always been the case. It is interesting to note that Ireland was never invaded by the Romans and was, therefore, never a part of the Roman Empire.[56] In fact, Ireland claims to have been an empire by herself, totally independent of all other empires:

> "It was in reference to this period," says O'Driscoll, "that Ireland, by the unanimous consent of the European nations, was placed in the rank of a third empire; the Roman, the Constantinopolitan, and the Irish."[57]

Ireland, in its early history, was an intellectual empire rather than an empire of military or religious conquest. Located off the west coast of England, the country was in effect "out of the line of fire" of the early barbarian invasions of the western Roman Empire. This "caused many learned men to flee to Ireland,"[58] thus raising the level of learning among Irish citizens. Eby and Arrowood provide insight into early Irish education:

> At a very early period the Druids and poets, who were the learned and literary class in Ireland, took students, who followed them from place to place, hearing their lectures. . . . In time, possibly in the third century, regular schools for law, military science, and literature began. Learning was held in the highest esteem, and the illiterate agricultural laborers were obliged to support the bards, while kings and other magnates were patrons of learning.
>
> Teachers were ranked in classes, the highest class of which was composed of men who were masters of Gaelic literature. . . . Twelve years of study were required for the completion of the bardic training.
>
> Fosterage, the practice of sending children from home at an early age to be reared and educated in the home and under the special care of a kinsman, was common among the leading people of the ancient Irish.[59]

Poetry and storytelling were a major focus of early Irish education. Bardic schools existed to train Irish poets. Dowling explains:

> The best description we have of a Bardic School at work is given in the Preface to the Clanrickarde Memoirs, published in London in 1722. It was a school of poetry, and open only to students who were themselves descendants of poets and already of some distinction in their tribes. The school was situated in a quiet spot away from the families and friends of the students so that their studies should suffer no

interruption. The school building was a simple construction with no windows, and furnished with a table, couch and chair for each student, who had a cubicle of his own. On the evening of the first day, the students were given a subject on which to write a poem; then they withdrew to their cubicles to compose their poems in complete darkness. There they remained till next evening when candles were brought and they wrote down their compositions. These were given to their professors in the assembly hall and examined by them. On Saturdays and the eves of Feasts, the students were entertained by the gentlemen and rich farmers of the neighbourhood. The school was open from Michaelmas to the 25th March, when the students returned to their homes, each one carrying with him an important document, namely, an Attestation of his Behaviour and Capacity, from the chief Professor, to those that had sent him.[60]

To this day there are Bardic Literary Societies in Ireland where members recount Irish poems and stories. A Protestant minister makes this observation:

The manner of preserving the accuracy of tradition is singular, and worthy of notice. In the winter evenings, a number of seanachies requently meet together, and recite alternately their traditionary stories. If anyone repeats a passage, which appears to another to be incorrect, he is immediately stopped, when each gives a reason for his way of reciting the passage, the dispute is then referred to a vote of the meeting, and the decision of the majority become imperative on the subject for the future.[61]

Ireland's introduction to Christianity came in the form of the ancient Celtic faith. It will surprise some to learn that St. Patrick, "the patron saint of Ireland," was not a Catholic but rather a Celtic Christian. While Celtic Christianity used ecclesiastical terminology similar to that used in Roman Catholicism such as the terms *abbot, monastery,* and *monk,* it was decidedly more Bible-based and was totally independent of Rome. Speaking of the Celtic Church, Andrew Miller says, "For many ages she maintained her independence of Rome, rejected all foreign control, acknowledged Christ only as Head of the Church."[62] In a similar vein, Elliott Binns says, "As the Irish had never been subject to the Roman Empire, they had no natural reverence for Rome or for its bishop, and adopted their own form of organization." [63]

Patrick, who grew up in Europe, was the son of a Celtic deacon and the grandson of a Celtic presbyter.[64] His main mission, beginning in A.D. 440, was to Northern Ireland. Because of the enduring ministry he founded, Ireland gained the reputation of being "dotted all over with churches, monasteries, and schools."[65]

Approximately a hundred years later another great Celtic missionary, St. Columba of Ireland, established a school and a missionary college on Iona, an island off the north coast of Scotland. His main mission was evangelization among the warlike tribes of the Picts in Northern Scotland. Students, many of whom had come from Europe to study under Columba on his small island, returned home to become missionaries to Britain, France, and Germany.[66] Miller says, "The fame of Ireland for its monasteries, missionary schools, and as the seat of pure Scriptural teaching, rose so high, that it received the honourable appellation of 'The isle of saints.'"[67] Godkin agrees: "The learning of the ancient Irish schools was unquestionably superior for those ages."[68] Sherrill captures the spiritual and academic spirit of Ireland in the pre-Catholic Era with these words:

> In Ireland a love of learning was kept alive; and those men had their own ideas about Easter and other churchly matters as well, seeing no sufficient reason why Rome should decide all questions.[69]

Regrettably, the good start in Ireland and Scotland changed dramatically at the hands of England's King Henry II, Pope Adrian IV, and the Viking invasions beginning in 795.[70] We will examine this unfortunate transition in chapter 5.

Figure 4. This statue of Charlemagne, the first emperor of the Holy Roman Empire, is near the entrance of Notre Dame Cathedral in Paris.

THE PALACE SCHOOL OF CHARLEMAGNE

In the meantime, Charlemagne, or "Charles the Great" as some called him, invited Alcuin, the famous schoolmaster of York, England, to come to his palace in Aachen, Germany, in 782,[71] to revive his palace school. This singular event shattered the academic darkness of Catholic Europe. Clearly, Pope Gregory's ban on Aristotle's liberal arts curriculum was not as tightly controlled at Charlemagne's palace school as it was at cathedral and monastic schools. Alcuin's mission was not only to serve as the principal teacher of Charlemagne's palace school but also to advance education throughout Charlemagne's empire.

Alcuin may have taught the most interesting collection of students in history. His class roll included the following:

1. King Charlemagne, "foremost in eagerness among his pupils."
2. Queen Liutgard, "the last and best beloved of [Charlemagne's] wives."
3. Gisela, sister of Charlemagne.
4. Charles, son of Charlemagne.
5. Pepin, son of Charlemagne.
6. Lewis, son of Charlemagne (would succeed his father as emperor of the Holy Roman Empire).
7. Rotrud, daughter of Charlemagne.
8. Gisela, daughter of Charlemagne.
9. Angilbert, son-in-law of Charlemagne.
10. Adelhard, nephew of Charlemagne.
11. Wala, nephew of Charlemagne.
12. Gundrada, niece of Charlemagne.
13. Einhard, the King's biographer.
14. Riculf, who would later become the Catholic Archbishop of Mayence.
15. Arno, who was later Archbishop of Salzburg.
16. Theodulf, who later became Archbishop of Orleans.[72]

Alcuin found it a challenge to teach the members of the royal household, most of whom were illiterate but eager to learn. Numerous historians record the following anecdote about Alcuin's royal class of students:

> He [Alcuin] had to be more than a skilful teacher of docile pupils, for their awakened minds roved restlessly about from one question and puzzle to another, and with these they plied their master assiduously, not the least persistent of his questioners being the king himself. Charles wanted to know everything and to know it at once. His strong, uncurbed nature eagerly seized on learning, both as a delight for himself and a means of giving stability to his government, and so, while he knew he must be docile, he was at the same time imperious. Thus, on one occasion when he had been informed of the great learning of Augustine and Jerome, he impatiently demanded of Alcuin, "Why can I not have twelve clerks such as these?" Twelve Augustines and Jeromes! and to be made to arise at the emperor's bidding! Alcuin was shocked. "What!" he discreetly rejoined, "the Lord of heaven and earth had but two such, and wouldst thou have twelve?"[73]

Not only did Alcuin serve Charlemagne as master educator of the royal household for the next eight years, but in 787 he assisted Charlemagne in writing his famous proclamation on Catholic education, the "first general charter on education" in the medieval period. It has been referred to as "perhaps the most important document of the Middle Ages" and "the charter of modern thought."[74] A portion of the king's charter, referred to as a "capitulary," is as follows:

> During past years we have often received letters from different monasteries informing us that at their sacred services the brethren offered up prayers on our behalf; and we have observed that the thoughts contained in these letters, though in themselves most just, were expressed in uncouth language, and while pious devotion dictated the sentiments, the unlettered tongue was unable to express them aright. Hence there has arisen in our minds the fear lest, if the skill to write rightly were thus lacking, so too would the power of rightly comprehending the Sacred Scriptures be far less than was fitting, and we all know that though verbal errors be dangerous, errors of the understanding are yet more so. We exhort you, therefore, not only not to neglect the study of letters, but to apply yourselves thereto with perseverance and with that humility which is well pleasing to God; so that you may be able to penetrate with greater ease and certainty the mysteries of the Holy Scriptures. Let there, therefore, be chosen for this work men who are both able and willing to learn, and also desirous of instructing others; and let them apply themselves to the work with a zeal equalling the earnestness with which we recommend it to them. —Adieu.[75]

Alcuin died in 804 in St. Martin's Monastery in Tours, a hundred miles south of Paris.[76] Charlemagne died eight years later in Aachen.[77] Regrettably, the succeeding emperors, including his son Lewis, did not perpetuate Charlemagne's enthusiasm for education in the Holy Roman Empire. The short-lived revival of learning created by Charlemagne and Alcuin came at the lowest point of the Middle Ages. Cubberley explains:

> The monastic and cathedral schools which had been established earlier had in large part been broken up, and the monasteries had become places for the pensioning of royal favorites and hence had lost their earlier religious zeal and effectiveness. The abbots and bishops possessed but little learning and the lower clergy, recruited largely from bondmen, were grossly ignorant, greatly to the injury of the Church. The copying of books had almost ceased, and learning was slowly dying out.[78]

COPYISTS

One of the "academic functions" of monasteries in this period was the hand-copying of books, including the Catholic Bible. Prior to the invention of the printing press in 1645, books were handwritten by copyists, usually by monks or nuns in monasteries. As words were read aloud, they were simultaneously written down by multiple copyists. It was a slow and tedious process. In the later Middle Ages, great care was given to the work, but this was not so during the Dark Ages. Brockett wrote:

> The ability to read and write was not considered, by any means, indispensable even to the bishops, much less to the inferior clergy. The monasteries generally contained libraries, and some of the monks could usually write well enough to transcribe such copies of the Scriptures or liturgy as were needed; but this was done in so imperfect and slovenly a manner that their manuscripts were full of errors, and a century or two later required the most strenuous efforts for their correction.[79]

Figure 5. The culmination of a fourteen-year chivalric education was knighthood celebrated, as depicted here, with a knighting ceremony.

Those who were literate and well educated during the Dark Ages had little status even in the monasteries. Cubberley says, "A knowledge of reading and writing was commonly regarded as effeminate."[80] This idea is indirectly affirmed by Reed and Prevost: "Many who copied the Bible and other documents did so because they were unable to survive the physical demands of monastic manual labor."[81] As we will see, this stigma diminished in the centuries to follow.

CHIVALRIC EDUCATION

We turn now to one of the more colorful forms of education to spring from the medieval period. It was a complete system of education for the Catholic nobility based on the feudalism that flourished in the Holy Roman Empire and to a limited degree in England and Scotland. It was called chivalric education, and its goal was knighthood. Like Spartan education, it involved little academic learning.

To understand chivalry, however, it is important to understand the feudalistic society of Catholicism's religious empire. A major responsibility of any government is to provide protection for its citizens, especially sudden attacks by invaders. Clearly the focus of the leaders of the medieval Catholic Church was preserving the church, not protecting the people from invaders. When the Catholic leaders failed to provide protection, a "privatized" form of protection emerged. This privatized protection began shortly after the fall of the old Roman Empire and the subsequent demise of the vast Roman army. Landowners devised their own system of protection, which in time grew into a formal system of feudalism that proved oppressive to the vast majority of the population. Professor Wilds writes:

> When the kings and princes gave of their lands to feudal lords, and these in turn granted sections to lesser lords, and so on down, the land so granted was called a "fief," or "feud;" the grantor was called "lord," or "liege;" and the one who received the grant was "vassal," or "retainer." The vassal

Figure 6. Warwick Castle in England is one of the best preserved medieval castles.

> made pledges of loyalty, military service, and other aid to his lord, and the lord in turn provided his vassal with counsel and protection. The great bulk of the population were serfs, who were bound to the soil and who passed with the land when it changed masters.[82]

The great castles of mainland Europe, England, and Scotland were created as fortresses against invaders. They were the protection centers for major landowners and their families during the medieval period. Each castle had a standing army of knights. It was this group that developed chivalric education.

Chivalric training began at age seven and continued through age twenty-one. Gangel and Benson describe the fourteen-year process as follows:

> At about the age of seven an applicant would be accepted as a page into a knight's household. After serving seven years the page would become a squire and accompany the knight to the battlefield as an assistant. Meanwhile the squire would learn courtly manners; how to fight on horseback; the art of hunting; care of armor, weapons, and horses; singing, reciting, and composing verses; and storytelling. At twenty-one the squire would become a knight, a title that carried various obligations.[83]

The ceremony of conferring knighthood, or "dubbing," took place most often in a Catholic Church. Frost and Bailey provide the following description:

> Part of the formality included fasting and a night of prayer before an altar where his sword rested. A lecture detailed his duties, and he swore three vows. He vowed loyalty to the church, honor and loyalty to his superiors, and gallantry and loyalty to his lady. Next, he was touched on each shoulder by a sword and proclaimed a knight. Symbolic of his rank, he received a gold chain, sword belt, sword, and spurs.[84]

Ideally, a knight was to be holy, gallant, honorable, humble, and generous. But as Reed and Prevost point out, knights were more likely to be "ruthless, selfish, cruel, scheming, and untrustworthy."[85] The knights and nobles were to play a major role in the eight Catholic crusades to oust the Islamic Turks from Jerusalem in the early medieval period. Of knights and medieval education, William Corkey says:

> Only two classes were educated, the Churchman and the Knight or Squire, and the course of instruction for the latter embraced hunting, riding, swimming, boxing, hawking, and shooting with the bow. This idea of educating only a select few for privileged positions was maintained throughout Europe until the dawn of the Reformation.[86]

EDUCATIONAL OPTIONS FOR COMMON PEOPLE

Ordinary citizens in the long Catholic era had two options for the education of their children. One led irrevocably to a life of service to the church in a Catholic monastery; the other, to life as a tradesman in one of the many guilds. The first option carried with it the promise of personal salvation and salvation for one's parents. When offering a son to a Catholic monastery the parental pledge was as follows:

> The dedication of children to the service of God is sanctioned by the example of Abraham and of many other holy men, as related in the Old and the New Testaments. Therefore, I, (name) now offer in the presence of abbot (name), this my son, (name), to omnipotent God and to the Virgin Mary, mother of God, for the salvation of my soul and of the soul of my parents. I promise for him that he shall follow the monastic life in this monastery of (name), according to the rule of St. Benedict, and that from this day forth he shall not withdraw his neck from the yoke of this service. I promise also that he shall never be tempted to leave by me or by anyone with my consent.[87]

The second option required parents to send their sons to live and work with a master craftsman so they could learn a craft and become tradesmen. Gangel and Benson describe the process:

Generally, a boy would work with a master craftsman for seven years as an apprentice. He would later become a journeyman, then finally a master craftsman. The trainer of the apprentice was to establish a written contract with the boy. He was responsible to give moral guidance as well as practical training in a trade (which included the provision of food, lodging, and a small allowance).[88]

THE PALACE SCHOOL OF ALFRED
THE GREAT

Before we look at the plight of evangelical Christians in the Catholic era, we must return to England and King Alfred the Great, "who alone among English kings is called Great."[89] Throughout much of the medieval period in England and in Europe, invasions by the Vikings, or "sea-warriors" from the Scandinavian countries, brought great havoc and distress to the population.

Figure 7. There is a bronze statue of King Alfred at Winchester, England, on which is inscribed: Alfred found learning dead, And he restored it; Education neglected, And he revived it; The laws powerless, And he gave them force; The Church debased, And he raised it; The land ravaged by a fearful enemy, From which he delivered it.

Alfred the Great distinguished himself for a number of reasons, not the least of which was that he protected the people of his kingdom of Wessex (the area around London) from the advancing Danish Vikings. He accomplished this by building a navy, by fortifying London, and by organizing a body of professional soldiers. He also provided a means of education for the upper-class families of his kingdom. Like Charlemagne he brought in scholars from other countries to his palace school to advance his educational objectives. Also like Charlemagne, he had educational objectives that, noble as they were, did not include schooling for common citizens. Bartley explains:

> The endeavors of King Alfred the Great, who must be looked upon as the father of English education, were chiefly directed to the improvement of those of his subjects who were in a superior position, and did not reach the working classes. This is shown, indirectly, by his enactment, that all freeholders who possessed two hides of land or upwards 'should send their sons to school and give them a liberal learning.' At the time this was considered a most extensive measure, and as embracing everyone who could possibly benefit by attendance at school. It is

evident, therefore, that in those days the idea of all, even the agricultural labourer, receiving a sound education, could hardly have existed.[90]

Because textbooks and other teaching aids were lacking, almost all instruction in the palace school was oral, requiring students to answer continuous teacher-initiated questions. Indeed, teachers asked many questions over and over again in monotonous drill form. This approach was similar to those of ancient Athens, Rome, and Jerusalem and later the catechetical schools of the early church Christians. Also in the tradition of the ancient educators, classroom discipline was severe. Aelfric's "Colloquy," written about 1005, gives us insight into discipline in eleventh-century English schools:

> The teacher asks: "Are you ready to be flogged while you learn?" The pupils answer: "We would rather be flogged for learning's sake than be ignorant," but they add ingratiatingly: "We know that thou art a humane man, and wilt not beat us unless our conduct compels thee."[91]

If students thought flogging by teachers was unjust, one example, repeated by numerous historians, affirms that students did retaliate when pushed too far. Scotus Erigena, one of the later scholars from Charlemagne's old palace school in Aachen, Germany, was invited to Alfred's palace school in England. For reasons not known he angered his students and "met his end by being stabbed to death with the pens of his infuriated pupils."[92]

In time, King Alfred's palace school suffered from the same lack of vision that brought about the demise of Emperor Charlemagne's palace school in Aachen. Both royals, however, are remembered in history for raising the lamp of learning in the grim darkness of the Dark Ages.

3. Stamping Out the Opposition

Simmering beneath the surface of human awareness during the long Catholic era is the largely untold story of evangelical Christians. These courageous followers of Christ lived in continuous dread of Catholic authorities, who offered the Catholic population "assured forgiveness of sin" in exchange for killing Waldensian Christians. This was a consistent pattern for a thousand years!

The Catholic Church often used its self-appointed authority of "sin-pardoning" to accomplish its purpose. Because of this nonbiblical practice, some critics referred to Catholic authorities as "pardon sellers."[93]

Establishing itself as the only mediator between God and man, the Catholic Church created its own monopoly on salvation and forgiveness of sin. Pope Leo XIII, in his encyclical "The Reunion of Christendom," declared that he, Leo, held "upon this earth, the place of God Almighty."[94] Pope Boniface VIII declared, "It is absolutely necessary for every human creature for salvation to be subject to the Roman pontiff."[95] Catholic authorities nowadays refer to Protestants as "separated brethren."[96] But until recent years Catholic authorities taught that all prayers for repentance for sins and for salvation must be offered exclusively through a Catholic clergyman. As Martin Luther would later point out, this practice was contrary to Romans 5:1–2:

> **Therefore, having been justified by faith, we have peace with God through our Lord Jesus Christ, through whom also we have access by faith into this grace in which we stand, and rejoice in hope of the glory of God.**

In 1517, the truth of these two Scriptures shook the Catholic world when Martin Luther declared, on biblical authority, "The just shall live by faith" (Romans 1:17 also see Habakkuk 2:4), and each of us has direct access to God. In the medieval centuries before Martin Luther, however, the Catholic Church used its self-given authority to forgive sins in exchange for:

1. money to rebuild St. Peter's Basilica,[97]
2. participation in the eight Catholic crusades to free Jerusalem from the Islamic Turks,[98]
3. attraction of gifts for the church,[99]
4. killing of heretics.[100]

"Sin pardons" for payment of cash and services to the church were offered at various times in the Middle Ages. The papal edict offering forgiveness of sin for killing heretics was aimed at the Waldensians. The Catholic Church attempted to stamp out the Waldensians over a period of eight hundred years.[101] Clarke claims that the Waldensians existed for a thousand years and have roots that go back to the first-century Christians, "a chain . . . connected with the first disciples of our Savior."[102]

> **For more than a thousand years, this community, organised in the region of the Cottian Alps, maintained its Religious independence against Papal supremacy. In vain it was attacked, desolated, driven out; it resisted every shock, the chain of its testimony to primitive Bible truth has never been broken. Scores of crusades were sent against it; myriads of its people were slaughtered, with every species of fiendish barbarity: by mercenary soldiery, or organised troops of popish monarchs, yet through all it remained stedfast.[103]**

There may well have been a strain of Anabaptists mingled with the Waldensians with "unbroken continuity from the Christians of the first century."[104] The Waldensians, or the Vaudois as they were called in France, perpetuated Christian schools like those first established in the early church in Rome, with the same diligence and conviction as their first-century forebears. Historian Eavey explains:

> However, it is known that among them was no insignificant amount of learning. Their children could read and write, their preachers and leaders possessed portions of the Gospels, and every member received instruction in the Scriptures. Not infrequently they learned the Gospels by heart and it was not uncommon for some of them to repeat from memory other long passages. Even the ignorant among them had a better knowledge of Scriptures than the scholars of the [Catholic] Church. What counted for most in terms of God-centered education was the fact that the evangelically-minded [Waldensians] sought for all people a knowledge of reading so that every individual might know the Scriptures for himself.[105]

A Waldensian pastor, Scipione Lentolo, writing to his former congregation in the Alps, asked, "How keen are you to send your sons to school, so that they may at least learn to read the Holy Scriptures?"[106]

Given the determination of Catholic leaders to eliminate heretics, it is amazing that the "chain" of Christian school education was broken neither in the Dark Ages nor in the Late Middle Ages, as we will discover. It appears from Waldensian Pastor Lentolo's question to his former congregation that teaching the Holy Scriptures to the next generation was still the fundamental reason for Christian school education.

In the latter half of the medieval period (1054–1517), the Late Middle Ages, the persecution of evangelical Christians intensified against such groups as the Waldensians, the Lollards, the Hussites, the Anabaptists, and others. As Tertullian had said, "The blood of martyrs is seed."[107] The Catholic authorities never fully succeeded in stamping out their opposition. Andrew Miller says, "The papal legate discovered that the open slaughter of heretics would never accomplish their utter extermination."[108]

THE GREAT DIVISION OF THE CATHOLIC CHURCH

We conclude this chapter with the division of the Catholic Church, the "Great Schism," which took place in 1054. Earlier, in 395, there had been a minor division of the Catholic Church along cultural lines resulting in a Western Latin Church in Rome and an Eastern Greek Church in

Constantinople, with the pope in Rome ruling over both divisions.[109]   Over time, however, theological differences began to appear:

> The eastern theology had its roots in Greek philosophy, while a great deal of western theology was based on Roman law. This gave rise to misunderstandings, and at last led to two widely separate ways of regarding and defining one important doctrine—the procession of the Holy Spirit from the Father or from the Father and the Son. Political jealousies and interests intensified the disputes; and at last, after many premonitory symptoms, the final break came in 1054, when Pope Leo IX smote Michael Cerularius and his adherents in the Eastern Church with an excommunication. There had been mutual excommunications before, but they had not resulted in permanent schisms. Now, however, the separation was final. . . . The eastern segment also resented the Roman enforcement of clerical celibacy.[110]

From the eastern segment of the great Catholic division grew the Slavic Orthodox Churches in Russia (the Russian Orthodox Church), Serbia, Bulgaria, Romania, and in other countries worldwide.[111]

After "The Great Schism" of 1054, it appears the Roman Catholic leaders became even more authoritarian than before. For example, Professor James writes:

> On ascending the papal throne as Gregory VII in 1073, he declared his determination to rule the world as a sovereign pontiff with a universal jurisdiction comparable to that of Caesar, and absolute power in ecclesiastical affairs.[112]

The Church's increased authoritarianism will appear as we move toward the Reformation. Like their Roman emperor predecessors, the popes of the Late Middle Ages assumed more and more personal power. Describing this phenomenon, Lewis Sherrill writes:

> With Innocent III, who was Pope from 1198 to 1216, the church became a world-state, in which the priesthood was superior to the kingship, and the Pope was the vicar of God; nor was it a cloistered dream, for this man disciplined kings, and regulated the affairs of a continent. In 1302 came the height of the development, in the famous bull of Innocent III entitled Unam Sanctam, setting forth that both secular and spiritual jurisdiction belonged ultimately to the Pope, who claimed the obedience of every creature on pain of forfeiting salvation.[113]

As we will see, the Catholic Church of the Late Middle Ages would leverage even further its self-appointed authority over salvation and sin-pardoning to gain even more power and control throughout the Western world.

Endnotes—Chapter Four

[1] Ellwood P. Cubberley, *The History of Education* (Boston: Houghton Mifflin Company, 1920), p. 141.

[2] *Encyclopaedia Britannica,* vol. 16 (Chicago: William Benton Publisher, 1961), p. 939.

[3] Pierre J. Marique, *History of Christian Education,* vol. 3 (New York: Fordham University Press, 1932), p. 3.

[4] See footnote 66 in chapter 3.

[5] Paul Helm, "Thomas Aquinas," *The New International Dictionary of the Christian Church,* J.D. Douglas, ed.(Grand Rapids, MI, 1974), p. 60.

[6] Thomas Aquinas, *Summa Theologiae* 2a, 2ae, Q. XI, a. 3, Trans. PTR, III, 6 (8), 17ff. quoted in Ray C. Petry, *A History of Christianity: Readings in the History of the Church,* vol. I (New York: Prentice Hall, Inc., 1962), 354–355. Also see Ellwood P. Cubberley, *Readings in the History of Education* (Boston: Houghton Mifflin Company, 1920), pp. 233–234.

[7] F. Hugh O'Donnell, *The Ruin of Education in Ireland,* Second Edition (London: David Nutt, 1902), opposite title page.

[8] Thomas Gascoigne, quoted in Will Durant, *The Reformation* (New York: Simon and Schuster, 1957), p. 23.

[9] C.B. Eavey, *History of Christian Education* (Chicago: Moody Press, 1964), p. 107.

[10] Cubberley, p. 307.

[11] Frank W. Blackmar, *History of Human Society* (University of Kansas), p. 350.

[12] A parish priest from the Styrian Village of Unzmarkt, 1752. Quoted in John Van Horn Melton, *Absolutism and the Eighteenth-Century Origins of Compulsory Schooling in Prussia and Austria* (Cambridge: University Press, 1988), p. 60.

[13] Bishop Graz-Seckau. Quoted in Karl Klamminger, "Leopold III. Ernst Graf Firmian," in Karl Amon, ed., *Die Bischöfe von Graz-Seckau 1218–1968* (Fraz, 1969), p. 350.

[14] Johann Schmut, *Erstes Eingreifen des Staates zur Hebung des niederen Schulwesens in der Steiermark unter Maria Theresia, Beiträge zur österreichischen Erziehungs und Schulgeschichte,* p. 11 (1909).

[15] Miller, pp. 516–517.

[16] Benson, p. 64.

[17] Loraine Boettner, *Roman Catholicism* (Philadelphia: The Presbyterian and Reformed Publishing Co., 1962), p. 97.

[18] Cubberley, p. 304.

[19] Loraine Boettner, *Roman Catholicism,* p. 97.

[20] Coulton, *Life in the Middle Ages,* vol. I, p. 205, quoted in Durant, *The Reformation,* p. 7.

[21] Elmer Wilds, *The Foundation of Modern Education* (New York: Rinehart and Company, Inc., 1936), p. 167.

[22] Ibid., p. 168. Wilds cites the accounts of Tacitus in his Germania and Annals.

[23] Ibid., p. 167.

[24] Barbara L. Faulkner, "Eastern Orthodox Church," *The New International Dictionary of the Christian Church,* J.D. Douglas, ed. (Grand Rapids, Michigan: Zondervan Publishing House, 1974), pp. 322–324.

[25] *Encyclopaedia Britannica* (Chicago: William Benton Publisher, 1961), p. 413.

[26] E.O. James, *In the Fullness of Time* (New York: The Macmillan Company, 1935), p. 165.

[27] *Encyclopaedia Britannica,* vol. 5 (Chicago, William Benton, Publisher, 1961), p. 58.

[28] Wallach Luitpoid, *Diplomatic Studies in Latin and Greek Documents from the Carolingian Age* (Ithaca, New York and London: Cornell University Press, 1977), p. 299.

[29] Ibid.

[30] Ibid., p. 339.

[31] Ibid., p. 301.

[32] Ibid., p. 304.

[33] Ibid.

[34] Robert L. Cooke, *Philosophy, Education and Certainty* (Grand Rapids, MI: Zondervan Publishing House, 1976), p. 88.

[35] Lewis Joseph Sherrill, *The Rise of Christian Education* (New York: The Macmillan Company, 1944), p. 213. Sherrill's quote within his quote is taken from Epistolae IV, 26; in MPL 77, col. 695.

[36] Kenneth Scott Latourette, *The First Five Centuries* (New York: Harper and Brothers, 1937), p. 194.

[37] Richard A. Todd, "Clergy, Bishops and Pope," *Introduction to the History of Christianity,* Tim Dowley, ed.(Minneapolis: Fortress Press, 1995), p. 203.

[38] Frederick Eby and Charles Flinn Arrowood, *The History and Philosophy of Education Ancient and Medieval* (New York: Prentice-Hall Inc., 1940), p. 657.

[39] A.F. Leach, *The Schools of Medieval England* (London: Methuen and Co., LTD., 1915), pp. 1–2.

[40] L.E. Elliot Binns, *The Beginnings of Western Christendom* (London: Lutterworth Press), p. 196.

[41] Joyce Horn, "Canterbury," *The New International Dictionary of the Christian Church,* J.D. Douglas, ed. (Grand Rapids, MI: Zondervan Publishing House, 1974), p. 190.

[42] Charles J. Burnett and Christopher J. Trabraham, *The Honors of Scotland: The Story of the Scottish Crown Jewels* (Edinburgh: Historic Scotland, 1992), pp. 16–17.

[43] Leach, p. 3.

[44] C.B. Eavey, *History of Christian Education* (Chicago: Moody Press, 1964), pp. 102, 107.

[45] William Boyd and Edmond J. King, *The History of Western Education* (London: Adam and Charles Black, 1921), p. 113.

[46] Ibid.

[47] Leach, p. 29.

[48] Eavey, 107.

[49] Lewis Joseph Sherrill, *The Rise of Christian Education* (New York: The Macmillan Co., 1944), p. 299.

[50] H.I. Marrow, *A History of Education in Antiquity* (New York: New American Library, 1964), p. 462.

[51] Boyd and King, p. 113.

[52] Eby and Arrowood, p. 665.

[53] D. Bruce Lockerbie, *A Passion for Learning* (Chicago: Moody Press, 1994), p. 100.

[54] Alcuin, quoted in A.F. Leach, pp. 58–59.

[55] Ibid., p. 59.

[56] Eby and Arrowood, p. 684.

[57] James Godkin, *The Religious History of Ireland* (London: Henry S. King & Co., 1873), p. 10.

[58] Eby and Arrowood, p. 685.

[59] Ibid.

[60] Clanrickarde Memoirs. clvii-clxi. Quoted in P.J. Dowling, *The Hedge Schools of Ireland* (Cork: The Mercer Press, 1935, Revised Edition, 1968), pp. 8–9.

[61] Mason: *Parochial Survey.* vol. I, 318. Quoted in Dowling, pp. 11–12.

[62] Andrew Miller, *Miller's Church History,* vol. II (London: Pickering and Inglis, 1924), p. 510.

[63] Binns, *The Beginnings of Western Christendom,* p. 207.

[64] *Encyclopaedia Britannica,* vol. 17, (Chicago: William Benton, Publisher, 1961), p. 385.

[65] Cubberley, *The History of Education,* p. 138.

[66] Miller, p. 511.

[67] Ibid., p. 509.

[68] Godkin, p. 11.

[69] Sherrill, p. 251.

[70] James Atkinson, "Reform," *Introduction of the History of Christianity,* Tim Dowley, ed. (Minneapolis: Fortress Press, 1977), p. 392.

[71] Andrew Fleming West, *Alcuin and the Rise of the Christian Schools* (New York: Charles Scribner's Sons, 1920), p. 39.

[72] Ibid., pp. 42–43.

[73] Ibid., pp. 45–46.

[74] Mullinger, p. 50; quoted in Sherrill, p. 252.

[75] 1 Migne, *Patrologia Latina, XCVIII,* p. 895. Mullinger, *Schools of Charles the Great,* pp. 97–99; quoted in West, pp. 49–51.

[76] Eby and Arrowood, p. 696.

[77] West, p. 196.

[78] Cubberley, *History of Education,* p. 141.

[79] Linas Brockett, *History and Progress of Education from the Earliest Times to the Present* (New York: A.S. Barnes and Burr, 1860), p. 139.

[80] Cubberley, *History of Education,* p. 166.

[81] James E. Reed and Ronnie Prevost, *A History of Christian Education* (Nashville: Broadman and Holman Publishers, 1993), p. 163.

[82] Wilds, p. 191.

[83] Gangel and Benson, p. 107.

[84] S.E. Frost Jr. and Kenneth P. Bailey, *Historical and Philosophical Foundations of Western Education,* 2d ed. (Columbus, Ohio: Charles E. Merrill Publishing Co., 1973), pp. 130–131.

[85] Reed and Prevost, p. 125.

[86] Corkey, *Episode in the History of Protestant Ulster* (Belfast: Dorman and Sons, Ltd.,1947), p. 13.

[87] From Migne, Patrologia, p. 66, col. 842. Quoted in Cubberley, *Readings in the History of Education,* p. 77.

[88] Gangel and Benson, p. 107.

[89] Eby and Arrowood, p. 673.

[90] George C.T. Bartley, *The Schools for the People* (London: Bell and Daldy, 1871), p. 1.

[91] G.G. Coulton, *Medieval Panorama,* p. 403, C.U.P., 1938. Quoted in Stanley J. Curtis, *History of Education in Great Britain* (London: University Tutorial Press, Ltd., 1948), p. 11.

[92] Ibid., p. 10.

[93] Thomas M. Lindsay, *A History of the Reformation* (Edinburgh: T. and T. Clark, 1906), p. 17.

[94] Pope Leo XIII, encyclical, "The Reunion of Christendom." Quoted in Loraine Boettner, *Roman Catholicism* (Philadelphia: The Presbyterian and Reformed Publishing Company, 1962), p. 127.

[95] Harold O.J. Brown, "Unhelpful Antagonism and Unhealthy Courtesy," *Roman Catholicism,* John Armstrong, ed. (Chicago: Moody Bible Institute, 1994), p. 163.

[96] Ibid., p. 168.

[97] Lindsay, p. 213.

[98] Lindsay, p. 224. (Pope Urban II offered complete remission of all cannical penances to those who participated in the crusades).

[99] Ibid.

[100] Clark, p. 121.

[101] Giorgio Tourn, *You Are My Witnesses: The Waldensians Across 800 Years* (Cincinnati: Friendship Press, 1989), cover page.

[102] Clarke, p. 120.

[103]Ibid.

[104]Kenneth Scott Latourette, *A History of Christianity* (New York: Harper and Row, 1953), p. 780.

[105]Eavey, p. 115.

[106]Lentolo, MS, p. 495; quoted in Evan Cameron, *The Reformation of Heretics, The Waldenses of the Alps* (Oxford: Clarendon Press, 1984), p. 209.

[107]Tertullian, Apol., 1, p. 13. Quoted in Will Durant, *Caesar and Christ* (New York: Simon and Schuster, 1944), p. 652.

[108]Miller, p. 486.

[109]Cubberley, *History of Education,* p. 102.

[110]*Encyclopaedia Britannica,* vol. 16 (Chicago: William Benton, Publisher, 1961), p. 939.

[111]Ibid., p. 940.

[112]E.O. James, p. 167.

[113]Sherrill, p. 212.

Illustration Sources

Figure 1   *Map*—Global Mapping International, Colorado Springs, CO.

Figure 2   *Coronation*—Photo by author (PBA).

Figure 3   *Cathedral*—PBA.

Figure 4   *Charlemagne*—PBA.

Figure 5   *Knighthood*—From an ancient manuscript, included in Ellwood P. Cubberley, *The History of Education* (Boston: Houghton Mifflin Company, 1920), p. 134.

Figure 6   *Castle*—PBA.

Figure 7   *King Alfred*—Included in Cubberley, *Readings in the History of Education* (Boston: Houghton Mifflin Company, 1920), p. 94.

Education in the Late Middle Ages

This next period of our study will take us to the Great Reformation beginning in 1517, which brought an end to the long night of the Middle Ages. We will look at the history of this era in this chapter and the next, and in so doing cover the period from 1054 to 1517, often called the Late Middle Ages. The three main divisions of chapter 5 are:

1. Educational Implications of the Crusades and the "Black Death"
2. The Liberalization of Ecclesiastical Education
3. The Rise of Catholic Universities

Our focus in this chapter is education. At the outset we will consider the educational impact of two historic tragedies that greatly influenced the lives of children and their parents in the Holy Roman Empire and the British Isles. Living in the Middle Ages was characterized by the uncertainty of life often created by wars and feuds of various kinds. The tragedies we will look at, however, were so unusual and so devastating to children that they deserve our special consideration. One of these events, the Crusades, was man-made. The other was the devastating plague known as "black death" that swept through England and mainland Europe.

Every educator knows that a secure, tranquil home environment is vital to the training of children and young people. As we consider the Crusades and the Black Death, imagine how disruptive and catastrophic these events were to the meager education and training opportunities available in the Middle Ages.

1. Educational Implications of the Crusades and the "Black Death"

The Crusades were conducted by the Catholic Church to free Jerusalem, "the sepulchre of Christ, from the hands of the unbelieving Turks."[1] The

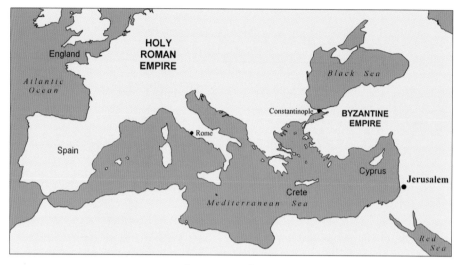

Figure 1. Crusader Map

city had been in the hands of Arabian Muslims since 637. These early "gatekeepers of Jerusalem" were tolerant of devout Catholics who came in great numbers to see the sacred places and to collect "sacred relics" such as "bones of martyrs, garments of saints, nails of the cross, and thorns of the crown."[2] This steady flow of pilgrims may have been the beginning of what we now call the "tourist industry." The clever Arabs collected a "reasonable" fee from every Catholic pilgrim.

This acceptable arrangement continued until 1067, when a change occurred. A new group of Muslims from Turkey took over Palestine. These new "proprietors" openly referred to the Catholic pilgrims as infidels, subjecting them to various indignities and sometimes to slavery.[3] In 1093, a pilgrim monk named Peter the Hermit visited Jerusalem and began a personal crusade to challenge the Catholics of France, Germany, and Italy to rid Jerusalem of the intolerant Turks.

It is important to understand the great dilemma of the Catholic Church and its shrinking Holy Roman Empire. The problem seemed to center on the steady encroachment of the followers of Mohammed, but church historian Clarence Benson believes the Catholic Church created its own problem:

> The impotence of the Church is best shown by the rise and spread of [Islam]. It seems almost unbelievable that this counterfeit religion should have taken such deep root and spread with such amazing rapidity after the Christian Church had been sufficiently strong to conquer the Roman Empire. Had the [Catholic] Church leaders been as

concerned about furthering the missionary movement in Asia and Africa as they were about determining whether Rome or Constantinople should have the primacy, all medieval history might have been changed.[4]

Thomas Lindsay, a noted scholar and a leader of the United Free Church of Scotland, describes the dilemma of the Catholic Church at the time of the Crusades:

> Christendom had shrunk greatly since the seventh century. The Saracens and their successors in Moslem sovereignty had overrun and conquered many lands which had formerly been inhabited by a Christian population and governed by Christian [Catholic] rulers. Palestine, Syria, Asia Minor, Egypt, and North Africa westwards to the Straits of Gibraltar, had once been Christian, and had been lost to Christendom during the seventh and eighth centuries. The Moslems had invaded Europe in the West, had conquered the Spanish Peninsula, had passed the Pyrenees, and had invaded France. [The Moslems were pushed back by the French at the battle of Tours in 732.] After they had been thrust back beyond the Pyrenees, the Spanish Peninsula was the scene of a struggle between Moslems and Christians which lasted for more than seven hundred years, and Spain did not become wholly Christian until the last decade of the fifteenth century. Serbia, Bosnia, Greece, Romania, Wallachia, and Moldavia were incorporated in the Moslem Empire. Germany was threatened by Turkish invasions, and for years the bells tolled in hundreds of German parishes calling the people to pray against the coming of the Turks. It was not until the heroic defence of Vienna, in 1529, that the victorious advance of the Moslems was stayed. [5]

The invasion of the Turks was of great concern to the popes in Rome. While the emperors of the Holy Roman Empire in Aachen, Germany, as well as the lesser civil authorities of Europe were, indeed, under the authority of the pope, their interests were not always the same as those of their superior in Rome. This situation created various factions throughout Europe. For example, when Pope Leo III crowned Charlemagne emperor of the Holy Roman Empire on Christmas Day in 800, he created a perpetual problem for the Catholic Church. Later emperors would not be as devoted to the church as Charlemagne, a fact that became particularly evident in the Late Middle Ages.

When "Peter the Hermit" presented the problem of the Turkish occupancy of Jerusalem to Pope Urban II in Rome, the pope viewed it as an opportunity to unite the factions in his religious empire and possibly raise funds for the Holy See. Understandably, the pope's motivations for the

Crusades were of little interest to his emperor in Aachen, Germany. Undoubtedly, the civil leaders of Germany would agree with a much later statement by Charles Beard: "Germany was the milch cow of the papacy, which it at once despised and drained dry."[6] Four hundred years later, Martin Luther would make the following observation about how Catholic leaders used their long struggle with the Islamic Turks to benefit the Catholic cause:

> Whenever there is any pretence of fighting the Turk, they send out commissions for collecting money, and often proclaim Indulgences under the same pretext. . . . and all this is done in the name of Christ and of St. Peter.[7]

In 1095 Pope Urban II persuaded two large church councils in Placentia and Clermont, France, to "stir up the laity in the cause of the Crusade."[8] In addition to the thousands of laity, four thousand Catholic bishops, monks, and priests attended these large gatherings.

In his lengthy speech at Clermont, where he was seeking to stir action, Pope Urban II said:

> Go forth, and God shall be with you. Redeem your sins—your rapine, [raping], your burnings, your bloodshed—by obedience. Display valour in a cause where death is the assurance of blessedness. Count it joy to die for Christ where Christ died for you. Think not of kindred or home; you owe to God a higher love.[9]

In other words, the pope promised those who joined the Crusade (there were eight Crusades between 1096 and 1270) that they would have forgiveness of sins and assurance of heaven if they died in the cause. Miller says:

> The blasphemous Pope offered absolution for all sins—the sins of murder, adultery, robbery, arson—and that without penance to all who would take up arms in this sacred cause. He promised eternal life to all who should suffer the glorious calamity of death in the Holy Land, or even on the way to it. The Crusader passed at once into paradise. The great battle of the Cross and the Crescent was to be decided for ever on the soil of the Holy Land. For himself, he said, he must remain at home: the care of the Church detained him.[10]

Picture, if you will, two waves of four hundred thousand and six hundred thousand Catholic Crusaders marching in the first Crusade across Europe through the perilous Byzantine Empire and on to the holy land and Jerusalem. In the process, hundreds of thousands died. Miller says this about the first wave of Crusaders:

They had no idea of the distance of Jerusalem, or of the difficulties to be encountered by the way. So ignorant were they, that, at the sight of the first city beyond the limits of their knowledge, they were ready to inquire if this was Jerusalem. In place of sobriety and order in their march, it was marked by murder, plunder, dissoluteness, and infamous habits of every kind. The unoffending Jewish inhabitants of the towns on the Moselle, the Rhine, the Maine, and the Danube, through which they marched, were plundered and slaughtered as the murderers of Christ and the enemies of the Cross. The population of Hungary and Bulgaria rose up against them because of their disorderly and plundering habits, and immense numbers of them were slain.[11]

Over the next 174 years, millions of Catholic Crusaders, some from as far away as England, lost their lives. Only a small percentage ever reached Jerusalem. While the Catholic Crusaders did indeed recapture Jerusalem for a time, their efforts never produced a permanent "Turk-free" Holy City. The Islamic community is still there today because Jerusalem is regarded as their Holy City as well. To this day the Mosque of Omar sits adjacent to the site of the Jewish temple.

The greatest tragedy of the Crusades was the Children's Crusade of 1212, which was approved by the Vatican.[12] Imagine thirty thousand children, under twelve years of age, marching from France and Germany to the Holy Land. There is no historical evidence that any of them reached Jerusalem— or that any ever returned to their homeland! Most died from thirst, hunger, and cold. Two shiploads of these children died in a shipwreck while crossing the Mediterranean, and five shiploads were sold to Moslem slave traders in Algiers by deceitful ship merchants.[13]

The tragedy is compounded by the fact that there is no historical documentation that the Catholic Church has ever apologized to the world for the deaths of thirty thousand children in the Children's Crusade and of millions of adults in the seven other Crusades.

The disruptive impact of the 174 years of the Jerusalem Crusades on the already fragile European systems of learning—whether ecclesiastical schooling in the monasteries, the palace schools, or the trade schools—was devastating and enormous.

THE "BLACK DEATH" PLAGUE OF 1349

Even more devastating to learning and to the normal life patterns of Europe was the "Black Death." A Jewish writer living in France describes it:

In the year 1349 there occurred the greatest epidemic that ever happened. Death went from one end of the earth to the other, on that side and this side of the sea, and it was greater among the Saracens [Muslims] than among the Christians. In some lands everyone died so that no one was left. Ships were also found on the sea laden with wares; the crew had all died and no one guided the ship. The Bishop of Marseilles and priests and monks and more than half of all the people there died with them. In other kingdoms and cities so many people perished that it would be horrible to describe.[14]

According to J.F. Hecker, "One-fourth of the population of Europe or 25,000,000 persons died in the epidemic."[15] The mortality rate was even higher in England. Writing on England's social and cultural history, Michael Alexander gives this account:

Striking England sometime between May and July 1348, the Black Death acquired its name from the dark blue patches that disfigured the skins of most victims of the disease, which consisted of three separate but related strains of plague—bubonic, pneumonic, and septicemic. Those who contracted the bubonic variety had at best a 35 percent chance of survival, whereas those who became infected with either of the other two forms almost never recovered. Indeed, the septicemic strain was so lethal that death often occurred within a day of the onset of the disease, before any outward symptoms had time to become apparent.

Because the mortality rate increased almost tenfold during the epidemic, some 35 to 40 percent of England's total population of approximately 6,000,000 died in less than a year.[16]

There have been other plagues in the history of mankind, but none on the scale of the worldwide "Black Death" of 1349. Both the Crusades (1096–1270) and the plague of 1349, left people with deep emotional scars. Now we turn our attention to the great reluctance of the Catholic Church to change its collective mind about education.

2. The Liberalization of Ecclesiastical Education

In Catholic dogma, "the toleration of non-Catholic ideas or beliefs was considered a deadly sin."[17] Therefore, the sixteenth-century writings of satirist Erasmus and even saintly Thomas Aquinas were to Catholic theologians "like vernal plants growing under the leaves."[18] To the Catholic mind in the Middle Ages, widespread literacy and learning led to heresy. And what constituted heresy? Anything that was contrary to Catholic dogma. You will recall that the church had placed even the Bible on

"The Index of Forbidden Books." Tragically, in Catholic England before the Reformation, a mother and father were burned at the stake for teaching their children the Lord's Prayer and the Ten Commandments in the English language.[19] No mercy was shown to those who posed a threat to the Catholic interpretation of the Latin Vulgate Bible and to Catholic dogma formulated by the popes and the general councils. It is accurate to say that in the Middle Ages the authority of the Catholic Church was regarded as supreme over the Bible.

This "higher than the Bible" authority carried over into Catholic education policy. Rather than provide universal private or public education to their constituency, as their Jewish and pagan predecessors had done, their policy was to provide strictly ecclesiastical education, and only for that ten percent of the population selected to perform as functionaries of the Catholic Church. In the Early Middle Ages there was no approved education other than ecclesiastical education, and that was designed to perpetuate dependence on the church and not to promote dependence on Christ and the Holy Scriptures nor to develop one's intellectual curiosity.[20]

In the Late Middle Ages, however, a pendulum-swing reaction that could not be controlled was setting in against the Catholic education policy. It began with the Crusades. In an attempt to fund the Crusades over their tumultuous 174-year history, European land barons sold their vast properties to the Catholic Church (the only monied buyer available) at greatly reduced prices. This development initiated a breakup of the medieval feudalistic society and stirred a new level of independence among the majority of the serf population. The Crusades, grim as they were, not only changed the relationship between classes of people but stimulated trade and travel by creating many new contacts between the Eastern and Western worlds. This sparked an interesting chain reaction. Suddenly there was a need for banking, factories to make salable products, and a higher level of literacy and scientific knowledge to keep pace with the growing economy. The demand for a new level of education was apparent. Ultimately these developments gave rise to more secondary schools and to Catholic universities.[21]

At this point, a brief step back in time to the church's first centuries will be helpful to our understanding of Catholic education policy. The early church Christians and the founding Catholic leaders had equal fears of paganism. They had vivid memories of the cruelties imposed on Christians by pagan Rome. Thousands of Christians died in the Roman Colosseum and in the Circus Maximus. These early Christians were also aware of the

Figure 2. Augustine (A.D. 354–430). The Catholic Church shifted its educational and theological philosophy from the teachings of Augustine to the teachings of Aristotle early in the 13th century. [Painting by Botticelli, Sandro (1444–1510). Saint Augustine in his study. Chiesa di Ognissanti, Florence, Italy.]

gross immorality of the pagan lifestyle. Understandably, the early Catholic Church fathers did everything in their power to prevent a wholesale return to paganism. Their strategy of stamping out the written works of pagans was successful for six centuries. The long censorship ended, however, when they inadvertently mixed their constituency (via the Crusades) with the Muslims, who had carefully preserved the classic works of the Greek and Roman empires.

Catholic leaders were so blinded by the many negative aspects of paganism that they failed to see the value of the Graeco-Roman achievements in medicine, botany, zoology, meteorology, literature, geometry, agriculture, and engineering, to name a few. Indeed, the course of history would have been substantially different had the Catholic community simply used biblical authority to determine the positive and negative aspects of pagan achievements, and if the church had adopted the good and rejected the grim paganism. It is interesting that the church listened to Augustine when he formulated his policy on heretics but failed to listen when he said, "Every good and true Christian should understand that wherever he may find truth, it is his Lord's."[22] In a similar vein, Frank Gaebelein says:

> Now Christian education, if it is faithful to its deepest commitment, must renounce once and for all the false separation between secular and sacred truth. It must see that truth in science and history, in mathematics, art, literature, and music belongs just as much to God as truth in religion. While it recognizes the primacy of the spiritual truth revealed in the Bible and incarnate in Christ, it acknowledges that all truth, wherever it is found, is of God. For Christian education there can be no discontinuity in truth, but every aspect of truth must find its unity in the God of all truth.[23]

Regrettably, the Catholic Church in the Middle Ages never fully accepted the mystery of the infallibility of the Holy Scriptures.

As mentioned in chapter 2, in regard to Roman education, excesses in one direction often create excesses in the opposite direction. This principle was true in Catholic education. Classical learning from ancient Greece and Rome began to filter into the Catholic world through Alcuin and the English schools and later through contact with the Muslims in Spain, Sicily, and Israel. As Catholic theologians began assimilating classical learning, it became clear that their filter for distinguishing the good from the bad in pagan scholarship was Catholic Church dogma and tradition, not biblical authority. As one might imagine, problems of assimilation rose not so much with the math and sciences, but with the pagan, pantheistic ideas in such studies as philosophy and logic. This dependence on dogma and tradition and neglect of the Scriptures facilitated Catholicism's drift toward Scholasticism and, in turn, influenced its ultimate acceptance of the Italian Renaissance.

SCHOLASTICISM

Scholasticism was an attempt to make faith and reason compatible—to literally make Catholic dogma blend with the philosophy of the Greek philosopher Aristotle. Ulich writes:

> In its essence, Scholasticism was the attempt to support the Christian [Catholic] creed by a philosophical structure of sufficient strength to withstand the ever rising doubts among Christian [Catholic] theologians who, partly because of Arabic influences, no longer felt as safe in their faith as did their predecessors of earlier centuries. Strangely enough, the tool that Christian [Catholic] Scholasticism used to reestablish unity was of pagan origin, the philosophy of Aristotle. Understandably, in the beginning the Church protested against the rapidly increasing interest in the works of the heathen, newly translated from Greek and Arabic; and conservative churchmen condemned the doctrines of Thomas Aquinas with their Aristotelian logic so that Albertus Magnus had to go to Paris in his defense (1277).[24]

Ulich says further that Scholasticism was "a kind of rationalization of the Gospel [that] placed Aristotle, called 'the Teacher' or 'the Philosopher' beside Jesus as the supreme authority."[25]   This, of course, is the essence of humanism, in which man is elevated to a level equal to, or above, Christ. In contrast, Ephesians 1:22 says (referring to Christ), "And He put all things under His feet, and gave Him to be head over all things to the church"; and Colossians 1:18, ". . . that in all things He [Christ] may have the preeminence" (NKJ).

There are differences of opinion as to when Scholasticism began and ended, but it was reflected in Catholic thinking mainly from the eleventh through the fourteenth centuries. The principal figure in the Scholastic movement was Thomas Aquinas (1225–1274), a theology professor at the University of Paris.[26] Colin Brown points out that Thomas Aquinas believed the Bible to be only one of many sources for truth:

Figure 3. Thomas Aquinas, (1225–1274), the champion of "consensus truth-making," became the patron of saint of Roman Catholic education. (Saint Thomas. Ss. Domenico e Sisto, Rome, Italy.)

Aquinas would start with a problem. He then would quote his authority. This could be a text of Scripture, a passage from one of the early Christian writers or a quotation from 'the philosopher'. The latter was never named; he did not need to be. It was Aristotle, the Greek philosopher from the fourth century BC, whose writings had been rediscovered and translated into Latin in the twelfth century. From now on his ideas set the tone. The Islamic philosophies of Avicenna and Averroes, as well as contemporary Jewish thinkers, were also taken into account. Only when he had taken note of all the relevant points both for and against would Aquinas give his own answer.[27]

Initially, conservative Catholic theologians raised their collective eyebrows at such "consensus truth-making," but over time the views of Thomas Aquinas became the official "logical theological system"[28] for the Catholic Church. *Summa Theologiae*, his principal written work, "remains today the authoritative exposition of Roman Catholic theology."[29] Regrettably, the works of Aquinas opened even further the floodgate of doubt about the authority of the Scripture. The great evangelical scholar Francis Schaeffer agrees:

It was all too easy for Greek and Roman thought forms to creep into the cracks and chinks of a faith which was less and less founded on the Bible and more and more resting on the authority of church pronouncements. By the thirteenth century the great Aquinas (1225–1274) had already begun, in deference to Aristotle (384–322 B.C.), to open the door to placing revelation and human reason on an equal footing.[30]

Isaac Doughton said, "What a strange prank of history that the pagan Aristotle, who died more than three hundred years before Christ was born, should have become the dominant master of mind in the Christian [Catholic] Church!"[31] Pope John XXII officially canonized Thomas Aquinas in 1323, and in 1879 Pope Leo XIII made him "the patron saint of Roman Catholic education."[32]

THE RENAISSANCE

The Renaissance, a by-product of Scholasticism, was underway within twenty-five years after the death of Thomas Aquinas in 1274.[33] It began in Italy and then spread to the rest of Europe. Cooke said it was clearly an attempt to "break away from the strong hand of the [Catholic] Church, and interest in pagan thought was ascendant."[34]

It must be remembered that all reforms that occurred in Catholicism's religious empire in the Late Middle Ages occurred at the hands of Catholic "insiders" who saw a need for change. These insiders were from various levels of the priesthood, and most had no intention of creating a worldwide "Renaissance" or "Reformation." In almost every case their initial attempt at reform was focused on local problems. Others quickly identified with their cause, and soon the reforms spread in an ever-widening circle.

The two main streams of reform, the Renaissance and the Reformation, were decidedly different from each other. The Renaissance, which preceded the Reformation by 215 years, was an attempt to return to humanistic ideals espoused by Socrates, Plato, and Aristotle, and was centered, for the most part, in the Italian peninsula. As we will see, Luther, the great reformer, had little regard for the pagan philosophers. He would later refer to Socrates as "that damnable heathen."[35] The Reformation, on the other hand, was centered in Germany and was a retreat from the authority of the Catholic Church to the authority of Christ as revealed in the Scriptures, which had been newly translated from the original languages. These forces for change were influenced directly and indirectly through Islamic contacts in Spain, Israel, and Sicily.

Along with the Italian Renaissance with its rediscovery of the good and bad qualities of the pantheistic world of ancient Greece and Rome, the Islamic contacts resulted in a return to the Greek and Hebrew languages, which had long been outlawed by the Catholic Church. Cubberley says:

> Greek was judged a heretical tongue. No one should lecture on the New Testament, it was declared, without a previous theological examination. It was held to be heresy to say that the Greek or Hebrew text read

thus, or that a knowledge of the original language is necessary to interpret the Scriptures correctly.[36]

This new access to the ancient languages made possible the direct translation of the Bible from its original languages. Therefore, the direction these early reformers took depended greatly on which of these two powerful forces they followed: the pantheistic philosophies of Greece and Rome or the Bible newly translated from the Greek and Hebrew languages.

The principal figures of the Renaissance were Petrarch, Boccaccio, Erigena, and Bacon. The principal leaders of the Reformation were Luther, Zwingli, Wycliffe, Huss, and Calvin. A case can be made that Desiderius Erasmus, "the greatest international scholar of the age,"[37] should be listed among the principal reformers of both camps. His unique contributions to the Renaissance and the Reformation will be covered in the last part of this chapter.

The Renaissance was more than a return to the pagan past, and it was more than an escape from the ecclesiastical and feudal despotism of the Catholic Church. Once Aquinas had created a cloud of doubt in the highest levels of the church with his ideas on "consensus truth-making," the traditional theological structure of the Catholic Church began to soften— some would say "unravel."

Of the two great movements, the Renaissance and the Reformation, the Catholic Church identified more closely with the Renaissance. With the rising spirit of independence and personal assertiveness, the Church was forced to adjust in order to maintain control. The most noticeable adjustment was in education. Whereas in the past the teaching of Aristotle's Seven Liberal Arts was regarded as a "crime"[38] and a "deadly sin,"[39] now church leaders began to embrace it. Eby and Arrowood write:

> No longer were the voices of influential churchmen raised in condemnation of the liberal arts and sciences; these were now the weapons, the armor, and the ornament of the Christian soldier.[40]

In a complete about-face, during the Renaissance "bishops, abbots, and the pope himself were promoting and fostering scholarship and schools."[41] Jewish historian Samuel Khan describes the change forced upon the Catholic Church:

> Medieval thought, with its one-sidedness, with its domination by the Church . . . with its unity forced upon it by religious intolerance, could not last for ever, and soon gaping fissures could be seen in that great Gothic edifice. The virile human mind became tired of the endless scholastic hair-splitting disputation and yearned for the creative activity and the freedom of thought which had been imprisoned for over a thousand years. Monastic life, with the course of time, turned traitor to its own

fundaments of poverty, asceticism, charity and humility; court life was exclusive, empty of ideal, especially after the crusades, arrogant and decadent; and there was stagnation in political, social and individual life.[42]

The new trend, or the "Revival of Learning" as it was called, resulted in an expansion of educational opportunities at all levels, but all education was still Catholic education. As Eavey points out, "Though there were schools in considerable number, the masses were illiterate."[43]

Before we examine the meteoric rise of the universities in the latter half of the Middle Ages, it is important to review the changes in Catholic education at the lower levels. Eavey provides the following overview:

> During the Early Middle Ages some secular authorities sponsored education, but they generally operated through the clergy. When secular rulers wanted schools established, these schools with few exceptions were set up in churches or cathedrals or monasteries. Kings and emperors sometimes stimulated educational activity among the clergy and in the church. The agency of control of most schools was the church. As the political power of the emperors declined during the ninth and tenth centuries, the pope and the church councils took more and more independent action in educational matters. Lay teachers were tolerated, but the cleric was officially the teacher prior to the Reformation. The most learned among the clergy taught the more advanced subjects, leaving the rudiments to be taught by the junior clergy or by priests who had little learning. There was no teaching profession, as distinguished from the clerical, until near the end of the Middle Ages.[44]

THE MONASTIC SCHOOLS

The mainstay of Catholic education during the Middle Ages had been the monastic boarding schools designed to prepare priests for service to the church. This was a low-level form of education that helped young men advance up the clerical ladder from "doorkeeper, reader, exorcist, acolyte, sub-deacon, deacon, and priest."[45] But as Lewis Sherrill says, "A man might advance through the minor orders and be ordained priest, and yet lack the simplest elements of an education."[46] The monastic schools were not only academically weak but almost devoid of Bible-centered learning. Eavey explains:

> Many monasteries accumulated libraries and became noted for literary and educational activity. In all this the Bible had only a small part. . . . the monasteries contributed comparatively little to pure Christianity or to true Christian education. . . ."[47]

A major function of the monastic schools had been copying manuscripts and preserving the handwritten books. But as the demand for better-written texts accelerated during the revival of learning, commercial copyists began to take the schools' place.[48] More and more the focus of monasteries was on managing their properties, which were extensive. In many monasteries the emphasis shifted from academics to "farming, the arts and crafts, stock breeding, and commerce."[49]

THE CATHEDRAL SCHOOLS

Understandably, the Catholic Church shifted its demand for academic training of its priests from monastic schools to church-sponsored schools.[50] Cathedral schools became the principal means of higher learning for Catholic clergy. Now that the Seven Liberal Arts had not only papal approval but papal support, what was once regarded as pagan was now the central focus of the growing cathedral schools. These schools endorsed the humanistic trends of the day and became the forerunners of the Catholic universities in the twelfth century. According to Reed and Prevost:

> More important than monastic education in the establishment of medieval universities was the cathedral school. The term *cathedral* comes from a Greek word meaning "seat." These schools existed at the administrative headquarters of the diocese where the bishop presided. Cathedrals became the center of public life with educational activities primarily for training clergy. In general, the bishops who led or supervised the cathedral schools were more receptive to new ideas and influences than the abbots of the monasteries. By the twelfth century, good teachers attracted many students in some of the cathedral schools. Abelard taught several thousand at the cathedral school of Notre Dame in Paris. His teaching attracted the students necessary to establish the university at Paris.[51]

Peter Abelard (1079–1142) was the most popular teacher of his time. It could be said that he was the Socrates of the Middle Ages. Catholic though he was, his acceptance on the faculty of the cathedral school at Notre Dame was amazing, given his promiscuous lifestyle and irreverence for Catholic theology.[52] Like Thomas Aquinas, he believed in "consensus truth-making" and reflected the spirit of the Renaissance. Eavey explains:

> He [Abelard] was critical of faith, condemning as credulity the acceptance of any doctrine without first subjecting it to examination by reasoning. One was to believe a doctrine not because God said it but because reason showed it to be true. Abelard found all the essential teachings of Christianity in the works of the classical writers and

Figure 4. (Below) The cathedral schools, symbolized by this work of art over the entrance to Notre Dame Cathedral in Paris, were the forerunners of the Catholic universitites in the 12th century.

Figure 5. (Above) Abelard, the "Socrates of the Middle Ages," drew thousands of students to the cathedral school at Notre Dame in Paris.

considered the difference between paganism and the Gospel not so great as the difference between the Old and the New Testament. He held that men have the right to question all dogmas and all teachings of the church fathers.[53]

If Socrates was the world's first hippie intellectual, Peter Abelard was the second. Like Socrates, he was popular with the masses, but understandably he made "the powers that be" uneasy.

PARISH SCHOOLS

Parish schools also developed in this period. They were the forerunners of the present-day Catholic parochial schools. The elementary students in these schools were taught by the priest, who often held classes in his home.[54] The emphasis in parish schools was elementary education with a particular focus on, "the rudiments of Latin, which was the vehicle for all western learning."[55] Durant describes the curriculum and discipline in England's parish schools, where education seems to have been more advanced than it was elsewhere:

> The curriculum stressed the catechism, the Creed, the basic prayers, reading, writing, arithmetic, singing, and flogging. Even in secondary schools flogging was the staff of instruction. A divine explained that "the boys' spirits must be subdued."[56]

SECONDARY SCHOOLS

Prior to the rise of the Catholic universities, secondary schools, most often housed in the cathedral complexes, reached a sophisticated level of instruction. The secondary schools were commonly referred to as "grammar schools" because of the heavy emphasis on grammar, composition, and languages, especially Latin. The classic literature of ancient Rome and Athens had become an accepted part of the curriculum. The Catholic high schools at Chartres and Laon in northern France were known as "centers of classical learning."[57] Of the secondary school at Chartres Cathedral, Eby and Arrowood quote John of Salisbury, who "asserted that the main peculiarity of the school of Chartres lay in its 'reverent dependence upon the ancients.'"[58] The fact that the leading secondary school of France had a "reverent dependence upon the ancients" is a clear example of the great philosophical shift under way in Catholic education. As we will see, this same new reverent dependence upon the ancients, an "education centering in man,"[59] was amplified and became the heart and soul of the Catholic universities that spread throughout Catholicism's religious empire in the twelfth century.

SCHOLASTIC GUILDS

In addition to the cathedral schools, another forerunner of the Catholic universities was the scholastic guild, which sprang from the trade schools and the apprentice programs that had developed early in the Late Middle Ages. Eavey explains:

> The eleventh and twelfth centuries were characterized by a new movement toward association, that is, the forming of guilds, or collections of like-minded men united for mutual benefit, protection, advancement, and self-government within the limits of their city, business, trade, or occupation. Also, there was at this time a revival of interest in learning, with the realization that the old schools were inadequate to meet the needs of a changing world. Certain of the cathedral schools enriched their program and attracted many students. The actual teaching function and the direct control of the school were often delegated by the bishop to a church official known as the "chancellor." The pope had authority over the bishop and the bishop over the chancellor.[60]

The larger and more sophisticated cathedral schools became known as "Studium Generale" with papal authority in the form of a "papal bull," or a "bull," from the emperor, who served under the pope to grant degrees and licenses to teach.[61]   Clearly, Catholic secondary schools were becoming college-level institutions. This phenomenon occurred almost simultaneously in England, on the Italian peninsula, and in mainland Europe. For example, Oxford was established in 1167,[62] and Cambridge, in 1209.[63] A.F. Leach points out that the rise of these two universities had the effect of "lowering the status of grammar schools."[64] This, of course, is understandable given the enlarged degree-granting role of the universities.

3. The Rise of Catholic Universities

Which university came into existence first? Eby and Arrowood disagree with those who claim that Plato founded the world's first university when he started The Academy:

> The ancient world had no true universities. There were, to be sure, centers of higher teaching and of productive scholarship in classical antiquity—Athens, Alexandria, Rome, Antioch, Pergamon, and Constantinople are notable examples—but classical antiquity did not develop the university.[65]

Reed and Prevost claim that Islamic universities came into being centuries before the Catholic universities of Europe:

> The existence of Arab universities before similar European institutions is not mere conjecture. The Egyptian University of Al-Azhar, founded in Cairo around 970, is one of the oldest universities in the world still in operation. Other Arab universities also existed before this time.[66]

Even libraries existed in the Islamic community long before they existed in the Vatican or other centers of the Holy Roman Empire. Early in the ninth century the ancient city of Baghdad had a library called a House of Wisdom, and the city became a center for university-level learning. Knight explains:

> When about the middle of the eighth century Baghdad became the capital of the Abbasid dynasty, influential Moslem leaders favored and fostered . . . learning; and Baghdad in time became one of the great centers of learning in the world, surpassing anything in western Europe. Harun-al-Rashid, who served as caliph from 786 to 809, and his son Mamun, who ruled from 813 to 833, encouraged schools; and the latter founded a great university, library, and observatory in the city of the Arabian Nights. There the scholars became interested in mathematics, learning much from the Hindus, including a system of computation which replaced the Roman notation and today is known as the Arabic numerals. Saracen [Islamic] learning in Spain was also extensive, and Cordova became a great center of education. Schools

and libraries flourished, and in many places conquered by the [Muslims] learned teachers are said to have become numerous.[67]

It is interesting that the Vatican Library and its "Biblioteca Archivio" did not come into existence until 1450, when Pope Nicholas V laid the foundation for what he hoped would become "the international center for Greek learning."[68]

According to Richard Gross, the basic organization of the Catholic universities of Europe in the twelfth century was "directly modeled after their earlier Islamic counterparts."[69] It is not known which of the Catholic universities was first; the University of Salerno, Italy, or the University of Paris. The founding dates of both are obscure. But we do know they were both established before the University of Bologna, Italy, in 1158 and Oxford University in 1167.[70]

Prior to the Reformation in 1517, there were seventy-nine universities in western Europe. Almost all of them had the approval of the pope and had been given a papal decree. By 1517 the most renowned Catholic universities were in Paris, Bologna, Pavia, and Prague.[71]

It is not an overstatement to say there is no modern institution that has more ties to the medieval past than a Western university. Understandably, this statement is more true in Europe than in North America. Professor Wilds provides the best description of a university in the Middle Ages with reference to its basic organization.

> It began as an association of teachers—in effect, a guild—which was chartered by pope, emperor, or king and was, therefore, much more independent of [local] ecclesiastical authority than was the cathedral school under the bishop or the monastic school under the abbot. It was also independent of any political or secular control. Many privileges, hitherto granted only to the clergy, were vouchsafed to its members under the charter; among them, exemption from taxation, exemption from military service, special courts outside of civil jurisdiction, and immunity from arrest by civil authorities.[72]

It is difficult for us to comprehend students attending a university at age fourteen, but as Wilds points out, this was the rule, not the exception.

> When a student entered the university about the age of fourteen, he attached himself to a master under whom he studied until he could "define and determine," which really meant until he was able to read, write, and speak Latin. When he could demonstrate by examination that he was adequately proficient, he was declared a "bachelor." He then continued his studies under several masters from four to seven years until he could "dispute," that is, until he could defend his thesis

or "masterpiece." The successful defense of his thesis entitled him to his *licentia docendi,* or license to teach. He was now admitted to the ranks of the masters and was allowed to enter into competition with the other masters for students and allowed to charge fees for his work.

By the end of the thirteenth century, most of the universities had become fully organized into four faculties: arts, medicine, law, and theology. [73]

There was nothing "politically correct" about the early universities. There were no women professors or women students. There was no concern about minorities of any kind. The universities were openly elitist, a fact that ultimately led to conflict with local townspeople. Lindsay writes:

> Medieval students sometimes assumed airs which roused the passions of the laity, and frequently led to tremendous riots. Thus in 1513 the townsfolk of Erfurt [Germany] battered in the gates of the University with cannon, and after the flight of the professors and students destroyed almost all the archives and library. . . . This pride of separa-tion between "clerks" and laity culminated in the great annual procession, when the newly capped graduates, clothed in all the glory of new bachelors' and masters' gowns and hoods, marched through the principal streets of the university town, in the midst of the university dignitaries and frequently attended by the magistrates in their robes. Young [Martin] Luther confessed that when he first saw the procession at Erfurt he thought that no position on earth was more enviable than that of a newly capped graduate.[74]

Will Durant records a similar "town and gown" conflict at Oxford University in England:

> In Oxford no love was wasted between town and gown—citizens and scholars. In 1355 the hostile camps rushed into open war, and so many heroes were killed that the year was known as that of the Great Slaughter. Despite the introduction of flogging into the universities of England (c. 1350), the students were a troublesome lot. Forbidden to engage in intramural athletics, they spent their energy in profanity, tippling, and venery; taverns and brothels throve on their patronage.[75]

The University of Paris was dissolved for six years because of student riots with the townspeople beginning in 1228. Soldiers were brought in to quell the riots, and several students were killed.[76] In 1209, Cambridge University was founded largely because "a band of scholars fled from riots in Oxford."[77] In the thirteenth and fourteenth centuries it was not uncommon for a breakaway colony of professors and students to leave a university and form a new one, or join a rival university in another city, in response to an "unwelcome royal or papal policy."[78]

The curriculum and organizational structure of these early universities reflected the spirit of the Renaissance with a feverish return to the ideals of Athens and Rome. The fact that students in some universities became the "rector," or in today's terms the "president," of the university harkens back to Athens, where every male citizen was deemed qualified to hold any political position in the city for a short term. There was in the universities a reverence for the name of Aristotle which, as Lindsay says, "almost took the form of a religious fervour."[79] The book list used at the University of Paris prescribed by the university's statute of 1254 for a B.A. and M.A. degree demonstrates how completely Aristotle had been adopted as the great authority in the intellectual community of Paris. This list was approved nine years before the pope banned Aristotle's writings and reflected a growing attempt by the university to supplant the pope's power over it.[80]

BOOKS REQUIRED AT PARIS FOR THE ARTS DEGREE

I. The "Old" Logic.
    1. Introduction to the *Categories* of Aristotle.
    2. *Categories* and *On Interpretation*, Aristotle.
    3. *Division* and *Topics* except Bk. IV, Boethius.

II. The "New" Logic.
    1. *Prior and Posterior Analytics*, Aristotle.
    2. *Sophistical Refutations*, Aristotle.
    3. *Topics*, Aristotle.

III. Moral Philosophy.
    1. *Ethics*, 4 Bks., Aristotle

IV. Natural Philosophy.
    1. *Physics*, Aristotle.
    2. *On the Heavens and the Earth*, Aristotle.
    3. *Meteorics*, Aristotle.
    4. *On Animals*, Aristotle.
    5. *On the Soul*, Aristotle.
    6. *On Generation*, Aristotle.
    7. *On Sense and Sensible Things*, Aristotle.
    8. *Sleep and Waking*, Aristotle.
    9. *Memory and Recollection*, Aristotle.
    10. *On Life and Death*, Aristotle.
    11. *On Plants*, Aristotle (?).

V. Metaphysics.
    1. *Metaphysics*, Aristotle.

VI. Other Books.
    1. *On the Six Principles*, Gilbert de la Porrèe.
    2. *Barbarismus* (Bk. 3, *Larger Grammar*), Donatus.
    3. *Grammar* (Major and Minor), Priscian.
    4. *On Causes*, Costa ben Luca.
    5. *On the Differences of Spirit and Soul* (another translation
       of *On Causes*).[81]

It is interesting to note that the Bible is not included on the University of Paris' book list. This is unfortunate but not surprising. You will recall from the previous chapter that in 1229 at the Catholic Council in Valencia, Spain, the Bible was placed on "The Index of Forbidden Books."[82] Prior to the ban on the Bible, the prevailing philosophy of the early Catholic universities was derived from the teachings of Augustine.[83] In 1229, the year the Bible was banned, the pope commissioned three professors at the University of Paris to examine the works of Aristotle, whose writings had been officially banned in 1210. There was a long ecclesiastical struggle over the issue, particularly at Paris. In 1263, Pope Urban IV lifted the ban and "officially recognized the Aristotelian philosophy and permitted it to be studied in the schools."[84] Years before, the climate for this major shift in educational philosophy was brought about by Albert of Cologne (1193–1280) and his famous student, Thomas Aquinas (1226–1274), who, as you recall, became the leading theology professor at the University of Paris. While the teachings of Augustine continued to be a major force in university schools of theology, a large number of the professors at Paris and Oxford had already shifted their allegiance to Aristotle and his philosophies of education, including his famous Seven Liberal Arts.[85]

Once the pope lifted the ban on him, Aristotle was elevated to prominence in an amazingly short time. In fact, Scottish historian Lindsay claims that the prevailing thought, not uncommon in the universities, was that Aristotle was a "forerunner of Christ" and "all who refused to accept his guidance were heretics."[86] English historian Rashdall said, "In the middle of the seventeenth century a Doctor of Medicine was compelled by the English College of Physicians to retract a proposition which he had advanced in opposition to the authority of Aristotle, under threat of imprisonment."[87]

The great Catholic shift from Augustine to Aristotle became official in 1263. It was, as A.F. Leach writes,

. . . the substitution of humanism for divinity, of this world for the next, as the object of living, and therefore of education, that differentiated the humanists from their predecessors. For a thousand years the attention of educated mankind had been concentrated on its latter end, or on what was feared to follow it. Not life but death had been the subject of culture. Not how to prepare for life but how to prepare for death was the sole object of education. The humanists' progress consisted in the adoption of the dogma, "The noblest study of mankind is man."[88]

In other words, the focus of education shifted from man studying God to man studying man—a shift from faith in God to faith in man—a major shift indeed!

What was the bottom-line result for the universities of their enormous commitment to Aristotle and to the philosophies of antiquity? There is no question that it led to a focus on some good outcomes of the general intellectual achievement, such as poetry, physics, botany, medicine, fine arts, navigation, geometry, grammar, astronomy, and architecture. It inspired individual achievement, intellectual curiosity, and the basic literacy that the Catholic Church had suppressed during the Middle Ages. This new emphasis resulted in some amazing human achievements, such as:

1. the invention of printing
2. the invention of gunpowder
3. the invention of the magnetic compass
4. Columbus' discovery of America

There is no question that the universities' emphasis on "the new learning" contributed to these achievements. It soon became apparent, however, that the same glaring omission present in the pagan educational institutions of Athens and Rome was now a serious omission in the universities of Europe. You will recall that Greek and Roman paganism taught no moral principles. Consequently, as Eby and Arrowood say, "The moral rottenness of their civilization is beyond description."[89] It is not surprising, therefore, that this same "moral rottenness" began to show up in the Catholic universities when their academic focus shifted to the teachings and lifestyle of the pagan philosophers. Linas Brockett notes:

Soon the students began to lead a vagrant life, and, under the name of Bacchantes, roamed over the different university towns of Europe, studying a little, but for the most part leading a riotous and lawless life, and often spending many years in their travels. Possessing many immunities and privileges as students, they took many more, and became, at last, the terror of the towns they visited.

Figure 6. Oxford University, like the other Catholic universities prior to the Reformation, experienced a declining enrollment. This is the entrance to the Bodleian Library at Oxford.

> It was their practice to attach to themselves very considerable numbers of young boys, whom they professed to teach the elements of reading and grammar, but whom they really employed to forage for them, requiring them, by begging or stealing, to procure their food, and beating them cruelly if they failed to do so.[90]

One might describe these student vagrants as "educated gangs." Reed and Prevost provide additional insight:

> Many students wandered from university to university, attended classes as they desired, and worried little about degrees. Since academic qualifications for basic study hardly existed, students could attend several universities before developing skills of reading and writing. This remained true until the Reformation.

> Some students left home in their early teens to study and did not return until they were thirty or forty years old. The average age of students at Paris was probably fifteen.[91]

Even as the lack of moral principles led to the demise of Athens and Rome, so too the lack of biblical morality led to a declining enrollment at the Catholic universities. Public enthusiasm for the universities waned as students became more and more burdensome to university towns. Attendance at the University of Paris dropped from a peak of five thousand to three thousand at the beginning of the fifteenth century. A similar decline occurred at Oxford, where enrollment declined from a peak of three thousand to under a thousand before the Reformation.[92]

LESSONS LEARNED

Originally the Catholic universities "were created by the clergy for the clergy,"[93] but as the great shift toward Aristotlelian philosophy settled in, most of the traditional religious courses vanished. Lewis Sherrill explains:

> **The church itself sowed the seed of the secularization of education in the very process of fostering an evolution whereby the liberal arts were separated from subjects for which, in Christianity, they had been preparatory; and the liberal arts were again made ends in themselves, precisely as they had been in paganism.[94]**

You will recall that the Seven Liberal Arts were academic divisions of study invented by Aristotle. It wasn't a "seven wonders of the world" kind of invention, nor was there anything either evil or divine about Aristotle's divisions of study. They did, however, become evil to the universities because, as the University of Paris book list reveals, they completely ignored the religious nature of the curriculum. To the evangelical mind, the mission of education is to teach truth. Therefore, the centerpiece, the keystone, the infallible point of reference for all teaching and learning is the sacred Scriptures and Christ Himself, who said, "I am the way, the truth, and the life" (John 14:6). The humanist maxim—that "the noblest study of mankind is man."—is simply not true. The biblical version of that maxim is, "The noblest study of mankind is God as revealed in the Scriptures."

ERASMUS

We conclude this chapter with one of the most interesting figures in education history—Desiderius Erasmus of Rotterdam, Holland. As one stands on the steps of St. Peter's Catholic Church in Leuven, Belgium, and looks to the far right of the church square (almost out of sight of the massive cathedral-like church) a small bronze statue of Desiderius Erasmus stands with only his name beneath it. There is no explanation of who he was. The size of the statue and its "almost out of sight" location undoubtedly symbolizes the "at arm's length" standing of Erasmus to the Roman Catholic Church.

Erasmus was an illegitimate son of a Catholic priest, who also became a priest. Though antagonistic to the Catholic Church, he remained a Catholic throughout his lifetime (1467–1536). Lockerbie claims Erasmus "may have been the greatest scholar of Europe."[95] With grants from Catholic Church officials and others, he studied, wrote, and taught at the universities of Paris, Oxford, and Cambridge. He earned his doctorate at Bologna University in Italy. Erasmus wrote his most famous book, *The Praise of Folly*, in seven days, and forty editions were published in his lifetime. The book, which was translated into twelve languages, was a satire on the errors of the Catholic Church.[96]

In a commentary that accompanied his own translation of the New Testament from the original languages, Erasmus suggested that the early church scholar, Jerome, who translated the Catholic version of the Bible, would be alarmed if he were to witness the current "goings on" in the Catholic church:

> What would Jerome say could he see the Virgin's milk exhibited for money, with as much honor paid to it as to the consecrated body of Christ; the miraculous oils; the portions of the true cross, enough, if collected, to freight a large ship? Here we have the hood of St. Francis, there our Lady's petticoat, or St. Anne's comb . . . not presented as innocent aids to religion, but as the substance of religion itself—and all through the avarice of priests and the hypocrisy of monks playing upon the credulity of the people.[97]

Though never excommunicated, Erasmus was not a darling of Catholic theologians. The pope himself was not beyond the reach of Erasmusian satire. While teaching at Cambridge, Erasmus wrote a dialogue or skit called, "Iulius exclusus." In the dialogue Pope Julius II has died and finds the gates of heaven closed to him by an obstinate St. Peter:

Peter: What? Popes with wives and children?

Julius: Wives? No, not wives, but why not children? . . .

Peter: Were you guilty of the crimes of which they accused you?

Julius: That is nothing to the purpose. . . .

Peter: Is there no way of removing a wicked pope?

Julius: Absurd! Who can remove the highest authority of all? . . . A pope can be corrected only by a general council, but no general council can be held without the pope's consent. . . . Thus he cannot be deposed for any crime whatsoever.

Peter: Not for murder?

Julius: No, not even if it were parricide.

Peter: Not for fornication?

Julius: Not for incest.

Peter: Not for simony?

Julius: Not for 600 acts of simony.

Peter: Not for poisoning?

Julius: No, nor for sacrilege.

Peter: Not for all these crimes gathered in a single person?

Julius: Add 600 more to them, there is no power that can depose the pope.

Peter: A novel privilege for my successors—to be the wickedest of men, yet be safe from punishment. So much the unhappier the Church that cannot shake such a monster off its shoulders. . . . The people ought to rise with paving stones and dash such a wretch's brains out. . . . If Satan needed a vicar he could find none fitter than you.[98]

Figure 7. Desiderius Erasmus, a contemporary of Martin Luther, was a major education reformer and Bible scholar. Some said, "Erasmus laid the egg that Luther hatched."

Erasmus was referred to as "the prince of the humanists."[99] He greatly admired the classics and classical Latin. Like Martin Luther, he was influenced by his early education in a Dutch system of Catholic schools called Brethren of the Common Life, founded by the Dutch scholar Gerhard Groote. Also like Luther, Erasmus was an education reformer. In 1529 he wrote a lengthy letter to his friend, the Duke of Cleves, on education. He began, "I desire to urge upon you, illustrious Duke, to take into your early and serious consideration the future nurture and training of the son lately born to you." Then he embarked on a profound treatise with thirty-seven points, each with a subject heading. Two of his points are as follows:

8. *Education of their children is a Duty owed by parents to the Commonwealth and to God.* Straightway from the child's birth it is meet that he should begin to learn the things which properly

belong to his well-being. Therefore, bestow especial pains upon his tenderest years, as Vergil teaches. Handle the wax whilst it is soft, mould the clay whilst it is moist, dye the fleece before it gathers stains. It is no light task to educate our children aright. . . . God will straitly charge the parents with their children's faults; therefore, except they bring up their little ones from the very first to live aright, they themselves will share the penalty. For a child rightly educated is a comfort and a joy to his parents, but a foolish child brings upon them shame, it may be poverty, and old age before their time. . . .

22. *The Disposition of the Teacher.* Seeing, then, that children in the earliest stage must be beguiled and not driven to learning, the first requisite in the Master is a gentle sympathetic manner, the second a knowledge of wise and attractive methods. Possessing these two important qualifications he will be able to win the pupil to find pleasure in his task. . . .

Fear is of no real avail in education: not even parents can train their children by this motive. Love must be the first influence; followed and completed by a trustful and affectionate respect, which compels obedience far more surely than dread can ever do. . . . [100]

In another letter to Duke George of Saxony, Erasmus explained his neutral position on the Reformation:

No wonder you are displeased at the aspect of things. None can deny that Luther had an excellent cause. Christ had almost disappeared, and when Luther began he had the world at his back. He was imprudent afterwards, but his disciples were more in fault than he. The fury is now so great that I fear the victors will exact terms which none who love Christ will endure, and which will destroy the Christian faith. You are a wise prince, and I will speak my mind freely. Christendom was being asphyxiated with formulas and human inventions. . . . The Gospel light had to be rekindled. Would that more wisdom had been shown when the moment came. Stupid monks and sottish filled the air with outcries, and made bad worse. Nothing was in danger but the indulgences; but they replied in language disgraceful to Christian men. They would not admit that Luther was right, and only cursed. Seeing how the stream was running, I kept out of it, merely showing that I did not wholly go with Luther. [101]

Erasmus had friends and enemies on both sides of the great Reformation issue. Luther was disappointed that Erasmus had not fully joined his cause. Some said, "Erasmus laid the egg that Luther hatched." [102] While Erasmus had friends in high places, he had enemies in even higher places. At the

Council of Trent, several of his books were publicly condemned and placed (along with the Bible) on Catholicism's list of forbidden books.[103] His books were even banished from his alma mater, the University of Paris.[104] Nonetheless, his writings were widely read, and he was second only to Luther as a popular writer. One Oxford book dealer claimed that one-third of all his book sales were the works of Erasmus.[105]

Even though Erasmus was regarded as a "Christian humanist," he was not an "evangelical," as Gangel and Benson explain:

> Though hardly embracing the worldly humanism of his colleagues to the South, Erasmus was a thoroughgoing humanist who believed that man was the measure of all things. As such, man's nature is fundamentally good, in contrast to the Reformation teachings of total depravity. As important as Erasmus was to the history of education, indeed to the history of Christian education, we dare not think of him as "evangelical" in the modern sense.[106]

It is interesting that forty-two days before the Reformation, Erasmus wrote from Antwerp to the Catholic Cardinal of York, England, this amazing prophetic line: "In this part of the world I am afraid a great revolution is impending."[107] On October 31, 1517, the Great Reformation occurred!

In our next chapter we will cover the same period, the Late Middle Ages, and will concentrate on the ecclesiastical and political climate in Catholicism's religious empire. We will also consider the great "morning stars" of the Reformation and the other "heroes of the faith" who maintained Christian schools during this turbulent period.

Endnotes—Chapter Five

[1] Andrew Miller, *Short Papers on Church History,* vol. 2. "The Crusades to the Days of the Reformation." (London: Pickering and Inglis, p. 353.

[2] Ibid., p. 355.

[3] Ibid., pp. 353–354.

[4] Clarence H. Benson, *A Popular History of Christian Education* (Chicago: Moody Press, 1943), pp. 51–2.

[5] Thomas Lindsay, *A History of the Reformation* (Edinburgh: T. & T. Clark, 1906), pp. 18–19.

[6] Charles Beard, *Martin Luther and the Reformation in Germany* (London: K. Paul, Trench & Co., 1889, 33; quoted in Frederick Eby, *The Development of Modern Education* (New York: Prentice-Hall, Inc., 1934), p. 11.

[7] Martin Luther, quoted in Lindsay, p. 245.

[8] Andrew Miller, "The Crusades to the Days of the Reformation," p. 355.

[9] Robertson, vol. 2., Milman, 630, vol. 3., 233; Waddington, vol. 2., p. 37.

[10] Miller, pp. 356–357.

[11] Ibid., p. 358.

[12] Kenneth Scott Latourette, *A History of Christianity,* vol. I (New York: Harper and Row, Publishers, 1953), p. 474. Note: Latourette said, "The Crusades were begun by the papacy. No Crusade was valid without papal endorsement."

[13] Jerald C. Brauer, ed., *The Westminster Dictionary of Church History* (Philadelphia: Westminster, 1971), pp. 183-184, quoted in James E. Reed and Ronnie Prevost, *A History of Christian Education* (Nashville: Broadman and Holman Publishers, 1993), p. 127.

[14] J. R. Marcus, *The Jew in the Medieval World: A Source Book*: 315–1791 AD (Cincinnati: The Sinai Press, 1938), pp. 45-46.

[15] J. F. Hecker, quoted in *Encyclopaedia Britannica,* vol. 17 (Chicago: William Benton, published, 1961), p. 990.

[16] Michael Van Cleave Alexander, *The Growth of English Education* (University Park, Penn: The Pennsylvania State University Press, 1990), p. 2.

[17] Samuel G. Kahn, *A Short History of Education* (Jerusalem: Yesodot Publishers, 1960), p. 34.

[18] Robert Ulich, *A History of Religious Education* (New York: New York University Press, 1968), p. 90.

[19] Christian History Institutes, "[Tyndale] God's Outlaw and Fugitive for Biblical Faith," Issue no. 59, p. 1. In 1408 the English Parliament passed the "Constitutions of Oxford," which forbade anyone translating or reading any part of the Bible in the English language without written permission from the Catholic Church.

[20] Benson, p. 62

[21] Ibid., pp. 720–721.

[22] Augustine, quoted in Frank E. Gaebelein, "Christian Education," *The New International Dictionary of the Christian Church,* J.D. Douglas, general editor (Grand Rapids: Zondervan Publishing House, 1974), p. 331.

[23] Frank E. Gaebelein, quoted by Kenneth O. Gangel in D. Bruce Lockerbie's work, *A Passion for Learning: The History of Christian Thought on Education* (Chicago: Moody Press, 1994), p. 398.

[24] Ulich, p. 70.

[25] Ibid., p. 71.

[26] *Encyclopaedia Britannica,* vol. 2 (Chicago: William Benton publisher, 1961), p. 166.

[27] Colin Brown, "Scholasticism," *Introduction to the History of Christianity (*Minneapolis: Fortress Press, 1995), p. 286.

[28] Elmer Harrison Wilds, *The Foundations of Modern Education* (New York: Rinehart & Company, Inc., 1936), p. 186.

[29] Ibid.

[30] Francis A. Schaeffer, *How Should We Then Live?* (Old Tappan, New Jersey: Fleming H. Revell, Company, 1976), p. 43.

[31] Isaac Doughton, *Modern Public Education* (New York: D. Appleton-Century Company, 1935), pp. 14–15. Quoted in Robert L. Cooke, *Philosophy, Education, and Certainty* (Grand Rapids: Zondervan Publishing House, 1940), p. 97. Note: Professor Cooke said the same thing as Doughton in a different way. He said, "Thomas Aquinas fixed for all time the position of the [Catholic] Church, making reason the interpreter and formulator of the doctrine and holding Aristotle as the "master mind." Ibid., p. 100.

[32] James E. Reed and Ronnie Prevost, *A History of Christian Education* (Nashville: Broadman Holman Publishers, 1993), p. 134.

[33] Cooke, p. 103.

[34] Ibid.

[35] Martin Luther, quoted in Frederick Eby, Th*e Development of Modern Education* (New York: Prentice-Hall Inc., 1934), p. 46.

[36] Ellwood P. Cubberley, *The History of Education* (Boston: Houghton Mifflin Company, 1920), p. 289 (see footnote).

[37] Ibid., p. 259.

[38] A. F. Leach, *The Schools of Medieval England* (London: Methuen & Co. Ltd. 1915), p. 29.

[39] Kahn, p. 4.

[40] Eby and Arrowood, p. 710.

[41] Ibid., p. 713.

[42] Kahn, p. 44.

[43] C. B. Eavey, *History of Christian Education* (Chicago: Moody Press, 1964), p. 107.

[44] Ibid., pp. 102–103.

[45] G. G. Coulton, *Medieval Panorama* (Cambridge: Cambridge University Press, 1940), p. 144. Quoted in Lewis Joseph Sherrill, *The Rise of Christian Education* (New York: The Macmillan Company, 1944), p. 263.

[46] Ibid.

[47] Eavey, p. 104.

[48] Eby and Arrowood, p. 724.

[49] Ibid.

[50] Harvey J. Graff, *The Legacies of Literacy* (Bloomington and Indianapolis: Indiana University Press, 1987), p. 58.

[51] James E. Reed and Ronnie Prevost, *A History of Christian Education* (Nashville: Broadman Holman Publishers, 1993), p. 141.

[52] *The New International Dictionary of the Christian Church*, J. D. Douglas, (Grand Rapids: Zondervan Publishing House, 1974), p. 3.

[53] Eavey, p. 111.

[54] Reed and Prevost, p. 141.

[55] Lewis Joseph Sherrill, *The Rise of Christian Education* (New York: The Macmillan Company, 1944), p. 259.

[56] Oxford Reformers, p. 211. Quoted in Will Durant, *The Reformation* (New York: Simon and Schuster, 1947), p. 235.

[57] Eby and Arrowood, p. 726.

[58] R. L. Poole, *Illustrations from the History of Medieval Thought*, pp. 114-119. Quoted in Eby and Arrowood, p. 726.

[59] Eavey, p. 114.

[60] Ibid., p. 107.

[61] *Encyclopaedia Britannica* (Chicago: William Benton, publisher, 1961), p. 862. NOTE: Education historian Ellwood Cubberley, *History of Education*, p. 17, quotes a decree adopted by the General Council of the Church of Rome in 1179, which required that the "scholacticus" "should have the authority to superintend all the schoolmasters of the diocese and grant them licenses without which none should presume to teach." Cubberley adds, "Thus we find, by 1200 a limited but powerful church school system, with centralized control and supervision of instruction, diocesan licenses to teach, and a curriculum adapted to the needs of the institution in control of the schools."

[62] Ellwood P. Cubberley, *Readings in the History of Education* (Boston: Houghton Mifflin Company, 1920), p. 154.

[63] Ibid.

[64] Leach, p. 157.

[65] Eby and Arrowood, p. 761.

[66] Reed and Prevost, p. 140.

[67] Edgar W. Knight, *Twenty Centuries of Education* (Boston: Ginn and Company, 1940), p. 157.

[68] Cubberley, *The History of Education,* p. 252.

[69] Richard E. Gross, ed., *Heritage of American Education* (Boston: Allyn and Bacon, 1962), p. 153. Quoted in Reed and Prevost, p. 141.

[70] Cubberley, *Readings in the History of Education,* p. 154.

[71] Frederick Eby, *The Development of Modern Education* (New York: Prentice-Hall, Inc. 1934), p. 22.

[72] Wilds, pp. 186–187.

[73] Ibid.

[74] Lindsay, p. 56.

[75] Will Durant, *The Reformation* (New York: Simon and Schuster, 1957), p. 236.

[76] Eby and Arrowood, p. 780.

[77] Michael Hall, *Cambridge: A Pevensey Heritage Guide* (Cambridge: The Pevensey Press, 1980), p. 5.

[78] Alan Corbban, *The Medieval English Universities: Oxford and Cambridge to 1500* (Berkeley: The University of California Press, 1988), p. 9. Also see P. Kibre, *Scholarly Privileges in the Middle Ages* (London: Medieval Academy of America), chapter 2.

[79] Lindsay, p. 56.

[80] Sherrill, p. 263.

[81] *Chartularium Universitatis Parisiensis,* vol. I, p. 119. Quoted in Cubberley, *Readings in History of Education,* pp. 168–169.

[82] Loraine Boettner, *Roman Catholicism* (Philadelphia: The Presbyterian and Reformed Publishing Co. 1962), p. 97.

[83] S. J. Curtis, *History of Education in Great Britain,* (London: University Tutorial Press LTD, 1948), p. 66.

[84] Ibid.

[85] Ibid.

[86] Lindsay, p. 56

[87] H. Rashdall, *The Universities of Europe in the Middle Ages,* vol. II, p. 703 (Oxford: 1895); quoted in Cubberley, *Readings in the History of Education,* p. 183.

[88] A. F. Leach, pp. 248–249.

[89] Eby and Arrowood, p. 513.

[90] Linus Brockett, History and Progress of Education (New York: A. S. Barnes & Burr, 1860), p. 165.

[91] Reed and Prevost, p. 147.

[92] Curtis, pp. 62-63. Note: Stanley Curtis points out that attendance figures at European universities were often exaggerated. He said, "Much has been written about the size of the student population of the mediaeval universities. People of the Middle Ages were much given to exaggeration, so that we should not be astonished at some of the amazing claims which were made. Thirty thousand seems to have been a favourite number both for Paris and Oxford, but such claims are fantastic, as both Rashdall and Coulton demonstrate."

[93] Sherrill, p. 165.

[94] Ibid.

[95] D. Bruce Lockerbie, *A Passion for Learning* (Chicago: Moody Press, 1994), 153.

[96] Will Durant, *The Reformation* (New York: Simon and Schuster, 1957), p. 277.

[97] Erasmus, *Commentary on Matthew 23:27,* quoted in Durant, *The Reformation,* p. 284.

[98] Erasmus, *Iulius exclusus, in Froude,* pp. 150-168, quoted in Durant, *The Reformation,* p. 280.

[99] Reed and Prevost, p. 181.

[100] Erasmus, On the Liberal Education of the Young. Quoted in Lockerbie, pp. 155, 157, and 160.

[101]Erasmus, *To Duke George.* Quoted in Ulich, p. 103.

[102]*The New International Dictionary of the Christian Church,* J.D. Douglas, ed. (Grand Rapids: Zondervan Publishing House, 1974), p. 350.

[103]Ulich, p. 102.

[104]Cubberley, *History of Education,* p. 289.

[105]Durant, p. 91.

[106]Gangel and Benson, p. 128.

[107]Erasmus, *III,* 48. Quoted in Durant, p. 292.

Illustration Sources

Figure 1   *Crusader Map*—Global Mapping International, Colorado Springs, CO.

Figure 2   *Augustine*—Alinari/Art Resource, NY.

Figure 3   *Thomas Aquinas*—Alinari/Art Resource, NY.

Figure 4   *Cathedral*—Photo by author (PBA).

Figure 5   *Cathedral*—PBA.

Figure 6   *Oxford University*—PBA.

Figure 7   *Erasmus*—PBA.

Decline of the Religious Empire

Before we give our attention to Martin Luther, the great education reformer, it is essential to understand the events and the political climate that led to the Reformation of 1517. There is little doubt that prior to the Reformation the Catholic world had become a political and ecclesiastical tinderbox waiting to be ignited.

No church before or since the Middle Ages has ruled the Western world as the Catholic Church ruled it between 590 and 1517, almost a millenium. It was, indeed, a time and situation unique in history, an attempt at complete control, of forced conformity to the dogma of a church whose leader saw himself as God on earth[1] and the king as "the mere deputy of the pope."[2] This chapter will address the long struggle between the kings of Europe and the Roman pontiff, drawing parallels between Rome as a political state and the Roman Catholic Church. The divisions of chapter 6 are:

1. *Understanding Papal Power*
2. *The Eve of the Reformation*
3. *Reformation Martyrs*

Historians generally agree that the apex of Catholicism's religious empire was the thirteenth century.[3] While it was a period when popes exercised enormous power, the relationship between the Vatican in Rome and the countries in the Holy Roman Empire was neither holy nor cordial. For example, in *Ranke's History of the Popes* we read:

> The domination of the Papacy was felt by the nations of Teutonic blood as the dominion of Italians, of foreigners, of men alien in language, manners, and intellectual constitution. . . . The sums which, under a thousand pretexts, were exacted by a distant court, were regarded both as a humiliating and as a ruinous tribute.[4]

Throughout Catholicism's constituency the power of the pope was held in varying degrees of reverence and fear. The pope evoked reverence because of a sincere but misguided belief in papal infallibility. His pronouncements were regarded as *ex cathedra* "immune from error."[5] He evoked fear because of his perceived ecclesiastical and civil authority, which were used most often to advance the wealth and power of the Catholic Church with little regard for the well-being of its people. It is important, therefore, to understand the basis for papal authority and why it was so widely accepted.

1. Understanding Papal Power

Pope Innocent III (1198–1216), the most powerful of all the popes,[6] defined the Catholic faith as follows at the Lateran Council in 1215:

> There is moreover one universal Church of the faithful, outside which no man at all is saved, in which the same Jesus Christ is both the priest and the sacrifice, whose body and blood are truly contained in the sacrament of the altar under the species of bread and wine, the bread being transubstantiated into the body and the wine into the blood by the divine power, in order that, to accomplish the mystery of unity, we ourselves may receive of His that which He received of ours. And this thing, the sacrament to wit, no one can make but a priest, who has

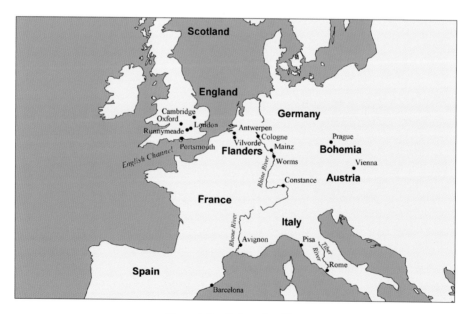

Figure 1. Pre-Reformation Map.

been duly ordained, according to the keys of the Church, which Jesus Christ Himself granted to the apostles and their successors.[7]

A reigning pope in the Middle Ages was regarded as Christ's one and only representative, the "Vicar of Christ" on earth. He saw himself as superior in authority to all other men. Pope Innocent III said, "All secular kings for the sake of God so venerate this Vicar, that unless they seek to serve him devotedly they doubt if they are reigning properly."[8] Pope Innocent III reaffirmed the doctrine of his predecessors with these words: "Those provinces which from old have had the Holy Roman Church as their proper teacher in spiritual matters should now in temporal things also have her as their peculiar sovereign."[9] His goal, and the goal of every pontiff in the Middle Ages, was to "dominate all human relationships"[10] in both religious and civil affairs.

At Jerusalem Jesus told the Sadducees, who were steeped in Jewish tradition, "You are mistaken, not knowing the Scriptures" (Matthew 22:29). Because of their emphasis on tradition, Christ would have said the same thing to the Catholic authorities in the Middle Ages. There are no examples in either the Old or New Testament of any infallible source for faith and practice for the church or its leaders other than the written Word of God. Like the religious patterns of the Jewish Sadducees, those of the Catholic Church were a composite of Scripture and man-made tradition that was often presented as canon law. In addition to papal infallibility, a host of Catholic religious practices were outside biblical authority. The Catholic Church of the Middle Ages was steeped in tradition and mysticism. Human traditions have their place, but John as Murray suggests:

> Tradition, even when it is the best, has no intrinsic authority. Tradition is always subject to the scrutiny and test of Scripture. Its rightness or value is always determined by its conformity to Scripture. This is just saying that it is never proper to appeal to tradition as having an intrinsic authority in matters of faith and morals. Tradition when right is always derived; it is never original and primary.[11]

Because so many religious practices in the Catholic Church in the Middle Ages were based on unsubstantiated claims to biblical authority (such as the sale of indulgences and the killing of heretics), it is little wonder that Catholic authorities suppressed literacy and Bible reading by the masses for fear their own practices would be challenged. As Pope Innocent III and the popes who followed him accelerated their man-made religious practices and carried them beyond human tolerance, they set in motion the events that led to the Great Reformation that would be ignited by Martin Luther, one of their own priests.

PAPAL POWER OVER KINGS

Papal authority over kings reached its zenith when Pope Innocent III excommunicated King John of England, who reigned from 1199 to 1216. It should be noted that King John was anything but a model king. Andrew

Miller says of him, "Never had a viler prince worn a crown." King John was "the most cruel, sensual, and faithless of monarchs."[12] Although John was unpopular among his English subjects, his defiance of the pope and later his groveling compliance to save his crown laid the foundation for civil independence of kingdoms from Catholic control "which led ultimately to the Reformation."[13] Additionally, King John's mismanagement of England's government and his personal excesses led to the great Magna Carta and ultimately to England's parliamentary form of government. On June 15, 1215, at a dramatic meeting in Runnymede, west of London, a group of English barons forced King John to sign his approval of the Magna Carta, a list of individual liberties. This event is important to Americans because England's Magna Carta was the foundational document that would inspire the American Bill of Rights in 1787.[14]

Figure 2. King John of England was the first monarch to challenge the authority of the pope. After a show of force by the pope, King John repented and gave England to the "Church of Rome."

The controversy between king and pope began when King John imposed royal taxes on the previously tax-exempt monasteries in his kingdom. It escalated when John interfered with the papal appointment of a new Archbishop of Canterbury—a seat first held by Augustine (not of Hippo). King John's actions led to an ultimate challenge of the pope's authority. Pope Innocent III responded by "smiting" England with an "interdict" which in effect, shut down its Catholic cathedrals, monasteries, and churches for four years.[15] He then excommunicated King John and finally, in November 1209, deposed him as King of England with these words:

> That John, King of England, be deposed from the royal crown and dignity; that his subjects be dissolved from their oath of allegiance, and be at liberty to transfer them to a person worthier to fill the vacant throne.[16]

No religious leader in history had exercised such power over an earthly king. Miller describes Pope Innocent III's amazing action:

The throne of England was now publicly and solemnly declared vacant, by the decree of the Pope, and the king's dominions the lawful spoil of whoever could wrest them from his unhallowed hands. Such was the power of the Pope in those days, and such the terror of his thunders. He struck great nations with his anathemas, and they fell before him as if withered and blasted; he hurled great kings from their thrones, and compelled them to bend before the tempest of his wrath, and humbly obey the mandate of his will. All, without exception, in Church and State, must accept his own terms of reconciliation, or die without salvation and be tormented in the flames of Hell for ever. . . .[17]

The pope often used rivalries between kingdoms to his advantage. Since King John did not voluntarily step down, the pope enlisted the services of King Philip Augustus of France to force him from his throne. A delegation of legates from the Vatican "placed in [Philip's] hand a formal commission, directing him by 'apostolic authority' to invade England, depose the king, and take his crown."[18] King Philip, not a friend of King John or of England, immediately assembled a large naval fleet and an army for the anticipated invasion of England. To ensure the success of the invasion, the pope sent a message to the other kingdoms of his religious empire announcing the reluctance of John to step down as the King of England. He then urged them to send soldiers to King Philip in France to participate in the invasion of England. The pope promised "to all who should take part in this holy war the remission of sins and the privileges of crusaders."[19]

Learning of the pope's army and naval forces forming across the English Channel in France, King John initiated the formation of a substantial army and navy of his own at Portsmouth, south of London. The pope, good strategist that he was, sent two "legates" from Rome to London to "brief" John on the magnitude of the military forces preparing to come against him. They warned that his crown would be taken from him by force and given to his archenemy, King Philip II of France.

Figure 3. English barons forced King John to sign his approval of the Magna Carta, one of the world's great documents on individual liberty.

The pope's strategy worked well. In an amazing about-face, King John, in order to save his crown and undoubtedly his neck, surrendered his kingly authority to Pope Innocent III on May 15, 1213, with this pledge:

> "I John, by the grace of God King of England and Lord of Ireland, in order to expiate my sins, from my own free will and the advice of my barons, give to the Church of Rome, to Pope Innocent and his successors, the kingdom of England, and all other prerogatives of my crown. I will hereafter hold them as the Pope's vassal. I will be faithful to God, to the Church of Rome, to the Pope my master, and to his successors legitimately elected. I promise to pay him a tribute of 1000 merks; to wit, 700 for the kingdom of England, and 300 for the kingdom of Ireland."[20]

King John, in the attempt to save his crown, gave away England, Ireland, and a "king's ransom" in future taxes to the Vatican. He also agreed to the pope's choice of Stephen Langton as England's Archbishop. Clearly, in this confrontation, the pope won.

To understand why Ireland was included in King John's "great giveaway," one must step back a few decades. The Norse invasions, over a three-hundred-year period, greatly weakened Ireland's Celtic Church. Seeing this weakness, the Catholic church began establishing a series of bishoprics and churches in Ireland. Finally, in 1171 at a meeting in Cashel, southwest of Dublin, "obedience to Rome" and "a system of tithes and papal tribute" were accepted.[21] On the issue of the Pope's right to give Ireland to King Henry II, Andrew Miller says:

> The ground on which the Pope rested his right to make this grant was thus expressed: "For it is undeniable, and your majesty acknowledges it, that all islands on which Christ the son of righteousness hath shined, and which have received the Christian faith, belong of right to St. Peter and the most holy Roman Church."[22]

As a political favor to England's King Henry II, Pope Adrian IV, the first English pope, deeded Ireland to him "as an inheritance."[23] Amazingly, the people of Ireland accepted the idea that the pope in Rome could legitimately give their country to a British king as a gift. It is equally amazing that King Henry's son John, heir to England's throne, in order to save his crown, could give Ireland back to the pope along with England. As Andrew Miller puts it, "Such was the power of the pope in those days. . . ."[24]

THE POPE WAS POWERFUL BUT UNPOPULAR

The pope may have had power over kings and kingdoms "in those days," but he did not have the good will of the people. Like the people of

Germany, who were filled with "scorn and disgust" for the papacy, the people in England were irate. In reference to the treatment of King John by Vatican authorities, a Church of England vicar wrote:

> They fomented the rebellion of his own subjects at home, sometimes of his barons, sometimes of his bishops, playing fast and loose on both sides for advantage. They disinherited him of his crown. They gave away his kingdom for a prey to a foreign prince. They incited strangers to make war against him. And they themselves by mere collusion and tricks had well near thrust him out of his throne.[25]

Meanwhile, what had happened to King Philip II in France, who under the directives of Pope Innocent III had been forming, for several months and at great expense, a massive military force to invade England? After the "restoration" of King John, the pope's "legate" rushed to the military camp of King Philip across the English Channel on the shores of France, where King Philip's forces were "on the point of embarkation for England."[26] One can only imagine the reaction of King Philip when he was informed that:

> there was now no further need for his services; and that in fact any attempt to invade the kingdom, or to annoy the King of England must be highly offensive to the Holy See, inasmuch as that kingdom was now part and parcel of the patrimony of the Church. It was therefore his duty to dismiss his army, and himself to return home in peace.[27]

King Philip knew he had been duped by the "Holy See":

> He had been drawn into enormous expense; he had called forth the whole strength of his dominions, under the delusive promise of a kingdom and the remission of his sins; all this he had done at the earnest entreaty of the Pope.[28]

Not wanting to lose face with their assembled military forces, both kings, Philip and John, led their forces in a confrontation, not in England or France but north of France in Flanders, now Belgium and Holland. Philip attacked the Flemings, and John joined the Flemings against Philip's army and naval forces. King John's forces prevailed,[29] but neither king benefited greatly from their misguided war. The sole purpose of the war was to save face for two proud kings, both of whom were victims of an egotistical pope.

This unfortunate series of events perpetuated the long feud between these cross-channel rivals. This legacy of hatred resulted in France and England's tragic Hundred Years' War, which lasted from 1337 until 1453, cost thousands of lives, and crippled both countries financially. The Hundred Years' War had an interesting side effect in England. The English population developed an intense dislike for the crude manners and customs of the French. Therefore, they accelerated their efforts in educating and training their children.[30] As a result, at the time of the Reformation, there were more Catholic schools in England than in France even though France had almost twice the population.

THE PROBLEM OF PAPAL TITHES AND TAXES

A growing number of pope–king confrontations, such as those experienced by Kings Philip and John, fueled a rising spirit of independence and nationalism in the various European countries. Catholic historian Pierre Marique acknowledges the problem:

> Meanwhile, there had developed in every country a national con-sciousness which, to a great extent, was antagonistic to Christian [Catholic] unity. Princes and governments were seeking to control all matters of a national character without any regard for the traditions of Western Christendom, or even the undeniable rights of the Church.[31]

In addition to the pope's forcing his civil authority beyond toleration in public confrontations, other factors were at work that widened even further the growing breach between the Vatican and its empire in the Western world. There were two gnawing problems: first, the amount of money that flowed to Rome in taxes, fees, and tithes; and second, the lifestyle of the clergy.

The first of these problems—papal taxes, fees, and tithes—was at the heart of much of the civil unrest. The Catholic Church is still a wealthy institution, but the affluence of today's church is limited compared with its wealth before the Great Reformation in 1517. The phrase "raking it in" might well have referred to the accumulated wealth brought by Catholic pilgrims to the Vatican in 1300. Pope Boniface VIII offered "plenary indulgences," ensuring immediate entry into heaven after death (bypass-ing purgatory) to pilgrims who brought gifts to Rome in a "Year of Jubilee," instituted for the first time in 1300. Robert Sencourt describes the pilgrims as follows:

> The press across the Tiber was so great that the traffic was regulated on the bridge by a law which kept those going on one side, those returning to the other. And when, at last, the pilgrims had passed up through the city into St. Peter's, they offered at the tomb of the Apostle their most generous gifts, gifts which were poured in with such profu-sion that priests literally gathered them with a rake.[32]

As an increase in trade throughout the empire increased the wealth of the general population, the Catholic Church appealed for gifts of every kind. Lindsay says:

> In those days of . . . prosperity and wealth, the town churches became "museums and treasure-houses." The windows were filled with painted glass; weapons, armor, jewels, pictures, tapestries were stored in the treasuries or adorned the walls. Ancient inventories have been preserved of some of these ecclesiastical accumulations of wealth. In the cathedral church in Bern, to take one example, the head of St. Vincentius, the patron, was adorned with a great quantity of gold, and with one jewel said to be priceless; the treasury contained 70 gold and 50 silver cups, 2 silver coffers, and 450 costly sacramental robes decked with jewels of great value. The luxury, the artistic fancy, and the wealth which could minister to both, all three characteristic of the times, were lavished by the Germans on their churches.[33]

Over the centuries the Catholic Church accumulated great wealth not only at Rome but in every country in its empire. The list of the church's estimated wealth, country by country, prior to the Reformation, is staggering:

1. France   *"A procurer-general of the parliament calculated in 1502 that three-quarters of all French wealth was ecclesiastical."*[34]

2. Germany   *"In the Centum Gravamina, or Hundred Grievances, listed against the church by the Diet of Nuremberg (1522), it was alleged that she [the Catholic Church] owned half the wealth of Germany."*[35] *"It was the papacy that drained Germany of Gold. . . ."*[36]

3. Denmark   *"In Scandinavia the rapidly rising wealth of the clergy, exempt from taxation, became an irritating burden to the people and state. Critics alleged that the church owned half the land in Denmark. . . ."*[37]

4. Scotland *"More than half the wealth of Scotland belonged to the clergy. . . ."* [38]

5. Italy   *"One-third of the peninsula belonged to the church as the Papal States, and she owned rich properties in the rest."*[39]

6. England   *"By 1500 the church owned, on a conservative Catholic estimate, about a fifth of all the property in England."*[40] *"It was estimated that more English money went to the pope than to the state or the king."*[41]

It is not an overstatement to say the Catholic Church of the Middle Ages had become obsessed with power and greed:

> She grew rich by appropriating the contributions that were raised for the purposes of the Crusades; and she grew strong through weakening the monarchs of Europe by exhausting their treasures and depopulating their countries. Every thought of the Papal mind, every feeling of the Papal heart, every mandate that issued from the Vatican, had but one object in view—the enriching and strengthening of the Roman See.[42]

THREE POPES AT ONE TIME

Near the end of the Roman Empire, you will recall, there was a rapid succession of Roman emperors—thirty-seven in thirty-five years! During the "second fall" of Rome, in the Catholic period, there was another rapid succession of leaders. Between 897 and 955, in the short span of fifty-eight years, seventeen popes followed each other to Catholicism's highest office. One, Pope John XI, was twenty-one when he assumed his duties![43] This instability of leadership eroded public confidence in the pope's claim to be the "Vicar of Christ" on Earth.

One interesting development in Catholic history was that unique period when there were three popes at one time. Understandably, the situation led to confusion and a further loss of prestige for the papacy. After all, how could all three popes be infallible? The three-pope controversy was referred to by some as the "Babylonian Captivity"[44] and by others as the "Avignon Schism"[45] (1378–1417). The Avignon Schism was the second of three schisms in the Catholic Church. The first was "The Great Schism" of 1054 at Constantinople, when the Greek Catholic Church separated from the Latin or Roman Catholic Church. The third and less known schism occurred in 1570 when the Church of England separated from Rome.[46]

The second schism is called the "Avignon Schism" because in 1309 the Vatican had been moved from Rome to Avignon in southern France. The moving of the papacy to France came in reaction to a series of "papal bulls," issued by Pope Boniface VIII, which limited the power of kings to tax the clergy and church landholdings.[47] As previously noted, European monarchs had been seething with resentment over the amount of money flowing from their kingdoms to Rome. Freeman Butts describes the confrontation:

Attacks upon the papacy by the kings grew in intensity during the fourteenth century. The principal contest involved Pope Boniface VIII and King Philip IV of France. Boniface issued a series of papal bulls in which he exhorted his clergy not to pay taxes to the kings, denied the right of secular courts to try the clergy, asserted his complete sovereignty over all secular rulers, and specifically declared Philip IV deposed. Philip IV in turn sent his agents to Italy to capture Boniface and demand that he quit the papacy. The result of the whole episode was a terrible fall in the prestige of the papacy.[48]

The kings of both England and France imposed restrictions on the flow of money to Rome. Germany, not having a strong monarch, and having in Aachen the seat of power for Catholicism's Holy Roman Empire, did not impose restrictions. Consequently, Germany, more than other countries, became the major source of revenue to satisfy the popes' ever-growing demands for money. Ultimately, the "heavy drainage of money" from Germany became a determining factor in the wide acceptance of Luther's Reformation in 1517.[49]

France, in addition to restricting funds to Rome, sought to restrict "ecclesiastical authority" further by demanding that the College of Cardinals elect a French pope. When Pope Boniface died the year after he was "humiliated to death" by the French king, and after another pope was elected and died soon after, the College of Cardinals bowed to the pressure from King Philip "The Fair" (Philip IV) and elected Clement V as the pope of the Roman Catholic Church. Clement V, from southern France, decided with the help of "Philip the Fair" to move the Catholic Church headquarters to Avignon on the east bank of the Rhone River in southern France. In 1348, a successor, Pope Clement VI, purchased the entire city of Avignon for the popes' residence and spent vast sums of money in building a "fortress-like" papal palace.[50]

Meanwhile, back in the "Eternal City," chaos prevailed. Once the home of the "Lord of the World,"[51] Rome now became an overgrown village. Poggio, a scholar in Rome during the long absence of the popes, pictured the city's desolation:

> The forum of the Roman people, where they assembled to enact their laws and elect their magistrates, is now enclosed for the cultivation of pot herbs, or thrown open to swine and buffaloes. The public and private edifices that were founded for eternity, lie prostitute, naked and broken—like the limbs of mighty giants; and the ruin is the more visible from the stupendous relics that have survived the injuries of space and time.[52]

Speaking of Rome during this period, Sencourt says, "The population of the city sank to 20,000 and grass grew in the most frequented streets."[53] Because the papacy had claimed Rome to be God's city, its decaying walls reflected a further erosion of public trust in ecclesiastical authority.

The phenomenon of the three popes occurred when Pope Gregory XI of Avignon suddenly moved the "Holy See" back to Rome. At his death a crowd of angry Romans demanded that the cardinals elect a Roman pope. The cardinals, most of whom were French, went along with them and elected Pope Urban VI. A faction of the cardinals, however, were unhappy with the majority decision and elected their own pope, Clement VII. After losing a bitter battle between the armies of the two popes for the control of the Vatican, Pope Clement moved to Avignon, the vacated papal throne in France. Now there were two popes in separate papal palaces, both with substantial finances and a large following.[54] During the first half of the Middle Ages, there had been short-term papal schisms, sometimes resulting in the coexistence of two and even three popes, but the schisms of the past had never been on the scale of the great Rome and Avignon Schism. The resulting unrest contributed significantly to the volatile environment that culminated in the Reformation. The schism not only divided the allegiance of nations but divided churches and high-level church leaders. Pope Urban VI of Rome, for example, ordered "some of his unbending cardinals tortured to death" because they failed to support him.[55] It was indeed a farcical situation.

In addition to two popes, there were two rival colleges of cardinals. In 1409, factions from both colleges met in Pisa, Italy, to resolve the dilemma of dual popes. Neither the Avignon pope nor the Roman pope recognized the validity of the Pisa General Council of Cardinals, and both refused to attend. Consequently, the cardinals, ignoring the principle of papal supremacy, deposed both popes and elected Alexander V as the one and only pope of the Catholic Church. However, the other two popes refused to step down, citing their papal supremacy established by canon law. Now there were three popes, one in Pisa, one in Rome, and the third in Avignon.

In 1415, almost one hundred years before the Reformation, a Catholic General Council convened in Constance, Germany, now Switzerland. It lasted more than three years! After forty-five general sessions, the three sitting popes were deposed and Benedict XIII from Spain was elected. Before the council adjourned, however, Benedict XIII was deposed, and in 1417 Martin V was elected. It was at this General Council in Constance that John Huss, the Rector or President of the Catholic University in Prague, was declared a heretic and burned at the stake for his belief that Scriptural authority held precedence over the authority of pope and cardinal.[56] Later in this chapter we will return to the amazing story of John Huss and two other martyrs.

2. The Eve of the Reformation

The tide of public support for the Catholic Church, and especially for its clergy, was ebbing in the decades immediately preceding the Reformation. The Catholic stronghold of Vienna, for example, in the twenty-year period before the Reformation, saw no recruits for the priesthood, once the most desired of all careers.[57] Durant outlines some of the concerns Catholic Europe had about the declining church:

> A thousand grievances swelled the case against the Church. Many of the laity resented the exemption of the clergy from the laws of the state, and the dangerous lenience of ecclesiastical courts to ecclesiastical offenders. . . .

> Further complaints alleged the divorce of religion from morality, the emphasis laid on orthodox belief rather than on good conduct, the absorption of religion in ritual, the useless idleness and presumed sterility of monks, the exploitation of popular credulity through bogus relics and miracles, the abuse of excommunication and interdict, the censorship of publications by the clergy, the espionage and cruelty of the Inquisition, the misuse, for other purposes, of funds contributed for crusades against the Turks, and the claim of a deteriorated clergy to be the sole administrators of every sacrament except baptism.

> All the foregoing factors entered into the anticlericalism of Roman Catholic Europe at the beginning of the sixteenth century. [58]

Durant's list does not include other areas of public concern such as a declining competence among the clergy, gross immorality, and the practice of simony.

SIMONY

The term "simony" is derived from the name of Simon Magus, the magician who attempted to purchase from Peter and Paul the gift of conferring the Holy Spirit on others and received his just punishment (Acts 8:18–24).[59] However, the Catholic Church had no reservation about awarding powerful positions, ecclesiastical and civil, to those who filled its coffers.

Pope Boniface IX was the first pontiff to raise money for Rome, "the central city of the earth,"[60] by selling positions in the Catholic Church. H.C. Lea records the following:

In 1483, when [Pope] Sixtus IV (l471–1484) desired to redeem his tiara and jewels, pledged for a loan of 100,000 ducats, he increased his secretaries from six to twenty-four, and required each to pay 2600 florins for the office. In 1503, to raise funds for Caesar Borgia, Alexander VI (1492–1503) created eighty new offices, and sold them for 760 ducats apiece. Julius II formed a 'college' of one hundred and one scriveners of papal briefs, in return for which they paid him 74,000 ducats. Leo X (1513–1521) appointed sixty chamberlains and a hundred and forty squires, with certain perquisites, for which the former paid him 90,000 ducats and the latter, 112,000. Places thus paid for were personal property, transferable on sale.[61]

Prior to becoming pope, Aeneas Sylvius claimed that "everything was for sale in Rome, and . . . nothing could be had there without money."[62] Outside Rome the high positions of abbot, bishop, archbishop, and cardinal could be purchased for a substantial sum paid to the Catholic Church. Some cardinals became millionaires by selling various church positions under their control.[63] Benson said, "The whole ecclesiastical system was used mainly either for money-getting or the gaining of secular power."[64]

INCOMPETENT CLERGY

There were indeed capable and brilliant men among the leaders of the Catholic Church, but there is ample evidence that great numbers were woefully uneducated and incapable of leadership. W.J. Heaton says:

We are told that Archbishop Mainz said of the Bible, "In truth I do not know what this Book is, but I perceive that everything in it is against us." When Hooper was bishop of Gloucester, he found that out of 311 of his clergy, 168 were unable to repeat the Ten Commandments. Thirty-one did not know where to find them. Forty could not tell where the Lord's Prayer is to be found and thirty-one did not know the Author.[65]

Lewis Sherrill points out that with the rise of the Catholic universities one might logically assume that all Catholic clergy were well educated. This, he says, was not the case:

Medieval catechisms grew out of the fact that many priests were unable to instruct their people in the simplest elements of the faith; and this was after the universities had arisen.

In 1411 the University of Paris, drawing up articles to be considered by the Council of Constance, called attention to the low state of learning. As late as 1552 Bishop Hooper found scores of clergy who did not know who was the author of the Lord's Prayer, or where it is to be found. In the thirteenth century some of the English clergy had to be ordered to go to school, very much as was the case in Gaul in the sixth century. The data concerning the ignorance of the clergy are abundant, but the point need not be pressed further if it is seen that the coming of the universities did not forthwith bring a generally educated clergy.[66]

IMMORAL CLERGY

The declining status of the Catholic clergy followed the declining status of the Catholic universities. The spirit of scholasticism and skepticism, originating in the universities, took its toll on traditional Catholic dogma—the glue that held the church together. The universities became increasingly independent of, and even hostile to, papal authority and to local civil authority. They became hotbeds of lawlessness and immorality. Dionysius, the Carthusian, wrote in the fifteenth century, "At the universities many lived in the abysses of vice, the fires of lust and the traps of bodily and spiritual perversion. . . ."[67] It is not surprising that, as Eby puts it, "The lack of discipline at the universities was the major cause of the dissolute behavior of the priests."[68] Additionally, there was a growing revolt against the rule of celibacy for Catholic clergymen. Durant explains:

Violations of the sacerdotal vow of chastity were frequent. . . . Thousands of priests had concubines; in Germany nearly all. In Rome it was assumed that priests kept concubines; and some reports estimated the prostitutes there at 6,000 in a population not exceeding 100,000. . . .

In fairness to these lusty priests we should consider that sacerdotal concubinage was not profligacy, but an almost universal rebellion against the rule of celibacy that had been imposed upon an unwilling clergy by Pope Gregory VII (1074).[69]

Referring to this period, Charles R. Swindoll writes:

Godless church prelates paraded their carnality, indulging in shameless acts of the flesh. Bibles, banned from the common people, were chained to ornate pulpits and printed only in Latin, the "secret language" of the clergy. Instead of demonstrating compassion, unselfishness, grace, and other servant-like characteristics, those who led were anything but models of Christ.[70]

Erasmus, at the time of the Reformation said, "Many convents of men and women differ little from public brothels."[71]

INQUISITIONS

Possibly the worst violations of human rights in history occurred in the name of Catholicism in the Middle Ages. Catholics around the world today, and all of us, cringe at the terror created by the infamous Catholic Inquisitions, which took place at an accelerated pace in the latter Middle Ages and continued to a lesser degree into the nineteenth century. It wasn't until 1816 that the pope "abolished torture in all the tribunals of the Inquisition."[72] The grim Catholic practice of torturing or killing people for crimes of conscience occurred in England, France, Italy, Germany, the Balkan States, and most notably, in Spain and her colonies in Latin America.[73] These crimes of conscience could be any matter of disagreement with Catholic dogma or practice and resulted in the label of "heretic." Thus, to protect the "purity" of the Catholic Church, the papacy felt justified in ordering the torture and death of such persons. There was no latitude for differences of opinion among believers.

It was the Roman Catholic Emperor Theodsius I, who in A.D. 380 set in motion the Catholic policy that made a nonbeliever (a heretic) guilty of a capital crime. Recall his statement:

> We ordain that the name of Catholic Christians shall apply to all those who obey this present law. All others we judge to be mad and dement- ed; we declare them guilty of the infamy of holding heretical doctrine; their assemblies shall not receive the name of churches. They shall first suffer the wrath of God, then the punishment which in accordance with divine judgment we shall inflict.[74]

In the centuries following there was an aggressive effort to stamp out all vestiges of heresy and heretics. But it was Pope Innocent III at the Fourth Lateran General Council in 1215 who greatly accelerated the hunt for heretics. Of him, Sherrill says:

> It was in . . . Pope [Innocent's] time . . . that the tracking down of heresy began to be a science, through the organization of the Inquisition, a spiritual court to detect and punish those whose beliefs were at variance with the doctrines of the church. . . .

> It now became the duty of bishop and parish priest to ferret out heresy, and the duty of the laity to inform the clergy concerning heretics. The Dominicans, famous for their educational work, were sometimes less respectfully known as "the Lord's dogs" (*Domini canes*), for Gregory IX, about 1232, made them responsible for spying out heresy in certain parts of Europe. In 1252 Innocent IV made it permissible to use torture to extract a confession. The permission was diligently used. Perhaps

faith has never fallen further from its first Galilean meanings than it did when the public execution of heretics came to be known as the *auto da fé*, which is to say, "the act of faith."[75]

Spain, more than any other country, developed a sophisticated system of "Inquisitors General" and an elaborate court process "where the accused were presumed to be guilty."[76] Many thousands were burned at the stake over the next three centuries, and tens of thousands more were tortured in an effort to gain a confession of "faith" in the Catholic religion or to bring about a testimony against others. Torture was "codified" and carefully regulated by Catholic authorities. Durant explains:

> Torture was to be kept short of permanently maiming the victim, and was to be stopped whenever the attendant physician so ordered. It was to be administered only in the presence of the inquisitors in charge of the case, and a notary, a recording secretary, and a representative of the local bishop. Methods varied with time and place. The victim might have his hands tied behind his back and be suspended by them; he might be bound into immobility and then have water trickle down his throat till he nearly choked; he might have cords tied around his arms and legs and tightened till they cut through the flesh to the bone. We are told that the tortures used by the Spanish Inquisition were milder than those employed by the earlier papal Inquisition, or by the secular courts of the age.[77]

In 1883, *The Catholic Banner*, a newspaper published in Barcelona, Spain, carried an article extolling the virtues of the Inquisition, which started in 1480 and continued 329 years until Napoleon stopped it in 1809. The article read in part:

> We have believed it right to publish the names of those holy men [Inquisitors General] under whom so many sinners suffered, that good Catholics may venerate their memory [the memory of the inquisitors, not the victims].

By Torquemada:—

    Men and Women burnt alive 10,220

    Burnt in effigy 6,480

    Condemned to other punishments 97,371

By Diego Deza:—

    Men and Women burnt alive 2,592

    Burnt in effigy 829

       Condemned to other punishments 32,952

By Cardinal Jimenez de Cisneros:—

       Men and Women burnt alive 3,564

       Burnt in effigy 2,232

       Condemned to other punishments .48,059

By Adrian de Florencia:—

       Men and Women burnt alive 1,620

       Burnt in effigy 560

       Condemned to other punishments 21,835

Total number of men and women burnt alive under the

       ministry of forty-five holy Inquisitors General 35,354

       Total number burnt in effigy 18,637

       Total number condemned to other punishments 293,533

General Total . . . . 347,704[78]

Catholicism had clearly drifted far from any theological moorings it may have had among the early church fathers. John Chrysostom, one of those early church fathers, was "the greatest preacher ever heard in a Christian pulpit."[79] He said, "To put a heretic to death would be to introduce upon earth an inexpiable crime."[80] Regretfully, Catholic policy was, "Those who doubted had either to be converted or to be eliminated."[81]

ROME AND ROMAN CATHOLICISM COMPARED

The Catholic Church became the heir to the Roman Empire largely because early in the fourth century Emperor Constantine had endowed it with ecclesiastical organization, imperial sanction, and material wealth. In its process of acquisition, the Catholic Church assimilated many characteristics of its predecessors, the Romans. In describing the Spanish Inquisition, Latourette illustrates Catholicism's pattern of assimilation. "In principle," he says, "The Inquisition was not new. The very words *inquisitio* and *inquisitor* came from Roman law and like so much else in canon law, were carried over from the Roman Empire."[82] Canon law, not the Bible, was the center of the Catholic Church. As Durant says:

> The Roman church followed in the footsteps of the Roman state; it conquered the provinces, beautified the capital, and established discipline and unity from frontier to frontier. Rome died in giving birth to the

church; the church matured by inheriting and accepting the responsibilities of Rome.[83]

With this introduction, we can compare Roman paganism and Roman
Catholicism as follows:

ROMAN PAGANISM	ROMAN CATHOLICISM
1. **Capital:** Rome	**Capital:** Rome
2. **Territory:** from Mesopotamia to England	**Territory:** (not all at the same time) Mesopotamia to Ireland
3. **Principal Authority Base:** Roman Law	**Principal Authority Base:** Canon Law
4. **Language:** Latin	**Language:** Latin
5. **Roman Education:** Prepared students for one profession—Oratory	**Catholic Education:** Prepared students for one profession—Clergy
6. **Worship:** Included: everlasting light before the altar, holy water, candles, incense and stole and vestments for priests[84]	**Worship:** Included: everlasting light before the altar, holy water, candles, incense and stole and vestments for priests[85]
7. **Name given to the** **highest priest of Rome:** Pontifex Maximus[86]	**Name given to Rome's** **Catholic bishop:** Pontifex Maximus, who is also the Pope[87]
8. **Lifestyle of Emperor:** highest in the empire, lived in a palace surrounded by opulent wealth	**Lifestyle of Pope:** highest in the empire, lived in a palace surrounded by opulent wealth
9. A period of rapid turnover of leadership: 37 emperors in 35 years, between 244 and 279[88]	A period of rapid turnover of leadership: 17 popes in 58 years, between 897 and 955[89]

ROMAN PAGANISM	ROMAN CATHOLICISM
10. **Heretics:** Death to those who disagree	**Heretics:** Death to those who disagree
11. Reasons for loss of public support:	Reasons for loss of public support:
a. The killing and torture of Christians in the Colosseum and Circus Maximus became less and less popular.	The killing and torture of heretics did not set well with the general population of Europe, especially in Spain.
b. Burdensome taxes.	As local kings grew more and more powerful, international papal taxes were increasingly resented.
c. Declining education system.	Catholicism was paranoid about education and Bible reading for the common people. Ultimately the Catholic Church could not stop the printing press or Wycliffe, Huss, Tyndale, Luther, and Calvin, who ignited, among other things, the world's most significant education revolution in history.
d. The emperors became more and more despotic.	The popes, like their ancient emperor counterparts, became increasingly despotic.

3. Reformation Martyrs

We now focus our attention on three Reformation heroes: John Wycliffe, John Huss, and William Tyndale. They had the following in common with each other and with Martin Luther: first, they were Catholic priests who exposed theological errors; second, they were university-level educators with doctorates in theology; third, they essentially championed the same issues; and fourth, all were declared heretics by the Catholic Church. John Huss and William Tyndale were burned at the stake. John Wycliffe died a natural death, but later the Catholic Church exhumed his remains, burned them, and had his ashes strewn on the River Swift.[90]

JOHN WYCLIFFE (1329–1384)

In the fourteenth century, Oxford University had surpassed the University of Paris as Europe's leading university. It was during that time that John Wycliffe was Oxford's foremost theologian and philosopher.[91] He wrote 200 books, which were mostly his sermons.[92] Professor Montagu Burrows, lecturing at Oxford University in 1881, said, "To Wycliffe we owe, more than to any one person who can be mentioned, our English language, our English Bible, and our reformed religion."[93] John Wycliffe is often referred to as "The Morning Star" of the Reformation. He deplored the fact that the Bible was not in the hands of the common people and in their own language. At great risk, Wycliffe translated the Vulgate Bible into a "middle

Figure 4. John Wycliffe (1329-1384), considered "The Morning Star of the Reformation," was the first of seven Catholic priests who championed biblical authority over papal authority and in so doing laid the foundation for the Great Reformation. The seven Reformation priests were Wycliffe, Huss, Tyndale, Zwingli, Luther, Calvin, and Knox. All were excommunicated from the Catholic Church.

English" language. It was not published until after his death in 1384. Regrettably, those caught reading the Wycliffe English Bible "often lost their lives"[94] because of the continuing Catholic ban on Bible reading. It should be noted that Wycliffe's Bible did not gain the wide circulation of the later Tyndale Bible because Wycliffe's was hand-copied, whereas Tyndale's was printed on the Gutenberg printing press. Indeed, the Gutenberg Press became a major factor in the Great Reformation.

Like the later reformers, John Wycliffe used strong words to describe the errors he saw in the Catholic Church:

1. **Monasteries**—"dens of thieves, nests of serpents, houses of living devils."[95]
2. **Indulgences**—"Men be great fools that buy these bulls of pardon. . ."[96]
3. **Purgatory**—"If the pope had the power to snatch souls from purgatory, why did he not, in Christian charity, take them out at once?"[97]

4. **Bishops**—"They pray only for show and collect fees for every religious service that they perform; they live in luxury, riding fat horses with harness of silver and gold; they are robbers . . . malicious foxes . . . ravishing wolves . . . gluttons . . . devils . . . apes."[98]

5. **The Pope**—"If he assumes earthly possessions, or political authority, he is unworthy of his office. Christ had not whereon to rest his head but men say this pope hath more than half the empire. . . . Christ was meek . . . the pope sits on his throne and makes Lords to kiss his feet."[99]

Wycliffe believed strongly that the Bible was the only authoritative guide for faith and practice. He believed that Christ was the true head of the church and that the doctrine of transubstantiation was false because, as his fellow Englishman, Robert Parkyn, said, "It is impossible for the natural body and blood of our Savior Jesus Christ . . . to be in more than one place at a time."[100]

Wycliffe was exceedingly popular with the common people of England. In 1382 a monastic chronicler said, speaking of Wycliffe's followers, "They multiplied exceedingly, like budding plants, and filled the whole realm. . . . You could scarce meet two men on the road but that one of them was a disciple of Wycliffe."[101] His followers were called Wycliffites and Lollards. The latter group had its origin among the scholars at Oxford University and soon spread to the English laity. After Wycliffe's death, the Lollards became an organized church, and many of their leaders were imprisoned in the Tower of London, burned at the stake, or hanged.[102]

In a bold manifesto to parliament in 1395, the Lollards drew up a statement called the Twelve Conclusions. Durant summarizes their beliefs:

> They opposed clerical celibacy, transubstantiation, image worship, pilgrimages, prayers for the dead, the wealth and endowment of the Church, the employment of ecclesiastics in state offices, the necessity of confession to priests, the ceremonies of exorcism, and the worship of the saints. In other pronouncements they recommended that all should read the Bible frequently, and should follow its precepts as superior to the decrees of the Church. They denounced war as unchristian, and luxury as immoral; they called for sumptuary laws that would compel a return to simple foods and dress; . . . already the Puritan mind and view were taking form in Britain.[103]

Two hundred thirty-five years later the Puritans, whose beliefs were similar to those of their Lollard ancestors, would sail to America to find relief from religious oppression and to provide literacy and learning so that all could read the Scriptures for themselves.

JOHN HUSS (1373–1415)

There is no question that John (Jan) Huss of Prague, Bohemia, now the Czech Republic, added greatly to the momentum of change that ultimately led to the Great Reformation. Huss was the popular rector (president) of the Catholic University of Prague and the daily preacher of Prague's Bethlehem Chapel. He learned of the teachings of John Wycliffe through a foreign student, Jerome of Prague, who studied under Wycliffe at Oxford. Referring to Jerome, Clarence Benson says:

> **He returned to his own city full of enthusiasm for the truths he had learned in England, and taught boldly the principal doctrines of the New Testament. One of his hearers was John Huss.**[104]

As a result, John Huss became imbued with the reform ideas of John Wycliffe and gave Wycliffe's writings wide circulation.

In 1403 the teachings of Wycliffe became so popular among the students at the University of Prague that the administrative clergy at the Cathedral, "submitted to the university masters forty-five excerpts from the writing of Wycliffe, and asked should these doctrines be barred from the university?"[105] A majority of the university professors agreed. Huss was among those who were opposed. He and several of his colleagues were excommunicated by the Archbishop of Prague, and 200 books by Wycliffe were burned at the Bishop's Palace. Pope John summoned Huss to appear before the papal court in Rome, but he refused.

Because of his popularity and his ties with the king of Bohemia, Huss was allowed to go into exile in "rural seclusion."[106] While in exile he wrote tracts and books that would ultimately be used against him at his heresy trial in Constance. In his writings he referred to the pope as a "money grabber." He spoke out against the sale of indulgences and collecting money to conduct war against

Figure 5. John Huss (1373–1415), burned at the stake for his faith on July 6, 1415, was the founder of the Christian school movement in Bohemia.

the king of Naples. He questioned the existence of purgatory and rejected image worship. He spoke out against the sale of high church positions (simony) and fees charged by priests for baptisms, confirmations, masses, marriages, and funerals. He said, "To rebel against an erring pope is to obey Christ."[107]

In November of 1414, Emperor Sigismund persuaded Huss to challenge the bulls of excommunication against him at the Catholic General Council at Constance. This was the same marathon council that attempted to settle the issue concerning the three popes. Emperor Sigismund promised Huss "safe conduct" with these official words: "You shall let John Huss pass, stop, stay, and return freely, without any hindrance whatever."[108] In a manner similar to Luther's famous journey from Wittenberg to his trial at Worms 100 years later, John Huss was met by huge crowds of well-wishers. John Foxe wrote in The Book of Martyrs:

> On his way he met with every mark of affection and reverence from people of all descriptions. The streets, and even the roads, were thronged with people, whom respect, rather than curiosity, had brought together. He was ushered into the towns with great acclamations; and he passed through Germany in a kind of triumph. "I thought," he said, "I had been an outcast. I now see my worst friends are in Bohemia."[109]

When Huss first arrived in Constance, he was treated courteously by the assemblage of Catholic ecclesiastical dignitaries and civil leaders. However, over a period of several months, as his writings were read and as his concurrence with many of the writings of John Wycliffe was affirmed, he was officially condemned as a major heretic. Standing before the council on July 6, 1415, bound by chains, John Huss said:

> I trust that by God's grace I am a sincere Christian, not deviating from the faith. I would rather suffer the dire punishment of death than to put forth anything contrary to the faith or to transgress the commands of the Lord Jesus Christ. . . . Hence I wish that the Fictor would show me today one precept of sacred Scripture that I do not hold. . . . And if I ever taught anything I should not have taught, I am ready humbly to revoke it. But I trust that I shall sooner appear before the tribunal of Christ before he finds me to deny one jot of the law of the Lord! [110]

After the proceedings were over, Huss was defrocked of his priestly attire and taken by civil authorities to a place outside the city, where he was bound to a martyr's stake. John Foxe describes the closing moments of Huss's life:

> Huss said, "I never preached any doctrine of an evil tendency; and what I taught with my lips I now seal with my blood." He then said to the executioner, "You are now going to burn a goose (the name of Huss

signifying goose in the Bohemian language), but in a century you will have a swan whom you can neither roast nor boil." If this were spoken in prophecy, he must have alluded to Martin Luther, who came about a hundred years after, and had a swan for his arms.

As soon as the faggots were lighted, the martyr sung a hymn, with so cheerful a voice, that he was heard above the cracklings of the fire and the noise of the multitude. At length his voice was interrupted by the flames, which soon put an end to his existence. His ashes were collected, and, by order of the council, thrown into the Rhine, lest his adherents should honour them as relics.[111]

Jerome, the Oxford student who had brought Wycliffe's teachings to Huss, followed Huss to his trial at Constance. Upon being identified by the authorities, he was tried by the council of bishops and declared a heretic. He was burned at the stake on the same spot where Huss had died.[112]

In the decades immediately following the death of John Huss, a revolt ensued in eastern Europe that had all the elements of the future Reformation to be ignited by Martin Luther. Like their Roman predecessors nearly a thousand years before, the Catholic leaders of Huss' era failed to realize that torturing and killing "heretics," most of whom were their own people, served only to accelerate the Catholic Church's downfall as a world power.

As couriers relayed back to Bohemia the news that John Huss had been killed at the Catholic Council in Constance, a fierce national revolt was set in motion.[113] The faculty at the University of Prague that had once waffled on Huss' strong stand against church errors now hailed him as a martyr and joined the groundswell for reform. Out of this movement came the Hussites and later the Moravians. These groups would form the "shock troops" of the coming Reformation, along with the Lollards of England and the ancient Waldensians, now spreading throughout Europe. They were the pre-protestant Protestants without whom the Great Reformation would not have been possible. It should be noted that the Waldensians were also called "The Brethren," their original name, which dates back to the first century.

HUNDREDS OF CHRISTIAN SCHOOLS

The common undertaking of these pre-Reformation groups was their secret distribution of the Bible, translated into the language of the people. To make the availability of the Scriptures meaningful, they became champions of basic literacy and established Christian elementary and secondary schools by the hundreds. Because these schools were often held in secret, their existence has been significantly "under-reported" by historians. Eby notes:

The educational activities of the many evangelical sects scattered throughout central Europe have uniformly been ignored by educational historians. The importance of their contribution to the evolution of popular culture can no longer be overlooked. According to a recent German authority, literacy was widespread among them.[114]

Referring to the evangelical schools that existed before the Reformation, German historian Thudichum brought to light the following:

All children could read and write . . . important passages of Scripture were given as copy for writing, and [were] also learned by rote. . . . Not only men, but women too, frequently learned the Gospels by heart, and in one instance a common countryman could repeat from memory the entire book of Job. The meeting places of these peoples were sometimes called schools (*scholae*). It was notorious that even the less learned among them knew the Scriptures more thoroughly than the scholarly doctors. The catechism of the Waldensians was used extensively among many of these sects. The training of the leaders of the evangelicals was generally confined to the vernacular, though individuals were often familiar with the Greek and Latin classics, as well as the writings of Church Fathers. Before Luther's Reformation, the Hussites had printed the Scriptures in the vernacular, and they possessed a good system of schools and a celebrated university.[115]

Gangel and Benson affirm these discoveries and point out the important tie between the Hussites and the Moravians:

The Hussites had printed the Scriptures in the vernacular before the time of Luther. They had developed a system of schools and an outstanding university for the purpose of promoting practical Christianity. If they had lived 150 years later they might have been part of the Anabaptist movement, rather like the Mennonites, stressing purity of conduct, self-denying love, and an absolute commitment to Scripture. Another very important educational group, the Moravians, were descendants of the Hussites.

Before Luther ever walked up to the Castle Church at Wittenberg, the Moravians were operating 300 churches and 300 schools with a denominational membership of 100,000 in Bohemia alone! That represented tremendous growth . . . from the days of Huss, after a persecution that had pretty well diminished by 1467.[116]

It should be noted, after John Huss was burned at the stake, the threat and fear of Catholicism diminished greatly in eastern Europe because the church had lost most of its public support. Durant claims that probably because of the declining threat, the "Moravian Brethren . . . became the first modern church to [openly] practice [biblical] Christianity."[117]

In contrast to the Catholicism of the Middle Ages, the three hallmarks of the four pre-protestant Protestant groups—the Waldensians, the Lollards, the Hussites, and the Moravians—was a strong commitment to the Bible, to public preaching, and to Christian school education. This pattern continued into the next century of reformers. As we will discover, Martin Luther spent nearly as much time establishing Bible-centered Christian schools as he spent establishing Bible-centered Christian churches.

We now conclude our study of the Middle Ages with the account of one of the great martyrs of the English speaking world.

WILLIAM TYNDALE (1494–1536)

Like Erasmus, William Tyndale was a contemporary of Martin Luther. Tyndale is important to us because of his English version of the Bible—the first to be translated directly from the original Hebrew and Greek languages. According to English historian Hughs, ninety percent of the authorized King James Bible, "the greatest and most influential classic in English literature, was unaltered Tyndale."[118] There is no question that William Tyndale laid the foundation for all future English language translations of the Bible.[119]

Tyndale was born in Wales. Between 1506 and 1521 he attended both Oxford and Cambridge Universities, where he mastered seven languages. He was a student at Cambridge when Martin Luther's books were publicly burned.[120] Incensed over the low status of the Bible at both universities, he wrote:

In the Universities they have ordained that no man shall look on the Scripture until he be noselled in heathen learning eight or nine years, and armed with false principles with which he is clean shut out of the understanding of the Scripture.[121]

Figure 6. William Tyndale

Tyndale was also incensed over the low status given the Bible by his fellow Catholic priests.Tyndale had been ordained a priest at age twenty-three at Oxford University.[122] Durant records an argument between Tyndale and a Catholic priest at the dinner table in Sir John Walsh's home. The priest said, "It would be better to be without God's law [i.e., the Bible] than without the pope's." Tyndale answered, "If God spare me life, ere many years I will cause the boy that driveth the plow to know more of the Scripture than you do."[123]

The absence of Bible literacy among both priests and laity convinced Tyndale that he should translate the sacred Scriptures from the original Greek and Hebrew into English. He said, "It was impossible to establish the lay people in any truth, except the Scripture were plainly laid before their eyes in their mother tongue."[124] Needing financial support for his work, Tyndale sought the patronage of London's Catholic Bishop Cuthbert Tunstall. Given the Catholic ban on Bible reading and the stirring of the Great Reformation in Germany, it is not surprising that his request was denied. Tyndale wrote, "Not only was there no room in my Lord of London's palace to translate the New Testament, but also there was no place to do it in all England."[125]

At this point it will help to step back to Tyndale's days at Cambridge. Although Martin Luther's books were publicly burned by Catholic authorities while Tyndale was a student there, Martin Luther's cause was very popular among the students, "a generation [that] was warming its hands at the fiercer fires of Martin Luther."[126] It is little wonder, therefore, that on being rejected by Bishop Tunstall, Tyndale sailed in 1524 for mainland Europe, first to Hamburg, then to Wittenberg to join Luther and the Protestant movement. As E.W. More explains it, Tyndale "gat him to Luther straight."[127] On May 27, 1524, Tyndale enrolled as a student for a period of nine or ten months at Wittenberg University, by now the world's first Protestant university.[128]

In 1525, Tyndale settled in Cologne, Germany, where he completed the translation of the New Testament. It was in Cologne that the first copies of any portion of the Bible were printed in English on the famous Gutenberg movable-type printing press. The press had been invented by Johann Gutenberg in Mainz, Germany, in 1454. There is no question that Gutenberg's printing press played a major role in the rapid spread of the Reformation and the Christian education revolution that accompanied it.[129]

In that year Germany was divided into Catholic towns and Protestant towns.[130] Tyndale soon learned that Cologne was a Catholic town when authorities, who had been alerted by a secret agent from England, raided the building where his New Testament was being printed. Fortunately, he had been forewarned in time to gather together the printed sheets and escape up the Rhine River to the Protestant city of Worms. Durant writes:

Tyndale fled from Catholic Cologne to Protestant Worms, and there printed 6,000 copies, to each of which he added a separate volume of notes and aggressive prefaces based on those of Erasmus and Luther. All these copies were smuggled into England, and served as fuel to the incipient Protestant fire.[131]

England's King Henry VIII immediately placed a watch on all English ports and issued a ban on "all printing, sale, importation, or possession of heretical works."[132]

Tyndale, for his own safety, moved to Antwerp, Belgium, where he stayed at the homes of sympathetic English merchants who attempted to protect him. In Antwerp he finished translating most of the Old Testament. Although he moved from place to place to avoid detection, it was only a matter of time until those determined to destroy him would succeed. W.E. Campbell describes the intense effort to capture Tyndale:

> Henry VIII, having tried unsuccessfully to capture Tyndale, made up his mind to treat him as an enemy, and instructed his ambassador in the Netherlands to demand his delivery from the Emperor. But Charles V, Holy Roman Emperor, being the nephew of Katherine of Aragon, was just then in no mood to oblige the King of England. Other expedients had therefore to be tried—Tyndale, in fact, was to be kidnapped and brought back to this country. It is not surprising under these circumstances that Tyndale did his best to elude arrest, hiding now in one place and now in another.[133]

Finally, King Henry's emissaries devised a plan that led to Tyndale's capture. Henry Phillips, a secret agent from England, befriended Tyndale in Antwerp posing as an evangelical Christian. Foxe describes Tyndale's capture:

> Phillips invited Tyndale to dine with him. No, said Master Tyndale; I go forth this day to dinner, and you shall go with me and be my guest, where you shall be welcome. So when it was dinner time, Master Tyndale went forth with Phillips, and at the going out of Poyntz's house [a merchant's home where Tyndale was staying] was a long narrow entry, so that two men could not go in a front. Master Tyndale would have put Phillips before him but Phillips would in no wise, but put Master Tyndale afore, for that he pretended to show great humility. So Master Tyndale, being a man of no stature, went before, and Phillips, a tall comely person, followed after him; who had officers on either side of the door upon two seats, which being there, might see who came in the entry; and coming through the same entry, Phillips pointed with his finger over Master Tyndale's head down to him, that the officers which sat at the door might see that it was he whom they

Figure 7. The Tyndale memorial at Vilvorde, Belgium. William Tyndale, more than anyone else, was responsible for the English translation of the Bible. The Catholic Church burned him at the stake for distributing copies of his translation to England and Scotland.

should take; as the officers that took Master Tyndale afterwards told Poyntz, and said to Poyntz, when they laid him in prison, that they pitied to see his simplicity when they took him. Then they took him and brought him to the Emperor's attorney or Procurer-General.[134]

On May 23, 1535, William Tyndale was taken to the state prison of the Netherlands at Vilvorde, six miles from Brussels.[135] Because of the lack of good will between Henry VIII and Emperor Charles V, Tyndale was not extradited to England but rather languished in the state prison for one hundred and thirty-five days.[136] In August 1536, under rule of the Spanish Inquisition, Tyndale was tried and convicted of being a heretic. On October 6 of that same year, he was burned at the stake. Today in Vilvorde, Belgium, at the edge of a city park, a small memorial to William Tyndale, bears these words:

WILLIAM TYNDALE

*Who suffered martyrdom under
Spanish rule on Oct. 6th, 1536
Was strangled and burnt at Vilvorde
Among his last words were these:
"Lord open the eyes of the King
Of England." This prayer was
Answered within a year by the
Issue under Royal Authority,
Of the whole Bible in English.*

In 1611, seventy-five years after the cruel martyrdom of Tyndale, the famous King James Bible, the most widely circulated book in history, was published and ultimately distributed throughout the English speaking world. While holding a Bible, we can easily forget the price that was paid by the likes of John Wycliffe, John Huss, William Tyndale, and countless others who preceded them.

Next, we will turn our attention to the Great Reformation, a historical event second in importance only to the birth of Christ. Consider the following:

1. The Reformation did not break the back of the Catholic Church as a church, but it broke the back of the Catholic Church as the most powerful, longest sustained, wealthiest, and among the cruelest civil powers in history.

2. The Reformation broke the tightly controlled religious monopoly held in the Western world by the Catholic Church for 927 years from 590 to 1517.

3. The Reformation obliterated Catholicism's ban on the Bible.

4. The Reformation overturned Catholicism's restrictions on literacy and learning for common people.

5. The Reformation opened the door for unfettered Christian school education, which existed continuously from the first century but was suppressed by the Catholic Church.

6. The Reformation opened the door for women to be educated and to play a much larger role in society.

7. The Reformation paved the way for democratic forms of government and a free and open society.

8. The Reformation opened the world to the influence of biblical principles upon which so many human freedoms are based.

The Reformation did not usher in heaven on earth, but it did usher in the dawn of a new era that the world desperately needed.

Endnotes - Chapter Six

1 Pope Leo XIII, encyclical, "The Reunion of Christendom," quoted in Loraine Boettner, *Roman Catholicism* (Philadelphia: The Presbyterian and Reformed Publishing Company, 1962), p. 127.

2 W. Ullmann, "A Medieval Document on Papal Theories of Government," *The English Historical Review,* vol. 61, 1946, pp. 180-181.

3 C.B. Eavey, *History of Christian Education* (Chicago: Moody Press, 1964), p. 125.

4 Leopold Ranke, *Ranke's History of the Popes*, translated from German by Sarah Austin, vol. III, p. 51, published in *Edinburgh Review*, October 1841.

5 Peter Toon, "Infallibility," *The New International Dictionary of the Christian Church,* J.D. Douglas, ed. (Grand Rapids: Zondervan Publishing House, 1974), p. 508.

6 R. Freeman Butts, *The Education of the West* (New York: McGraw-Hill, 1947), p. 159.

7 Innocent III, Lateran Council, 1215, cited by Alexander Hamilton Thompson, *Cambridge Medieval History,* vol. 6, p. 635.

8 Innocent III, *Selected Letters of Pope Innocent III Concerning England,* Ep. 67, "Rex Regum," *Medieval Texts* (Edinburgh: Thomas Nelson and Sons, Ltd., 1953), pp. 177-182, quoted in Ray C. Petry, ed. *A History of Christianity,* vol. I (Ann Arbor: Baker Book House, 1962), p. 319.

9 Ibid.

10 Robert G. Clouse, "Innocent III," *The New International Dictionary of the Christian Church,* J.D. Douglas, ed. (Grand Rapids: Zondervan Publishing House, 1974), p. 509.

11 John Murray, "Tradition: Romish and Protestant," in *Studies in Theology,* vol. 4 of *Collected Writings of John Murray* (Carlisle: Banner of Truth, 1982), p. 271, quoted in John Armstrong, ed., *Roman Catholicism* (Chicago, Moody Press, 1994), p. 238.

12 Andrew Miller, *Short Papers on Church History,* vol. II, "The Crusades to the Reformation" (London: Pickering and Inglis), p. 442.

13 Ibid.

14 Ibid.

15 Ibid., pp. 445-446.

16 Pope Innocent III, Greenwood's "Cathedra Petri," book xiii, p. 582; Milman's "Latin Christianity," vol. iv, p. 90; Waddington's "History of the Church," vol. ii, p. 167.

17 Miller, p. 447.

18 Ibid.

19 Ibid.

20 Ibid., p. 448.

21 *Encyclopaedia Britannica,* vol. 12 (Chicago: William Benton, Publisher, 1961), p. 617.

22 Miller, p. 510.

23 *Encyclopaedia Britannica,* vol. 12 (Chicago: William Benton, Publisher, 1961), p. 602.

24 Miller, p. 447.

25 James Brogden, Vicar, Trinity College, Cambridge, *Catholic Safeguards Against the Errors, Corruptions, and Novelties of the Church of Rome,* vol. I (London: Spottiswoods and Shaw, 1851), p. 384.

26 Miller, p. 449.

27 Pandulph, papal legate, "Cathedra Petri," book xiii., p. 588, quoted in Miller, p. 449.

28 Ibid.

29 Ibid.

30 Michael Van Cleave Alexander, *The Growth of English Education* 1348-1648 (University Park, Pennsylvania, The Pennsylvania State University Press, 1990), pp. 30-31.

31 Pierre J. Marique, *History of Christian Education,* vol. II (New York: Fordham University Press, 1926), p. 83.

32 Robert Sencourt, *The Genius of the Vatican* (London: Jonathan Cape, 1935), pp. 45-46. He references Migne, cli, 1181 quoted in Lagarde, *Latin Church in the Middle Ages,* p. 306.

33 Thomas M. Lindsay, *A History of the Reformation,* vol. I (Edinburgh: T. and T. Clark, 1906), pp. 116-117.

34 La Tour, *Les Origins de la Reforme,* I, 361, quoted in Will Durant, *The Reformation* (New York: Simon and Schuster, 1957), p. 17. Note: The author has boldfaced "three-quarters," "half" etc. in 1-6.

[35] Robertson, *History of the Reign of Charles* V, vol. I, p. 126. quoted in Durant, *The Reformation*, p. 17.

[36] Lindsay, p. 76.

[37] Durant, *The Reformation*, p. 153.

[38] Brogdon, p. 514.

[39] Durant, *The Reformation*, p. 17.

[40] Belloc, *How the Reformation Happened*, p. 117, quoted in Durant, *The Reformation*, p. 530.

[41] Rogers, *Economic Interpetation of History*, p. 75. quoted in Durant, *The Reformation*, p. 30.

[42] Miller, p. 520.

[43] Kenneth Scott Latourette, *Christianity Through the Ages* (New York: Harper and Row, Publishers, 1965), p. 98.

[44] Ibid., p. 148.

[45] J.G.G. Norman, "Schism," *The New International Dictionary of the Church*, J.D. Douglas, gen. ed. (Grand Rapids: Zondervan Publishing House, 1974), p. 883.

[46] Ibid.

[47] Ronald Finucane, "An Age of Unrest," *Introduction to the History of Christianity*, Tom Dowley, ed. (Minneapolis: Fortress Press, 1990), p. 330.

[48] Butts, p. 161.

[49] James Harvey Robinson and Charles A. Beard, *Outlines of European History*, Part II (Boston: Ginn and Company, 1907), p. 18. Also see W. Ullman, "A Medieval Document on Papal Theories of Government," *The English Historical Review*, vol. 61, 1946, pp. 180-181.

[50] Finucane, "An Age of Unrest," *Introduction to the History of Christianity*, pp. 331-333.

[51] "Roman Catholic Church," *Encyclopaedia Britannica*, vol. 19, 1961, p. 418. Note: Pope Alexander III referred to himself as "Lord of the World."

[52] Poggio, quoted in Sencourt, pp. 46-47.

[53] Ibid.

[54] Finucane, "An Age of Unrest," *Introduction to the History of Christianity*, p. 335.

[55] Ibid.

[56] Ibid., pp. 335-337.

[57] Lea, Auricular Confession, III, p. 429, quoted in Durant, *The Reformation*, p. 25.

[58] Durant, *The Reformation*, p. 24.

[59] James DeJong, "Simony," *The New International Dictionary of the Christian Church* (Grand Rapids: Zondervan Publishing House, 1974), p. 906.

[60] Sencourt, p. 22.

[61] H.C. Lea, *Cambridge Modern History*, I. p. 670, quoted in Lindsay, p. 16.

[62] Ibid., quoted in Durant, p. 18.

[63] Durant, p. 19.

[64] Clarence H. Benson, *A Popular History of Christian Education* (Chicago: Moody Press, 1943), p. 64.

[65] W.J. Heaton, *The Bible of the Reformation*, quoted in Benson, p. 64.

[66] Lewis Joseph Sherrill, *The Rise of Christian Education* (New York: The Macmillan Company, 1944), p. 264. Sherrill cites: Coulton, *Medieval Village*, pp. 258-259, Coulton, *Medieval Panorama*, p. 158, and Leach, *Educational Charters*, pp. 147, 148, and 155.

[67] Dionysius the Carthusian, *On Scholars* (Article 4) quoted by Robert Ulich, *A History of Religious Education* (New York: New York University Press, 1968), p. 88.

[68] Frederick Eby, *The Development of Modern Education* (New York: Prentice-Hall, Inc., 1934), p. 107.

[69] Lea, *Historical Sketch of Sacerdotal Celibacy*, pp. 429-432, and *Cambridge Modern History*, vol. I, p. 672, quoted in Durant, *The Reformation*, p. 21.

70 Charles R. Swindoll, *The Finishing Touch* (Dallas: Word Publishing, 1994), p. 146.

71 Erasmus, Epistle 94 in Froude, *Life and Letters of Erasmus,* p. 352, quoted in Durant, *The Reformation,* p. 20.

72 *The Encyclopaedia Britannica,* vol. 12 (Chicago: William Benton, Publisher, 1961), p. 382. See H.C. Lea's important work: *History of the Inquisition in the Middle Ages* (3 volumes, 1888).

73 Ibid., pp. 380-382

74 Edgar W. Knight, *Twenty Centuries of Education* (Boston: Ginn and Company, 1940), p. 91.

75 Sherrill, pp. 213-214.

76 *Encyclopaedia Britannica,* vol. 12 (Chicago: William Benton, Publisher, 1961), p. 378.

77 Lea, *Inquisition in Spain,* vol. III, p. 2, H. Ellis, *Soul of Spain,* p. 42, quoted in Durant, *The Reformation,* p. 211.

78 C. Leopold Clarke, *The Christian Church and the See of Rome* (London: Protestant Truth Society), (no date given) p. 180.

79 *Catholic Encyclopedia* (New York: The Encyclopedia Press, Inc., 1913), vol. VIII, p. 452, quoted in Robert L. Cooke, *Philosophy, Education and Certainty* (Grand Rapids: Zondervan Publishing House, 1940), p. 82.

80 *Encyclopaedia Britannica,* vol. 12 (Chicago: William Benton, Publisher, 1961), p. 377.

81 Robert Ulich, *A History of Religious Education* (New York: New York University Press, 1968), p. 92.

82 Kenneth Scott Latourette, *A History of Christianity,* vol. I (New York: Harper and Row, Publishers, 1953), p. 457.

83 Durant, *Caesar and Christ* (New York: Simon and Schuster, 1944), p. 619.

84 Ibid., p. 618.

85 Ibid.

86 Clyde Currey Smith, "Pontifex Maximus," *The New International Dictionary of the Christian Church,* J.D. Douglas, ed. (Grand Rapids: Zondervan Publishing House, 1974), p. 792.

87 Ibid.

88 Durant, *Caesar and Christ,* p. 628.

89 Kenneth Scott Latourette, *Christianity Through the Ages,* (New York: Harper and Row Publishers, 1965), p. 98.

90 Robert Clouse, "John Wycliffe," *The New International Dictionary of the Christian Church,* J.D. Douglas, gen. ed. (Grand Rapids: Zondervan Publishing House, 1974), p. 1064.

91 A.K. Curtis, *Christian History Magazine,* vol. II, no. 2, issue 3 (Worchester, PA: Christian History Institute, 1983), p. 4.

92 Ibid., p. 1.

93 Ibid.

94 James E. Reed and Ronnie Prevost, *A History of Christian Education* (Nashville: Broadman and Holdman Publishers, 1993), p. 172.

95 Wycliffe, "On The Pope," in *English Works,* p. 80, quoted in Durant, *The Reformation,* p. 34.

96 Wycliffe, "Of Prelates," in *English Works,* quoted in Durant, Ibid.

97 Ibid., p. 81.

98 Ibid., pp. 96-104.

99 Wycliffe, "De Officio Pastorali", in *English Works,* p. 457, quoted in Durant, *The Reformation,* p. 34. Also see "Wycliffe's reply to the Papal Condemnation," *Select English Works of Wycliffe,* III, pp. 504-506, PTR, II, 5 (3), pp. 13-14, quoted in Ray C. Petry, ed. *A History of Christianity,* vol. 1 (New York: Prentice-Hall, Inc., 1962), pp. 356-357.

[100] Robert Parkyn, "Reformation Revoked Transubstantiation," *The English Historical Review,* vol. 62 (London: Longmans, Green and Co., 1947), p. 75.

[101] Durant, *The Reformation,* pp. 112-116.

[102] Ibid., p. 117.

[103] Ibid., p. 116.

[104] Clarence H. Benson, *History of Christian Education* (Chicago: Moody Press, 1943), p. 56.

[105] Durant, pp. 163-164.

[106] Ibid., p. 164.

[107] John Huss, *De Ecclesia,* pp. 220-221, quoted in Durant, *The Reformation,* p. 165.

[108] John Foxe, *Actes and Monumentes* (Foxe's *Book of Martyrs*) (London: John Daym, 1563), p. 155.

[109] Ibid.

[110] John Huss, Contra Paletz, p. 325, quoted in Matthew Spinka, *John Huss' Concept of the Church* (Princeton: Princeton University Press, 1966), p. 237.

[111] John Foxe, p. 159.

[112] Durant, *The Reformation,* p. 167.

[113] Ibid.

[114] Eby, p. 28.

[115] Frederich Thudichum, *Papsttum and Reformation im Mittelalter,* (Leipzig: Eduard Schmidt, 1903), p. 11, quoted in Eby, p. 29.

[116] Gangel and Benson, pp. 132 and 171.

[117] Durant, *The Reformation,* p. 172.

[118] P. Hughs, *The Reformation in England,* vol. I, p. 146, quoted in Durant, *The Reformation,* p. 534. Also see R. W. Chambers, *Man's Unconquerable Mind,* pp. 190-191.

[119] G.E. Duffield, *The Work of William Tyndale* (Appleford, Berkshire, England: The Sutton Courtenay Press, 1964), Introduction, p. xi.

[120] W.E. Campbell, *Erasmus, Tyndale and More* (London: Eyre and Spottiswoode, 1949), p. 100.

[121] Tyndale, *Works,* P.S. II, p. 291, quoted in Duffield, *The Work of William Tyndale,* Introduction xv. Also see Tyndale, *Works,* "The Obedience of a Christian Man" (1528), vol. I, pp. 157-158.

[122] Campbell, pp. 99-100.

[123] Durant, *The Reformation,* p. 533. Also see G. E. Duffield, Introduction, xiv.

[124] G.E. Duffield, "William Tyndale," *The New International Dictionary of the Christian Church,* J.D. Douglas, ed. (Grand Rapids: Zondervan Publishing House, 1974), p. 990.

[125] Tyndale, Foxe, vol. V, p. 34, quoted in G. E. Duffield, Introduction, xv.

[126] Demaus, *William Tyndale,* p. 242, quoted in W.E. Campbell, p. 103.

[127] E.W. More, *Dialogue Concerning Tyndale,* bk. iv, c. 17, p. 283 B, and bk iii, c. 8, p. 227 A.

[128] Mozley, *William Tyndale,* p. 53, quoted in G.E. Duffield, Introduction, xv.

[129] Linas Brockett, *History and Progress of Education* (New York: A.S. Barnes and Burr, 1860), p. 184.

[130] Durant, p. 533.

[131] Ibid.

[132] Ibid.

[133] Campbell, p. 267.

[134] Foxe, quoted by Mozely, *William Tyndale,* quoted by Campbell, pp. 269-270.

[135] Campbell, p. 270.

[136] Mozely, *William Tyndale,* pp. 296-297, after Foxe, quoted in Campbell, p. 270.

Illustration Sources

Figure 1   *Map* - Global Mapping International, Colorado Springs, CO.
Figure 2   *King John* - Royal England Readers, Our Kings and Queens (London: Thomas Nelson and Sons, 1893) p. 77.
Figure 3   *Magna Charta* - Ibid., p. 79.
Figure 4   *Wycliffe* - Image Select/Art Resource, NY.
Figure 5   *Huss* - John Foxe, "Acts and Monuments," in *Foxes Book of Martyrs* (London: John Daym, 1563), p. 152.
Figure 6   *Bronze Relief of Tyndale* - Photo by author (PBA).
Figure 7   *Tyndale Memorial* - PBA.

Martin Luther, the Great Education Reformer

It is not an overstatement to say that the Reformation of 1517 was the second most important event in history, surpassed in significance only by the birth of Christ.[1] The Reformation, as Latourette says, "ushered in a new stage in the history of mankind."[2] It all began at noon, October 31, 1517, when Martin Luther, a young Augustinian monk, rector (president) of Wittenberg University, nailed his handwritten Ninety-five Theses to the Castle Church door in Wittenberg, Germany.[3] In so doing, he unwittingly ignited a world-class revolution. Frederick Eby concurs:

The Reformation was the most far-reaching and profound awakening in the history of western civilization. To think of it merely as a reform of church organization or moral practices and doctrine is to misinterpret its broader significance for human progress. No aspect of human life was untouched, for it involved political, economic, religious, moral, philosophical, literary, and institutional changes of the most sweeping character.[4]

The great theological issues of the Reformation were about justification by God's grace through faith in Christ and the Bible's ultimate authority taking precedence over Catholic tradition, dogma, and canon law. These theological

Figure 1. Luther nailed his Ninety-five Theses to the Castle Church door in Wittenberg, Germany, at noon, October 31, 1517.

issues were fundamental and affected not only the church but every area of society, including education.

As we will see, Luther was as concerned about education reform as he was about church reform. As Painter says, "Though it is not generally recognized, yet Luther brought about as important a reformation in education as in religion."[5] Professor Kittelson carries the point further:

Figure 2. Martin Luther (1483-1546)

> **"Luther the Educational Reformer," is by no means just one more slice of the reformer's career. It is an issue that lies at the very heart of understanding Luther. . . . Certainly, he was a great theologian, a pastor, and a biblical scholar, but from the beginning of his career to its end, he was also an educational reformer, who not only spoke his mind but also acted on his convictions.**[6]

Before examining Luther as an education reformer, we will review further the amazing events that brought him into prominence. The three divisions of chapter 7 are:

Figure 3. The famous Wittenberg door as it appears today.

1. *Martin Luther, the "David" Who Took On "Goliath"*
2. *Dramatic Changes Caused by the Reformation*
3. *Luther as the Education Reformer*

More has been written about Martin Luther than any other figure in history except Jesus Christ Himself.[7] Luther has been characterized many ways. The Catholic Church ultimately determined that he was a "notorious heretic and a devil."[8] Audin called him "The Samson of the Reformation."[9] He might better be characterized as the "David"—the Catholic monk who took on "Goliath"—his own church.

1. Martin Luther, the "David" Who Took On "Goliath"

While Luther was unaware of the multifaceted revolution his call for an academic debate would bring, it would be foolhardy to suggest that he was unaware of the wide ramifications of the issues he set forth in his Ninety-five Theses. He posted his theses on the church door the day before the biggest church day of the year. Thomas M. Lindsay describes the setting:

> The Church of All Saints (the Castle Church) in Wittenberg had always been intimately connected with the University; its prebendaries were professors; its doors were used as a board on which to publish important academic documents; and notices of public academic "disputations," common enough at the time, had frequently appeared there. The day of the year which drew the largest concourse of townsmen and strangers to the church was All Saints' Day, the first of November. It was the anniversary of the consecration of the building, and was commemorated by a prolonged series of services.[10]

It is not known whether Martin Luther was privy to the fact that his Ninety-five Theses were removed from the Castle Church door and translated from Latin into German. The document was subsequently typeset on the university's Gutenberg press and distributed throughout Germany. We do know that Luther's Ninety-five Theses "went through the entire land [western Europe] in fourteen days,"[11] and that the university's printing house presses "could not throw them off fast enough to meet the demand which came from all parts of Germany."[12] Frederick Mecum (Myconius), a Franciscan friar of the time, said, "It is as if they had been circulated by angelic messengers."[13] Luther's theses resonated well in the academic community:

Figure 4. (left) Johannes Gutenberg (1397-1468) of Mainz, Germany, invented the moveable type printing press. His presses were a major factor in the rapid spread of the Reformation.
(Musée Gutenberg, Mayence)

Figure 5. (below) A sixteenth-century printing press.

Within a fortnight every university and religious center was agog with excitement. All marveled that one obscure monk from an unknown university had stirred the whole of Europe.[14]

Clearly, the invention of Gutenberg's movable-type printing press contributed in a major way to the lightning-like spread of the Reformation.

What had Luther written in his Ninety-fiveTheses that shook the Catholic world on October 31, 1517? The following are selected portions of his famous theses:

THE NINETY-FIVE THESES, 1517

Out of love and zeal for truth and the desire to bring it to light, the following theses will be publicly discussed at Wittenberg under the chairmanship of . . . Martin Luther. . . . He requests that those who cannot be present to debate orally with us will do so by letter. In the Name of Our Lord Jesus Christ. Amen.

21. Thus those indulgence preachers are in error who say that a man is absolved from every penalty and saved by papal indulgences.
27. They preach only human doctrines who say that as soon as the money clinks into the money chest, the soul flies out of purgatory.
28. It is certain that when money clinks in the money chest, greed and avarice can be increased; but when the church intercedes, the result is in the hands of God alone.
32. Those who believe that they can be certain of their salvation because they have indulgence letters will be eternally damned, together with their teachers.
33. Men must especially be on their guard against those who say that the pope's pardons are that inestimable gift of God by which man is reconciled to Him.
36. Any truly repentant Christian has a right to full remission of penalty and guilt, even without indulgence letters.
43. Christians are to be taught that he who gives to the poor or lends to the needy does a better deed than he who buys indulgences.
46. Christians are to be taught that, unless they have more than they need, they must reserve enough for their family needs.
52. It is vain to trust in salvation by indulgence letters, even though the indulgence commissary, or even the pope, were to offer his soul as security.
54. Injury is done the Word of God when, in the same sermon, an equal or larger amount of time is devoted to indulgences than to the Word.

62. The true treasure of the church is the most holy gospel of the glory and grace of God.

79. To say that the cross, emblazoned with the papal coat of arms and set up by the indulgence preachers, is equal in worth to the cross of Christ is blasphemy.

86. Again, "Why does not the pope, whose wealth is today greater than the wealth of the richest Crassus [a rich Roman ruler], build this one basilica of St. Peter with his own money rather than with the money of poor believers?"[15]

Luther's Ninety-five Theses touched on numerous topics, but the dominant theme was the sale of indulgences. What was an indulgence? The Catholic Church had become a master at "marketing" forgiveness of sin. Instead of repenting of one's sin in personal prayer to God through His Son, Jesus Christ, as Christians are admonished to do in 1 John 1:9, the Catholic Church claimed that access to forgiveness and spiritual restoration was available only through the Catholic Church. Confession of sin was to be made to a priest, who would determine the magnitude of one's sin and assign an appropriate form of repentance or "penance" such as exclusion from the church communion service or committal to prayer, fasting, and almsgiving. It was the almsgiving that grew into what some called "the holy trade."[16] The purchase of an indulgence could apply toward a release from pain in purgatory after death and thus provide immediate access to heaven. Luther alluded in his theses to a popular saying of the time: "As soon as the money in the coffer rings, the soul from purgatory springs."[17]

Indulgences were not new. For generations past Catholic popes had issued them as incentives to participate in the massive Catholic Crusades against the Turks in Jerusalem, and as incentives to join King Philip's army against the stubborn King John of England. They were also issued as an enticement to Catholic pilgrims to bring gifts to the Vatican in Rome, a tradition begun in 1300.

At the time of the Reformation, indulgences had come to be so valued that they were now sold as a commodity "on the open market" to raise funds to remodel St. Peter's Basilica in Rome. In 1517, Pope Leo X, who "lived lavishly,"[18] commissioned their sale over the protest of the rulers in England, France, Spain, and Germany, who strongly objected to Rome's constant demand for money.[19] Ignoring these objections, the Roman pontiff enforced his demand through his archbishop in each country. In Germany, the pope called upon Archbishop Albrecht of Mainz, who had paid the Vatican 20,000 florins for his position, to conduct the special indulgence sale. Archbishop Albrecht delegated the task to a well-known fund-raiser for the Catholic Church, a Dominican friar named Johann Tetzel. A Franciscan friar of a rival order said of Tetzel:

> It is incredible what this ignorant monk said and preached. He gave sealed letters stating that even the sins which a man was intending to commit would be forgiven. The pope, he said, had more power than all the Apostles, all the angels and saints, more even than the Virgin Mary herself; for these were all subject to Christ, but the pope was equal to Christ.[20]

Myconius described the grand entrance of Tetzel into the town of Annaberg:

> When the Commissary or Indulgence-seller approached the town, the Bull (proclaiming the Indulgence) was carried before him on a cloth of velvet and gold, and all the priests and monks, the town council, the schoolmasters and their scholars, and all the men and women went out to meet him with banners and candles and songs, forming a great procession; then all the bells ringing and all the organs playing, they accompanied him to the principal church; a red cross was set up in the midst of the church, and the Pope's banner was displayed; in short, one might think they were receiving God Himself.[21]

Citizens of Wittenberg who had purchased indulgences from Tetzel asked Luther for his opinion of the papal letters that described their "efficacy." These papal letters became the trigger that ignited the Reformation.[22] Luther's response was his now famous Ninety-five Theses, which he nailed to the Castle Church door "after many of his friends had urged him to interfere, and in deep distress of mind, . . . he resolved to protest."[23] Incidentally, the formal debate Luther called for never took place.[24] One might say, on the other hand, it took place on a much larger scale!

THE RESPONSE TO THE NINETY-FIVE THESES

Volumes have been written about Luther's courageous action and the subsequent reaction in the Western world. In a simplified form, the following is a brief chronology of events that occurred in the days and years immediately following those few hammer blows with which Luther nailed the Ninety-five Theses to the now-famous door in Wittenberg—the door that tourists by the busload still come to see.

A drop in sales: The sale of indulgences suddenly dropped, not only for Johann Tetzel, but for all indulgence-sellers throughout Catholicism's religious empire. Lindsay says, "The desire to purchase indulgences cooled and the sales almost stopped."[25]

A Dominican attack on Luther: In January 1518, the German Dominicans met in Frankfurt and formulated an official complaint to the pope in Rome in which they described Martin Luther as a heretic and the author of "schism."

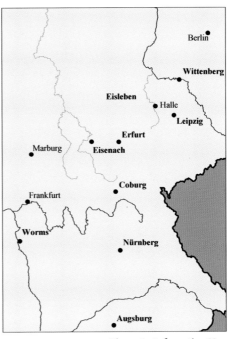

Luther summoned to Rome: On August 7, 1518, Luther received a citation to appear in Rome[26] to defend himself against the charge that he was a "heretic and a rebel against ecclesiastical authority."[27] Luther appealed to his friend, Elector (Governor or Prince) Frederick, for protection. Frederick had founded Wittenberg University and was fond of Luther because of his reputation as a

Figure 6. Reformation Map

popular professor. It was said that "multitudes of students flocked to Wittenberg to hear him."[28] With the help of Emperor Maximilian, who disliked the pope, Frederick arranged for Luther's summons to Rome to be canceled; but Luther was later summoned to appear before Cardinal Cajetan in October 1518 at the Imperial Diet (a national assembly) in Augsburg, Germany,[29] where he was asked to retract unconditionally the views expressed in his Ninety-five Theses. Luther said he would retract any statements proven from Scripture to be in error. Since no attempt was made to prove the error of Luther's statements, the meeting ended in a stalemate, and Luther left the city secretly for fear of his life.[30]

Luther condemned: Meanwhile, the writings of Martin Luther were read throughout Europe, especially in Germany. Luther's words resonated particularly well with the Germans when he wrote:

> Some have estimated that every year more than 300,000 gülden find their way from Germany to Italy. . . . We here come to the heart of the matter. How comes it that we Germans must put up with such robbery and such extortion of our property at the hands of the pope. . . . If we justly hang thieves and behead robbers, why should we let Roman avarice go free? For he is the greatest thief and robber that has come

or can come into the world, and all in the holy name of Christ and St. Peter! Who can longer endure it or keep silence?[31]

Luther's words may have been well received by Germans, but understandably they were strongly denounced by Pope Leo. On June 15, 1520, Martin Luther was condemned by the pope and declared a heretic. Durant tells it this way:

> On June 15, 1520, Leo X issued a bull, *Exsurge Domine*, which condemned forty-one statements by Luther, ordered the public burning of the writings in which these had appeared, and exhorted Luther to abjure his errors and return to the fold. After sixty days of further refusal to come to Rome and make a public recantation, he was to be cut off from Christendom by excommunication, he was to be shunned as a heretic by all the faithful, all places where he stayed were to suspend religious services, and all secular authorities were to banish him from their dominions or deliver him to Rome.[32]

Figure 7. The site in Wittenberg where Luther and his students publicly burned the Papal Bull and several books of canon law.

Luther now found himself on Catholicism's "most wanted" list. He was to be treated as a fugitive, and any community that protected him was to be deprived of all Catholic religious and civil services. In a daring act of defiance, Luther, with the help of his students at Wittenberg University, publicly burned the Papal Bull, *Exsurge Domine,* along with several books of canon law[33] within a few yards of his home "with all the jollity of undergraduate high spirits."[34] Today, in Wittenberg at the corner of Am Bahnhof and Lutherstrasse, there is a memorial park commemorating Luther's historic action.

Luther on trial at Worms: This act of defiance prompted Charles V, the newly crowned emperor of the Holy Roman Empire, to summon Martin Luther to another Imperial Diet, this time at the Bishop's Palace in Worms, Germany. It was an awesome assembly. On April 17 and 18, 1521, Luther, in his monastic garb, stood before the emperor, six German electors, and an impressive array of nobles, prelates, and burghers. The meeting was held in a chamber "so crowded that even the electors found it difficult to reach their seats, and most of those present stood."[35]

Only a few weeks before, Luther's friends had urged him not to go to Worms. Even though the emperor had issued a safe-conduct order, his friends were skeptical and reminded him of the tragic burning of John Huss at a similar setting one hundred years before. Fully aware of the danger, Luther determined to go to Worms. In scenes reminiscent of John Huss' journey from Prague to Constance, Luther was met by crowds of well-wishers as he made the two-hundred-mile journey southwest from Wittenberg to Worms, located on the Rhine—the same river on which John Huss' ashes had been strewn July 6, 1415. Durant describes the crowds:

> April 2 Luther left Wittenberg. At Erfurt a large crowd, including forty professors from the university [his alma mater], hailed him as a hero. When he approached Worms, Spalatin [a friend] rushed a warning to him not to enter, but rather to hurry back to Wittenberg. Luther answered: "Though there were as many devils in Worms as there are tiles on the roofs, I will go there." A band of knights rode out to meet him and escort him into the city (April 16). The streets filled at news of his arrival; 2,000 people gathered around his carriage; all the world came to see him.[36]

The crowd soon became his source of protection. On the second day of the National Assembly, Luther affirmed that the collection of books and pamphlets on display was his. Now Johann Eck, the pope's emissary, asked him to repudiate what he had written, saying:

> Martin, your plea to be heard from Scripture is the one always made by heretics. You do nothing but renew the errors of Wyclif and Huss. . . . How can you assume that you are the only one to understand the sense of Scripture? Would you put your judgment above that of so many famous men and claim that you know more than all of them? You have no right to call into question the most holy orthodox faith, which we are forbidden by the Pope and the Emperor to discuss, lest there be no end to debate. I ask you, Martin—answer candidly and without distinctions—do you or do you not repudiate your books and the errors which they contain?[37]

Luther answered in Latin, then repeated his historic response in German:

> "If His Imperial Majesty desires a plain answer," said Luther, "I will give it to him, *neque cornutum neque dentatum,* and it is this: It is

impossible for me to recant unless I am proved to be in the wrong by the testimony of Scripture or by evident reasoning; I cannot trust either the decisions of Councils or of Popes, for it is plain that they have not only erred, but have contradicted each other. My conscience is thirled [bound] to the word of God, and it is neither safe nor honest to act against one's conscience. God help me! Amen!"[38]

Figure 8. The spot where Luther stood before the Emperor at Worms.

As the session ended, Luther, sensing that his life was in danger, was heard to say, "God, come to my help."[39] The emperor's soldiers lunged toward him and shouted, "To the fire with him, to the fire!"[40] Luther need not have worried. More than five thousand people had gathered outside the Bishop's Palace. As soon as Luther appeared, "the Germans, nobles and delegates from the towns, ringed him round to protect him . . . Luther in the midst of them, . . . they accompanied him to his lodging."[41] Thomas Carlyle, in his book *Heroes and Hero Worship*, described the above scene as "the greatest moment in the modern history of man!"[42]

Later in the Diet proceedings, Luther's books were publicly burned, undoubtedly in response to the burning by Luther and his university students in Wittenberg of the canon law books and the Papal Bull. Bainton records a further attempt to humiliate Luther: "An anonymous pamphleteer reports that on top of the bonfire was placed an effigy of the heretic with the inscription in French, German, and Latin: 'This is Martin Luther, the Doctor of the Gospel.'"[43] This title was intended to offend, but in reality was a badge of honor to Luther.

Luther kidnapped: Knowing that Luther's safe-conduct order would expire on May 6, his friend and benefactor Elector (Prince) Frederick feared that the emperor's police might arrest him. With Luther's reluctant approval, they arranged to have him ambushed as he journeyed home to Wittenberg. He was taken to Frederick's Castle in Wartburg, where he remained for nine months.[44] Luther wrote later that his time at Wartburg Castle was his "Patmos."[45] Latourette describes Luther's remarkable productivity at the castle:

In his nine months in the Wartburg, in spite of ill health Luther wrote nearly a dozen books and translated the New Testament from Greek into German. His translation of the entire Bible, completed later and polished by him again and again, continued to be standard and through its dignity and felicity of expression was epoch-making in the literary history of Germany.[46]

Luther returns home: In March 1522[47] Luther, against the counsel of his protector, Elector Frederick, began the long journey home. Because of his new "outlaw" status with the Catholic Church, he had to travel disguised in the clothes of a knight. He wore a beard and went under the name "Junker (Knight) George."[48] On arriving back in Wittenberg, Luther quickly resumed his duties as president of his fast-growing university and led the ever-widening revolt against the Catholic Church.

2. Dramatic Changes Caused by the Reformation.

Before we examine Luther's role as an education reformer, we need to understand some of the sweeping changes that were occurring as a result of the Reformation. The Reformation sparked spiritual, economic, social, and political changes unprecedented in human history. It closed the door on the Middle Ages and opened the door to the modern world. Some changes first appeared beneficial but later proved to be less than positive. Studying the rapid changes that took place in general will help us better understand the context of Luther's ideas on education.

Positive Change

Upon his return from Wartburg, Luther began a preaching campaign, eight days straight in Wittenberg, then traveled to other German cities where he preached to thousands more. This event stimulated the phenomenon of open-air preaching, which became necessary to accommodate the large crowds. Whole cities turned out to hear not only Luther but other "powerful evangelical preachers" such as Martin Bucer and Matthew Zell.[49]

Negative Change

Luther opposed the use of force to advance the Reformation, saying:

I will not use force or compulsion with anyone; for faith must be of freewill and unconstrained. . . . If I employ force, what do I gain?. . . What becomes of the sincerity of the heart, of faith, of Christian love? What we want is the heart, and to win we must preach the gospel.[50]

However, there were those in Wittenberg and in other cities who raided Catholic churches and monasteries, stoned worshipers praying before statues of Mary, demolished altars, and pulled down statues and religious paintings.[51]

Positive Change

The enrollment at Wittenberg University grew to more than two thousand students. Many of them "carried Bibles under their arms" and saluted each other as "brothers at one in Christ."[52] Latourette says:

Students came from all parts of Germany and from several countries to drink of the new spring at its source. Returning home, they profoundly influenced the Reformation in state after state and country after country.[53]

Among those students at Wittenberg University was Szegedi Kis Istvan from what is now Mezotur, Hungary, who returned home and established the first Reformation Christian school in 1530. The Mezotur Christian School has been in continuous operation since 1530 except for 43 years (1948–1991) when Hungary was under Communist oppression. A sister school, Debrecen Christian School in Debrecen, Hungary, founded in 1538, has been in continuous operation from its beginning. If not the oldest, these two schools are among the oldest Christian schools in the world.[54]

Negative Change

With the closing of the monasteries, the monastery schools were closed as well. The Pre-Reformation populace had been conditioned to send their children to monastic schools for the single purpose of preparing them for service to the Catholic Church. A monastic school education was a passport to a guaranteed salary provided by the church, the wealthiest employer in the land. The Catholic population had come to see no other purpose for education. Therefore, as we will see when we study Luther's education reforms, Luther had difficulty persuading parents to send their children to school. Consequently, in the early years of the Reformation, as Catholic institutions of learning closed, many students simply did not attend school.[55] This was understandable but nonetheless a very serious problem.

Positive Change

Luther advocated a new policy of rebuking heretics. He said, "We should vanquish heretics with books, not with burning."

Negative Change

Luther had difficulty finding pastors for churches because "under the new order there was as yet no certainty that the pastorate would provide a livelihood."[56]

Positive Change

One of Luther's evangelical doctrines that stimulated noticeable change was his teaching that the clergy should marry "as a moral and spiritual necessity."[57] Consequently, as monks, priests, and bishops converted to biblical doctrine, they married. Durant records the phenomenon:

On October 23 [1521] the Mass ceased to be said in Luther's monastery. On November 12, thirteen of the monks walked out of the cloister and headed for marriage; soon a similar exodus would empty half the monasteries of Germany.[58]

Luther himself married Catherine (Katy) Von Bora, a former nun, "who bore him a family of three sons and two daughters."[59] Luther enjoyed telling the story of a parish priest who in reading the Bible for the first time was startled to find that "bishops and priests ought to be husbands of one wife."[60]

Negative Change

The new religious freedom created opportunity for heresies and cults to appear. One "radical," Carlstadt, "proclaimed that schools and studies were deterrents to piety, and that real Christians should shun all letters and learning.[61] One of the followers of Carlstadt, George Mohr, dismissed the school where he served as master and told the parents to "keep their children innocent of letters."[62] This, of course, did not help Luther's cause of providing education for the children of all believers.

Positive Change

Durant says that "the Bible was accepted by nearly all Europe as the infallible Word of God."[63] Luther's writings and translation of the Bible were widely read. The presses in Wittenberg alone produced 100,000 copies of the Scriptures. Poet Heinrich Heine said, "Luther created the German language and he did so by translating the Bible."[64] Luther's writings had an impact far beyond Germany:

There were no newspapers yet, nor magazines; battles were fought with books, pamphlets, and private letters intended for publication. Under the stimulus of Luther's revolt the number of books printed in Germany rose from 150 in 1518 to 990 in 1524. Four-fifths of these favored the Reformation. Books defending Romanism were hard to sell, while Luther's were the most widely purchased of the age. They were sold not only in bookstores but by peddlers and traveling students; 1,400 copies were bought at one Frankfurt fair; even in Paris, in 1520, they outsold everything else. As early as 1519 they were exported to France, Italy, Spain, the Netherlands, England. "Luther's books are everywhere and in every language," wrote Erasmus in 1521; "no one would believe how widely he has moved men."[65]

It was reported that Ferdinand, the archduke of Germany, told Emperor Charles V that "Luther's doctrine has taken such deep root that among a thousand persons there is not one who is not to some extent touched by it."[66]

Negative Change

The Pre-Reformation schools were sad excuses for schools. They were devoid of academic competition and the Catholic Church assured salaries whether or not the students performed well, so there was little incentive for excellence. A European proverb reflected the negative attitude toward education: "Whom the gods despise, they make a scribe or a schoolmaster."[67] As in

Roman schools, flogging was standard procedure. Luther, never at a loss for descriptive words, had this to say about Pre-Reformation schools:

> Was it not a burning shame that formerly a boy must needs study twenty years or longer only to learn a jargon of bad Latin, and then to turn priest and say mass? And he, who finally arrived at this pinnacle of his hopes, was accounted happy. . . . But, for all this, he remained a poor illiterate man all his days, and was neither good to cluck nor to lay eggs. Such are the teachers and guides that we have had to put up with, who knew nothing themselves, and accordingly were unable to teach anything that was either good or true.[68]

Positive Change

Music received a major boost as a result of the Reformation, largely because of the emphasis given by Martin Luther, himself the author of thirty-seven hymns. Reformation music impacted both churches and schools. Coleridge said, "Luther did as much for the Reformation by his hymns as by his translation of the Bible."[69] Some might disagree with the theological implications of that claim, but few would disagree that Luther's great hymns have played a major role in lifting the spirits of Christians for the past five centuries. Luther's most enduring hymn, "A Mighty Fortress Is Our God," is still sung in many churches today.

Negative Change

There was a serious lag time between the close of the Catholic medieval schools and the coming of the new evangelical schools. As Eby points out, every form of Catholic education was in decline because of the Reformation:

> The universities were affected as seriously as were the lower schools. The University of Cologne, which had 370 students in 1516, 8 years later matriculated only 54. Erfurt, the foremost seat of humanistic learning in Germany, enrolled 311 during the year 1520–1521, and by 1527 the number had declined as low as 14. The celebrated University of Vienna enrolled 661 new matriculants in 1519; by 1532 only 12 students were enrolled.[70]

At the University in Heidelberg, "there were as many professors as students."[71] Many of the students defecting from the old Catholic institutions were enrolling in Luther's Wittenberg University.

3. Luther as the Education Reformer

Martin Luther was more than an ivory tower ideologue. He saw the larger picture and had the leadership skills to bring about dramatic change. He knew, for example, that church reform could not move forward without education reform. He saw Christian schools as an essential ally in restoring the evangelical church:

> When schools prosper, the Church remains righteous and her doctrine
> pure. . . . Young pupils and students are the seed and source of the
> Church. If we were dead, whence would come our successors, if not
> from the schools? For the sake of the Church we must have and main-
> tain Christian schools.[72]

Luther was a strong advocate of Christian schools and of Bible-centered
learning. He did not simply champion literacy. Neither did he view Christian
school education as just a tool to build church attendance. His own church
was thriving. Every citizen in and around Wittenberg already belonged to
his church. Nor did he promote Christian school education as a money-
maker. Christian schools never have been, nor will they ever be, a financial
bonanza for the church. Luther advocated Christian schools not for what
they could give the church in numerical or monetary gain but for their basic
purpose of preserving the integrity of the gospel of Christ.

His appeals for the establishment of Christian schools were often based
on the Scriptures. A good example is found in his famous treatise "Letters
to the Mayors and Aldermen of All the Cities of Germany in Behalf of
Christian Schools":

> Moses so repeatedly urges and demands of parents to teach their chil-
> dren; hence, also Psalm 78 says: "He commanded our fathers, that they
> should make them known to their children: that the generation to come
> might know them, even the children which should be born; who should
> arise and declare them to their children." . . . And what other reason is
> there why we old folks are living, than that we are to tend, teach, and
> bring up the young people? It is impossible that these hobbledehoys
> should be their own teachers and keepers; hence God has commended
> them to us old and experienced people for their well being, and shall
> demand of us a solemn account of them. Accordingly, also Moses com-
> mands, [in] Deut. 32, saying: "Ask thy father, and he will shew thee:
> thy elders, and they will tell thee."[73]

Again and again, Luther drew from the Scripture in building his case for
Christian schools.

LUTHER'S PLACE IN HISTORY AS AN EDUCATOR

As previously mentioned, Martin Luther was as much an education
reformer as he was a church reformer. Dr. F.V.N. Painter, writing early in
this century, agreed: "Luther deserves henceforth to be recognized as the
greatest, not only of religious, but of educational reformers."[74] In reference
to Luther's treatise quoted above, Painter said it was "the most important
educational treatise ever written."[75] G.M. Bruce says in a similar manner:

"Luther . . . stands forth as the greatest educator of his age."[76] James Kittelson agrees with both:

> There can be no doubt, that Luther the educational reformer, contributed to the modern world not only by insisting that basic education be available to all—and by making it so—but also by bringing to common people the fundamental notion that true religion could be a matter of the mind as well as of the heart and public behavior. From the training of pastors, to the catechisms, to the hymns, Luther's educational reforms in fact did much to create the modern world, with its typical distinction at the popular level between religion of the head and religion of the heart.[77]

LUTHER'S PHILOSOPHY OF EDUCATION

Luther's educational philosophy can be summed up in one word—Bible-centered. Luther was biblical about everything, including education. He said:

> Above all, in schools of all kinds the chief and most common lesson should be in the Scriptures. . . . But where the Holy Scriptures are not the rule, I advise no one to send his child. Everything must perish where God's word is not studied unceasingly.[78]

In 1524 Luther wrote his letter to mayors and aldermen about Christian schools. He wrote his second most important treatise on Christian schools, "Sermon on the Duty of Sending Children to School," in 1530. Copies of his sermon were delivered by messenger to all the pastors in Germany with the instructions that it be read to their congregations. Because of its importance, substantial sections are quoted in this chapter and the next one. In his sermon, in classic Luther style, he reiterated his commitment to biblical principles with these words:

> For if the Scriptures and learning perish, what will remain in Germany, but a lawless horde of Tarters or Turks, yea, a multitude of wild beasts.[79]

Then he referred to the devil, which he often did, and said:

> Such results he [Satan] does not allow to appear at present, and powerfully blinds the people, that when the evil does come, and they are obliged to learn it from experience, he may laugh at their misery and lamentation, which they can no longer do any thing to help. They will then be forced to say, "We have waited too long," and would give a hundred florins for half a scholar, while now they would not give five florins for a thorough one.[80]

Like the true Christian school educator he was, Luther believed that the Bible must have the central place in Christian schools, including Christian universities. For example, the slogan of the University of Marburg was, in 1527, "Let him be accursed, whoever teaches anything contrary to the Scriptures." The Marburg University was designed to teach everything according to "the pure Word of God" which included law, medicine, the liberal arts, and the Latin, Greek, and Hebrew languages. Twelve evangelical universities were thus established in Germany along these same academic lines of biblical authority.[81]

LUTHER'S SERIOUS PROBLEM OF TRANSITION

It is difficult for us to comprehend just how dominant Catholicism in the Middle Ages had become. There was barely an individual or civil transaction made that did not go through the bureaucratic structure of the Catholic Church—a church orchestrated by one man, the pope, who lived in unbelievable opulence in Rome.[82]

The impact of the Reformation was tantamount to a giant shift of the earth's center of gravity. Society suddenly shifted from Catholic authority to biblical authority—from a world where the church is church-centered to a new world where the church is Bible-centered. Imagine, if you will, people from every level of society in town after town, country after country, defecting from medieval Catholicism to the new world of "the priesthood of believers." While there was indeed a euphoric feeling of liberation, aspects of the transition were difficult.

Wherever the Reformation flowered, the medieval Catholic infrastructure died. Living without that infrastructure, flawed though it had been, was no doubt similar to living today without public utilities, police and fire protection, the court system, and welfare programs. As the Great Reformation gained momentum and crossed political boundaries, it took away the "guaranteed livings" that the Catholic Church had provided to multiplied thousands of priests, monks, and church clerics of all kinds, paid for by the burdensome ecclesiastical taxation.

A "guaranteed living" for a son was available when he was, in effect, given to the Catholic Church and educated in the "one-occupation" schools of the monasteries, cathedrals, and parish churches. As Eby points out, the demise of the Catholic system left an enormous vacuum that Luther and his fellow reformers attempted to fill:

> The vast number of ecclesiastical livings can be guessed from a single example. In the city of Lübeck there were five parishes, each with its

large church and numerous chapels. The city itself had a population between 30,000 and 50,000 people. At the time of the Reformation, the cathedral supported 66 priests and another church had 68, while the total number of priests in the city was about 800. This meant a priest for every 10 or 12 families in the town. In addition to these offices, monasteries and convents, as well as brotherhoods, existed in abundance.

Before the Reformation, education had trained the young directly for the kind of living and type of work expected of the individual.

The overthrow of the Roman Church, together with all the monasteries and ecclesiastical foundations, threw Germanic civilization into wild disorder. All the offices, livings, and appointments within the gift of the ecclesiastical order were threatened with extinction.[83]

These changes, Eby points out, greatly affected parental attitudes toward education:

As a consequence of the changed order of things, with no certainty of future appointments to offices and livings, parents lost all incentive to educate their children. Luther belabored the mercenary attitude of those parents who preferred rather to train their children for manual and commercial vocations than to send them to the school to become pastors, teachers and civil servants. A new civilization was being born, involving a new order of vocational life. Until these new livings could be established, and new schools could be organized that would train for the new posts, parents did not know what training to give their children.[84]

At this point it is helpful to reintroduce Desiderius Erasmus. He was, you will recall, a lukewarm participant in the Reformation. He was a powerful critic of papal errors, but he never became an evangelical believer and never wholeheartedly joined the Reformation cause. While he wrote many favorable words about Luther, he also criticized him, especially on issues pertaining to education. In his sharpest statement about Luther and education, he said that "wherever Luther prevails, the cause of literature and learning is lost."[85] These oft quoted words were an accurate description of the early years of the Reformation, but Erasmus lacked an understanding of Luther's larger vision. Luther was well aware of the transition problem:

First of all we see how the schools are deteriorating throughout Germany. The universities are becoming weak, the monasteries are declining, and, as Isaiah says, "The grass withereth, the flower fadeth, because the spirit of the Lord bloweth upon it" (Isaiah 40:7) through the Gospel. For through the word of God the unchristian and sensual character of these institutions is becoming known. And because selfish parents see that they can no longer place their children upon the bounty of monasteries and cathedrals, they refuse to educate them. "Why should we educate our children," they say, "if they are not to become priests, monks, and nuns, and thus earn a support?"[86]

In nautical terms, Luther found that his "Reformation ship" turned much more slowly than he had envisioned. There was more to his task as a reformer than nailing papers to the front door of his church. He had to re-create the whole of society according to biblical principles. It was indeed an enormous task.

LUTHER'S PLAN FOR EDUCATION REFORM

As we will see, Luther's plan for education reform took several turns. Ultimately Luther placed his churches and schools under civil government, but that was not his original plan. His first choice for Christian schooling was an alliance between parents and the churches. As Boyd and King point out, "The assumption on which he proceeded was that the new church should take over the educational work of the old."[87] In this issue Luther, courageous and forceful as he was, fought an enormous uphill battle on all fronts. As previously mentioned, his number one challenge was parental apathy. In each of his writings on education, he gives considerable space to an appeal to parents based on the great worth of an educated society taught under a rigorous curriculum much broader in design than the "single-occupation schools" of the past. But as he learned:

> Parents were loath to pay the necessary school fees, although formerly they might well have paid far larger sums under the guise of charity or church exactions, sums which had made possible the maintenance of the church schools. Moreover some of the more extreme sectarians also began to question the need for education if everything came from the spirit.[88]

He faced apathy in another direction as well—namely, the civil leaders, who had reclaimed vast, income-producing properties formerly owned by the Catholic Church. Like John Knox, who would later establish Christian schools in Scotland, Luther learned that civil authorities, often motivated by greed, had priorities other than his new church ministry schools for the income from the properties now being returned to the people. As Durant says:

> The Reformers had expected that the revenues of ecclesiastical properties appropriated by the state would in part be devoted to establishing new schools to replace those that were disappearing with the closing of the monasteries; but "princes and lords," Luther complained, "were so

busily engaged in the high and important affairs of the cellar, the kitchen, and the bedchamber that they had no time" to help education.[89]

Impatient civil leaders saw local infrastructure needs such as bridges, roads, and muskets as more important than funding the new Christian schools. Luther appealed to them:

> Dear Sirs, if for the temporal peace and safety of a city we must every year spend such large sums to purchase muskets, to build roads, paths, dikes, and to procure innumerable other things, why should we not much more cheerfully expend as much upon our poor, needy youths, by supporting one or two experienced persons as schoolmasters.[90]

Luther was faced with yet another problem, inept church pastors, most

of whom were former Catholic priests. As Kittelson explains, "One of the most common complaints about the pre-Reformation parish priest was that he was an ignorant lout, little different from the rude peasants he served."[91] This was also true of pre-Reformation schoolmasters. Luther learned through a church and school survey—a survey that he and Elector (Governor) John of Saxony had authorized, that pastors and schoolmasters were woefully ill prepared academically and doctrinally to give leadership to the new Christian schools. Luther himself visited some of the churches. He exclaimed, "What

Figure 9. Luther's desk at Lutherhalle in Wittenberg is regarded as a national treasure in Germany. Permission granted — (Lutherhalle Wittenberg)

miseries we see here." Obviously, it would take time to bring the pastors and schoolmasters to the level of professional excellence Luther required for the schools he had in mind. Therefore, Luther found himself retreating from his first plan of a simple alliance between churches and parents.

Now Luther was forced to consider a second choice—a three-way alliance among parents, the churches, and city governments. The involvement of government was not, as we have said, his first choice. Government would either force parents to send their children to Christian schools or would establish its own schools This situation is well explained by Gerald Strauss in his excellent work *Luther's House of Learning:*

Luther's first thoughts on the subject of Christian education were considerably at variance with the compromise he eventually came to accept. His many remarks on teaching and learning show him arriving most reluctantly at the conclusion that voluntary effort, parental direction, and community enterprise were weak reeds from which to construct a vigorous educational program. It caused him a good deal of pain to admit the failure of his early conviction that a change of heart must precede the imposition of doctrines and rules.[92]

Several other factors influenced Luther to make what some would regard as a serious philosophical error. Eby explains:

> A turning point in Luther's experience and attitudes came during the years 1525 to 1528. Three contacts profoundly affected his judgment and altered his views on education. These were the Peasants' War in 1525, the church-school survey in 1527, and the rapid spread of Anabaptist doctrines [which he opposed]. Therefore he revised his views as to the relation of church and state. . . . Every individual must be brought up in subserviency to the state, and outwardly at least he must be submissive to the religious doctrines and practices of his prince. Schools and universities must be established and conducted by the state.[93]

The idea of placing individuals, churches, and their educational institutions under local and state "subserviency" represented a major concession for Luther. He did not live to see the long-range impact of his decision. He would weep if he could see the cold, half-empty state-run Lutheran churches in most "Lutheran countries" today.[94] He would weep again if he could see the non-Christian character of today's state-run schools in Germany—all of which are descended from Martin Luther's Christian schools. Painter agrees:

> It is to be noted . . . that in handing over education to the State [and city governments] Luther did not contemplate, as will be readily understood, a complete secularization of the schools, but desired them to have a distinctly Christian character.[95]

Eby provides the best description of Luther's dramatic change of mind:

> In his earlier period Luther had proclaimed the thesis: "A Christian man is the most free lord of all, and subject to none." He had looked upon the church as an independent organism, separate from the state and founded upon the Scriptures. Hereafter the church was more and more completely subordinated to the civil power. Luther came to regard civil rulers as divinely commissioned to rule, not only in temporal, but in ecclesiastical affairs as well.[96]

Luther's assumption was that civil authorities, being "divinely commis-sioned," would rule over churches and schools in a manner that would not violate biblical principles. Quite obviously, civil authorities became, over time, less and less dependent on biblical authority for moral guidance.

Later we will discover that those secular state schools in northern Germany (Prussia), descendent schools of Martin Luther's Christian schools, were the models for the first state-sponsored public schools established in 1837 in Massachusetts by Horace Mann.

Meanwhile, back in Reformation Germany, Luther was discouraged by parental apathy, a lack of income from former Catholic lands, and inept human resources for leadership. He began to steer the ever-growing evangelical movement toward his second choice for education reform—a three-way alliance that not only included civil government but gave it dominance. Gerald Strauss says:

> Reacting to the events of these early years, Luther too veered from excited optimism to deepest gloom. But whether encouraged or despondent, he made it evi-dent now, as did his colleagues, that they no longer counted on individual effort and personal zeal. Only dimly aware of the fateful consequences of their decision, they [Luther and Melanchthon] welcomed the good offices of political authority and embraced them as the most promising agent for accomplishing their pedagogical objectives.[97]

Figure 10. Philip Melanchthon (1497-1560) was Luther's right-hand man in education reform.

The driving force behind the new education reform plan that gave preeminence to civil government was Philip Melanchthon, Luther's "right-hand man" at Wittenberg University. He later became known as the "Preceptor (Educator) of Germany" because of the many textbooks he wrote and his innovative contributions to German education, particularly at the secondary level.[98] Melanchthon was a popular professor of Greek and theology at the university and was considered one of the "greatest scholars of his time."[99] According to Reed and Prevost:

> His greatest contribution was writing textbooks on ethics, physics, reli-gions, history, rhetoric, dialectic, and psychology. His Greek grammar, first written when he was sixteen, passed through twenty-six editions before his death, and his Latin grammar passed through fifty-five editions.[100]

Luther, Melanchthon, and a third professor, Johann Bugenhagen, who was also the beloved pastor of the Wittenberg University Church, were the prime movers of the Reformation's evangelical Christian school movement that ultimately spread throughout the Western world and were the "main attractions" at Wittenberg University. Under their leadership, the university's enrollment climbed to 2,000 students in the 1520s and '30s at a time when other universities were in serious decline.[101] Bugenhagen would later play a major role in the spread of Christian school education in northern Germany and in the Scandinavian countries, particularly Denmark.[102]

Once Luther accepted the new school plan, he supported it aggressively:

> **Luther gave his support to this shift of educational authority from private to public jurisdiction, from voluntary to compulsory participation, and from associative to institutional organization.[103]**

The new plan, called the Saxony school plan, had its genesis in the town of Leisnig in the Dutchy of Saxony in northern Germany. A brief abstract of the elementary school plan follows:

> **Each school was to consist of three classes. In the first class there was to be taught the beginnings of reading and writing, in both the vernacular and in Latin, Latin grammar (Donatus), the Creed, the Lord's prayer, and the prayers and hymns of the church service. In the second class Latin became the language of instruction, and Latin grammar was thoroughly learned. Latin authors were read, and religious instruction was continued. In the third class more advanced work in reading Latin (Livy, Sallust, Vergil, Horace, and Cicero) was given, and rhetoric and dialectic were studied.[104]**

Even though civil government was now involved, financing the schools was still a challenge. Luther, who was opposed to forming rigid administrative plans,[105] as Germans were prone to do, believed that the new community-based Christian schools could be financed through a variety of sources. Painter explains:

> **Circumstances were allowed to determine the way in which schools should be supported. In some cases a tuition fee was charged, and in others the teacher was paid out of the common treasury of the congregation. . . . The people were urged to contribute liberally to the support of schools, and Luther recommended education as a suitable object for bequests. "Therefore," says Luther, "If the father is poor, let the child be aided with the property of the Church. The rich should make bequests to such objects, as some have done, who have founded scholarships; that is giving money to the Church in a proper way."[106]**

It sounds strange to us today, but in some communities "a small fee for tuition was charged and collected by city officers."[107] In the rural areas, students from poor families were allowed to meet their portion of the tuition requirement by bringing a stick of wood each day for the classroom's fireplace.[108] Some families could pay tuition by having students bring to school a loaf of bread to supplement the teacher's salary.[109] With financial support difficult to obtain from Germany's magistrates for education, this type of "creative financing" became a necessity.

The major advantage Luther saw in the alliance with civil government was that the government had the potential to force families to send their children to school. As we saw earlier, Martin Luther was not the first to advocate compulsory school attendance, but he was indeed the first to ask civil authorities to require students to attend Christian schools. His logic was as follows:

> But I maintain that the civil authorities are under obligation to compel the people to send their children to school, especially such as are promising, as has elsewhere been said. For our rulers are certainly bound to maintain the spiritual and secular offices and callings, so that there may always be preachers, jurists, pastors, scribes, physicians, school-masters, and the like; for these can not be dispensed with. If the government can compel such citizens as are fit for military service to bear spear and rifle, to mount ramparts, and perform other martial duties in time of war; how much more has it a right to compel the people to send their children to school, because in this case we are warring with the devil, whose object it is secretly to exhaust our cities and principalities of their strong men, to destroy the kernel and leave a shell of ignorant and helpless people, whom he can sport and juggle with at pleasure.[110]

Throughout his writings Luther refers to Germany's reputation as a land of unlearned brutes. In his famous sermon, read in the new evangelical churches throughout the country, he appeals to German pride:

> We have, alas! lived and degenerated long enough in darkness; we have remained German brutes too long. Let us use our reason, that God may observe in us gratitude for His mercies, and that other lands may see that we are human beings, capable both of learning and of teaching, in order that through us, also, the world may be made better.[111]

THE IMPACT OF LUTHER'S BROADSIDES ON EDUCATION

Martin Luther issued, in the parlance of naval warfare, three "broadsides" to three different audiences in Germany, and these were effective in piercing through the prevailing apathy toward evangelical education or education of any kind:

1. In 1520, Luther wrote his famous letter "To the Christian Nobility of the German Nation on Improvement of the Christian Estate." In his list of proposed improvements, he wrote, "Each city should have schools for boys and girls, where the gospel should be read to them either in Latin or German."[112] His intended audience was Germany's highest levels of civil leadership—such as the emperor and the electors—who represented national and state governments.

2. In 1524, Luther wrote his "Letter to the Mayors and Aldermen of All the Cities of Germany in Behalf of Christian Schools." Of the three broadsides, this was the most effective. Cities in Germany in the sixteenth century were still in the traditional mode of city-states and were not greatly influenced by a centralized national government. City magistrates quickly responded to Luther's appeal, and by the end of the sixteenth century there were 300 Christian schools in Germany.[113] Luther was alarmed, however, at how quickly and how tightly regulated the city-sponsored schools became. He referred to their voluminous regulations as "piles of laws."[114] Strauss explains:

    > School ordinances tended to be wordy documents exhibiting to a fault the preoccupation with minutiae, and the paternalistic inclination to direct every activity, that are so typical of their age. As early codes were modified in response to changing circumstances, they grew ever longer and more unyielding. In many cases their fastidious pettiness all but destroyed the religious and pedagogical principles on which they had been based. One senses the old nagging distrust at work, the fear of leaving anything unregulated, no matter how trivial.[115]

3. In 1530, Luther wrote his third broadside, entitled "Sermon on the Duty of Sending Children to School." It was aimed at the general population and, as previously mentioned, was delivered in Sunday services by evangelical pastors. Parishioners in the sixteenth century were accustomed to hearing strongly worded admonitions from their pastors. Even so, one wonders whether the following words from Luther's written sermon did not, indeed, sting their ears:

    > For you support neither schools nor pastors, though according to the Gospel you are under obligation to do so; and besides, you show yourselves such accursed and ungrateful wretches that you are unwilling to give your sons to be educated for maintaining these gifts of God, but possess every thing in vain, not manifesting a

> drop of gratitude, but on the contrary letting the kingdom of God and the salvation of souls be neglected, to their destruction. Ought not God to be angry?
>
> Yea, it would be no wonder if God should open the doors and windows of hell, and let all the devils loose upon us, or if He should rain fire and brimstone from heaven and sink us all in the abyss of hell, as He did Sodom and Gomorrah.[116]

While Luther was capable of writing scorching words such as these, he was equally capable of writing gracious words. Near the end of his sermon he wrote the following about teachers:

> If I had to give up preaching and my other duties, there is no office I would rather have than that of school-teacher. For I know that next to the ministry it is the most useful, greatest, and best; and I am not sure which of the two is to be preferred. For it is hard to make old dogs docile and old rogues pious, yet that is what the ministry works at, and must work at, in great part, in vain; but young trees, though some may break in the process, are more easily bent and trained. Therefore let it be considered one of the highest virtues on earth faithfully to train the children of others.[117]

LUTHER'S DEATH

Martin Luther died on February 18, 1546, in Eisleben, Germany, where he was born sixty-three years before. He had gone there to settle a dispute between two counts. There is no question that Luther was uniquely suited for the assignment God had given him. There is also no question that he was a man of exceptional character. Regarding his character, Brady says:

> Mighty in intellect, strong in common sense, eloquent in speech, dauntless in courage, tender in spirit, warm in affection; all his natural gifts and virtues were consecrated to God, and he was as superior to most men in spiritual graces as in intellectual and moral endowments. With faith like that of one of the old prophets or apostles, he exhibited also a humility and self-sacrifice equal to that which had been seen in the greatest saints and confessors and martyrs. To the authority of Holy Scripture he ever showed the profoundest submission, along with extreme tenderness of conscience. He had deep perception and made clear avowal of all the special doctrines of the Gospel. To him we owe the recovery, after long eclipse, of that great cardinal doctrine of evangelical truth, "justification by faith"; the doctrine of salvation by Christ, not by human merit. This truth was taught to him by the Holy Spirit out of the Word of God, and this Gospel of glad tidings he proclaimed anew to the world. Whether in his person or in his work, we can never sufficiently admire the grace of God in him.[118]

CONCLUSION

We conclude this chapter with one of the more interesting modes of communicating the message of Christ employed by Luther and Melanchthon. It was known as their book of contrasted engravings entitled *The Passional Christi et Antichristi*. Lindsay explains it best:

> Luther planned the book, Luke Cranach designed the pictures, and Melanchthon furnished the texts from Scripture and the quotations from Canon Law. It is a series of pairs of engravings representing the lives of our Lord and of the Pope, so arranged that wherever the book opened two contrasting pictures could be seen at the same time. The contrasts were such as these: Jesus washing the disciples' feet; the Pope holding out his toe to be kissed: Jesus healing the wounded and the sick; the Pope presiding at a tournament: Jesus bending under His Cross; the Pope carried in state on men's shoulders: Jesus driving the money-changers out of the Temple; the Pope and his servants turning a church into a market for Indulgences, and sitting surrounded with strong boxes and piles of coin. It was a "good book for laity," Luther said.[119]

The brief comparative study that follows is much less dramatic than that of Luther and Melanchthon, but it is nonetheless useful.

Reformation Evangelicalism	Medieval Catholicism
1. **Access to God:** People have direct access to God through faith in Christ (Romans 1:17).	**Access to God:** People have access to God only through the Catholic Church.
2. **Preaching:** The centerpiece of an evangelical church service was the sermon.	**Preaching:** Catholic worshipers seldom heard sermons—the centerpiece was ceremony and pageantry.
3. **Principal Authority Base:** Authority resides in the Bible translated from the original languages.	**Principal Authority Base:** Authority resides in Catholic tradition, canon law patterned after Roman law,[122] and the Catholic Vulgate Bible. "The Bible was hardly ever read. When it was, it was interpreted at four levels—the literal, spiritual, allegorical, and analogical (that is, its heavenly meaning). Hardly anybody knew what the Bible really said or meant."[123]
4. **Music:** Hymn singing by evangelical congregations was a valued innovation of the Reformation. Luther wrote thirty-seven hymns.	**Music:** The priests sang chants. There was no congregational singing.

Reformation Evangelicalism	Medieval Catholicism
5. **Bible:** The Bible was available in the language of the common people.	**Bible:** The Vulgate Bible was on the "List of Forbidden Books" and not available to the laity.[124] The translation of the Bible into the vernacular was forbidden.
6. **Laity:** The status of the laity was elevated. Luther, in his second treatise "The Freedom of a Christian Man," spoke of the individual "priesthood of all believers" and in so doing, according to Eby, "added vitally to the self-respect of the lower classes."[120]	**Laity:** The status of the laity was suppressed and the status of the clergy was elevated. Popes and bishops lived in palaces surrounded by luxury unparalleled elsewhere in society.
7. **Education:** Evangelicals attempted to provide Christian education and basic literacy for all levels of society.	**Education:** Literacy was suppressed for all those not destined to serve the Catholic Church. As Andrew Miller says, "Learning was branded as the parent of heresy."[125]
8. **Teaching:** Teachers and teaching as a profession enjoyed an elevated status. Luther said, "Let it be considered one of the highest virtues on earth faithfully to train the children of others."[121]	**Teaching:** The "teaching profession," such as it was, was not held in high regard.
9. **Civil Government:** Civil government was elevated above the church.	**Civil Government:** Civil government remained subservient to the church.

The Great Reformation was not a phenomenon limited to Germany, although Luther, of course, was the great igniter. He lit the original match that brought flame to embers that had been at the point of ignition for centuries. The Reformation quickly spread throughout the Western world. Everywhere the evangelical Reformation flourished, Christian school education was right there on the front line and provided depth and durability to its noble objectives. In the next chapter we will consider, in greater detail, what Luther believed about education.

Endnotes—Chapter Seven

[1] F.V.N. Painter, *Luther on Education* (St. Louis: Concordia Publishing House, 1889), p. 9. Painter's exact statement was "The most important event in history since the advent of Christ, is the Reformation of the sixteenth century."

[2] Kenneth Scott Latourette, *Christianity Through the Ages* (New York: Harper and Row, Publishers, 1965), p. 159.

[3] Kurt Aland, ed., *Martin Luther's Ninety-five Theses* (Saint Louis: Concordia Publishing House, 1967), p. 12. Note: In reference to the size of the *Ninety-five Theses,* Aland said, "about twice the size of a piece of typing paper."

[4] Frederick Eby, *The Development of Modern Education* (New York: Prentice-Hall, 1934), p. 1.

[5] Painter, Preface iv.

[6] James M. Kittelson, "Luther the Education Reformer," *Luther and Learning*, Marilyn J. Harran, ed. (London: Associated University Presses, Inc., 1985), p. 96.

[7] *The New International Dictionary of the Christian Church*, J.D. Douglas, ed. (Grand Rapids: Zondervan Publishing House, 1974), p. 611.

[8] Roland Bainton, *Here I Stand: A Life of Martin Luther* (New York: 1950), p. 186, quoted in Durant, *The Reformation*, p. 362.

[9] Painter, p. 11.

[10] Thomas M. Lindsay, *A History of the Reformation*, vol. 1 (Edinburgh: T. and T. Clark, 1906), p. 214.

[11] *Encyclopaedia of Living Divines*, vol. II, Philip Schaff, ed. (Toronto: Funk and Wagnalls Company, 1891), p. 1364.

[12] Lindsay, p. 215.

[13] Frederick Mecum (Myconius), quoted in Lindsay, p. 230.

[14] James Atkinson, *Introduction to the History of Christianity*, Tim Dowley, ed. (Minneapolis: Fortress Press, 1995), p. 366.

[15] Martin Luther, trans. by C.M. Jones and H.J. Grinn, *Martin Luther's Ninety-five Theses*, Kurt Aland, ed. (Saint Louis: Concordia Publishing House, 1967), pp. 50, 52-57.

[16] Atkinson, p. 366.

[17] Ludwig Pastor, *History of the Popes*, (St. Louis, 1898); quoted in Will Durant, *The Reformation* (New York: Simon and Schuster, 1957), p. 339.

[18] Lindsay, p. 231. Lindsay, speaking of Pope Leo X, said, "He had a huge income, much greater than that of any European monarch, but he lived beyond it."

[19] Durant, *The Reformation*, p. 338.

[20] Ibid., p. 339.

[21] Lindsay, p. 213.

[22] Durant, *The Reformation*, p. 340.

[23] Lindsay, p. 214.

[24] *Encyclopaedia Britannica*, vol. 14 (Chicago: William Benton, Publisher, 1961), p. 493.

[25] Lindsay, p. 229.

[26] Aland, p. 6.

[27] *Encyclopaedia Britannica*, vol. 14 (Chicago: William Benton, Publisher, 1961), p. 493.

[28] J. Köstlin, p. 1364. Also see Aland, p. 8: "Students were streaming into Wittenberg from all areas, hundreds of them sitting at Luther's feet."

[29] H.G. Haile, *Luther, A Biography* (Garden City, New York: Doubleday and Company, Inc., 1980), Foreword "Important Events."

[30] "Martin Luther," *Encyclopaedia Britannica*, vol. 14 (Chicago: William Benton, Publisher, 1961), p. 495.

[31] "An Open Letter to the Christian Nobility of the German Nation Concerning the Reform of the Christian State," *Luther Works*, II, pp. 83-99. Quoted in Durant, *The Reformation*, p. 353.

[32] Ibid, p. 352.

[33] Aland, p. 7.

[34] Joseph Clayton, *The Protestant Reformation in Great Britain* (London: The Bruce Publishing Company, 1934), p. 9.

[35] Durant, *The Reformation*, p. 360.

[36] Ibid. The Luther quote within the Durant quote is taken from Charles Beard, *Martin Luther and the Reformation* (London 1899), p. 432.

[37] Johann Eck, quoted by Roland Bainton, *Here I Stand: A Life of Martin Luther* (New York: 1950), p. 185, quoted in Durant, *The Reformation*, p. 361.

[38] Martin Luther, *Reichstagsakten*, ii, p. 636; quoted in Lindsay, p. 291. Note: There are numerous versions of Luther's famous speech, especially the last lines. Köstlin, along with Painter and others, adds the familiar words, "Here I stand, I cannot do otherwise. God help me. Amen!" *(Hier stehe ich, ich kann nicht anders; Gott helf mir, Amen!)* Köstlin, p. 1365.

[39] Ibid.

[40] Ibid.

[41] Ibid.

[42] Thomas Carlyle, *Heroes and Hero Worship*, p. 360. Quoted in Durant, *The Reformation*, p. 361.

[43] Bainton, *Here I Stand: A Life of Martin Luther*, p. 191, quoted in B.A. Gerrish, "Doctor: Doctor Martin Luther: Subjectivity and Doctrine in the Lutheran Reformation," *Seven-Headed Luther,* Peter Newman Brooks, ed. (Oxford: Clarendon Press, 1983), p. 2.

[44] Scott H. Hendrix, *Luther and the Papacy* (Philadelphia: Fortress Press, 1981), p. 121.

[45] Köstlin, p. 1365. Note: The Apostle John wrote the Book of Revelation on the Isle of Patmos off the coast of Asia Minor.

[46] Latourette, p. 172. Note: Durant claims that 100,000 copies of Luther's New Testament were sold in his lifetime. (Durant, p. 369).

[47] Hendrix, p. 122.

[48] Durant, *The Reformation*, p. 363.

[49] Lindsay, p. 310.

[50] Lindsay, p. 318. Note: Luther, however, was not above some lightheartedness at papal expense. Scott Hendrix records, "Wittenberg students dressed up as the pope, cardinals, and bishops and marched through town mocking the hierarchy. Luther approved of their fun since the 'enemy of Christ' deserved such ridicule." Hendrix, p. 124. Hendrix cites: WABr 266.29 (February 17, 1521).

[51] Durant, *The Reformation,* pp. 364-366.

[52] Ibid., p. 311.

[53] Latourette, p. 172.

[54] Author's interview with administrators of Mezotur Christian School and Debrecen Christian School in Hungary in 1996.

[55] Eby, pp. 65-66. Note: Eby, in reference to parental motivation for sending a child to a monastic school, quoted Charles Beard, who said, "A butcher's son might become a cardinal; a fisherman's boy [might] fill the chair of Saint Peter." Charles Beard*, Martin Luther and the Reformation in Germany* (London: K. Paul, Trench, Trübner, and Company, 1889), p. 14.

[56] Eby, p. 68.

[57] Lindsay, p. 313.

[58] Durant, *The Reformation*, p. 364.

[59] *Encyclopaedia Britannica,* vol. 14, p. 495.

[60] Lindsay, p. 305.

[61] Durant, *The Reformation,* p. 366.

[62] Ibid., p. 366.

[63] Durant, *The Reformation,* p. 370.

[64] Ernist Christian Helmreich, *Religious Education in German Schools* (Cambridge, Mass.: Harvard University Press, 1959), p. 9.

[65] Durant, *The Reformation,* p. 368. Durant quotes Erasmus from J.A. Froude, *Life and Letters of Erasmus* (New York: 1894), p. 294. Note: It is interesting that Luther took no royalties for his writings although as Durant said, "They made a fortune for his publisher." (see Durant, p. 417).

[66] *Encyclopaedia Britannica,* vol. 14, p. 495.

[67] Stephen C. Perks*, The Christian Philosophy of Education Explained* (Whitby, North Yorkshire, England: Avant Books, 1992), p. 3.

[68] Martin Luther, quoted in Henry Barnard, *German Teachers and Educators* (Hartford: Brown and Gross, 1878), p. 149; cited by Painter, p. 63.

[69] Coleridge, quoted by Painter, p. 105.

[70] Eby, p. 64. Eby cites Johannes Janssen, vol. XIII, p. 258 for the declining university enrollment figures.

[71] Ibid.

[72] Luther, quoted in Painter, *Luther on Education*, pp. 132-133.

[73] Luther, "Letter to the Mayors and Aldermen of All the Cities of Germany in Behalf of Christian Schools," translated by W.H.T. Dau (Hickory, North Carolina: A. L. Crouse, 1895), pp. 8-9.

[74] Painter, p. 168.

[75] Ibid.

[76] G.M. Bruce, *Luther as an Educator* (Minneapolis: Augsberg Publishing House, 1928), p. 229, quoted in Eby, p. 67.

[77] Kittelson, p. 111.

[78] Martin Luther, quoted in Painter, p. 147.

[79] Luther, quoted in Painter, *Luther on Education,* p. 216.

[80] Ibid.

[81] Eby, *The Development of Modern Education,* p. 88.

[82] Andrew Miller, "The Crusades to the Reformation," *Short Papers on Church History,* vol. II, (London: Pickering and Inglis), p. 520.

[83] Eby, *The Development of Modern Education,* p. 66. Eby cites: Walter M. Rucus, John Bugenhagen, Pomeranus, (Philadelphia: United Lutheran Publishing House, 1924), p. 75.

[84] Ibid.

[85] F. Paulsen, *German Education Past and Present* (London: 1908), p. 54. Quoted in T.G. Cook, *The History of Education in Europe* (London: Methuen & Co. Ltd., 1974), p. 24.

[86] Luther, "Letter to Mayors and Aldermen . . . in Behalf of Christian Schools," quoted in Painter, pp. 170-171.

[87] William Boyd and Edmund J. King, *The History of Western Education* (London: Adam and Charles Black, 1921), p. 188.

[88] Ernst Christian Helmreich, *Religious Education in German Schools* (Cambridge, Mass.: Harvard University Press, 1959), p. 13.

[89] Durant, *The Reformation*, p. 786.

[90] Luther, "Letter to Mayors and Aldermen . . . About Christian Schools," Dau, p. 6.

[91] Kittelson, p. 105.

[92] Gerald Strauss, *Luther's House of Learning* (Baltimore: The Johns Hopkins University Press, 1978), p. 4.

[93] Eby, *Early Protestant Educators,* p. 18.

[94] Note: It is tragic that during the second world war very few pastors of the German Lutheran churches spoke out against Hitler's mass killing of millions of Serbs, Croats, and Jews. Since then, the German people have publicly apologized for this grievous sin. Luther would have grieved even more.

[95] Painter, p. 136.

[96] Eby, *The Development of Modern Education,* p. 71.

[97] Strauss, p. 10. Strauss cites Luther's Letter to Elector Johann of Saxony of May 30, 1530, WA, Br, 5, no. 1572, and WA, 30-32: 582-585.

[98] Ellwood P. Cubberley, *The History of Education* (Boston: Houghton Mifflin Company, 1920), p. 316.

[99] Painter, *A History of Education*, p. 166.

[100] James E. Reed and Ronnie Prevost, *A History of Christian Education* (Nashville: Broadman and Holman Publishers, 1993), p. 194.

[101] Ibid.

[102] Cubberley, *The History of Education,* p. 315.

[103] Strauss, p. 7.

[104] Cubberley, *The History of Education,* p. 316.

[105] Strauss, p. 4.

[106] Painter, *Luther on Education*, pp. 140-141.

[107] Strauss, p. 4.

[108] Ibid., p. 26.

[109] Ibid., p. 27.

[110] Luther, "Sermon on the Duty of Sending Children to School," quoted in Painter, *Luther on Education,* pp. 269-270.

[111] Ibid., p. 202.

[112] Luther, "To the Christian Nobility of the German Nation on Improvement of the Christian Estate," quoted in Helmreich, p. 13.

[113] Durant, *The Reformation*, p. 787.

[114] Strauss, p. 20.

[115] Ibid.

[116] Luther, "Sermon on the Duty of Sending Children to School," quoted in Painter, *Luther on Education,* pp. 265-266.

[117] Ibid., p. 264.

[118] Gary Brady, *A Few Luther Anecdotes* (London: The Evangelical Library Bulletin, 1996), pp. 16-17.

[119] Lindsay, p. 308. Lindsay's note: *The Passional Christi et Antichristi* has been reproduced in facsimile by W. Scherer (Berlin, 1885).

[120] Eby, *The Development of Modern Education,* p. 63.

[121] Luther, "Sermon on the Duty of Sending Children to School," quoted in Painter, *Luther on Education,* p. 264.

[122] Kenneth Scott Latourette, *A History of Christianity,* vol. 1 (New York: Harper and Row, Publishers, 1953), p. 457.

[123] James Atkinson, "Reform," *Introduction to the History of Christianity,* Tim Dowley, ed. (Minneapolis: Fortress Press, 1995), p. 372.

[124] Loraine Boettner, *Roman Catholicism* (Philadelphia: The Presbyterian and Reformed Publishing Co., 1962), p. 97.

[125] Andrew Miller, *Miller's Church History,* vol. II (London: Pickering and Inglis, 1924), p. 516.

Illustration Sources

Figure 1   *Theses* - Permission granted — Lutherhalle at Wittenberg, Germany.

Figure 2   *Luther* - Helen Pierson, *History of Germany* (New York: George Routledge and sons, 1884, p. 129

Figure 3   *Wittenberg door* - Photo by author (PBA).

Figure 4   *Gutenberg* - Museum of Gutenberg, Mainz, Germany.

Figure 5   *Printing press* - Frederick Eby, The Development of Modern Education - Second Edition - (New York: Prentice Hall, Inc. 1934) p. 17.

Figure 6   *Map* - Global Mapping International, Colorado Springs, CO.

Figure 7   *Memorial* - (PBA).

Figure 8   *Memorial* - (PBA).

Figure 9   *Luther's Desk* - Permission granted - Lutherhalle at Wittenberg, Germany.

Figure 10 Melanchthon - Ellwood P. Cubberley, Readings in the History of Education (Boston: Houghton Mifflin Company, 1920) p. 247.

What Luther Believed About Education

Martin Luther wrote more about education than any other reformer. Therefore, it is important to study his writings and analyze the impact of his ideas on the Great Reformation and their relevance for Christian school educators today.

In its simplest terms, the Great Reformation was a return to biblical authority. Luther himself claimed that it was the power of the Scriptures that brought about the Reformation. In his Sunday morning sermon on March 9, 1522, at the Town Church in Wittenberg, with reference to the Reformation Luther said that "the Word so greatly weakened the papacy that no prince or emperor ever inflicted such losses upon it. I did nothing; the Word did everything."[1] The authority of the Scriptures became the central theme of the Reformation. As Durant says, "The Bible was accepted by

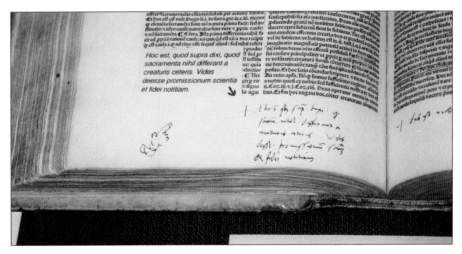

Figure 1. This is Luther's personal Bible at the Lutherhause Bibliotheca (Library) Academica in Wittenberg. The man's hand was drawn by Luther. His note in Latin reads in part: "...This is what I have said before that (the) sacraments are not different from the rest of (the) created things." The Wittenberg Bible in Luther's German translation was completed in 1534.

Figure 2. The Wittenberg Town Church where Luther often preached. Both Luther and Melanchthon are buried in the nearby Palace Church—the church of the famous "Wittenberg door."

nearly all Europe as the infallible Word of God."[2] This dramatic shift from papal authority to biblical authority affected every segment of society, including education. Luther was committed to education reform, viewing it as second only to church reform.

This chapter will explore in some detail Luther's strong beliefs about education, under three divisions:

1. *How Luther's Educational Background Influenced His Views on Education*
2. *Luther's Ideas on Education*
3. *Lessons from Luther's Shortcomings*

There is no question that Luther's home environment, his personal reading of the Scriptures, and his educational training shaped his views as a theologian and as an education reformer.

1. How Luther's Educational Background Influenced His Views on Education

Luther was born November 10, 1483, in Eisleben, not far from Wittenberg, in northern Germany. He was the first of seven children born to Hans and Grethe Luther. Numerous historians hint at the possibility that Luther's father, Hans, was a Hussite. Whether that was true or not, there is little doubt that the atmosphere of the Luther household was a pious one. Painter says, "His home training was exceedingly strict in its austere piety."[3] It is noteworthy, as Lindsay states, that young Martin was "a dreamy, contemplative child; and the unseen world was never out of his thoughts."[4]

LUTHER'S ELEMENTARY YEARS
Luther's first school experience was in a strict Catholic Latin school in Mansfield where he "endured the cruelties of a merciless pedagogue."[5] Like

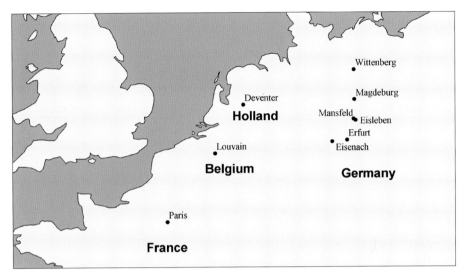

Figure 3. Luther Map

the ancient Augustine, Luther would later complain about the cruel floggings inflicted on him by his early schoolmasters. Durant describes the curriculum of the pre-Reformation Catholic schools:

They stressed basic prayers, reading, writing, arithmetic, singing and flogging. Even in secondary schools flogging was the staff of instruction.[6]

Martin was flogged fifteen times in one day for misdeclining a noun.[7]

From his earliest years in school, it is clear that Martin Luther was "a diligent and apt pupil."[8] Melanchthon, writing about Luther's education, said, "he . . . manifested a keen power of intellect, and was, above all, gifted for eloquence."[9]

LUTHER'S SECONDARY EDUCATION

There is no question that the persona of the teachers, and what they teach both directly and indirectly, impacts the lives of their students. This biblical principle (see Luke 6:40) is illustrated by the fact that three of the great sixteenth-century education reformers—Desiderous Erasmus, Johannes Sturm, and Martin Luther—all attended schools sponsored by, or influenced by, Brethren of the Common Life. The Brethren of the Common Life, sometimes referred to as the Brethren of the Common Lot, or simply "The Brethren," was a conservative Catholic group that leaned toward pietistic theology and championed the causes of common people. For nearly two centuries "The

Brethren" established or loosely controlled hundreds of elementary and secondary schools throughout Holland and Germany.[10]

Gerard Groote, the founder of the group, was from a family of respected burghers in Deventer, Holland (now Belgium). He held a master's degree from the University of Paris[11] and was widely known as a speaker. He gave two- and three-hour sermons twice every day. He soon became a source of irritation to Catholic authorities, however, and was barred from preaching because he spoke out against the vices of the Catholic clergy. He also distributed portions of the Bible that had been translated into the Dutch language.[12] This was a dangerous pattern, of course, given the fact the Catholic Church had issued a strict ban on Bible reading by the laity at the Council at Valencia, Spain, in 1229.[13] This ban remained in force well beyond the Reformation as was painfully demonstrated at Louvain, Belgium, in 1543 with the public execution of a Flemish couple whose sole crime was reading the Scriptures.[14]

Gerard Groote died in one of Europe's many plagues during the formative years of the Brethren of the Common Life schools, but his followers dutifully continued to practice his ideas on education. Julia Henkel describes the educational goals of Brethren of the Common Life Schools:

> The Brethren schools, whose policies and practices were firmly grounded in Groote's ideas, sought to make their pupils, above all else, good Christians, disciples whose primary desire was to imitate Christ and His apostles. Having a religious goal in education was not a new thing, but such a goal had usually been limited to the education of the clergy. The Brethren's concept of educating the common man, and of giving him a religious education at that, was unique. The burden of their teaching (and preaching) was more purity, more charity, more tolerance, more enlightenment, and more respect for human faculties. Their concern for the common man was behind their use of the vernacular—even to the point of translating parts of the Bible into Dutch, a move that was attacked by many in the Roman church. But the Brethren, despite their mystical orientation, did not limit their educational goals to the central religious one; they were also concerned about the intellectual, physical, and social lives of their pupils.[15]

The Brethren of the Common Life schools all but disappeared in the mid-seventeenth century, but many of their ideals were adopted by Luther, Sturm, Calvin, Knox, and later the Puritans who established Christian schools in America.[16] Some of their educational ideals and ideas were as follows:

1. Brethren of the Common Life teachers believed that "learning without piety was rather a curse than a blessing."[17]
2. "Brethren" teachers went beyond the typical religious instruction of the cathedral, monastic, and parish Catholic schools, which was generally limited to "an elaboration of the Lord's Prayer, the Apostle's Creed, and the Ten Commandments."[18] The religious instruction in the Brethren of the Common Life schools was noticeably more extensive. George Durance points out that, "the Brethren hoped that through direct exposure to the Scripture the students would grow"[19] and learn "to love and fear God, to search the Scriptures, and to lead virtuous lives."[20] This pattern of exposing students to the Scriptures in the vernacular was, to say the least, living on the edge of Catholic law.
3. Brethren teachers also practiced biblical integration. Durance says, "The Brethren . . . sought to weave religious education throughout the curriculum in such a way that each subject such as mathematics or geography was taught in a 'Christ-centered' manner."[21] This represented a major innovation that Christian school educators practice to this day.
4. Brethren teachers were committed to a higher level of academic excellence and to textbook reform. Durance said, "Several of the Brethren wrote new textbooks in order to improve the academic quality of school books."[22] He then cited Erasmus, who said that their purpose was to introduce "something of a higher standard"[23] into the schools.
5. Julia Henkel, in her doctoral dissertation, "An Historical Study of the Educational Contributions of the Brethren of the Common Life," found the following curricular innovations, which were revolutionary at the time: (a) student research projects and class reports; (b) story-telling sessions; (c) question-and-answer sessions; (d) visual aids; (e) plays with moral principles, and (f) grade-level divisions.[24]

The numerous philosophical and academic innovations introduced by the Brethren of the Common Life schools will become apparent in the learning styles later advocated by Martin Luther and the other education reformers whose lives were impacted by the Brethren teachers.

Luther was enrolled in the Brethren of the Common Life School in Magdeburg, Germany,[25] at age fourteen. It is not known why he later transferred to the School of St. George in Eisenach. It is known that "he had relatives there."[26] He studied three years at the School of St. George and earned his board, room, and tuition by singing and begging in the streets.[27] Luther recounted this experience in his famous "Sermon on the Duty of Sending Children to School," "Do not despise the boys," he says, "who beg from door to door 'a little bread for the love of God.' . . . I have, myself, been such a beggar pupil, and have eaten bread before houses, especially in the dear town of Eisenach."[28] The curriculum at the School of St. George included advanced courses in Latin grammar, composition, rhetoric, and poetry, "in which he easily outdistanced his fellow pupils."[29]

LUTHER AT THE UNIVERSITY OF ERFURT

In the meantime, in the mining town of Mansfield, Luther's father had become one of four members of the village council and had advanced economically as the operator of three smelting furnaces. This turn of events made it possible for Martin, in 1501 at age eighteen, to enroll in the University of Erfurt, "then the most famous in Germany."[30] Like all the pre-Reformation institutions of higher learning, it was solidly Catholic. Lindsay notes,

> The University of Erfurt was strictly allied to the Church. Different Popes had enriched it with privileges; the Primate of Germany, the Archbishop of Mainz, was its Chancellor; many of its professors held ecclesiastical prebends, or were monks; each faculty was under the protection of a tutelary saint; the teachers had to swear to teach nothing opposed to the doctrines of the Roman Church; and special pains were taken to prevent the rise and spread of heresy.[31]

In the brief span of four years Martin Luther, the miner's son from Mansfield, would graduate second in his class with a master's degree in scholastic philosophy.[32] Although the University of Erfurt, like all Catholic universities, was steeped in humanism and the teachings of Aristotle—"the father of scientific investigation"[33]—Luther developed a profound dislike for humanism and regarded Aristotle as a "blind heathen teacher."[34]

Scottish historian Thomas Lindsay, who provides the best account of Luther's university years, writes:

> The scanty accounts of Luther's student days show that he was a hardworking, bright, sociable youth, and musical to the core. His companions called him "the Philosopher," "the Musician," and spoke of his lute-playing, of his singing, and of his ready power in debate. He took his various degrees in unusually short time. He was Bachelor in 1502, and Master in 1505.[35]

Figure 4. There are numberous memorials to Luther throughout Germany. This memorial in Worms, The Lutherplatz, is the most elaborate. Luther, the central statue, is surrounded by his fellow reformers including such forerunners as John Wycliffe and John Huss.

But as Lindsay says,

He was never a member of the Humanist circle; he was too much in earnest about religious questions, and of too practical a turn of mind.[36]

Later in his life Luther said that his greatest discovery at the University of Erfurt was "the accidental finding of a copy of the Bible, the first complete Bible he had ever seen."[37]

MONASTERY

After graduation from the university, life took an unexpected turn for Martin Luther. In 1505, terrified by a summer lightning storm that struck him to the ground, and saddened by the recent death of two of his university classmates, Luther began to think deeply about his spiritual life. His response was to join an Augustinian monastery in Erfurt in an attempt to quell his inner anxiety.[38] When Luther requested a copy of the Bible, he was told by his superior in the monastery that "reading the Bible simply breeds unrest."[39] Although he was ordained a priest in 1507, his anguish of soul continued. He fasted. He whipped himself, but to no avail. Finally, John Staupitz, the local vicar-general of Erfurt, on his visits to the monastery observed Luther's distress. He "revoked Nathin's (Luther's superior) order that Luther should not read the Scriptures."[40] He gave him a Bible and a commentary, and encouraged him to read.

Peace of soul came to Luther when he read Roman's 1:17 and realized that "the just shall live by faith."[41]

In 1508 Luther was assigned to the small university at Wittenberg as the "Chair of Philosophy."[42] In 1512 he earned a doctoral degree in theology from Wittenberg University, but his graduate studies took him back to Erfurt University for three semesters.[43] Upon receiving his doctorate, he was made a full professor of theology, the senior position at the university.

This review of Luther's rather extensive educational background will help us better understand his ideas on education, which in many ways were revolutionary for the time. As mentioned before, Martin Luther was Bible-centered about everything, including education. His ideas sprang from biblical authority—the hallmark of the Reformation.

2. Luther's Ideas on Education

No reformer in history has faced a greater challenge than Luther in his quest to transform the schools of Germany at every level. On the other hand, few people in history were as spiritually and academically prepared for the enormous task before him.

LUTHER'S TRANSFORMATION OF THE UNIVERSITIES

We begin with Luther's perception of Germany's system of higher education—a system well known to him. Luther gets quickly to the point with these colorful words:

> Heretofore what did a person learn in the universities and monasteries but to become a dunce, a dolt, and a blockhead? A person would study twenty, yea, forty years, and yet know neither Latin nor German. The scandalous vicious life by which our precious youth were miserably corrupted, I shall not mention.

> True, rather than have the universities and monasteries remain what they have been heretofore, so that our young people would have no other mode of instruction and life, I should wish that no boy would learn anything and be a mute. For, it is my serious opinion, prayer, and desire that these hog-pens and Satan's schools be either sunk into the abyss or changed into Christian schools.[44]

Luther denounces the Catholic universities of his day as "dens of murderers," "Temples of Moloch," and "synagogues of corruption," and says "they are only worthy of being reduced to dust."[45] In his letter of 1520 "To the Christian Nobility of the German Nation on Improvement of the Christian Estate," Luther said:

> What are the universities, as at present ordered . . . [but] schools of Greek fashion and heathenish manners, full of dissolute living, where very little is taught of the Holy Scriptures and of the Christian faith, and the blind heathen teacher, Aristotle, rules even further than Christ. Now my advice would be that the books of Aristotle, the 'Physics,' the 'Metaphysics,' 'Of the Soul,' and 'Ethics,' which have hitherto been considered the best, be altogether abolished, with all others that profess to treat of nature, though nothing can be learned from them, either of natural or spiritual things. Besides, no one has been able to understand his meaning, and much time has been wasted, and many vexed with much useless labor, study, and expense.[46]

As Martin Luther assumed more and more of the leadership role at the university in Wittenberg, it is not surprising that a dramatic philosophical shift took place in the curriculum and the faculty. The amazing result was an equally dramatic increase in enrollment. The student enrollment at Wittenberg University in 1513 was approximately 400.[47] As Luther's reforms flowered and flourished, the school grew to 2,000 students[48] and quickly became the most popular university in Germany.

Figure 5. A Pre-Reformation school (after an illuminated engraving in Brulefer's Bonaventure sententiar, *printed at Venice in 1504).*

Basing his work on his Bible-centered philosophy, Luther set about to establish a Bible-centered curriculum. Gritsch says:

> By 1517, he had persuaded most of the faculty, particularly Dean Karlstadt, to reform the curriculum along the lines he advocated. Luther successfully used the academic debates—designed to examine students and advance scholarly positions—to draw radical distinctions between what he called a "theology of the cross" centered in Christ, and a "theology of glory" grounded in the notion of human cooperation with divine grace. By 1521, Augustine had supplanted Aristotle at Wittenberg University, and the biblical languages of Hebrew and Greek were taught along with Latin. Aristotelian logic and physics now took a back seat, soon to be abolished altogether. . . . Matthias Goldhahn

was assigned to teach Hebrew and Philip Melanchthon, called at Luther's urging to teach Greek in 1518, was soon one of the most popular teachers as well as, at age 21, one of the youngest. Luther had put together a successful team to teach the new curriculum.[49]

Kittelson adds:

Aristotle's dialectic, the disputations, and canon law were removed from the curriculum and their place taken by rhetoric, grammar, the ancient languages, and, above all, the Bible.[50]

Thankfully, as mentioned earlier, the curricular reforms at Wittenberg University spread rapidly to other universities in Germany and to the Western world.

Luther's reforms did not end at the university level. As Kittelson says, "Suddenly, it became apparent to Luther and his colleagues that preaching at the Castle Church in Wittenberg or lecturing at the university would not accomplish the reform."[51] Luther set out on a bold plan to reform all levels of education.

LUTHER AND ELEMENTARY EDUCATION

Like the true Christian school educator he was, Luther believed that the Bible must have the central place in a school's curriculum. This is not to suggest that Luther believed in a narrowly focused curriculum. On the contrary, Luther advocated a much broader curriculum than had been utilized in the Catholic schools of the Middle Ages. He was committed, however, to the idea that books, other than the Bible, "should be read only for a time so that through them we may be led into the Scriptures."[52] To Luther, everything must point to the truth of the Scriptures. It was for that reason that Luther advocated the use of the ancient fables of Aesop in the school curriculum because their common sense moral messages often correspond to biblical precepts. Luther personally translated Aesop's fables into high German and regarded them "next to Scripture in importance"[53] in the elementary curriculum.

ELEMENTARY EDUCATION FOR EVERYONE

Luther broke the educational mold when he promoted the concept of a basic education for everyone. His principal objectives were to advance literacy so that everyone could read the Scriptures and be useful to themselves and to society. In his appeal for mayors and aldermen to establish Christian schools, Luther wrote:

Even if there were no soul and men did not need schools and the languages for the sake of Christianity and the Scriptures, still for the establishment of the best schools everywhere, both for boys and girls, this consideration is of itself sufficient, namely, that society, for the maintenance of civil order and the proper regulation of the household, needs accomplished and well-trained men and women. Now such men are to come from boys, and such women from girls; hence it is necessary that boys and girls be properly taught and brought up.[54]

Although Luther was not "politically correct" by today's standards, he was light-years ahead of his predecessors in his emphasis on schools for girls. He did, however, suggest that secondary schools were primarily for boys. We see in Luther's letter to the mayors and aldermen another important gender innovation, that of women teachers. We are also provided insight into Luther's broad view of curriculum:

But were they instructed in schools or elsewhere by thoroughly qualified male or female teachers, who taught the languages, other arts, and history, then the pupils would hear the history and maxims of the world, and see how things went with each city, kingdom, prince, man, and woman; and thus, in a short time, they would be able to comprehend, as in a mirror, the character, life, counsels, undertakings, successes, and failures, of the whole world from the beginning. From this knowledge they could regulate their views, and order their course of life in the fear of God, having become wise in judging what is to be sought and what avoided in this outward life, and capable of advising and directing others.[55]

A VERY SHORT SCHOOL DAY

Because the parents of Luther's day were prone to ignore their children's education altogether, he advocated a one- or two-hour school day. In his letter to mayors and aldermen on behalf of Christian schools, Luther wrote:

My idea is that boys should spend an hour or two a day in school, and the rest of the time work at home, learn some trade and do whatever is desired, so that study and work may go on together, while the children are young and can attend to both. They now spend tenfold as much time in shooting with cross-bows, playing ball, running, and tumbling about.

In like manner, a girl has time to go to school an hour a day, and yet attend to her work at home; for she sleeps, dances, and plays away more than that. The real difficulty is found alone in the absence of an earnest desire to educate the young, and to aid and benefit mankind with accomplished citizens. The devil much prefers blockheads and drones, that men may have more abundant trials and sorrows in the world.[56]

MUSIC

Luther, himself an accomplished musician and hymn-writer, believed the school curriculum was not complete without music, and he said:

> I have always loved music. He who knows this art is in the right frame, and fitted for every good pursuit. We can not do without music in our schools. A schoolmaster must know how to sing, or I would not allow him to teach. Nor ought we to ordain young theologians to the sacred office, unless they have first been well-tried and practiced in the art in the school.

> Music is a fair, glorious gift of God; and it lies very near to theology. I would not part with my small faculty of music for vast possessions. We should practice the young continually in this art, for it will make able and polished men of them.[57]

DISCIPLINE

Perhaps because of his own experience of being "flogged fifteen times in one day for misdeclining a noun,"[58] Luther was opposed to the ancient tradition of flogging as a means of school discipline. In 1523, Luther wrote:

> It is impossible that a disciple, or a scholar, can love the teacher who is harsh and severe; for, how can he prevail on himself to love one who immures him . . . ? Nevertheless, the child needs the discipline of the rod; but must be tempered with admonition, and directed to his improvement; for, without this, he will never come to any good, but will be ruined, soul and body. . . . A miserable teacher, indeed, would that man be, who should only know how to beat and torment his scholars, without ever being able to teach them any thing. Such schoolmasters there have been, whose schools were nothing but so many dungeons and hells, and themselves tyrants and gaolers; where the poor children were beaten beyond endurance and without cessation, and applied themselves to their task laboriously and with overpushed diligence, but yet with very small profit. . . . A well-informed and faithful teacher, on the other hand, mingles gentle admonition with punishment, and incites his pupils to diligence in their studies, and to a laudable emulation among themselves; and so they become rooted and grounded in all kinds of desirable knowledge, as well as in the proprieties and the virtues of life, and they now do that spontaneously and with delight, which formerly, and under the old discipline, they approached with reluctance and dread.[59]

CATECHISMS

Luther wrote two catechisms for school children, a "shorter catechism" for elementary students and a "larger catechism" for secondary students and for "ignorant adults."[60] Catechisms, of course, were not new. The early Christians used them to educate the great influx of new converts,[61] which were coming to them by the thousands for baptism—most of whom were pagans. The Catholic Church had used them extensively in their clergy preparatory schools.

There were at least two reasons why Luther wrote catechisms: first, his visits to the churches and schools in 1527 and 1528 revealed an alarming ignorance of basic evangelical doctrine; and second, the churches were losing converts to the growing Anabaptist movement, whose ideas Luther regarded as heretical. Eby explains:

> Luther composed the catechisms for the purpose of making them the textbooks for the instruction of all children and ignorant adults. In his great enthusiasm for the Scriptures during his earlier years he wished the Bible to be the only book used. . . . the teachings of the Anabaptists made him distrustful of the free use of the Scriptures by the common people. Under this conviction he threw all emphasis upon the teaching of the catechism.[62]

Luther's catechisms, especially the shorter catechism, was immediately popular, not only in Germany but throughout the Western world. By the end of the sixteenth century the shorter catechism had been translated into seventeen languages.[63] Helmreich says:

> The catechism was central to Luther's plan of elementary education, since faith was the first principle of a moral life. For all his emphasis on learning and languages, on understanding of the Bible and individual responsibility to God, faith in "the redemption of the world by our Lord Jesus Christ" was the rock on which he built. This faith, then, must be presented to the child at the earliest possible moment, and made an integral part of his educational experience.[64]

The shorter catechism centered on the Lord's Prayer, the Ten Commandments, and the Creed (a statement of faith). A sample of the "Ten Commandment" questions and answers are as follows:

The First Commandment

Thou shalt have none other gods but me.

What does that mean?

Answer. We are to fear, love, and trust God above all things.

The Second Commandment

Thou shalt not take the name of the Lord thy God in vain.

What does that mean?

Answer. We are to fear and love God, so that we use not His name in cursing, swearing, witchcraft, lying, or deceiving, but in all our necessities call upon it, with prayer, praise, and thanks.

The Third Commandment

Remember that thou keep holy the Sabbath day.

What does that mean?

Answer. We are to fear and love God, that we despise not preaching nor His Word, but keep that Word holy, and gladly hear it and learn it.[65]

The catechisms were to be taught not only at school but also at home and at church. The following are Luther's instructions to pastors in teaching the catechisms to children and adults:

When those whom you are instructing have become familiar with the words of the text, then teach them to understand the meaning of those words, so that they may become acquainted with the object and purport of the lesson. . . . Allow ample time for the lessons. For it is not necessary that you should, on the same occasion, proceed from the beginning to the end of the several parts; it will be more profitable if you present them separately, in regular succession. When the people have, for instance, at length correctly understood the First Commandment, you may proceed to the Second, and so continue. By neglecting to observe this mode the people will be overburdened, and be prevented from understanding and retaining in memory any considerable part of the matter communicated to them.[66]

In teaching the catechism Luther would have agreed with the pedagogical principle espoused by fellow German educator, Wolfgang Ratichius (1571–1635), who said, "Teach only one thing at a time, and often repeat the same thing."[67] In his teaching instructions to parents, Luther wrote:

Not simply that they may learn and repeat the words by heart, as has hitherto been the case, but let them be questioned from article to article, and show what each signifies and how they understand it. If everything can not be asked at one time, take one article to-day, and another to-morrow. For when parents or guardians will not take the

trouble through themselves or others, there no catechetical instruction can ever be successful.[68]

Luther's educational objective in writing the shorter and larger catechisms was to simplify the truths of the Bible and adapt them to the understanding of children and young people. Luther said that he felt so strongly about the catechisms that he would be willing to have all his books perish except for them and his essay on "Unfree Will."[69]

LUTHER ON SECONDARY EDUCATION

The maxim that "we teach the way we were taught" holds true in our study of Luther's views on secondary education. Among his ideas on educational reform, we see shades of Luther's childhood experiences in the city Latin school in Mansfield, in the Brethren of the Common Life School in Magdeburg, and in the St. George School in Eisenach. Luther's solid understanding of biblical principles and his own common sense helped him to ferret out the good from the

Figure 6. A Luther memorial on the Wittenberg town square or "market place."

bad in his educational experience and forge a system of academic reform that was unprecedented in human history.

Britain's famous conservative prime minister Benjamin Disraeli (1804–1881) said, "If you would converse with me define your terms." This becomes necessary in understanding the levels of education in the sixteenth century. For example, when Luther speaks of "primary schools," he means, in today's terminology, "secondary schools." While Luther was light-years ahead of the Catholic educators of the Middle Ages, that he was not "politically correct" by today's standards becomes quickly apparent in the following excerpt from a letter he wrote to the Margrove George of Brandenberg, in which he suggested:

> It is well that in all towns and villages good primary schools should be established out of which could be picked and chosen those who are more fit for the universities, out of which the men can then be taken who are to serve your land and people.[70]

In Luther's mind, secondary education and the world of civic and religious leadership were the domain of gifted members of the male population—a societal pattern destined not to change appreciably until the twentieth century.

LANGUAGE STUDY

At the center of Luther's Reformation emphasis was that the Bible should be distributed everywhere in the vernacular of the people. However, when it came to the education of children and young people, it is interesting that he insisted their education be given in Latin. Nearly one-third of Luther's long letter to the mayors and aldermen has to do with his commitment to education that includes Latin. At the secondary level, in addition to Latin, he insisted on Hebrew and Greek. The teaching of three languages may seem idealistic, but one must understand his perspective, which he explained well:

> And let this be kept in mind, that we will not preserve the Gospel without the languages. The languages are the scabbard in which the Word of God is sheathed.
>
> For God had a purpose in giving the Scriptures only in two languages, the Old Testament in the Hebrew, and the New Testament in the Greek. What God did not despise, but chose before all others for His Word, we should likewise esteem above all others.
>
> Therefore it is evident that where the languages are not preserved, there the Gospel will become corrupted. Experience shows this to be true. For immediately after the age of the apostles, when the languages ceased to be cultivated, the Gospel, and the true faith, and Christianity itself, declined more and more, until they were entirely lost under the Pope.
>
> ... it is our evident duty earnestly to cultivate the languages, now that God has restored them to the world through the revival of learning.[71]

For nearly a thousand years the Catholic Church had attempted to reduce the languages of the Western world to Latin, the language of the old Roman Empire. It was another means of controlling their world. Luther advocated Latin for education because it was the universal language of the educated world. Luther was committed to Hebrew and Greek for secondary students because he wanted to protect the integrity of the Gospel. In addition to pastors knowing the ancient languages, he wanted physicians, lawyers, judges, teachers, clerks, accountants, secretaries, notaries, and civil leaders to have direct access to the Scriptures in their original languages so that the leaders of society would be on an even playing field

Figure 7. A village in Germany, typical of villages where Christian schools and churches were established after the Reformation.

with the clergy and would not be easily led into false doctrine as they had been under Catholicism. Luther wrote:

> For the preacher or teacher may publicly read the whole Bible as he chooses, right or wrong, if there be no one present to judge whether he does it correctly or not. But if one is to judge, there must be an acquaintance with the languages; otherwise, the judging will be in vain. Hence, although faith and the Gospel may be preached by ordinary ministers without the languages still such preaching is sluggish and weak, and the people finally become weary, and fall away. But a knowledge of the languages renders it lively and strong, and faith finds itself constantly renewed through rich and varied instruction. In the first Psalm the Scriptures liken such a study to "a tree planted by the rivers of water, that bringeth forth its fruit in its season; its leaf also shall not wither."[72]

The common people of Luther's day did not share his commitment to Greek, Hebrew, and Latin. Frederick Eby describes the attitude of parents toward Luther's admonition to study the ancient languages:

> What made matters still worse was the attitude of the common people toward the study of the learned languages. Having obtained the Scriptures in German, the people saw no reason why their sons should spend years in the study of the forgotten tongues in which they were originally written.[73]

An exasperated Luther lashed out at parents with these strong words:

> But, you say again, if we shall and must have schools, what is the use to teach Latin, Greek, Hebrew, and the other liberal arts? Is it not enough to teach the Scriptures, which are necessary to salvation, in the mother tongue? To which I answer: I know, alas! that we Germans must always remain irrational brutes, as we are deservedly called by surrounding nations.[74]

As to the worth of languages, Luther's own testimony was, "I should have failed in my work, if the languages had not come to my aid, and made me strong and immovable in the Scriptures."[75]

HISTORY AND HISTORIANS

Luther was not married when he wrote his famous letter to the mayors and aldermen on behalf of Christian schools. He and the former nun, Catherine Von Bora (Katy), were married later when Luther was forty-two. In his letter he wrote:

> As for myself, if I had children and were able, I would have them learn not only the languages and history, but also singing, instrumental music, and the whole course of mathematics. For what is all this but mere child's play, in which the Greeks in former ages trained their children, and by this means became wonderfully skillful people, capable for every undertaking? How I regret that I did not read more poetry and history, and that no one taught me in these branches. Instead of these I was obliged with great cost, labor, and injury, to read Satanic filth, the Aristotelian and Scholastic philosophy, so that I have enough to do to get rid of it.[76]

Luther believed that history should be taught at both the elementary and secondary levels. He held history and historians in high regard:

> Therefore historians are most useful people and most excellent teachers, whom we can never sufficiently honor, praise, and thank, and it should be a care of our great lords, as emperors and kings, to have histories of their times written and preserved in libraries, and they should spare no expense to procure persons capable of teaching. . . . But it requires a superior man to write history, a man with a lion-heart, who dares without fear to speak the truth.[77]

GYMNASTICS AND MUSIC

Luther was not the first to advocate gymnastics (sports) and music as basic to school curriculum. In ancient Athens students typically attended three different schools at three different locations. The first school of the day was, "The Letters School," the second was, "The Music School," and the third was, "The Gymnastic School," or "Palaestra."[78] Luther acknowledged his debt to the "ancients" with these words:

> It was well considered and arranged by the ancients that the people should practice gymnastics, in order that they might not fall into revelling, unchastity, gluttony, intemperance, and gaming. Therefore these two exercises and pastimes please me best, namely, music and

Figure 8. A flowering tree in the courtyard of Luther's home is a likely symbol of Luther's commitment to teach natural sciences by direct study and observation of God's creation.

gymnastics, of which the first drives away all care and melancholy from the heart, and the latter produces elasticity of the body and preserves the health. But a great reason for their practice is that people may not fall into gluttony, licentiousness, and gambling, as is the case, alas! at courts and in cities. Thus it goes when such honorable and manly bodily exercises are neglected.[79]

NATURAL SCIENCE

One of Luther's more significant educational innovations was his admonition to teach the natural sciences by direct study and observation of God's creation. We will forgive Luther for believing the sun revolved around the earth. He said, "I believe the Holy Scripture, for Joshua commanded the sun to stand still, not the earth" (Joshua 10:12).[80] It was a "giant leap" for people of Luther's day to believe in the heliocentric theory set forth by the Polish astronomer Nicolas Copernicus (1473–1543) that, "In the middle of all sits the sun on his throne, as upon a royal dais ruling his children, the planets, which circle about him."[81]

That issue aside, Luther "broke the mold" in natural science studies with these words, which include a mild insult to his friend Erasmus:

We are at the dawn of a new era, for we are beginning to recover the knowledge of the external world that we had lost through the fall of

Adam. We now observe creatures properly, and not as formerly under the Papacy. Erasmus is indifferent, and does not care to know how fruit is developed from the germ. But by the grace of God we already recognize in the most delicate flower the wonders of divine goodness and omnipotence. We see in His creatures the power of His word. He commanded, and the thing stood fast. See that force display itself in the stone of a peach. It is very hard, and the germ it encloses is very tender; but, when the moment has come, the stone must open to let out the young plant that God calls into life. Erasmus passes by all that, takes no account of it, and looks upon external objects as cows look upon a new gate.[82]

LIBRARIES

Near the end of his long letter to mayors and aldermen about Christian schools, Luther set forth his appeal for the establishment of libraries. He wrote:

Finally, this must be taken into consideration by all who earnestly desire to see such schools established and the languages preserved in the German states: that no cost nor pains should be spared to procure good libraries in suitable buildings, especially in the large cities, which are able to afford it. For if a knowledge of the Gospel and of every kind of learning is to be preserved, it must be embodied in books, as the prophets and apostles did, as I have already shown. This should be done, not only that our spiritual and civil leaders may have something to read and study, but also that good books may not be lost, and that the arts and languages may be preserved. . . .[83]

Later in the same letter Luther was more specific about the criteria for selecting books. He began with a negative statement about libraries established by Catholic monks:

No books have been accessible but the senseless trash of the monks and sophists. How could the pupils and teachers differ from the books they studied? A jackdaw does not hatch a dove, nor a fool make a man wise. That is the recompense of our ingratitude, in that we did not use diligence in the formation of libraries, but allowed good books to perish, and bad ones to survive.

But my advice is, not to collect all sorts of books indiscriminately, thinking only of getting a vast number together. I would have discrimination used, because it is not necessary to collect the commentaries of all the jurists, the productions of all the theologians, the discussions of all the philosophers, and the sermons of all the monks. Such trash I would reject altogether, and provide my library only with useful books; and in making the selection, I would advise with learned men.[84]

3. Lessons from Luther's Shortcomings

Philip Melanchthon, Martin Luther's friend and able associate, said, "Without knowledge of history, human life is, in a way, nothing but a perpetual childhood."[85] Melanchthon, who was an avid student of Greek and Roman literature, might well have gleaned this thought from Rome's greatest philosopher, Cicero, who said, as noted earlier, "Not to know what took place before you were born is to remain forever a child."[86]

The study of human history provides valuable lessons, both good and bad. There is little doubt that Martin Luther was God's man to change the course of human history. As Painter says, "In education as in religion, Luther showed himself great, a seer in advance of his age, the founder of a new and higher culture."[87] Speaking of Luther, Benson says, "His life kindles admiration.[88] However, great as he was, Luther had his shortcomings, and there are valuable lessons to be learned from his shortcomings as well as from his monumental achievements. His shortcomings appeared mostly in his latter years. Durant says, "Luther should never have grown old."[89]

Luther seemed at his best when the battle was "white hot." In the early years of the Reformation, he always faced an enemy, be it the papacy, the Roman Catholic Church, or the devil himself. He became what some called "a godly fugitive" whose life was in constant danger. He was at the epicenter of the second most important event in history. Luther had flourished well under the pressure of his God-given assignment. In time, however, as the Reformation matured, Luther changed. By 1542, two-thirds of Germany had become Protestant.[90] McGrath says, "In Germany, more than fifty of the sixty-five imperial free cities responded positively to the Reformation, with only five choosing to ignore it altogether."[91] The enemy seemed further removed from Luther, and as the pressure receded, Luther's public statements, rather than mellowing, became increasingly harsh. Luther himself said, "When I am angry I can write, pray, and preach well, for then my whole temperament is quickened, my understanding sharpened."[92] Added to that, Luther's health became a problem. Erwin Lutzer writes:

> In Luther's last days, when the irritability of age and disease took over, he said many things that would have been best left unsaid. Whether it was regarding the papacy or the Anabaptists or the Jews, Luther always spoke in colorful, condemning language.[93]

Figure 9. On the southeast corner of the choir room of the Town Church, the church where Luther preached, is the so called "Jewish pig." This reviling and mocking bit of statuary was placed there by the Catholic authorities during an early attempt to "rid" Germany of the Jewish population around 1304. Regretfully, Luther did not remove this offensive symbol. The present-day Wittenberg community has placed a memorial to the Jews on the pavement below the offensive caricature.

THE JEWS

In the early years of the Reformation, on the Jewish issue, Luther said, "Whoever is anti-Jewish is anti-Christian."[94] In his declining years he referred to the Jews as "venomous," "bitter worms," and "disgusting vermin,"[95] and much more that need not be mentioned. This change was unfortunate. Because of his remarkable influence, Luther might well have turned the tide of history and lessened Germany's legendary hatred of the Jews. Germany's hatred of the Jews dated back to the Catholic crusades and to Bishop Augustine of Hippo, who claimed the entire Jewish race was responsible for Christ's death and therefore the Jewish race should be "cursed by the [Catholic] Church."[96] Rather than complying with Hitler's awful mass annihilation of Germany's Jews, Luther's German Lutheran churches, centuries later, might well have stood up to Hitler had Luther, in his declining years, strongly reaffirmed his earlier statement that "whoever is anti-Jewish is anti-Christian." Understandably, some Lutheran bodies have since publicly denounced Luther for his serious error regarding the Jews.[97]

TEACHER TRAINING

From the standpoint of education, at least one historian has faulted Luther and the other reformers for not giving more energy to establishing teacher training programs for the new evangelical schools. As Benson says:

Had the reformers concerned themselves as much with training teachers as they did with preparing catechisms, universal education for religious purposes would have been attained centuries earlier.[98]

Luther, Calvin, Zwingli, and Knox were all theologians. They were "big picture" reformers who clearly saw that long-term church reform required education reform at all levels—elementary, secondary, and university. And given their limited resources of time, talent, and funds, their achievements in Christian school education are remarkable. On the other hand, their efforts in Bible-centered education would have had more staying power had the teachers and masters of the new evangelical schools been trained more specifically in the philosophy of Christian school education and the art of placing the Scriptures at the center of the curriculum. The lack of professional training was a serious shortcoming of Reformation educators.

We will discover in the next chapter how John Calvin and John Knox, standing on the foundation of Luther's work, gave added momentum to the Great Reformation through both church and school reform.

Endnotes—Chapter Eight

1   Luther, "Eight Sermons at Wittenberg," 1522, LW 51:77, quoted in Eric W. Gritsch, *Academia and Forum: Luther's Reformation in Wittenberg* (Luther Theological Seminary Bulletin, vol. 70, winter, 1990), p. 17. Note: The term "Reformation" was not used at the time of Luther.

2   Will Durant, *The Reformation* (New York: Simon and Schuster, 1957), p. 370.

3   F.V.N. Painter, *A History of Education* (New York: D. Appleton and Company, 1905), p. 154.

4   Thomas M. Lindsay, *A History of the Reformation*, vol. 1 (Edinburgh: T and T Clark, 1906), p. 194.

5   Ibid.

6   Durant, *The Reformation*, p. 235.

7   Ibid., pp. 341–342.

8   Mathesius, *Historien von Martini Lutheri*, Anfang, Lehre, Leben and Sterben (1896). quoted in *Encyclopaedia Britannica*, vol. 14 (Chicago: William Benton, Publisher, 1961), p. 491.

9   J. Köstlin, "Luther, Martin," *Encyclopaedia of Living Divines*, vol. 2 (Toronto: Funk & Wagnals Co., 1891), p. 1363.

10 James E. Reed and Ronnie Prevost, *A History of Christian Education* (Nashville: Broadman and Holman Publishers, 1993), p. 180.

11 George M. Durance, *From Brethren to Humanists* (Master's Thesis, The University of Calgary, 1978), p. 57.

12 Will Durant, *The Reformation* (New York: Simon and Schuster, 1957), p. 128.

13 Loraine Boettner, *Roman Catholicism* (Philadelphia: The Presbyterian and Reformed Publishing Co., 1962), p. 97.

14 Ellwood P. Cubberley, *The History of Education* (Boston: Houghton Mifflin Company, 1920), p. 304. Cubberley's footnote reads: "Very severe measures were enacted to prevent the spread of the contagion of heresy. All Protestant literature was forbidden circulation in Catholic lands. The printing-press, as a disseminator of heresy, was placed under strict license. Certain books were ordered burned. Perhaps the most extreme and ruthless measure was the prohibition, under penalty of death, of the reading of the Bible. That this harsh act was carried out the record of martyrs shows. As one example may be mentioned the sister of the Flemish artist Matsys and her husband, he being decapitated and she buried alive in the square fronting the cathedral at Louvain, in 1543, for having been caught reading the sacred Book."

15 Julia Hinkel, "Geert Groote," quoted in *Towns*, p. 86, and in Kenneth O. Gangel and Warren S. Benson, *Christian Education: Its History and Philosophy* (Chicago: Moody Press, 1983), p. 126.

16 Reed and Prevost, p. 181.

17 Lindsay, pp. 51–52.

18 Durance, p. 43.

19 Ibid.

20 Albert Hyma, *The Christian Renaissance: A History of the Devotio Moderna*, 2nd ed. (Hamden, Conn.: Archon Books, 1965), p. 9, cited by Durance, p. 43.

21 Durance, p. 43. Durance cites Henkel, "Educational Contributions," p. 104, for the hyphenated word, "Christ-centered."

22 Ibid.

23 Erasmus, *Works*, vol. 4, p. 405.

24 Julia Smith Henkel, "An Historical Study of the Educational Contributions of the Brethren of the Common Life" (Ph.D. dissertation, University of Pittsburgh, 1962), pp. 73–144, cited by Durance, p. 44.

25 Lindsay, p. 194.

26 Köstlin, p. 1363.

27 Reed and Prevost, p. 191.

28 Luther, "Sermon on the Duty of Sending Children to School," quoted in Painter, p. 93.

29 *Encyclopaedia Britannica*, vol. 14 (Chicago: William Benton, Publisher, 1961), p. 491.

30 Lindsay, p. 195.

31 Ibid., p. 196.

32 Ibid., p. 197.

33 Samuel G. Kahn, *A Short History of Education* (Jerusalem: Yesodot Publishers, 1962), p. 20.

34 Frederick Eby, *Early Protestant Educators* (New York: McGraw-Hill Book Company, Inc., 1931), p. 35.

35 Lindsay, p. 197.

36 Ibid.

37 Gustav M. Bruce, *Luther as an Educator* (reprint; Minneapolis: Augsburg Press, 1928), p. 71, quoted in Reed and Prevost, p. 191.

38 Cf. Georg Oergel, *Von Jungen Luther* (Erfurt, 1899), pp. 35–41, quoted in Lindsay, p. 197.

39 *The Tischreden* (Preger, Leipzig, 1888), I 27, quoted in Lindsay, p. 200.

40 Lindsay, p. 202.

41 Ibid.

42 Köstlin, p. 1363.

43 Ibid.

44 Luther, "To the Magistrates and Councilmen of All the Cities of Germany in Behalf of the Establishment and Maintenance of Christian Schools," translated by W.H.T. Dau. *Luther, Christian Schools* (Hicklry, N.C.: A. L. Crouse, Printer, 1895) p. 7.

45 Frederick Eby, *The Development of Modern Education* (New York: Prentice-Hall, Inc. 1934) p. 77, Eby cites Johannes Janssen, *History of the German People at the Close of the Middle Ages*, vol. 3 (London: Kegan, Paul, Trench, Tvübner, and Company, 1905), p. 355.

46 Luther, "To the Christian Nobility of the German Nation on Improvement of the Christian Estate," quoted in Painter, p. 144.

47 Eric W. Gritsch, "Academia Forum: Luther's Reformation in Wittenberg," *Luther Theological Seminary Bulletin*, vol. 70, Winter 1990, p. 18.

48 Kenneth Scott Latourette, *Christianity Through the Ages* (New York: Harper and Row, Publishers, 1965), p. 159.

49 Gritsch, p. 19.

50 James M. Kittelson, "Luther the Educational Reformer," *Luther and Learning*, Marilyn J. Harran, ed., The Wittenberg University Symposium (London: Associated University Presses, 1985), p. 98. Kittelson cites Schwiebert, *Luther and His Times*, 293 ff.

51 Ibid., p. 107.

52 Martin Luther, WA 6:461, 4–5; LW 44:205, quoted in James L. Kittelson, "Luther the Educational Reformer," *Luther and Learning* (The Wittenberg University Luther Symposium) Marilyn J. Harran, ed. (London: Associated University Presses Inc., 1985, p. 109.

53 Eby, p. 76.

54 Luther, "Letter to the Mayors and Aldermen of All the Cities of Germany in Behalf of Christian Schools," quoted in Robert Ulich, *Three Thousand Years of Educational Wisdom: Selections from Great Documents* (Cambridge, Mass: Harvard University Press, 1965), p. 232.

55 Ibid.

56 Luther, "Luther's Letter to the Mayors and Aldermen of All the Cities of Germany in Behalf of Christian Schools," quoted in Painter, *Luther on Education*, pp. 199–200.

57 Luther, "The Value of Music," translated by Henry Barnard, "German Teachers and Educators," pp. 158–159, translated from Karl von Raumer, "Geschichte der Päagogik," vol. I, pp. 143–145. Original in Georg Walch, "Luthers sämtliche Schriften," Vol. 22, pp. 2249-2253. Compare Preserved Smith, and Herbert Percival Gallinger, "Conversations with Luther," pp. 98–100. Quoted in Eby, *Early Protestant Educators*, p. 159.

58 Durant, *The Reformation*, pp. 341–342.

59 Luther, translated by Henry Barnard, "German Teachers and Educators," p. 152. *Commentary on the Epistle to the Galatians*, "D. Martin Luthers Werke," Weimar, ed., vol. 40, I, p. 529. Quoted in Eby, *Early Protestant Educators*, pp. 32–33.

60 Eby, *Early Protestant Educators*, pp. 86–87.

61 A.F. Leach, *The Schools of Medieval England* (London: Methuen & Co. Ltd., 1915), p. 8. Also see Frederick Eby and Charles Flinn Arrowood, *The History and Philosophy of Education Ancient and Medieval* (New York: Prentice-Hall Inc., 1940), p. 634.

62 Eby, *Early Protestant Educators*, p. 87.

63 Ernst Helmreich, *Religious Education in German Schools* (Cambridge, Mass.: Harvard University Press, 1959), p. 11.

64 Ibid.

65 Eby, *Early Protestant Educators, pp. 93–94. Eby cites Wace, Henry and C.A. Buchheim, Luther's Primary Works*, pp. 6–9.

66 Luther, quoted in Painter, *A History of Education*, p. 151.

67 Note: Wolfgang Ratichius developed a rapid method for teaching Latin. His work had a profound impact on Comenius and others. Quoted in Painter, *Luther on Education*, p. 151.

68 Luther, quoted in Painter, *Luther on Education*, p. 153.

69 Helmreich, p. 11.

70 Luther, "Luther's Correspondence and Other Contemporary Letters," trans. and ed. by Preserved Smith, Ph.D., and Charles M. Jacobs, D.D., pp. 486–488. Quoted in Eby, *Early Protestant Educators*, p. 99.

71 Luther, "Letter to the Mayors and Aldermen of All the Cities of Germany in Behalf of Christian Schools," quoted in Painter, *Luther on Education*, pp. 186–193.

72 Ibid., pp. 192–193.

73 Eby, *The Development of Modern Education*, p. 68.

74 Luther, "Letter to the Mayors and Aldermen of All the Cities of Germany in Behalf of Christian Schools," quoted in Painter, *Luther on Education*, p. 183.

75 Ibid., p. 193.

76 Luther, "Letter to the Mayors and Aldermen of All the Cities of Germany in Behalf of Christian Schools," quoted in Painter, *Luther on Education*, pp. 198–199.

[77] Luther, "Luther on Studies and Methods," quoted in Painter, *Luther on Education*, p. 161.

[78] H.G. Good, *A History of Western Education* (New York: The Macmillan Company, 1960), pp. 24–25.

[79] Luther, quoted in Painter, *Luther on Education*, p. 166.

[80] Luther, *Table Talk*, January 4, 1539. no. 4638. LW 54:359. Quoted in Gritsch, "Academia and Forum: Luther's Reformation in Wittenberg," *Lutheran Theological Seminary Bulletin*, vol. 70, winter 1990, p. 25.

[81] Nicholas Copernicus, quoted in R.E.D. Clark "Copernicus, Nicolas," *The New International Dictionary of the Christian Church*, J.D. Douglas, ed. (Grand Rapids: Zondervan Publishing House, 1974), p. 262. Note: The greatest damage created by the Copernicus discovery was to the ancient practice of astrology (see Clark).

[82] Luther, quoted in Painter, *Luther on Education*, p. 163.

[83] Luther, WML, 4:126, quoted in Painter, *Luther on Education*, p. 203.

[84] Ibid., pp. 206–207.

[85] Lutherstadt Wittenberg, "The Historic Mile" (Wittenberg: Drei Kastanieu Verlag, 1995), p. 9.

[86] Edwin Yamauchi, "The Religion of the Romans," *Introduction to the History of Christianity*, Tim Dowley, ed. (Minneapolis: Fortress Press, 1995), p. 14.

[87] Painter, *Luther on Education*, p. 146.

[88] Clarence H. Benson, *A Popular History of Christian Education* (Chicago: Moody Press, 1943), p. 77.

[89] Durant, *The Reformation*, p. 422.

[90] Frank W. Blackmar, *History of Human Society* (New York: Charles Scribner's Sons, 1926), p. 385.

[91] Alister E. McGrath, *The Life of John Calvin* (Cambridge, Mass., Blackwell Publishers Inc. 1990), p. 80.

[92] Luther, *Table Talk*, 319, quoted in Durant, The Reformation, p. 418.

[93] Erwin W. Lutzer, *Hitler's Cross* (Chicago: Moody Press, 1995), p. 86.

[94] Ibid., p. 88.

[95] Ibid., p. 86.

[96] Ibid., p. 87.

[97] Ibid., p. 88. (See *Chicago Tribune*, Nov. 14, 1994, "Lutherans Publicly Repudiate Founder)".

[98] Benson, p. 76.

Illustration Sources

Figure 1   *Bible* - Photo by author (PBA).

Figure 2   *Church* - PBA.

Figure 3   *Map* - Global Mapping International, Colorado Springs, CO.

Figure 4   *Luther Memorial in Worms* - PBA.

Figure 5   *School*- Ellwood P. Cubberley, *Readings in the History of Education* (Boston: Houghton Mifflin Company, 1920), p.224

Figure 6   *Luther Memorial in Wittenberg* - PBA.

Figure 7   *Countryside* - PBA.

Figure 8   *Tree* - PBA.

Figure 9   *Symbol* - PBA.

CHAPTER

9

1505—TIME PERIOD—1572

John Calvin and John Knox—The Great Church School Educators

Figure 1. John Knox (left); John Calvin (right)

John Calvin of Geneva, Switzerland, and John Knox of Edinburgh, Scotland, were great Protestant reformers, and both were also, like Luther, aggressive education reformers committed to Bible-centered Christian schools. Their schools were more closely aligned with the church than Luther's Christian schools, which he reluctantly turned over to civil government along with his churches and universities.

We are fortunate that both Calvin and Knox left behind ample written documents about their beliefs on Christian school education. This chapter will draw heavily on those documents along with an abundance of other sources. These are the chapter divisions:

1. The Historic Setting of Calvin and Knox
2. A Comparison Between the Calvin and Knox Schools
3. What Calvin and Knox Wrote About Christian School Education

John Calvin and John Knox were the foremost leaders of the second generation of the evangelical Protestant reformers. All the reformers were former Catholic priests who came to realize that "the just shall live by faith" (Romans 1:17 and Romans 5:1). Like the independent reformers they were, they developed doctrines that varied from those of other reformers, but they were nonetheless united on the essentials of biblical authority and the Gospel of Christ. Ultimately their influence, especially Calvin's, exceeded that of Martin Luther. The Calvinist movement spread to larger population centers than did the Lutheran movement. Calvinism impacted Switzerland, France, England, Hungary, Holland, Scotland, and America.[1] Kerr says:

> **Calvinism, or the Reformed faith as it became known, spread from Switzerland into the Rhine valley and became the theological impulse of the Huguenots of France, the Protestants of Holland, the Puritans of England and New England, and the Presbyterians of Scotland and of America.[2]**

Lutheranism spread throughout the Western world, but the areas of its greatest concentration were Germany and the Scandinavian countries.[3] In future chapters we will discover that the English Pilgrims and Puritans who came to America in 1620 and 1630 were essentially Calvinists with minor variations in their doctrinal positions. America's earliest schools, established by the Puritans, bore the undeniable imprint of Knox's and Calvin's Bible-centered educational philosophy.

1. The Historic Setting of Calvin and Knox

John Calvin (1509–1564) was a Frenchman born in Noyan, sixty miles northeast of Paris. His father, Gerard Calvin (Cauvin), was a notary public for the Catholic bishop of Noyan.[4] In 1523, at age fourteen, John Calvin enrolled as a student at the University of Paris.[5] By today's standards, age fourteen is much too young to begin a university education, but as McGrath says, "by the standards of the [sixteenth century], fourteen could possibly have been considered a late age to begin such an education."[6] A few years before his death, Calvin's father "incurred the displeasure of the Roman Church,"[7] and in 1528 he persuaded his son Calvin to turn away from his preparation for the priesthood in Paris and study law at the University

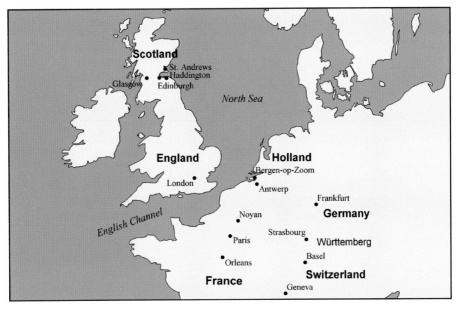

Figure 2. The Knox/Calvin map

of Orleans, seventy miles southwest of Paris. After his father's death in 1531, Calvin returned to the University of Paris.[8] While a student at the university, Calvin experienced a "sudden conversion" to Christ, which he described as follows:

> And at first, whilst I remained thus so obstinately addicted to the superstitions of the papacy that it would have been hard indeed to have pulled me out of so deep a quagmire by sudden conversion, [God] subdued and made teachable a heart which, for my age, was far too hardened in such matters. Having thus received some foretaste and knowledge of true piety, I was straightway inflamed with such great desire to profit by it, that although I did not attempt to give up other studies I worked only slackly at them. And I was wonderstruck when, before the year was out, all those who had some desire for the true doctrine ranged themselves around me to learn, although I was hardly more than a beginner myself.[9]

On another occasion Calvin said, "At last, God turned my course in a different direction by the hidden bridle of His providence."[10]

It is not known what influenced Calvin's conversion, but we do know that the University of Paris, like other Catholic universities, was impacted by the writings of Martin Luther. McGrath describes Luther's influence in Paris:

Figure 3. John Calvin's signature.

During 1523, the faculty of theology had been obliged to meet 101 times, far in excess of the thirty or so meetings usually held. The cause for these additional meetings was a distant and largely unknown figure—Martin Luther—whose ideas threatened to take city, university and church by storm. Lutheranism did indeed come to dominate the affairs of both city and university, making it difficult for any informed person within the city to avoid at least some familiarity with its ideas. As contemporary witnesses make abundantly clear, the works of Martin Luther found a substantial and enthusiastic readership within the intellectual elite of Paris as early as 1519.[11]

Had the faculty at the University of Paris met a few times to counter the growing influence of Luther's Bible-based teaching, the history of France would not have included the dreadful massacre of the French Huguenots in the second half of the sixteenth century. As we will see, the Huguenots were strong advocates of Christian school education. Thousands died for their faith.

John Calvin, now a Protestant in a Paris increasingly hostile to evangelicals, escaped in December 1534 to Basel, Switzerland, a Protestant stronghold.[12] Two years later, Calvin published his first edition of *The Institution of the Christian Religion*, often referred to as "The Institutes."[13] Later Calvin expanded his writings, and they became a major tool in the spread of Calvinism.

Calvin's move to Geneva in 1536 proved historically significant. He had gone to Geneva at the request of Guillaume Farel, a fiery preacher referred to as "the reformer of Geneva."[14] Calvin said, "Guillaume Farel detained me in Geneva, not so much by counsel and exhortation as by a dreadful curse, as if God had from heaven laid His hand upon me to arrest me."[15] Geneva, Switzerland, became the center of Calvinism and was often referred to as the "Rome of Protestantism."[16] John Calvin, who brought unsolicited notoriety to the city, was called by one historian a "God-intoxicated man."[17] When Calvin arrived, Geneva was considered a Protestant city, but Geneva's "conversion" to Protestantism was a "political conversion," not the result of a spiritual revival. Bouwsma explains:

> . . . although no towns were born Protestant, and some towns achieved Protestantism, others had Protestantism thrust upon them. Geneva

belonged to this last group, compelled to turn Protestant by political circumstances rather than by any significant wave of evangelical fervor.[18]

In 1536, Geneva, the city of 10,000 inhabitants on the southern shore of Lake Geneva, was in reality neither Catholic nor Protestant. Fuhrmann said:

...the city was a religious and spiritual desert. In previous years the Genevese had expelled the Roman Catholic bishop and ruler of the city, but their Protestantism then consisted merely in no longer attending Mass. They had freed themselves from the yoke of the bishop but were unwilling to accept the yoke of Christ. Rejecting all religious authority, they did not have the least idea of what the Christian faith might be. Their main concerns were money, business, pleasure, and sports.[19]

Before he left in 1535, the Catholic bishop of Geneva, in retaliation, "excommunicated the entire population of the city."[20] The city council of Geneva took over all former Catholic Church properties,

Figure 4. John Knox, one of the most eloquent and powerful preachers of his time, was also a champion for Christian school education. This striking statue of Knox is near the entrance of the New College Library in Edinburgh.

including the imposing St. Peter's Cathedral, which still stands in the center of Geneva. The former Catholic cathedral now became the international center of Calvinism.

JOHN KNOX

John Knox (1505–1572) was born in Haddington, Scotland. He attended the University of Glasgow and the University of St. Andrews and became a priest and a lawyer for the diocese of St. Andrews. He would later be known as a "renegade priest."[21]

Evangelical Protestantism came to Scotland, as it did to so many other countries, through her Catholic universities, where faculty and students were fascinated with Martin Luther's writings. Catholic authorities, alarmed at the invasion of Luther's literature and the influx of Tyndale's English New Testaments, asked the Scottish Parliament to take action:

...within a few years of Luther's doctrinal revolt in 1517, action in Scotland was considered necessary to stem the invasion of Lutheran heresy from the continent through east-coast ports, and, with it, the threat of doctrinal turmoil and confusion. In July 1525 Parliament banned the importation of any books or works of the said Luther, his disciples or servants, and it strove to suppress the recitation of 'his heresies or opinions' throughout the realm; the lords of council strengthened the measure in 1527; and Parliament, in ratifying the statute in 1535, required all who harboured Lutheran literature to hand it over to their bishops. Such action was less than fruitful. Despite James V's orders to his sheriffs in Aberdeenshire in August 1525, at his bishop's behest, to search out 'sundry strangers and others within his diocese' who possessed 'books of that heretic Luther and favoured his errors and false opinions,' Reformation literature continued to be smuggled into east-coast ports: from Antwerp and Bergen-op-Zoom, it was reported in 1527, Scottish merchants readily shipped home Protestant works and English New Testaments, particularly to the university town of St. Andrews and to Edinburgh.[22]

It is not known when John Knox became an evangelical believer. We do know that in 1546 he was carrying a two-handed sword as a bodyguard for Protestant reformer George Wishart. Later, Wishart and another reformer, Patrick Hamilton, were arrested by the Catholic archbishop and burned at the stake at St. Andrews. Knox, who witnessed the burning of Patrick Hamilton, described the cruel execution:

The innocent servant of God being bound to the stake in the midst of some coals, some timber, and other matter appointed for the fire, a train of [gun] powder was made and set afire. This gave a glaise to the blessed martyr of God, scrimpled his left hand and that side of his face, but kindled neither the wood nor yet the coals. And so remained he in torment, until men ran to the Castle again for more powder, and for wood more able to take fire. When at last this was kindled, with loud voice he cried, "Lord Jesus, receive my spirit! How long shall darkness overwhelm this realm? And how long wilt Thou suffer this tyranny of men?"[23]

In 1546, John Knox became pastor of the new Protestant congregation at St. Andrews Castle.[24] Knox was soon captured by French soldiers who had crossed the North Sea at the request of Scotland's Catholic parliament to assist them in their determination to stamp out "the growing menace of Protestantism."[25] He was made a chained galley-slave on a French galley for nineteen months. Knox said that he and his fellow prisoners were "miserably" treated and were under constant pressure to renounce their Protestant faith.[26] Lindsay describes what Knox endured:

For nineteen months he had to endure this living death, which for long drawn out torture can only be compared with what the Christians of the earliest centuries had to suffer when they were condemned to the mines. He had to sit chained with four or six others to the rowing benches, which were set at right angles to the side of the ship, without change of posture by day, and compelled to sleep, still chained under the benches by night; exposed to the elements day and night alike; enduring the lash of the overseer, who paced up and down the gangway which ran between the two lines of benches; feeding on the insufficient meals of coarse biscuit and porridge of oil and beans; chained along with the vilest malefactors. The French Papists had invented this method of treating all who differed from them in religious matters.[27]

Miraculously he was released in 1549, largely through the intervention of England's young Protestant king, Edward VI.[28]

It is not surprising, therefore, that upon his release from the French galley in 1549, Knox made his way to England, where he distinguished himself as a Protestant preacher.[29] In 1551, he was appointed chaplain to King Edward VI.[30] Upon King Edward's premature death in 1553, his Catholic sister, Mary Tudor, or "Bloody Mary" as she became known because of her many executions of Protestants, became England's queen.[31] Knox referred to her as the "wicked English Jezebel."[32] In January 1554, to avoid execution, John Knox headed for mainland Europe where, at Calvin's suggestion,

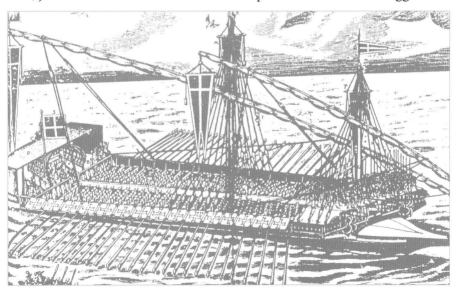

Figure 5. When John Knox defected from the Catholic priesthood and became a Protestant, he was captured and forced to serve for nineteen months as a galley slave on a French galley.

Figure 6. Knox referred to England's Catholic Queen Mary as "that wicked English Jezebel." She was also known as "Bloody Mary" for her many executions of Protestants.

he became the pastor of the growing English congregation in Frankfurt, Germany. Most members of his congregation, like Knox himself, were exiles from England or Scotland. Later, after a nine-month speaking tour in Scotland, he returned to Switzerland and accepted Calvin's call to pastor the English church in Geneva.[33] It was there that Knox observed Calvin's citywide system of Christian schools.

In the meantime, Protestantism had gained considerable strength in Scotland. Knox was asked by a group of Scottish nobles, known as "Lords of the Congregation," to return to his homeland to provide leadership to the growing Protestant movement. Upon his return he was elected pastor of Edinburgh's Protestant congregation, which now met in St. Giles, the former Catholic cathedral that to this day dominates the skyline of downtown Edinburgh.[34] Nichols says:

Knox preached constantly and with fiery eloquence in St. Giles', Edinburgh, strengthening the cause with every word. Meanwhile a Scottish Reformed Church was organized with great rapidity, under his direction.[35]

So pervasive was the spiritual transformation of Scotland that most members of the Scottish Parliament attended Knox's church at St. Giles. It is not surprising, therefore, that he along with five other Protestant ministers was asked by Parliament to draw up what became known as the "Scot's Confession," a statement of faith that was passed by Parliament on August 17, 1560.[36] At that point John Knox, from his St. Giles Cathedral, became the central figure of the newly formed Scottish Presbyterian Church, which to this day is the State Church of Scotland.

2. A Comparison Between the Calvin and Knox Schools

Both Calvin and Knox were strong advocates of Christian school education. The clearest distinction between their Christian schools was that Calvin's schools were a city system, whereas Knox's Christian school system was for all of Scotland.

GENEVA ACADEMY

Calvin's mentor in Christian education was Johannes Sturm of Strassburg, Germany (now Strasbourg, France), 150 miles north of Geneva. Sturm, like Luther and Erasmus, had attended a Brethren of the Common Life School. Sturm's citywide system of schools incorporated many ideas from his own experience at the Brethren of Common Life School in Deventer, Holland (now Belgium). Calvin had observed Sturm's city system of schools firsthand from 1538 to 1541, while he served as an evangelical pastor in Strasbourg and part-time teacher in Sturm's Christian school.[37] Calvin and Farel had been banished from Geneva for three years as a result of their unfavorable standing among influential religious factions in Geneva. Amazingly, in 1541, because of

Figure 7. This is St. Giles Cathedral in Edinburgh, where John Knox preached and where he is buried. This photo was taken on a Sunday when Scotland's military was being honored.

a dramatic change of leadership on the Geneva City Council, they were strongly urged to return to Geneva and, in effect, were given the "keys to the city."[38]

Speaking of Calvin's exposure to Sturm's citywide Christian schools, Boyd and King write:

> From his association with Sturm he not only learned a great deal about school organization, but acquired some idea of the limited capacities of children, such as he had obviously not possessed when he drew up his Catechism for juvenile instruction in 1537. The result was evident in the Ecclesiastical Ordinances he prepared in 1541, when recalled from banishment and given a new status as chief minister of the Genevan Church. In these Ordinances it was expressly laid down that a college [high school], in which the children could learn "the languages and the secular sciences" as a preparation for the ministry and for civil offices, was necessary for the well-being of the Church and of the community as a whole. At the head of this college [high school] was to be "a man of learning and experience," and

under him there were to be "readers" to give higher instruction, and "bachelors" to teach the younger children. The teacher was to rank as an officer of the Church and to be subject to ecclesiastical discipline like the ministers.[39]

Geneva Academy, a secondary school, opened with a ceremony at St. Peter's Cathedral on June 5, 1559, with John Calvin presiding. Calvin had raised the funds for the property and the building of the new Christian school.[40] Theodore Beza, who became Calvin's counterpart to Luther's Philip Melanchthon, was installed as the first rector of Geneva Academy and gave the opening address.[41] The enrollment at the school, five years later, reached fifteen hundred students, "the majority of them from abroad."[42] There was a rigorous and pious atmosphere to Calvin's year-round academy. Painter writes:

> In the summer the recitations began at six in the morning; in winter at seven. The students were required to attend divine worship once every school-day, and thrice on Sunday. The Lord's Prayer and the Creed were in the course of study, and all the students were taught to sing and intone the Psalms. As in the gymnasia of Germany, the ancient languages, as an aid to biblical exercises, occupied a large part of the seven years' course. Calvin himself was one of the teachers, and it is said that his auditors daily numbered a thousand.[43]

In his inaugural prayer, Calvin asked God for His blessing on the new school and on those who had responded to his appeal for funds. He had personally gone door-to-door seeking funds for the new classroom building—which stands to this day. Amazingly, Calvin persuaded the Geneva City Council to donate the revenue from all civil court fines to his school's building fund.[44] Vander Walt writes:

> Calvin's Genevan school was a Christian school even to the tiniest physical detail. . . . On the doors of the school building, for example, slogans were painted which spoke of the lifeview of the founder and of the community served by the school. The first was in Hebrew: "The fear of the Lord is the principle of wisdom . . . ;" the second in Greek: ". . . because Christ has become for us the wisdom out of God . . ." and the third in Latin: "But the wisdom from above is in the first place pure, then peaceable, friendly . . ." and higher up there was the city coat of arms. . . . Calvin's personal motto for his school was, "How can this school honor God?"[45]

The rules were strict at Calvin's school and the consequences for infractions were severe. Vander Walt says,

Students were forbidden to dance, to play cards, to gamble, to visit taverns, to use profanity, to participate in masquerades or to sing obscene or improper songs. Jail sentences or fines could be imposed for transgressions.[46]

In organizational structure, Calvin's schools were substantially different from our schools today and from the Christian schools established by Luther or Knox. Calvin showed only moderate interest in elementary education. As Luther did, he regarded elementary schools, or "folk schools," as "screens" for quality students for his secondary schools. With reference to Calvin's view of elementary education, Frederick Eby writes:

> [Calvin] complained to the council of Geneva that there were too many small schools, and the number was reduced to four, one for each quarter of the city. A small fee was charged to these schools. He required that only those boys should be allowed to attend these elementary schools who could not learn Latin. Even then in the interest of uniformity, he demanded that all the pupils in these schools should be assembled every Wednesday at the great college [high school] so that there might be some religious instruction in common. The teachers of the elementary schools were required to be examined and supervised.[47]

In Calvin's schools the course of study was substantially more rigorous than that of the schools established by Luther and Knox. In Geneva all students were required to attend school six and one-half days a week. There were no formal classes on Wednesdays, but all students were required to attend a morning-long chapel service at the cathedral or at the secondary school.[48]

Geneva Academy was two schools in one, a high school and an upper-level school. The upper-level school was, in effect, a seminary that ultimately became the University of Geneva, and it continues to this day as a highly respected educational institution. It is interesting that Calvin's high school also admitted elementary students who had proven capable of learning Latin. Grade placement was determined by achievement and ability, not age level.[49]

THE CHURCH AND SCHOOL AS ONE

There is no question that Calvin saw the church and school as one united ministry. Professor Vander Walt says, "According to [Calvin], church and school were mutually dependent and one could not think of one without involving the other. In distinguishing the two, Calvin in no way separated them."[50] Nor did Calvin separate education into sacred and secular categories. Vander Walt says:

Calvin found the division into secular/sacred alien to his mind; no facet of schoolwork was excluded from the influence of the Scriptures and the Christian lifeview. There was for example a special prayer prior to the first lesson, recited by a pupil, in which God was exhorted to impart to them strength, wisdom and support. The singing of a psalm likewise was intended for relaxation, but also served to help the pupils to assimilate Christian concepts of faith. The school day closed with a brief divine service. In the school the Word of God was the foundation of all learning and also of education. The Scriptures carry the authority of God, because they were inspired and revealed by Him. For this reason they then also have authority for the sphere of teaching and education. The Lord uses the enlightened—the teachers—to introduce the unenlightened to the mysteries of the Scriptures.[51]

John Calvin's position on the unity of the church and school and of sacred and secular education in Christian schools becomes not only an important philosophical principle but a valid legal precedent in today's world. This is especially significant among those who naively suggest, for example, that a math or science teacher in a Christian school need not be an evangelical Christian. Calvin established the principle that all truth is God's truth and must be taught God's way by godly teachers.

A KEY TO THE REFORMATION'S DURABILITY
Like all of the Reformation leaders, Calvin accomplished as much with education reform as with church reform—or more. The two went hand in hand. A reformation on the scale of the Great Reformation required a great army of godly civil leaders, pastors, and Christian school educators. The reformers would not have been nearly as effective had they not established Bible-centered elementary and secondary schools. Christian school education became the keystone of the Reformation's durability. A close look at the curriculum of Calvin's schools reveals his commitment to training Christian leaders. Cubberley says:

These colleges [secondary schools] became famous as institutions from which learned men came forth. The course of study in the seven classes of one of the Geneva colleges, which has been preserved for us, reveals the nature of the instruction. The lowest class began with the letters, reading was taught from a French-Latin Catechism, and the usual Latin authors were read. Greek was begun in the fourth class, and, in addition to the usual Greek authors, the New Testament was read in Greek. In the higher classes, . . . logic and rhetoric were taught to prepare pupils to analyze, argue, and defend the faith. Elocution was also given much importance in the upper classes as preparation for the

Figure 8. Guillaume Farel, John Calvin, Theodore Beza (Geneva Academy's first administrator), and John Knox are the central figures at the International Reformation Monument in Geneva. Inscribed at the base of the monument are the first three letters in Greek of the name Jesus.

ministry, two original orations being required each month. Psalms were sung, prayers offered, sermons preached and questioned on, and the Bible carefully studied. The men who went forth from the colleges of Geneva to teach and to preach the Calvinistic gospel were numbered by the hundreds.[52]

NO THEOCRACY

Some have suggested that John Calvin established a theocracy in Geneva. There is little doubt that Calvin was a seminal figure in the Great Reformation and in the history of that city. The beautiful hundred-yard Reformer's Wall and Calvin's fifteen-foot-tall statue in the University Park in Geneva attest to Calvin's great influence in the city. But as McGrath says, "The notion that Calvin was the 'dictator of Geneva' is . . . totally devoid of historical foundation."[53] In reality, Geneva was a city-state in the tradition of a Greek city-state. Again, McGrath says, "If any political entity of the sixteenth century may be compared to a Greek city-state, it is the city of Geneva."[54] It was, in fact, a city-state republic called "The Republic of Geneva," which meant that the elected city council was the final authority on all matters including religious issues. Calvin was an employee of the city who had been called by the city council to head the city's council of ministers—a body that made recommendations to the city council. Clearly, the council revered Calvin, but because he was not born in Geneva, he was regarded as a foreigner. Consequently, said McGrath:

> Calvin was thus denied access to the city's decision-making machinery. He could not vote; he could not stand for office. . . . His influence over Geneva was exercised indirectly, through preaching, consultation and other forms of legitimate suasion. Despite his ability to influence through his moral authority, he had no civic jurisdiction, no right, to coerce others to act as he wished. Calvin could and did urge, cajole and plead; he could not, however, command.

Again, McGrath says:

> The image of Calvin as the 'dictator of Geneva' bears no relation to the known facts of history.[55]

Understanding the city government of Geneva and Calvin's relationship to it clarifies the governance of Calvin's churches and schools, which in reality were the city's churches and schools. This fact explains why Geneva's council of ministers, headed by Calvin, screened and selected teachers for Geneva's Christian schools, but it was the city council that ultimately employed them. As Vander Walt notes, "According to the decrees of 1541, the council of ministers . . . had the responsibility for recommending the appointment of teachers . . . but the actual appointments were made by the city council."[56] This same pattern of governance was followed by John Knox in Scotland and by the English Puritans who settled in America's Massachusetts Bay Colony in 1630. Therefore, it can be said there was no theocracy in Geneva, nor was there a theocracy in Edinburgh or the American colonies. In each case an elected body was the governing authority. Regrettably, the "governing authority" did not include

Figure 9. POST TENEBRAS LUX ('after the darkness, light'), the motto of Geneva and of the Reformation, is inscribed behind the Reformers Wall.

women and racial minorities, but compared to the Catholic past, it was a giant leap toward a democratic form of government.

MEANWHILE IN SCOTLAND

In Scotland as elsewhere, the wide distribution of the Bible created an insatiable thirst for learning. When one looks at the genesis of the Great Reformation in each of the Reformation countries, one finds that the simple act of distributing the Bible in the language of the people created the first spark of spiritual transformation. In Germany, Martin Luther was spiritually transformed by the Gospel of Christ when he read Romans 1:17, "The just shall live by faith." Luther affirmed the power of the Scriptures when he said, "I did nothing: the Word did everything."[57]

Before Farel or Calvin arrived in Geneva, the city had already been influenced by traveling merchants who sold copies of Luther's writings and the sacred Scriptures to the citizens.[58] On their newly-struck coins the Genevans inscribed, "After darkness, light," indicating it was the release of the Bible among the people that brought light to Geneva. The same was true in Scotland. The foundation stones for the Reformation in Scotland were laid by the wide reading of the Scriptures, which were secretly distributed among those who were literate. Renwick explains:

> As soon as Luther started his great movement in 1517, evangelical books and pamphlets began to infiltrate into Scotland and England often through Scottish ports, in spite of all that the [Catholic] Church and Parliament could do. Tyndale's English translation of the New Testament came to have a marked influence when thus smuggled into the country. In 1525 and 1527 Parliament passed Acts to keep Scotland clean of what they called 'all sic filthe and vice' and threatened imprisonment and forfeiture of goods against any who should bring in the works of Luther. Notwithstanding this, the people were deeply stirred; the tide rose strongly against the abuses in the [Catholic] Church, and a chorus of criticism resounded throughout the land.[59]

As in the other Reformation countries, the infusion of the Bible in Scotland created an unprecedented thirst for learning and for basic literacy for all classes of people—not just the aristocracy.

In 1543, much to the chagrin of the Catholic authorities, the Scottish Parliament, now leaning toward Protestantism, had "legalized the reading of the Scriptures in the vernacular."[60] Later in 1555, John Knox made a nine-month preaching tour of Scotland and spoke to great crowds in several towns and cities. He said they were "night and day sobbing and groaning for the Bread of Life. If I had not seen it with my eyes in my own country, I could not have believed it."[61]

The growing spiritual awakening among the Scottish people that Knox witnessed in 1555 led to the dramatic events of 1560, which became a major turning point for Scotland. Today in Edinburgh, in the pavement just west of St. Giles Cathedral, brass tablets mark the location of the historic 1560 meeting of Parliament that transformed Scotland from a Catholic to a Protestant nation. Renwick describes the momentous event:

> Immediately after the session was constituted, a petition was presented from certain Protestant barons, gentlemen, burgesses, and others. . . . They asked that the 'many pestiferous errors' of the Roman Church be disavowed, that the purity of worship and the primitive discipline of the Church be restored, and that the ample ecclesiastical revenues be applied to three noble ends, viz. the support of a gospel ministry, the promotion of education, and the care of the poor.[62]

John Knox, who had been called back to Edinburgh in 1559 by the "Lords of the Congregation," was now the Protestant pastor of St. Giles Cathedral. Knox and five other Protestant leaders (all with the first name of "John") were asked to draw up a confession of faith for Scotland. Largely because of John Knox, who had been exposed to several Protestant confessions on the continent, they presented their confession of faith within four days. Its acceptance by Scotland's Parliament took place on August 17, 1560. In Scottish history, the event is equivalent in importance to America's Declaration of

Figure 10. This bas-relief shows The Reformers Wall in Geneva, John Knox preaching in St. Giles Cathedral, Edinburgh. An Englishman said of Knox's preaching, "The voice of one man is able in one hour to put more life in us than five hundred trumpets continually blustering in our ears." Knox was known as "The Thundering Scott."

Independence, signed on July 4, 1776. Some have described Scotland's historic date as "the birthday of a people."[63] Dr. Thomas McCrie says:

> The nation, by its rulers and representatives, passed from Popery to Protestantism; and in its civil capacity, ratified (not the gospel indeed, which no acts of parliament can ratify) but the profession of the gospel, which the people, in their religious capacities, had already embraced. And thus it appears that there was a civil establishment of the true religion in Scotland, before there was even an Established Church, for the Reformed Church of Scotland was not as yet regularly organized, much less endowed. The legal recognition of the Presbyterian Church, as an organized society, was a subsequent step, and indeed not fully obtained for many years after this.[64]

Seeing the need for an established Protestant church, the Parliament asked the same six ministers who had drafted Scotland's Confession of Faith to draw up a plan showing how the new church should be governed. This document is significant because it included a comprehensive plan for Christian school education. Their finished work was called *The First Book of Discipline*.[65] It was a remarkable document, but it was not ratified by Parliament largely because of a disagreement over funding. *The First Book of Discipline* required Parliament to use the new source of income generated by the vast territories formerly owned by the Catholic church, which was equal to half of Scotland,[66] to be used to support the gospel ministry, to promote education, and to care for the poor.[67]

What Knox and his fellow authors of *The First Book of Discipline* (as well as many members of Parliament) did not know was that when it became evident that the Protestant Reformation was going to succeed, Catholic officials quickly deeded over many of their church properties and buildings to Catholic laymen, thus keeping them out of the hands of Protestants. There were also "ruthless and selfish barons," some of whom were members of Parliament, who illegally confiscated large territories that had formerly been owned by Catholic monasteries.[68] While these factors were indeed a setback, the plan for a nationwide system of Christian education set forth by Knox and his five co-authors "laid hold on the mind of Scotland, and the lack of endowments was more than compensated by the craving of the people for education."[69] Therefore, in spite of the setback created by a lack of endowment funds, the plan moved forward, albeit at a slower pace. Lindsay says:

> Scottish students who had been trained in the continental schools of learning (many of whom were from Geneva), and who had embraced the Reformed faith, were employed to superintend the newly-organised

educational system of the country, and the whole organisation was brought into sympathy with the everyday life of the people by the preference given to day schools over boarding schools, and by a system of inspection by the most pious and learned men in each circle of parishes.[70]

THE SCOTTISH SCHOOL PLAN

The genius of the plan was that it was comprehensive and available to all students, boys and girls, from all levels of society. As Edgar points out, it was "a system starting from the village school and ending with the university."[71]

While Scotland's school plan was theologically Calvinistic, Eby claims its organizational pattern followed the Lutheran school plan in Würtemberg, Germany:

> . . . it proposes a national system of schools according to the Calvinistic principles under state and church control. Comparison should be made with the "School Ordinance" of Würtemberg [Germany]. Provision is made for family instruction, church instruction, parish schools, grammar schools, and universities. Supervision is provided for in each case.

Then he makes the following interesting observations:

> From the time of the great Celtic missionary movement in the eighth and ninth centuries, the Scottish people had retained an unusual devotion to education. The Reformation built the new institutions upon this interest which had so long been active.[72]

Boyd and King provide the following concise description of Scotland's national school plan:

> The pupil in the remotest country district might spend two years learning reading, catechism, and the elements of grammar; then pass to a town grammar school to study grammar and Latin for three or four years more; next go for four years to a high school . . . in one of the larger towns to get a knowledge of logic, rhetoric, and the ancient languages (including Greek), and finally to the university for a three years' course in philosophy (including dialectic, mathematics and natural philosophy), to be followed by a course in law, medicine or theology, which he would complete about his twenty-fifth year.[73]

The John Knox ideal was a church and Christian school in every community.[74] He said, "It is necessary that every church have a schoolmaster appointed."[75] Often the pastor of a small village church also served as the teacher of the village school.[76] We will find this same pattern carried over to New England's Puritan schools a few decades in the future.

Because *The First Book of Discipline* and its school plan were rejected by the Scottish Parliament, the primary authority for compulsory school attendance and other school ordinances came from the vigorous church community. Because the Scottish Christian schools were a national system, their grade levels were more clearly defined than those of the Christian schools in Geneva, which included students of all age levels.[77]

What was the practical outcome of Scotland's plan for a national system of Christian schools? While the plan was not perfect, it became a model for other developing Reformation countries. Renwick says:

> The record of the Church in Scotland in promoting education is without equal, and caused the Scottish peasantry to be the best educated in the world. As an example of what the Reformed Church ideal of popular education did for Scotland, we may recall that in the year 1800, there were 1000 students in Oxford and Cambridge combined, the only universities in England. Scotland had four universities and in Edinburgh alone there were 993 students. In 1830 the English universities had less than 3,000 students, while the Scottish universities had 4,400 in spite of the fact that the population of England was eight times that of Scotland. What would the position of Scotland have been if the misguided nobles had not grabbed the revenues which John Knox had designated for education?[78]

We move now to the written statements of Calvin and Knox about Christian school education. Because it is not central to our purpose, we are setting aside the fascinating account of the political struggle between John Knox and the queens, namely, Mary Queen of Scots—a Catholic who sought to undermine the Protestant Reformation in Scotland and who argued often with John Knox—and Elizabeth I, England's Protestant queen who might have been of greater help to Knox had he not written his famous treatise "The First Blast of the Trumpet Against the Monstrous Regiment of Women," a thunderous "blast" against women in authority.[79]

We are also setting aside the plots and intrigues of the Catholic Church to retake Scotland, "to have it as a jumping-off place to attack Protestant England."[80] These historic events, fascinating and valuable in their own right, we leave to historians with a much broader focus.

3. What Calvin and Knox Wrote About Christian School Education

"Everywhere Protestantism went—Christian schools were founded."[81] This classic quotation by Eavey is true because the great reformers of the sixteenth century had a clear and sustained vision for Christian schools. We are fortunate indeed that the words they wrote about Christian school education have been preserved. As you might expect, Luther wrote the most about Christian schools. Incidentally, the fifty-four volumes of *Luther's Works*, published in English in 1958, require eighteen feet of shelf space. The writings of Calvin and Knox on Christian schools are not so voluminous as Luther's but are no less profound.

JOHN CALVIN'S WORDS ON CHRISTIAN SCHOOLS
The following is from a sermon by Calvin from the Book of Titus:

Those to whom God has given the honor of having children, let them know that they are all the more obligated to take pains that their children are duly instructed. Thus if they wish to have good instruction, it is always necessary to begin with faith. For children could give the appearance of having all the virtue in the world, but that would be worth nothing, unless God be feared and honored by them. How frequently we see those who take great pains that their children be indoctrinated in the business of the world! It is true that they provide excellent teachers for their children, but for the purpose of making a grand show, so that they might know some three words of Latin and be able to display at the dinner table that they converse easily and can put up a good front according to the world. Yet it is never a question of knowing God! It is the wrong way to proceed! It is putting the cart before the horse![82]

Calvin, like Luther, was committed to teaching a catechism to children. He saw it as an indispensable tool for perpetuating the basic doctrines of the church among the children and thus preserving the integrity of the Gospel for the next generation of believers. In a letter he wrote:

Believe me, Monseigneur, the Church of God will never preserve itself without a Catechism, for it is like the seed to keep the good grain from dying out, and causing it to multiply from age to age. And therefore, if you desire to build an edifice which shall be of long duration, and which shall not soon fall into decay, make provision for the children being instructed in a good Catechism. . . . This Catechism will serve two purposes, to wit, as an introduction to the whole people, so that every one may profit from what shall be preached, and also to enable them to discern when any presumptuous person puts forward strange doctrine . . . the Catechism ought to serve as a check upon such people.[83]

The following is an interesting side note having to do with Calvin's published catechisms. It is difficult for us to comprehend a world without a free press and free speech. Books in Calvin's day, published in Geneva (a Protestant city), were regarded by the Catholic Church as heresy and were specifically placed on their list of "forbidden books." In 1560 Philippe Berry, a journeyman cobbler, was arrested at Dijon, France, for the "crime" of having in his possession a catechism, published in Geneva, called, "Primer for Christians Containing Questions for Children, etc."[84] The Catholic law specifically stated that it was a crime to possess books which were a "Primer for children containing the following: The Lord's Prayer, etc., showing the form for making one's profession of faith, for which it is especially to be condemned."[85]

Calvin, like Luther, was concerned that teaching the catechism to children would not be a mere exercise in rote memory. He admonished that one should not cram full the head of a child nor cause him or her "to lose the little bit of courage he [or she] has."[86] In his commentary on Isaiah 28:10, where Isaiah gives us one of the great principles of education, "precept upon precept, line upon line," Calvin said,

> . . . let their masters not fill little children with large readings in as much as they are not capable of doing it, rather let it distill in them like little drops. In this way one repeats to them two or more times the same thing, and shows them often the same precepts; in short, the students keep to the rudiments until they come to judgment and reason.[87]

Calvin was particularly concerned that children know how to "give a reason for their faith":

> It is most important for the due preservation of purity of doctrine that children from their youth should be instructed how to give a reason for their faith, and therefore some simple catechism or confession of faith ought to be prepared and taught to the children. At "certain seasons of the year" the children ought to be brought before the pastors, who should examine them and expound the teachings of the catechism.[88]

The following is an excerpt from Calvin's "Catechism of the Church of Geneva Being a Form of Instruction for Children in the Doctrine of Christ:"

Master: What is the chief end of human life?

Scholar: To know God by whom men were created.

Master: What reason have you for saying so?

Scholar: Because he created us and placed us in this world to be glorified in us. And it is indeed right that our life, of which himself is the beginning, should be devoted to his glory.

Master: What is the highest good of men?

Scholar: The very same thing.

Master: Why do you hold that to be the highest good?

Scholar: Because without it our condition is worse than that of the brutes.

Master: Hence, then, we clearly see that nothing worse can happen to a man than not to live to God.

Scholar: It is so.

Master: What is the true and right knowledge of God?

Scholar: When he is so known that due honour is paid to him.

Master: What is the method of honouring him duly?

Scholar: To place our whole confidence in him; to study to serve him during our whole life by obeying his will; to call upon him in all our necessities, seeking salvation and every good thing that can be desired in him; lastly, to acknowledge him both with heart and lips, as the sole Author of all blessings.

Master: To consider these points in their order, and explain them more fully—What is the first head in this division of yours?

Scholar: To place our whole confidence in God.

Master: How shall we do so?

Scholar: When we know him to be Almighty and perfectly good.

Master: Is this enough?

Scholar: Far from it.

Master: Wherefore?

Scholar: Because we are unworthy that he should exert his power in helping us, and show how good he is by saving us.

Master: What more then is needful?

Scholar: That each of us should set it down in his mind that God loves him, and is willing to be a Father, and the author of salvation to him.

Master: But whence will this appear?

Scholar: From his word, in which he explains his mercy to us in Christ, and testifies of his love towards us.[89]

The children's catechism continues and then concludes with a Statement of Faith.

Calvin's school by-laws refer only to education for boys. It is assumed that, if he followed such other reformers as Luther, Melanchthon, Bugenhagan and Sturm, girls were given at least elementary education in separate schools. The Calvin documents are not clear on this issue.

CALVIN'S SEVEN LEVELS OF INSTRUCTION

The class levels that follow begin with level seven, which is in reverse order from American grade levels. In other words, Calvin's class seven was the equivalent of an American first grade. A student's placement in any given class was determined by ability to achieve, not by chronological age. Therefore, we can be reasonably sure there were no "social passes" in the Christian schools of Geneva. Calvin's school by-laws for class levels were as follows:

Special rules for class seven

Here the pupils shall be taught to recognize the letters of the alphabet, then to form syllables from the Latin-French alphabet, then to read French fluently and finally Latin also, from the Latin-French catechism. If age permits, here the boys shall learn to write.

Rules for class six

In this class, the first and simplest elements of declension and conjugation shall be given in the first six months. In the remaining six months, there shall be given a thorough elementary explanation of the parts of speech and of their properties so that the pupils may compare French with Latin and in addition practice simple exercises in Latin. Here also the boys shall be improved in writing and become accustomed to using Latin.

Rules for class five

In this class, a more exact explanation of the parts of speech and the more elementary rules of syntax shall be given. The "Bucolics" of Vergil shall be offered. Some practice in style begins here.

Rules for class four

In this class, the rules for Latin syntax shall be completed. The shorter and more intimate letters of Cicero shall be offered, Short easy subjects shall be assigned for themes in imitation of the style of these letters.

The pupils shall have explained to them the quantities of syllables, embraced in a few rules, with reading from Ovid's "Elegies," "De Tristibus" ("Tristia") and "De Ponto" ("Epistulae ex Ponto").

Finally, the boys shall be taught in the simplest possible manner the reading, declension, and conjugation of Greek.

Rules for class three

Here Greek grammar shall be taught with more detail, so that the boys may closely observe the rules of both languages (i.e. Latin and Greek) and practice composition in them alternately. From among the authors, these especially are to be read: Cicero's "Letters," "De Amicitia," "De Senectute" in Greek and Latin, Vergil's "Aeneid," Caesar's "Commentaries," Isocrates' parenetic orations (the hortatory orations, two to Nicocles and one to Demonicus) as circumstances admit.

Rules for class two

Here history shall be taught, in Latin from Livy, in Greek from Xenophon, Polybius, or Herodian. Of the poets, Homer shall be read by each in turn. The elements of dialectic, i.e. the divisions of propositions and the figures of argumentation (nothing more) shall be explained. They shall be taught as thoroughly as possible propositions and arguments from the writers who are studied, and especially from Cicero's "Paradoxa" and his shorter orations but without any attention to the technique of oratory.

On Saturdays, from three to four, the Greek Gospels shall be read to them directly.

Rules for the first class

In this class, finally there shall be added to the rudiments of dialectic which have along been taught, the five voices, categories, places, and proofs, but from some scholarly manual. They shall add the elements of rhetoric and especially those which pertain to stylistic expression.

The use of the individual rules shall be carefully and thoroughly shown in the more artistic speeches of Cicero and also in the "Olynthiacs" and "Philippics" of Demosthenes, likewise in Homer and Vergil, in such a way that the bare propositions may be carefully sorted out, then their adornments explained and compared with the rules themselves.

They are to practice style carefully. They are to have two declamations a month, as we have said, on Wednesdays.

Saturdays from three to four, let them hear read some one of the letters of the apostles.[90]

Calvin's school by-laws, which had become an official document of Geneva's city ordinances, provide a clear description of the position of the school's chief administrator, or "rector." Reference made to the "honorable senate" means the elected city council of Geneva.

CONCERNING THE RECTOR OF THE SCHOOL

The rector of the school, a man of conspicuous piety and learning shall be chosen in the fear of and reverence for God, on the first of May, from the board of ministers and professors, by the general vote of this board. When chosen, he shall be presented to the honorable senate and his election confirmed by its authority.

He shall attend to the administration of the entire institution. Negligent professors and teacher, even the principal, are to be reminded by him of their duty. If disagreements arise among students, he shall settle them either by the weight of his own influence, or if it becomes necessary, by resorting to the authority of the ministers.

All students who are to attend the lectures of public professors, shall come to consult with him and be advised by him to present themselves first of all to the honorable senate and according to custom, receive from it the right of domicile. After this, they shall then subscribe in their own writing to the confession of faith (in the form in which we shall append it to these by-laws) and be recorded on the roll of the students.

Likewise he shall give a testimonial of character and attainments, after carefully making inquiry, to such students as ask it.

He shall never call a meeting of the students beyond those stated, unless the senate has given him permission.

He shall fill his office for two years. Then either another man shall be chosen or the same re-elected.[91]

The best window into the workings of Calvin's school can be found in his school by-laws on "promotions." It is interesting that the by-laws specify such details as "a short speech" and "proper modesty." Note the obvious close tie among the leaders of the city council (the senate), the church, and the school.

CONCERNING PROMOTIONS

Each year, three weeks before the first of May, a public theme in French shall be proposed in the assembly hall at noon by some one of the public professors in turn. The individual students in each class shall take this down according to their own degree of proficiency.

Then the pupils of each class, changing rooms, at sight, without recourse to books, without outside aid, shall by themselves translate the assigned theme into Latin within five hours.

And that there may be no dishonesty, the teacher of the second class shall supervise the pupils of the first class, the teacher of the first the second, etc. Those in charge shall maintain a careful supervision and conduct the examination in all fairness.

When the themes have been collected and arranged in order in groups of ten, the individual teachers shall bring them without any tampering to the principal.

The next and following days, up to the first of May, the rector with the aid of the public professors shall examine the exercises of the individual classes in order. After the corrections are indicated, and the boys called in, in groups of ten and questioned in the presence of their teacher, the class to which each is to be promoted shall be decided in accord with the opinion of the examiners.

On May first, (unless it happens to fall on a Sunday, in which case the ceremony shall be postponed to the next day) the entire school shall assemble in St. Peter's church. If it seems advisable to the honorable senate, there shall be present some one of the syndics or senators, together with the ministers of the gospel and the professors, the principal and the assistant teachers. In this assembly, the rector of the school shall read these by-laws aloud and recommend them in a short speech. Then from each class, the two pupils who have shown themselves superior to the rest in application and scholarship shall receive at the hand of the syndic or senator who is present some small prize which may seem appropriate to the honorable senate and they shall respectfully express their thanks. Then after the rector has made a short commendatory address, students of the first or second class shall with proper modesty read some original composition in either prose or verse, if available. Finally after the rector has given the benediction and prayers have been recited, the gathering shall be dismissed.

That day shall be a holiday for the entire school.

If any student seems to his teachers to have made so much progress that he can be promoted to a higher class before the end of the year, the teacher shall mention him to the principal, who shall make written record of all students of this type. Then on the first of October, the rector shall meet with the teachers in the gymnasium and make a decision in regard to the matter. But if at some other time of the year, any student seems fit to be promoted out of order, he shall be promoted out of order, with the full consent of the rector.[92]

THE WHOLE CITY OF GENEVA WAS AN EDUCATIONAL ENTERPRISE
Harro Hoepfl has suggested that because of the unusual cooperation among Geneva's city, church, and school officials, "the entire city was, in a very real sense, an educational enterprise."[93] Calvin's school programs evoked a higher level of city and church cooperation than any other aspect of his ministry. Over time, however, Calvin's relationship with the Geneva city council wore thin. At one point in 1551, Calvin wrote in a letter to a friend, "You cannot believe how much I am displeased with the present state of our republic."[94] A year later he wrote, "Our fellow citizens occasion as much concern; the disorder of this republic is so great that the church of God is tossed about like Noah's ark in the waters of the deluge."[95] It appears, however, that any disenchantment Calvin may have had with the city fathers of Geneva did not carry over to the jewel of his ministry— his Christian schools. His system of Christian education in Geneva became the prototype for Christian school education wherever the Calvinist Reformation spread, particularly in Holland, Scotland, and the American colonies.

Figure 11. There are three copies of Calvin's chair—two in Geneva and one in Edinburgh. There appears to be no way of knowing which one of the three is the original. This one is located in the rare books section of the University of Geneva Library.

Professors Eby and Arrowood provide an excellent summary of Calvin's philosophy:

> According to [Calvin's] view, church and state have the same objective—namely, to carry out the Will of God. They have, however, different but complementary functions. They operate as two organs which form a unitary organism. The church interprets the Will of God and also sets the moral standard, and the state endeavors to realize both in the conduct of the members of the community. This point of view was adopted by the Huguenots in France, the Reformed Church people in Holland, the Presbyterians in Scotland, and the Puritans in England. The school according to the Calvinistic theory is the offspring of both church and state. This conception dominated education in the American colonies and wherever Calvinists held sway.[96]

We conclude this chapter with the words of John Knox in his famous "Book of Discipline," when he wrote to Scotland's Parliament on "The Necessity of Schools." In his usual eloquent style he said:

> Seeing that God hath determined that His Church here on earth shall be taught not by angels but by men; and seeing that men are born ignorant of all godliness; and seeing, also, how God ceaseth to illuminate men miraculously, suddenly changing them, as He changed His Apostles and others in the primitive Church: it is necessary that your honours be most careful for the virtuous education and godly upbringing of the youth of this realm, if ye now thirst unfeignedly for the advancement of Christ's glory, or desire the continuance of His benefits to the generation following. For as the youth must succeed to us, so ought we to be careful that they have knowledge and erudition, for the profit and comfort of that which ought to be most dear to us, to wit, the Church and Spouse of the Lord Jesus.
>
> Therefore, we judge it necessary that every . . . church have a schoolmaster appointed.[97]

As previously quoted, John Knox continued describing his plan for Christian school education for his beloved Scotland. Knox and Calvin believed that Bible-centered academic education was an essential ministry of the church community. Writing on the legacy of Calvin, Peter DeJong says:

> A systematic and sustained program of child education by the church was integral to Calvin's conception of the truly Christian life. To neglect this would not only mean losing priceless opportunities for the welfare of individuals, the church, and the whole community; it would be tantamount to disobeying God and thus depriving men of his

blessing. Where this blessing was lost, man's life was plunged into ever-increasing errors and unhappiness.[98]

DeJong cites James Smart, who said, "Teaching belongs to the essence of the Church, and a church that neglects this function of teaching has lost something that is indispensable to its nature as a church."[99]

There is little doubt that the great gains of the sixteenth century Reformation would have been lost had they not been accompanied by the establishment of Christian schools. In chapter 10 our focus will be on the "lesser reformers" who carried out the mission of providing Christian school education for the common people of Europe.

Endnotes—Chapter Nine

[1] William Boyd and Edmond J. King, *The History of Western Education* (London: Adam and Charles Black, 1921), p. 197.

[2] Hugh T. Kerr, ed., *By John Calvin* (New York: Association Press, 1960), p. 12.

[3] Carl S. Meyer, "Lutheranism," *The New International Dictionary of the Christian Church*, J.D. Douglas, ed. (Grand Rapids: Zondervan Publishing House, 1974), p. 613.

[4] Ibid., p. 177.

[5] Alister E. McGrath, *A Life of John Calvin* (Cambridge, Mass.: Blackwell Publishers, Inc., 1990), p. 21.

[6] Ibid., p. 22. McGrath cites, J. Toussaert, *Le sentiment religieux en Flandre à la fin du Moye Age* (Paris, 1963).

[7] Frederick Eby, *The Development of Modern Education* (New York: Prentice-Hall, Inc., 1934), p. 116.

[8] Elmer Towns, *A History of Religious Education* (Grand Rapids: Baker Book House, 1975), p. 167.

[9] John Calvin, preface to his commentary on Psalms, quoted by John Woodbridge, "Calvin's Damascus," in *Table Talk*, (Orlando, Fl., Oct., 1995), p. 9.

[10] McGrath, p. 70.

[11] Ibid., pp. 47–48.

[12] Will Durant, *The Reformation* (New York: Simon and Schuster, 1957), p. 460.

[13] A. Lint, "John Calvin," *Introduction to the History of Christianity*, Tim Dowley, ed (Minneapolis: Fortress Press, 1995), p. 380.

[14] Ibid.

[15] W. de Greef, *The Writings of John Calvin* (Grand Rapids: Baker Books, 1989), pp. 28–29.

[16] Ellwood P. Cubberley, *Readings in the History of Education* (Boston: Houghton Mifflin Co., 1920), p. 272.

[17] Durant, *The Reformation*, p. 462.

[18] William J. Bouwsma, "The Peculiarity of the Reformation of Geneva," *Religion and Culture in the Renaissance and Reformation*, vol. XI, Steven Ozment, ed. (Kirksville, Mo.: Sixteenth Century Journal Publishers, Inc., 1989), p. 65.

[19] Paul T. Fuhrmann, "A Historical Foreword," *Instruction in Faith* (1537), by John Calvin (Philadelphia: The Westminster Press, 1947), p. 7.

[20] de Greef, p. 91.

[21] J. Kirk, "Scottish Reformation," *Dictionary of Scottish Church History and Theology* (Edinburgh: T. and T. Clark, 1993), p. 695.

[22] Ibid., pp. 693–694.

[23] John Knox, *The History of the Reformation of Religion in Scotland*, Twentieth Century Edition (London: Andrew Melrose, 1905), p. 7.

[24] Richard N. Greaves, "John Knox," *The New International Dictionary of the Church*, J.D. Douglas, ed. (Grant Rapids: Zondervan Publishing House, 1974), p. 570.

[25] Robert Hastings Nichols, *The Growth of the Christian Church* (Philadelphia: The Westminster Press, 1945), p. 216.

[26] Jasper Ridley, John Knox, *The Thundering Scott, Christian History*, vol. XIV, no. 2, p. 47.

[27] Thomas M. Lindsay, *A History of the Reformation*, vol. II (Edinburgh: T. & T. Clark, 1908), p. 286.

[28] *Encyclopaedia Britannica*, vol. 13 (Chicago: William Benton, Publisher, 1961), pp. 462–463.

[29] Nichols, p. 216.

[30] Kirk, p. 465.

[31] William Cormish, *"John Knox," The Reformation: Many Men with One Idea* (Geneva: Foundation of Les Clefs de Saint Pierre, 1985), p. 21.

[32] Ridley, p. 11.

[33] R.G. Kyle, "John Knox," *Dictionary of Scottish Church History and Theology* (Edinburgh: T. and T. Clark, 1993), p. 465.

[34] Ridley, p. 14.

[35] Nichols, p. 217.

[36] Kyle, p. 465.

[37] Boyd and King, p. 199.

[38] Reid, p. 178.

[39] Boyd and King, p. 199.

[40] de Greef, p. 53. de Greef cites Charles Borgeaud, *Histoire de l'Université de Genèva*, vol. I, L`Académie de Calvin, 1559–1798 (Geneva, 1900).

[41] Ibid., p. 55.

[42] Ibid., p. 56.

[43] F.V.N. Painter, *A History of Education* (New York: D. Appleton and Company, 1905), p. 172.

[44] J.L. Vander Walt, *The School That Calvin Established in 1559* (Transvaal, Republic of South Africa: Institute for Reformational Studies, 1984), pp. 308–312.

[45] Ibid., pp. 309, 312, 316. Vander Walt cites Van Niekerk, 1940, p. 112.

[46] Ibid., 308.

[47] Frederick Eby, *Early Protestant Educators* (New York: McGraw Hill Book Company, Inc. 1931), pp. 234–235.

[48] de Greef, p. 54

[49] Vander Walt, p. 324. Vander Walt cites: Nordman, W. 1964: Calvin; der Mensch, das Werk, die pädagogische Bedeutung. *Der evangelische Religionslehrer und der Berufsschule*, 12(4): 113–122, p. 121.

[50] Ibid., p. 334.

[51] Ibid., p. 336. Vander Walt cites: White, R, 1969: "The School in Calvin's Thought and Practice," *Journal of Christian Education* 12:5–6, p. 19.

[52] Ellwood P. Cubberley, *The History of Education* (Boston: Houghton Mifflin, 1920), p. 331.

[53] McGrath, p. 86.

[54] Ibid., p. 107.

[55] Ibid., p. 109.

[56] Vander Walt, p. 335. Vander Walt cites: Bratt, J.H. 1959: "John Calvin and the Genevan Schools," *Christian Home and School*, 37(7): 12–13, March.

57 Luther, "Eight Sermons," 1522, LW 51:77, quoted in Eric W. Gritsch, *Academia and Forum: Luther's Reformation in Wittenberg* (Luther Theological Seminary Bulletin, vol. 70, winter 1990), p. 17.

58 Ibid.

59 A.M. Renwick, *The Story of the Scottish Reformation* (London: Inter-Varsity Fellowship, 1960), p. 24.

60 Ibid., p. 24.

61 Ibid., p. 48.

62 Ibid., p. 89. Renwick cites John Knox, *History*, vol. I, pp. 335–338.

63 Ibid., pp. 91–92.

64 Ibid., pp. 92–93. Renwick cites T. McCrie, *Sketches of Scottish Church History*, (1841), pp. 65–66.

65 Boyd and King, p. 201.

66 Renwick, p. 116.

67 Ibid.

68 Ibid.

69 Lindsay, *A History of the Reformation*, vol. II, p. 307.

70 Ibid.

71 John Edgar, *History of Early Scottish Education* (Edinburgh: James Thin, Publisher to the University), p. 243. Note: Edgar cites Cunningham but provides no reference.

72 Eby, *Early Protestant Educators*, pp. 275–276.

73 Boyd and King, p. 202.

74 Renwick, p. 118.

75 John Knox, *The History of the Reformation of the Religion of Scotland* (included in Knox's *Confession* and *The Book of Discipline*), A Twentieth Century Edition-revised and edited by Cuthbert Lennox (London: Andrew Melrose, 1905), p. 382.

76 Edgar, p. 251.

77 Boyd and King, p. 202.

78 Renwick, p. 118.

79 Kyle, p. 19. Note: Knox wrote "The First Blast of the Trumpet . . ." in 1558. It was directed at Mary Tudor, but it was offensive to all queens, including Elizabeth I.

80 Renwick, p. 45.

81 C.B. Eavey, *History of Christian Education* (Chicago: Moody Press, 1964), p. 156.

82 Calvin, *Sermon 4 on the Epistle to Titus*, OC.LIV, p. 429.

83 Calvin, J. Bonnet, *Letters of John Calvin*, vol. II (Philadelphia: Presbyterian Board of Publications, 1858), pp. 191–192.

84 John H. Leith, *Colloquium on Calvin Studies*, V. at Davidson College, Davidson, North Carolina, January 19–20, 1990. Leith provides the following narrative footnote: "On the arrest of this young man, 18 years old and a native of Caen, in Normandy, see *Archives communales de Dijon*, D 65. The legal record is dated 3 February 1560 (=1561, the new year beginning at Easter). Cf. Henri Hauser, *Les compagnonnages d'arts et métiers á Dijon aux XVII and XVIII siècles*, Paris, 1907, pp. 71–72.

85 Ibid., Leith's footnote: "*Cf. Edict faict par le Roy sur certains articles faictz par la faculté de Théologie de Paris touchans et concernana nostre foy et religion chrestienne, avec le cathologue des livres censurez*. Paris. Jean André, 1545. 8vo, [36] pages, A-I4. Our citation is found on page H1 verso. Copy in Paris, Bibliothèque Sainte-Geneviève, number D.8.4285. Room 4.

86 Calvin, *L'ABC francois* [Geneva] [Jean Crespin] 1551, p. 3. Cited by John H. Leith, *Calvin Studies V*, p. 138.

87 Calvin, *Commentary on Isaiah 28:10*, Geneva, Francois Perrin, 1572, 20, 165 pages verso and 166 recto. The original Latin: OC XXXVI, 468 cited by John H. Leith, *Calvin Studies V*, p. 160.

[88] Calvin, Articles (*Articuli de regimine ecclesiae*), cited by Lindsay, *History of the Reformation*, vol. 2, p. 107.

[89] Calvin, "Catechism of the Church of Geneva . . ." Translated by Henry Beveridge, vol. II, pp. 37–39. Cited by Eby, *Early Protestant Educators*, pp. 248–249.

[90] Calvin, "By-laws of the Academy of Geneva," translated by Ernestine F. Leon, cited by Eby, *Early Protestant Educators*, pp. 259–262.

[91] Ibid., pp. 262–263.

[92] Ibid., pp. 263–265.

[93] Harro Hoepfl, *The Christian Polity of John Calvin* (Cambridge: Cambridge University Press, 1992), pp. 202–204. Cited by John Heath, *Calvin Studies VI*, p. 62.

[94] Calvin, Letter of Viret, January 24, 1551, CO, 14:27. Cited by William J. Bouwsma, "The Peculiarity of the Reformation in Geneva," *Religion and Culture*, Steven Ozment, ed., vol. XI (Kirksville, MO: Sixteenth Century Journal Publishers, Inc., 1989), p. 75.

[95] Ibid., Calvin's Letter to Baurer, February 14, 1552, CO, 14:474.

[96] Frederick Eby and Charles Flinn Arrowood, *The Development of Modern Education* (1st ed.), (New York: Prentice-Hall, Inc., 1934), p. 34.

[97] John Knox, *The History of the Reformation of the Religion of Scotland* (included in Knox's *Confession* and *The Book of Discipline*), A Twentieth Century Edition-Revised and edited by Cuthbert Lennox (London: Andrew Melrose, 1905), p. 382.

[98] Peter Y. DeJong, "Calvin's Contribution to Christian Education," *Calvin's Theological Journal*, vol. 2, no. 2, November 1967, p. 200.

[99] James E. Smart, *The Teaching Ministry of the Church* (Philadelphia: Westminster Press, 1964), p. 11. Cited by DeJong, p. 200.

Illustration Sources

Figure 1   *Knox and Calvin* - The Knox rendering is from a title page of a twentieth-century edition of *The History of the Reformation of Religion in Scotland* by John Knox—revised and edited by Cuthbert Lennox (London: Andrew Melrose, 1905). The rendering of Calvin is from a booklet by Arnold Mobbs, *The Calvin Auditorium, John Knox Chapel* (Geneva: Eglise Nationale Protestante de Geneva, 1985) p. 9 (used by permission).

Figure 2   *Map* - Global Mapping International, Colorado Springs, CO.

Figure 3   *Calvin's signature* - *A History of Calvinism* (author unknown).

Figure 4   *Statue* - Photo by author (PBA).

Figure 5   *Galley* - Alison Grant and Ronald Mayo, *The Huguenots* (London: Longman Group Limited, 1973), p. 71.

Figure 6   *Queen Mary* - Royal England Readers, *Our Kings and Queens* (London: Thomas Nelson and Sons, 1893), p. 145.

Figure 7   *St. Giles* - (PBA).

Figure 8   *Reformers* - (PBA).

Figure 9   *City motto* - (PBA).

Figure 10   Knox preaching - (PBA).

Figure 11   *Calvin's chair* - (PBA).

The Lesser Reformers as Educators

The "lesser reformers"—Philip Melanchthon, Johann Bugenhagen, Johann Sturm, Martin Bucer, and Ulrich Zwingli—were the great educators of the Reformation era. As educators, they were equal or superior to their mentors—Luther, Calvin, and Knox. God used Luther, Calvin, and Knox as well as Wycliff, Huss, and Tyndale to set the larger stage for the return to biblical authority, but it was the lesser reformers who carried out the details of education reform. Almost all of them, as we will see, were educated in the philosophy of Renaissance humanism, and that education affected, in varying degrees, their philosophy of Christian school education. For the lesser reformers, we will examine:

Figure 1. Philip Melanchthon was called the "Preceptor [teacher] of Germany." This statue is a part of the Luther memorial at Worms.

1. *Their Place in History*
2. *Their Achievements in Christian School Education*
3. *A Critique of Their Educational Philosophy*

As previously stated, the Great Reformation was as much a reform of education as a reform of the church. The dramatic shift from educating ten percent of the population for ecclesiastical purposes, which existed under Catholicism, to educating everyone is regarded to this day as the most significant educational event in history. This powerful revolution in education, which jolted the Western world out of the Middle Ages, took place largely at the hands of the lesser reformers. We begin with Luther's most trusted advisor and Germany's foremost educator.

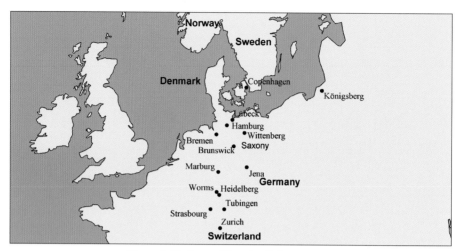

Figure 2. The Lesser Education Reformers' map

PHILIP MELANCHTHON (1497–1560)

There is little doubt that Philip Melanchthon, one of the great scholars of the Reformation era, deserved the title "Preceptor (Teacher) of Germany." Boyd and King provide the following concise description of this close associate of Martin Luther:

> Among the great men to whose efforts Protestant Germany owed the creation of her educational institutions, Philip Melanchthon stands out as the first and the greatest. In a long and arduous career, extending over forty years spent in working out the theological groundwork of the new faith, he devoted himself to an extraordinary variety of educational enterprises. He made the university of Wittenberg the centre of Protestant studies by his own lectures on the classics and on theology; he kept a private school in his house for youths going on to the study of the arts, and wrote a series of grammatical and other textbooks so admirable that some of them were still in use in the Eighteenth Century; he established the school systems of several towns (notably in Saxony), re-organized some of the old universities like Heidelberg, and organized the new Protestant universities of Marburg, Königsberg, and Jena. The title of *Præceptor Germaniæ*, which is his by general consent, was assuredly well deserved.[1]

In northern Germany today there are numerous memorials to Martin Luther, but in Wittenberg, where the Great Reformation began, almost as many statues and other forms of recognition are for Philip Melanchthon as for Luther. In the town square of Wittenberg, for example, the bronze statues of Luther and Melanchthon are of equal size. Thousands of tourists each year visit the former residences of both. This is not to suggest that Melanchthon is remembered in Wittenberg as an equal to Luther but rather to recognize Melanchthon for his contribution to the reform of Germany's educational system. With reference to his lifestyle, Painter writes:

> During his whole life Melanchthon was a student of remarkable industry. He often arose as early as two or three o'clock in the morning to pursue his studies, and many of his works were written between that hour and dawn. . . . Melanchthon exerted an influence upon the educational progress of Germany in

Figure 3. Philip Melanchthon's statue in Wittenberg is equal in size to Luther's statue.

> various ways. First of all, he was an able teacher, whose instruction was largely attended. Two thousand students, from all parts of Europe, thronged his lecture-room at Wittenberg, and bore away the precious seed both of the gospel and of ancient learning. . . . Many of the leading educators of Protestant Germany . . . were once his students.[2]

Before we look at the curriculum advocated by Melanchthon, it is important to understand his philosophy of education. While his views on education were similar to Luther's, there were some marked differences. According to Gangel and Benson:

> One wonders how Luther and Melanchthon dealt with their differences "behind closed doors." Apparently, Philip was able to tone down his obvious love for a classical curriculum sufficiently for Martin to ignore the differences and emphasize his strengths as theologian and historian.[3]

Figure 4. A nineteenth-century replica of Melanchthon's desk and chair at Lutherhalle in Wittenberg.

It is well known that Martin Luther was not a lover of the pagan classics. He referred to Aristotle as "that blind heathen teacher."[4] Luther agreed with Peter Ramus of France, who commented, "All that Aristotle said was false."[5] Melanchthon, on the other hand, had been steeped in humanism as a student at Tübingen University and regarded the pagan classics as essential to advanced learning. Hendrix cites Oberman, who claims that "Philip Melanchthon and other reformers with humanist backgrounds robbed Luther's admonitions of their eschatological urgency."[6] Boyd and King write:

> The triumph of humanism through the effort of Melanchthon and his disciples prevented this obvious extension of the ideals of the Reformation, and made the study of an alien culture the central interest of the higher schools for more than three hundred years.[7]

Surprisingly Luther, over time, compromised on the issue of including pagan classics at the secondary and university levels. Marsden says:

> The Protestant university curriculum as established by Melanchthon was a mix of progressive and conservative elements. Despite Luther's earlier strictures, Melanchthon persuaded him by the 1530's that Aristotle was useful to the university curriculum, even if not a reliable guide in theology or ethics.[8]

Professor Freeman Butts claims that Melanchthon was selective in his use of pagan writings, "being careful to select only those authors who were duly pious."[9] It is paradoxical, of course, to ascribe biblical piety to the pagans of antiquity, who believed there was a multiplicity of gods. Gangel and Benson point out that "though [Luther and Melanchthon] . . . differed on the value of the classics, they were of one mind on the centrality of Scripture and theology in the curriculum of all ages."[10] Both Luther and Melanchthon were committed to the idea that their Christian school curriculum should be taught in Latin and that its primary purpose was to train students for the ministry and for service to the people as civil servants.[11]

MELANCHTHON'S PLAN FOR EDUCATION REFORM

In 1527 and 1528 Luther, Bugenhagen, and Melanchthon conducted school visits in various cities in Germany and observed firsthand the need for change in the schools. As a preamble to what became known as the Saxony School Plan, Melanchthon detailed some of their findings:

> There are now many mistakes in the schools. In order that the young may be properly instructed, we have drawn up the present form. In the

first place, teachers should instruct the children only in Latin, and not in German or Greek, as some have hitherto done, who burden the poor children with a multiplicity of subjects, which is not only not profitable, but even hurtful. It is evident that such schoolmasters seek not the welfare of the children in teaching so many languages, but their own reputation. In the second place, they should not burden the children with many books, but in every way avoid a multiplication of studies.[12]

What follows is the complete Saxony School Plan written by Philip Melanchthon in 1528 and approved by Martin Luther. The three-level plan is of particular interest to the English-speaking world because it not only became the curriculum model for all of Germany but it had considerable influence on education in England and Colonial America.[13] As with Calvin's seven grade levels at Geneva Academy, a student's academic progression through the three grade levels of Melanchthon's Saxony School Plan was achieved by mastery of the academic material and was not designed to reflect the age level of the student, nor was each group or grade level designed to be achieved in a single school year. Melanchthon said, "it is indispensable that the children be classified into distinct groups,"[14] an innovation at the time. Melanchthon's Saxony School Plan was as follows:

The First Group.—The first group should consist of those children who are learning to read. With these the following method is to be adopted: They are first to be taught the child's-manual, containing the alphabet, the creed, the Lord's prayer, and other prayers. When they have learned this, Donatus and Cato may both be given them; Donatus for a reading book, and Cato they may explain after the following manner: the schoolmaster must give them the explanation of a verse or two, and then in a few hours call upon them to repeat what he has thus said; and in this way they will learn a great number of Latin words, and lay up a full store of phrases to use in speech. In this they should be exercised until they can read well. Neither do we consider it time lost, if the feebler children, who are not especially quick-witted, should read Cato and Donatus not once only, but a second time. With this they should be taught to write, and be required to shew their writing to the schoolmaster every day. Another mode of enlarging their knowledge of Latin words is to give them every afternoon some words to commit to memory, as has been the custom in schools hitherto. These children must likewise be kept at music, and be made to sing with the others, as we shall show, God willing, further on.

The Second Group.—The second group consists of children who have learned to read, and are now ready to go into grammar. With these the following regulations should be observed: The first hour after noon every day all the children, large and small, should be practiced in music. Then the schoolmaster must interpret to the second group the fables of Aesop. After vespers, he should explain to them the "Paedology" of Mosellanus; and, when this is finished, he should select from the "Colloquies" of Erasmus some that may conduce to their improvement and discipline. This should be repeated on the next evening also. When the children are about to go home for the night, some short sentence may be given them, taken perhaps from a poet, which they are to repeat the next morning, such as *Amicus certus in re incerta cerniture.*—A true friend becomes manifest in adversity. Or *Fortuna, quem nimium fovet, stultum facit.*—Fortune, if she fondles a man too much, makes him a fool. Or this from Ovid: *Vulgus amicitias utilitate probat.*—The rabble value friendships by the profit they yield.

In the morning the children are again to explain Aesop's fables. With this the teacher should decline some nouns or verbs, many or few, easy or difficult, according to the progress of the children, and then ask them the rules and the reasons for such inflection. And at the same time when they shall have learned the rules of construction, they should be required to construe (parse), as it is called; this is a very useful exercise, and yet there are not many who employ it. After the children have thus learned Aesop, Terence is to be given to them; and this they must commit to memory, for they will now be older, and able to work harder. Still the master must be cautious, lest he overtask them. Next after Terence, the children may take hold of such of the comedies of Plautus as are harmless in their tendency, as the "Aulularia," the "Trinummus," the "Pseudolus," etc.

The hour before mid-day must be invariably and exclusively devoted to instruction in grammar: first etymology, then syntax, and lastly prosody. And when the teacher has gone thus far through with the grammar, he should begin it again, and so on continually, that the children may understand it to perfection. For if there is negligence here, there is neither certainty nor stability in whatever is learned beside. And the children should learn by heart and repeat all the rules, so that they may be driven and forced, as it were, to learn the grammar well.

If such labor is irksome to the schoolmaster, as we often see, then we should dismiss him, and get another in his place,—one who will not shrink from the duty of keeping his pupils constantly in the grammar. For no greater injury can befall learning and the arts, than for youth to grow up in ignorance of grammar.

This course should be repeated daily, by the week together; nor should we by any means give children a different book to study each day.

However, one day, for instance, Sunday or Wednesday, should be set apart, in which the children may receive Christian instruction. For some are suffered to learn nothing in the Holy Scriptures; and some masters there are who teach children nothing but the Scriptures; both of which extremes must be avoided. For it is essential that children be taught the rudiments of the Christian and divine life. So likewise there are many reasons why, with the Scriptures, other books too should be laid before them, out of which they may learn to read. And in this matter we propose the following method: Let the schoolmaster hear the whole group, making them, one after the other repeat the Lord's prayer, the creed, and the ten commandments. But if the group is too large, it may be divided, so that one week one part may recite, and the remaining part the next.

After one recitation, the master should explain in a simple and correct manner the Lord's prayer, after the next the creed, and at another time the ten commandments. And he should impress upon the children the essentials, such as the fear of God, faith, and good works. He must not touch upon polemics, nor must he accustom the children to scoff at monks or any other persons, as many unskillful teachers use to do.

With this the schoolmaster may give the boys some plain psalms to commit to memory, which comprehend the sum and substance of the Christian life, which inculcate the fear of the Lord, faith, and good works. As the 112th Psalm, "Blessed is the man that feareth the Lord" the 34th, "I will bless the Lord at all times" the 128th, "Blessed is every one that feareth the Lord, that walketh in His ways"; the 125th, "They that trust in the Lord shall be as Mount Zion, which can not be removed, but abideth forever"; the 127th, "Except the Lord build the house, they labor in vain that build it"; the 133d, "Behold how good and how pleasant it is for brethren to dwell together in unity!" or other such plain and intelligible psalms, which likewise should be expounded in the briefest and most correct manner possible, so that the children may know, both the substance of what they have learned and where to find it.

On this day too the teacher should give a grammatical exposition of Matthew; and, when he has gone through with it, he should commence it anew. But, when the boys are somewhat more advanced, he may comment upon the two epistles of Paul to Timothy, or the 1st Epistle of John, or the Proverbs of Solomon. But teachers must not undertake any other books. For it is not profitable to burden the young with deep and difficult books as some do, who, to add to their own reputation, read Isaiah, Paul's Epistle to the Romans, St. John's Gospel, and others of a like nature.

The Third Group.—Now, when these children have been well trained in grammar, those among them who have made the greatest proficiency should be taken out, and formed into the third group. The hour after mid-day they, together with the rest, are to devote to music. After this the teacher is to give an explanation of Virgil. When he has finished this, he may take up Ovid's "Metamorphoses," and in the latter part of the afternoon Cicero's "Offices," or "Letters to Friends." In the morning Virgil may be reviewed, and the teachers, to keep up practice in the grammar, may call for constructions and inflections, and point out the prominent figures of speech.

The hour before mid-day, grammar should still be kept up, that the scholars may be thoroughly versed therein. And when they are perfectly familiar with etymology and syntax, then prosody (metrica), should be opened to them, so that they can thereby become accustomed to make verses. for this exercise is a very great help toward understanding the writings of others; and it likewise gives the boys a rich fund of words, and renders them accomplished many ways. In course of time, after they have been sufficiently practiced in the grammar, this same hour is to be given to logic and rhetoric. The boys in the second and third groups are to be required every week to write compositions, either in the form of letters or of verses. They should also be rigidly confined to Latin conversation, and to this end the teachers themselves must, as far as possible, speak nothing but Latin with the boys; thus they will acquire the practice by use, and the more rapidly for the incentives held out to them.[15]

However pedagogically and politically incorrect Melanchthon's Saxony School Plan may appear to us today, it was the original academic touchstone that stimulated education reform throughout Germany and the Western world. Melanchthon died at age sixty-three, the same age as Luther at his death. The two are buried within a few feet of each other in the Palace Church in Wittenberg.

The brief comparative study that follows provides insight into the tension that existed between the philosophies of Renaissance humanism, centered in Greek and Roman literature, and evangelical Protestantism, centered in biblical authority. An appropriate preamble to the comparison is provided by professors Eby and Arrowood:

[Renaissance humanism and evangelical Protestantism] were like two great rivers which flow together but are never completely united; in the center of the stream they are individually indistinguishable, but on the sides each retains its identity virtually unchanged. No slight difficulty presents itself when one attempts to understand the varied relationships

in which these two movements stood toward each other. They presented a unified attack upon a common enemy, [Catholicism] and agreed
generally upon the organization, aim, and curriculum of the schools.
But in other respects they were quite antagonistic.[16]

Renaissance Humanism	Evangelical Protestantism
1. Opposed scholasticism	Opposed scholasticism
2. Opposed Catholicism	Opposed Catholicism
3. Believed in the virtues of man as the basis of authority	Believed in God as revealed in the Scriptures as the basis of authority
4. Advocated the use of Latin and sometimes Greek in the schools as "the gateways to the ancient classical literatures of Rome and Greece"[17]	Advocated the use of Latin in the schools as it was the language of the early church fathers, and the use of Greek and Hebrew in the schools as they were the languages of the Bible
5. Originated in Italy	Originated in Germany
6. Humanists tended to be elitist and were among those characterized as rich and aristocratic	Evangelicals generally identified with the spiritual and academic welfare of the lower and middle classes[18]

Note: Eby and Arrowood point out that both the humanists and the
evangelicals were committed to the ancient languages because, as they said:

Students read Aristotle in the original Greek and found that he actually
contradicted what they had found in their round-about translations
from the [Muslims]. The religious reformers, on the other hand, found
that the church of the New Testament was quite different from the
Roman [Catholic] Church that they knew.[19]

JOHANN BUGENHAGEN 1485–1558)

Johann Bugenhagen's role in the Great Reformation was much more
than that of a theology professor at Wittenberg University and the popular
pastor of the Wittenberg University Church. Bugenhagen, even more than
Luther and Melanchthon, "aided the cause of Protestant schools in
Germany,"[20] particularly in northern Germany, and in the Scandinavian

countries. His main emphasis was elementary education. Bugenhagen was to elementary education what Melanchthon was to secondary education in the great education reform movement of the sixteenth century. One of his great gifts was his ability to organize.[21]

In the years immediately prior to the Reformation, a growing number of private schools, referred to as "reading and writing schools," had been established in Germany by the rising commercial class, quite independent from Catholicism's ecclesiastical schools. Eby says, "Those schools taught only the secular arts and were greatly disliked by the various church schools."[22] In the wake of the Great Reformation, the Catholic schools closed, but the secular private schools remained open. The town councils of Brunswick, Hamburg, Lübeck, Breman, and other cities in northern Germany and the Kingdom of Denmark[23] called upon Bugenhagen to make these "reading and writing schools" over into evangelical Protestant schools. Under Bugenhagen's plan there were to be German language schools for the lower classes, Latin schools for the upper-class students, and separate schools for girls. Eby explains:

Figure 5. Johann Bugenhagen was the champion of Christian elementary education in Northern Germany and the Scandinavian countries. He was the only Christian school educator in all of history to crown a king.

> Into the old root Bugenhagen sought to graft a new order, a system of Latin and vernacular schools under the control of the city authorities in which the Protestant religion was taught together with the secular subjects. Due to the favorable conditions which existed in this part of the country, the city councils were willing to establish some town schools for boys and separate schools for girls in which the vernacular was used; also Latin schools for the higher class of students.[24]

One might ask, Just how 'Christian' were these Protestant schools that functioned under the combined authority of the town and church councils? History reveals that over time they lost most of their original evangelical fervor, but the introduction to the Brunswick school ordinance, written in 1528 by Bugenhagen, is revealing:

School Ordinance from the Church Ordinance
of the Town of Brunswick

Before all else, therefore, it is considered necessary here at Brunswick through the honorable council and the entire community to establish good schools and to employ honorable, well-grounded, scholarly masters and assistants to the honor of God the Almighty for the welfare of the youth and the satisfaction of the entire city. Therein the poor, ignorant youth may be properly trained, learn the ten commandments, the creed, the Lord's prayer, the Christian sacraments, with as much of explanation as is suitable for children, also learn to sing the psalms in Latin, and read passages every day from the Latin scriptures. In addition they are to study the humanities from which one learns to understand such matters. And not merely that, but also that in time there may come good schoolmasters, good preachers, good jurists, good physicians, God-fearing, decent, honorable, well-grounded, obedient, sociable, scholarly, peaceable, sober but happy citizens, who henceforth may train their children in the best way, and so on to the children's children.

This will God have from us, he will also be with us through his grace, that this may take place and be successful. The Jews taught their children in the homes, and had schools in every town, which were called synagogues, so that they learned well the law of Moses, and could defend their faith. Furthermore, the Jews still teach their children in their own way. Among us Christians it is certainly disgraceful that we do not learn to know Christ rightly in whom we are baptized; furthermore it is a shame that we do not have the youth taught such arts as will help them to be of service to themselves and to the world, and serviceable to the salvation of their souls and to the good government in these lands and cities.

If our industry does not succeed with some children, it will with many others. A tree that bears many good apples should not be hewn down because two or three are wormy. We must not neglect to do good, because it is thrown away on some individuals.[25]

While these early Christian schools were operating under the auspices of the city and the city's evangelical churches, they were financed primarily with tuition paid by parents, with one interesting feature that sounds strange to us today. Eby explains:

These schools were to be supported from fees paid by the parents. The new feature of great importance, however, was that the teachers were to receive, from the municipal treasury, a bonus for teaching catechism, religion, and church music. In this manner the old town school was now linked up with religious instruction, and was on its way as the elementary school of the common people.[26]

The famous hornbook, used so effectively in teaching the fundamentals of reading to young students in the American colonies, had its beginning in Europe and was used in Bugenhagen's Christian schools. Elmer Wilds describes the hornbook and its use:

> The Protestant schoolmaster early developed a simple course of study for the teaching of reading. A child in learning to read began with the hornbook, a thin board on which a printed leaf containing the alphabet and the Lord's Prayer was pasted, covered over with a thin sheet of transparent horn to preserve it from wear. The child learned his letters from this device until it was superseded by the primer. The earliest primer was a simple A-B-C book, a sheet of cardboard folded to form four or six pages, containing an illustrated alphabet with a verse beneath each letter. From this developed the type of primer introduced into the American colonies, containing the alphabet, the illustrated alphabet with verses, the syllabarium, and short reading passages consisting of selections from the Psalter and the New Testament, and hymns. Having learned to read, the child passed to the catechism, the Psalter, and the Bible, which constituted the entire range of reading in the early Protestant schools.[27]

Bugenhagen is undoubtedly the first and only Christian school educator in history to be called upon to crown a king. James Atkinson records this unusual event:

> King Christian III succeeded to the Danish throne in 1536 and the transition [in Denmark] to Protestantism was virtually completed. He stripped the [Catholic] bishops of their lands and property at the Diet of Copenhagen (1536), and transferred the church's wealth to the state.

> Christian III then turned to Luther for help. In 1537 Luther sent Bugenhagen—the only Lutheran theologian at Wittenberg who could speak the dialects of Denmark and the German border. Bugenhagen crowned the king and appointed seven superintendents. This severed the old line of [Catholic] bishops and established a new line of [Protestant] presbyters. At the synods which followed church ordinances were published, and the Reformation recognized in Danish law.[28]

Understandably, this event gave Bugenhagen considerable status in Denmark. He spent five years establishing Christian school education throughout the country.[29] From Denmark the Reformation spread to the other Scandinavian countries and on to Greenland. As Eavey says, "everywhere Protestantism went—Christian schools were founded."[30]

JOHANN STURM (1507–1589)

Johann Sturm of Strassburg, Germany (now Strasbourg, France), was the most humanistic of the new generation of Protestant educators. In fact, as Eby says, "religion was not Sturm's supreme concern, but was utilized chiefly as a help to the study of Latin."[31] Sturm's humanistic philosophy reflected his early education in the Brethren of the Common Life School and the Catholic University at Louvain.[32]

Sturm's Strassburg school, the Gymnasium, was important to the Reformation education movement, not for its philosophy or lack thereof but for its patterns of organization. In fact, his citywide school system became the organizational model for John Calvin's Geneva Academy and for countless other

Figure 6. Thousands of students attended Johann Sturm's secondary school in Strassburg, Germany (now Strasbourg, France). His motto: "All subjects to be kept within range of the pupil's ability; all teaching to be made clear and definite; little at a time."—C.W. Bardeen - 1901

secondary schools as the Reformation spread throughout the Western world. You may recall that Calvin lectured at Sturm's secondary school in Strassburg when he was there as an exile from Geneva. Later, as Calvin organized his citywide system of Christian schools, he drew heavily on Johann Sturm's ideas. Sturm expanded Melanchthon's three levels of learning to ten levels. Freeman Butts says:

> In his school at Strassburg Sturm divided the curriculum into ten graded classes, each to be taught by a different teacher and each to follow a prescribed curriculum. Learning Latin was the exclusive task of the first three years, then Greek was added from the fourth class on. In the senior section of six years the course branched out to the seven liberal arts and the lectures were open to the public.[33]

In Sturm's course of study called "Classic Letters," written as a curriculum guide for his faculty, one will note the reverse order of grade levels, the emphasis on Latin and Greek (the gateway languages to the pagan classics), and the strong emphasis on Rome's foremost thinker and philosopher, Cicero. Sturm's curriculum outline was as follows:

Tenth Class [Equivalent to first grade]. The alphabet, reading, and writing simple Latin; Latin declension and conjugation; the German catechism.

Ninth Class. The pupil committed to memory a few Latin words each day, so as to acquire a vocabulary. This was to be done systematically: each pupil was to make a small dictionary of related words. He was also to be thoroughly grounded in declining and conjugating Latin nouns and verbs.

Eighth Class. Vocabularies of words in common use were enlarged as in the former class. Pupils were grounded in the eight parts of speech. They read the selected letters of Cicero, with constant study of the grammatical construction of the language. Exercises in style now began to take the place of the vocabulary exercises.

Seventh Class. Latin syntax as exemplified in the daily reading of Cicero's letters; exercises in style. On Sundays, translation of the catechism into classical Latin.

Sixth Class. The longer letters of Cicero were translated into German; Greek was commenced. A greater elegance in Latin style was sought. Saturday and Sunday the catechism and pious literature were translated into Latin.

Fifth Class. Poetry was studied; scansion, varieties of metre and verse; mythology; Cicero's *Cato* and *Laelius*, and the *Eclogues* of Virgil. Their encyclopedias of Latin words were completed; Greek was continued; style was more thoroughly cultivated, and versification begun. Passages of great elegance were translated into German and then back into Latin, extempore; the Epistles of Paul were translated in this manner on Saturday and Sunday.

Fourth Class. The study of Latin and Greek grammar was now completed; the pupils could speak these languages; Cicero's *Oration against Verres* and Horace were studied, and Greek was continued. Daily practice in style, reviews, and Paul's Epistles.

Third Class. Rhetoric was begun—based, in Latin, on Cicero's speech for Cluentius; and, in Greek, on Demosthenes. The first book of the *Iliad*, and that of the *Odyssey*. Greek orations were translated into Latin, and from Latin into Greek. The odes of Pindar and Horace were changed into a different metre. The comedies of Plautus and Terence were acted. Style was incessantly practiced and improved.

Second Class. The scholars themselves now interpreted Greek poets and orators; the same was done for Latin authors. Logic and rhetoric were studied. This latter subject was illustrated by passages from Demosthenes and Cicero. Daily exercises in style and the writing of short dissertations were given. Plays of Aristophanes, Euripides, or Sophocles were studied and acted.

First Class. Logic and rhetoric were further studied, and their rules applied to Demosthenes and Cicero. Virgil and Homer were to be completed. Thucydides and Sallust were to be translated in writing.[34]

Cicero was the centerpiece of Sturm's curriculum. His objective for every student was "the acquisition of pure, fluent Ciceronian eloquence,"[35] for he said:

Cicero was but twenty years old when he delivered his speeches in behalf of P. Quintius and Sextius Roscius; but, in these latter days, where is the man, of fourscore even, who could bequeath to the world such masterpieces of eloquence? And yet, there are books enough, and there is intellect enough. What, then, do we need further? I reply, the Latin language, and a correct method of teaching. Both these we must have, before we can arrive at the summit of eloquence.[36]

Clearly, Sturm's school had an elitist flare with an aristocratic clientele. Eby says:

The success of Sturm's school was phenomenal. Its enrollment reached several thousand students, for all northern Europe sent boys for him to train. The nobility were amply represented. At one time, two hundred noblemen, twenty-four counts and barons, and three princes were enrolled.[37]

Johann Sturm can legitimately be counted among Germany's Protestant education reformers, but the center of his educational focus was on Cicero, not on Christ and the Holy Scriptures. He was far adrift of the Bible-centered philosophy of education espoused by Martin Luther, who said, "Above all in the schools of all kinds the chief and most common lesson should be in the Scriptures. . . . everything must perish where God's word is not studied unceasingly."[38]

MARTIN BUCER (1491-1551)

Like all the Protestant reformers, Martin Bucer (or Butzer), of Strassburg, was a converted Catholic priest. And like so many other reformers he was converted through reading the Bible, through the writings of Martin Luther, and in his case through a private meeting with Luther himself. Stephens claims that this latter event, which took place in 1518, "shaped the rest of [Bucer's] life."[39]

Bucer's effort in Christian school education predated that of Calvin and Sturm. Bucer was one of the most successful of the reformers in persuading a Protestant town council to turn over revenues from the former Catholic

lands to the Christian school education of the town's children. Eby and Arrowood describe this amazing development:

> In 1524, Martin Bucer, the most noted reformer of Strassburg, approached the magistrates with a plan for a system of free schools. The money for their support was to be derived from the revenues of the former religious orders, for Bucer believed that by right these revenues should be used for the aid and education of the poor and not for the expenditures of the town government. Several Latin schools were organized, as well as elementary schools in which reading and writing of German, catechism, and music were taught.[40]

Figure 7. Martin Bucer, the founder of Christian school education in Strassburg, Germany (now Strasbourg, France), said the purpose of his schools was "that Christ might reign more fully over the 'republic'."

In those years immediately following the Great Reformation, civil leaders maintained a close relationship with religious leaders. Town councils welcomed recommendations from church pastors. Martin Bucer had become the leading spokesman for the evangelical pastors of Strassburg and presented a series of fourteen recommendations to the civil leaders. His first recommendation had to do with establishing Christian schools for all children. William Nottingham says:

> In the Code of Fourteen Recommendations, which Bucer lists, Christian education of youth is in first place. . . . This was, indeed, the first article of the law against idleness, and the second was that all children of Christian parents, both boys and girls, including the poorest, learn to read and write, in order that Christ might reign more fully over the "republic." Then suitable trades will be taught them according to their proven abilities, while some continue the study of the liberal arts.[41]

Strassburg was the geographical crossroads between France, Germany, Switzerland, and the Netherlands. Consequently, the educational ideas of both Bucer and Sturm had a wide sphere of influence, including John Calvin in Geneva. Through Calvin their ideas were spread throughout the Western world.

ULRICH [OR HULDREICH] ZWINGLI (1484–1531)

Ulrich Zwingli, a young Catholic priest in Switzerland, after reading the newly published New Testament translated from the original Greek by Erasmus, suddenly realized that many doctrines of the Catholic Church were in error. The year after Luther, in Wittenberg, took his famous stand against the sale of indulgences (1517), Zwingli "drove the indulgence-seller, Sampson, out of the canton [county] by his open denunciations."[42] He also closed down a Catholic shrine that had these words over its gate, "Full forgiveness of all sin can be had here."[43] His bold actions created no small alarm among Catholic authorities. Because of the firestorm created by Luther the year before, Zwingli's Catholic bishop thought it best, rather than excommunicating him, to transfer him to the cathedral at Zurich and to give him the title "papal chaplain." It is a matter of history that the bishop's strategy did not work. Lowndes explains:

Figure 8. Ulrich Zwingli, the first Protestant reformer in Switzerland, wrote the first treatise on Christian school education.

> On New Year's Day, 1519, he entered the pulpit of the cathedral of Zurich for the first time, and announced to his hearers, that, in a continuous series of sermons, he would preach on the life of Christ such as it was set forth in the gospel of St. Matthew, and such as he had come to understand it by looking at it by its own inherent light to the exclusion of all human authorities. Thus he asserted what the Church was not willing to grant, —the freedom of the pulpit; and the impression he made was very great. Distinguished persons in the city who long before had ceased to frequent the church, because they derived no good from their visits, returned, and became active and zealous members of his flock.[44]

Within two years Zwingli persuaded the town council of Zurich, after a public debate with Catholic authorities, to abandon Catholicism and to assume ownership for the people of Zurich of all Catholic properties. And like the other reformers, he then appealed to the city fathers to channel the income from the former Catholic properties toward a citywide system of Christian schools. In 1523 he published a short treatise entitled *The Christian Education of Boys*, which Boyd and King say was "the first book to be written on education from the Protestant point of view."[45] The following year Zwingli wrote a second book, *How to Educate the Young in Good Manners and Christian Discipline*. The book was divided into three parts: instruction in (1) the things that belong to God, (2) the things that pertain to self, and (3) the things that concern our fellow men. The following short excerpt gives insight into Zwingli's understanding of the Christian philosophy of education:

Although it is not in human power to bring the heart of man to believe in God, even with an eloquence greater than that of Pericles; and, although our heavenly Father alone, who draws us to himself, can accomplish that work, yet faith, as Paul teaches, comes by hearing, namely, the hearing of the Word of God. Therefore, we must seek to instill faith in youth by the clearest and commonest words from the mouth of God, at the same time praying that He who alone begets faith would enlighten him whom we instruct. It also seems to me not discordant with the teaching of Christ, if we lead the young through visible things to the knowledge of God, placing before their eyes the beauties of the whole world, and showing them under the mutations of Nature an immutable Being who holds the manifold world in such admirable order.[46]

Like the other reformers, Zwingli was committed to the study of languages. Under Catholicism, Hebrew and Greek, the languages of the Bible, had been outlawed. Painter says:

Figure 9. Zwingli (on the left) challenges Luther on theological issues having to do with communion at the Marburg Colloquy.

Zwingli advocated a study of Hebrew and Greek as an aid to the clear and assured apprehension of Scripture truth. Latin was to be studied for its general utility. Yet these linguistic attainments should not be associated with pride, but with a sincere and unpretentious love of truth. Christ was held up as the prototype of every virtue, upon which life should be formed. Zwingli encouraged the study of mathematics and gymnastics, and urged especially the learning of a trade, by which, in case of necessity, a livelihood might be earned.[47]

In 1525, Zwingli was elected to the newly formed Protestant School Board. From that position he was given a greater opportunity to influence education in the city-state of Zurich.

As we said at the outset of this chapter, all the reformers were humanists, in varying degrees, Luther being the least humanistic. The identification by the reformers with humanists such as Erasmus was due in part to their mutual disdain for the Catholic Church. In that sense Zwingli was a strong advocate of humanism. Eavey says:

He was a zealous supporter of humanism, which he had studied at several universities. Under the influence of Erasmus and others he had become convinced that traditional [Catholic] theology had no biblical basis, and he carefully read the Scriptures in the original Greek and Hebrew. In charge of the cathedral at Zurich, he attacked the dogmas and traditions of the church and supported by the town, gradually dropped one church form after another. He made the extension of education a part of his work of reform, fostering humanistic learning and founding a number of humanistic institutions. He introduced elementary schools into Switzerland and also published an educational treatise recommending a course of studies similar to that of Luther.[48]

Some have referred to Zwingli as "the third man of the Reformation,"[49] with Luther and Calvin. Zwingli is remembered for his public debate with Martin Luther in 1529, at Philip of Hesse's castle in Marburg, Germany, where the two of them agreed on fourteen points of doctrine but disagreed on the nature of the presence of Christ in the elements of the Lord's Supper. Luther believed it was literal rather than symbolic.[50] These days, tourists visit Philip of Hesse's picturesque castle in Marburg to see the room in which Luther and Zwingli conducted their famous "Marburg Colloquy."

Zwingli died in an "unnecessary" civil war at the age of forty-seven. At his death he said, "They can kill the body, but not the soul."[51]

We conclude this chapter with C.B. Eavey's insightful observation about the error in judgment the reformers made in their practice of mixing the teachings of the pagans of antiquity with the teachings of the sacred Scriptures. Eavey observes:

Virtually all of the reformers were humanists or at least had been trained in humanistic schools and were altogether willing to borrow from humanistic sources. . . . Consequently, official Protestantism from its very beginning failed in spite of the spiritual heights achieved, to do for the world of mind what it did for the world of spirit. Thus, once more, when men were given the opportunity to accept as true knowledge the revelation coming from God, they chose instead, though in education now rather than in religion, to weaken the truth of God by means of an admixture of human wisdom which would in the future, just as the human had done in the past, fail to satisfy the yearning of men for truth. And it was by the choice then made that there was introduced into modern education, general and Christian, the leaven of worldly intellectual paganism.[52]

As one writer said, "The church married the enemy and became corrupted by it."[53]

We turn now from the unique history of the great Protestant reformers to the subsequent Christian school movements which, like tidal waves, spread rapidly throughout the Western world.

Endnotes - Chapter Ten

[1] William Boyd and Edmond J. King, *The History of Western Education* (London: Adam and Clark Black, 1921), p. 191.

[2] F.V.N. Painter, *A History of Education* (New York: D. Appleton and Company, 1905), p. 166.

[3] Kenneth O. Gangel and Warren S. Benson, *Christian Education: Its History and Philosophy* (Chicago: Moody Press, 1983), p. 142.

[4] Frederick Eby, *Early Protestant Educators* (New York: McGraw-Hill Book Company, Inc., 1931), p. 35.

[5] Frederick Eby, *The Development of Modern Education* (New York: Prentice-Hall, Inc., 1934), p. 100.

[6] Scott H. Hendrix, "Luther's Impact on the Sixteenth Century," *The Sixteenth Century Journal* XVI, no. 1 (spring 1985}, p. 3. Hendrix cites Heiko A. Oberman, "Martin Luther: Vorläufer der Reformation," in *Verifikationen, Festschrift für Gerhard Ebeling zum 70. Geburtstag,* ed. E. Jüngel, J. Wallmann, W. Werbeck (Tübingen: Mohr [Siebeck], 1982), pp. 91–119.

[7] Boyd and King, p. 193.

[8] George M. Marsden, *The Soul of the American University: From Protestant Establishment to Established Nonbelief* (New York: Oxford University Press, 1994), p. 36.

[9] R. Freeman Butts, *The Education of the West* (New York: McGraw-Hill Book Company, 1947), p. 255.

[10] Gangel and Benson, p. 143.

[11] Martin Luther, *Letter to the Mayors and Alderman of all the Cities of Germany in Behalf of Christian Schools,* cited by Painter, *Luther on Education,* pp. 200–201.

[12] Painter, *A History of Education,* p. 169.

[13] Ibid.

[14] Philip Melanchthon, *Book of Visitation School Plan,* translated by Henry Barnard, *German Teachers and Educators,* pp. 169–171, translated from Karl von Raumer, *Geschichte der Pädagogik,* vol. I, pp. 155–158; Reinhold Vorbaum, *Evangelische Schulordnungen,* vol. I, pp. 1–8. Cited by Eby, *Early Protestant Educators,* p. 180.

15 Ibid., pp. 182–187.
16 Frederick Eby and Charles Flinn Arrowood, *The Development of Modern Education* (New York: Prentice-Hall, Inc., 1934), p. 51.
17 Ibid., 52.
18 Ibid., pp. 52–53.
19 Ibid.
20 James E. Reed and Ronnie Prevost, *A History of Christian Education* (Nashville: Broadman and Holman Publishers, 1993), p. 195.
21 Eby, *The Development of Modern Education,* p. 80.
22 Eby, *Early Protestant Educators,* p. 191.
23 Eby, *The Development of Modern Education,* p. 80.
24 Eby, *Early Protestant Educators,* p. 192.
25 Johann Bugenhagen, translated from original in Friedrich Koldewey, *Braunschweigische Schulordnungen, Monumenta Germaniae Paedagogica,* vol. I, pp. 27–38. Cited by Eby, *Early Protestant Educators,* pp. 193–194.
26 Ibid., pp. 80–81.
27 Elmer Harrison Wilds, *The Foundations of Modern Education* (New York: Rinehart and Company, Inc., 1936), pp. 289–290.
28 James Atkinson, "Reform," *Introduction to the History of Christianity* (Minneapolis: Fortress Press, 1995), p. 385.
29 Hugh J. Blair, "Johann Bugenhagen," *The New International Dictionary of the Christian Church,* J.D. Douglas, ed. (Grand Rapids: Zondervan Publishing House, 1974), p. 164.
30 C.B. Eavey, *History of Christian Education* (Chicago: Moody Press, 1964), p. 156.
31 Eby, *The Development of Modern Education*, p. 92.
32 J.G.G. Norman, "Johannes Strum," *The New International Dictionary of the Christian Church*, p. 937.
33 R. Freeman Butts, *The Education of the West* (New York: McGraw-Hill Book Company, 1947), p. 255.
34 Eby and Arrowood, *The Development of Modern Education* (New York: Prentice-Hall, Inc., 1934), pp. 111–112.
35 Ibid.
36 Johann Sturm, translated by Henry Barnard, *German Teachers and Educators* (Hartford: Brown and Gross, 1878), p. 195. Cited by Eby and Arrowood, *The Development of Modern Education,* p. 109.
37 Ibid., p. 112.
38 Martin Luther, quoted by F.V.N. Painter, p. 147.
39 W.P. Stephens, *The Holy Spirit in the Theology of Martin Bucer* (New York: Cambridge University Press, 1970), p. 5.
40 Eby and Arrowood, *The Development of Modern Education,* pp. 116–117.
41 William Jesse Nottingham, *The Social Ethics of Martin Bucer* (New York: a doctoral dissertation, Columbia University, 1962), p. 206.
42 *Encyclopaedia of Living Divines* (Toronto: Funk and Wagnalls Company, 1891), p. 2577.
43 Ibid.
44 Ibid.
45 Boyd and King, p. 197.
46 Ulrich Zwingli, *How to Educate the Young in Good Manners and Christian Discipline*, cited by Painter, pp. 172–173.
47 Painter, p. 173.
48 E.B. Eavey, *History of Christian Education* (Chicago: Moody Press, 1964), p. 149.

[49] Henry Babel, "Ulrich Zwingli," *Men—An Idea: The Reformation* (Geneva: Foundation of Les Clefs de Saint-Pierre, 1985), p. 9.

[50] Keith Randell, *Luther and the German Reformation* (London: Edward Arnold, A Division of Hodder and Stoughton, 1988), pp. 64–70.

[51] Lowndes, p. 2579.

[52] Eavey, p. 157.

[53] Source unknown.

Illustration Sources

Figure 1   *Melanchthon* - Photo by author (PBA).

Figure 2   *Map* - Global Mapping International, Colorado Springs, CO.

Figure 3   *Melanchthon* - (PBA).

Figure 4   *Desk and chair* - (PBA).

Figure 5   *Bugenhagen* - Ellwood P. Cubberley, *The History of Education* (Boston: Houghton Mifflin Company, 1920), p. 314.

Figure 6   *Sturm* - Ellwood P. Cubberley, *Readings in the History of Education* (Boston: Houghton Mifflin Company, 1920).

Figure 7   *Bucer* - Gottfried Hammann, "Martin Bucer," *The Reformation: Many Men with One Idea* (Geneva: Foundation of Les Clefs de Saint-Pierre, 1985), p. 47.

Figure 8   *Zwingli* - Cubberley, *The History of Education*, p. 297.

Figure 9   *Marburg Colloquy* - Keith Randell, *Luther and the German Reformation*, 1517-55 (London: Edward Arnold, A Division of Hodder & Stoughton, 1988), p. 67.

The Appearance and Disappearance of the Protestant Schools of France

It is an almost unknown fact that there were two thousand evangelical Protestant Christian schools and churches in France in the sixteenth century.[1] The estimated number of French evangelical believers, usually referred to as "Huguenots" or "Gospellers,"[2] varies widely from 750,000[3] to two million[4] at a time when the total French population was fifteen million.[5] Without a doubt, the story of the French Huguenots is among the saddest in history. Carlos Martyn writes:

> The venerable muse of history recites many lessons which are full of tears, but upon no occasion does her voice sink into deeper pathos than when she relates the story of French Protestantism.[6]

Historian Roche refers to the long ordeal of the Huguenots as "two and a half centuries of terror and triumph"[7]—terror because multiplied thousands of Protestants were brutally killed, and triumph because in the face of enormous persecution Protestants (mostly French Calvinists) built churches and schools and laid the foundations for democracy that culminated in the French Revolution of 1789.

The suffering endured by the Huguenots at the hands of the medieval Catholic Church is incomprehensible. Bayle, a sixteenth-century philosopher, claimed that "the persecutions of the early Christians at the hands of the pagan emperors of Rome were far easier to withstand than the persecutions of the French Protestants."[8]

The most under-reported story of the Great Reformation is the massacre and dispersion of the French Protestants. From the standpoint of Christian school educators, to overlook this page of history, as many historians do, is to disregard one of the most important education histories of all time—the appearance and disappearance of the two thousand Protestant schools of France. These schools and their churches vanished with the near eradication of the French Huguenot population. The divisions of this chapter are as follows:

1. *The Events Leading to the "Death to the Heretics" Campaign*
2. *The Huguenots and Their Commitment to Christian School Education*
3. *The Extirpation of All Protestant Schools in France*

Clearly, the concept of separation of church and state did not exist in France during this period. "The established [Roman] church,"[9] or the "old church"[10] as it was called, was the force behind the French throne throughout the long persecution of Protestants. This is not a characterization of the Catholic Church today, but it was the pattern of the medieval Catholic Church at the time of Luther, Calvin, and the French Huguenots.

In order to understand the Huguenots as possibly the most determined Christian school educators in history, one must examine their historical roots and particularly the harsh religious and political environment of their era.

1. The Events Leading to the "Death to the Heretics" Campaign

The Vaudois of France, like the Waldensians of the Italian Alps and eastern Europe, were pre-Reformation reformers committed to biblical authority and to basic literacy for their children. Martyn said, "The Vaudois supported their doctrines by the authority of the Holy Scriptures—the most unlearned among them could repeat large portions of the Bible by heart."[11] For five hundred years prior to the Great Reformation, these courageous believers suffered unbelievable terror at the hands of Catholic authorities.[12]

> Monks marched from city to city . . . pillaged towns and villages and castles; outraged women, and even little girls; and then formed circles around the blazing stakes at which the Vaudois were burning, with an impious affectation of devotion, chanted in unison the hymn *Veni Creator*, while the wail of their tortured victims ascended to the pitying heavens.[13]

The Reformation of the 1500s began in France as in numerous other countries where devout Catholic priests, who were university scholars, were secretly reading the Scriptures in the original languages. In France that scholar was Jacques Lefèvre, "one of the most distinguished professors in the University of Paris."[14]

> The study of the Bible produced the same effect upon [Lefèvre's] mind that it had done on that of Luther; but he was a man of far different

temperament—gentle, retiring, and timid, though no less devoted to the cause of truth. He was, however, an old man of seventy; his life was fast fleeting; yet here was a world lying in wickedness around him. What he could do he nevertheless did. He translated the four Gospels into French in 1523; had them printed at Antwerp; and put them into circulation.[15]

More important to Lefèvre than the approval of his colleagues at the Sorbonne, "the powerful school of theology that now dominated the University of Paris,"[16] was the truth of the gospel. Durant says:

> Lefèvre, like Luther, demanded a return to the Gospel; and, like Erasmus, he sought to restore and clarify the authentic text of the New Testament as a means of cleansing [the Catholic Church] from medieval legends and sacerdotal accretions. "How shameful it is," said one of his comments, "to see a bishop soliciting people to drink with him, caring for naught but gambling . . . constantly hunting . . . frequenting bad houses!"[17]

Two of Lefèvre's early converts were his former students Guillaume Farel, regarded as the "John the Baptist of John Calvin,"[18] and Guillaume Briconnet, the bishop of Meaux (a short distance east of Paris). These three men and their dissemination of the sacred Scriptures ignited the Great Reformation in France. Smiles wrote:

> The bishop [Briconnet], on taking charge of his diocese, had been shocked by the disorders which prevailed there, by the licentiousness

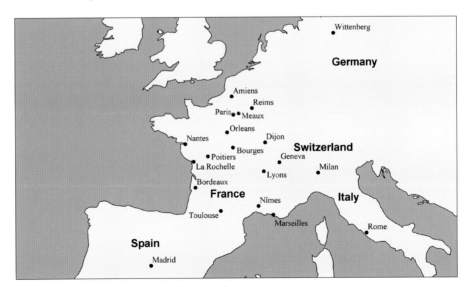

Figure 1. The Huguenot Map

of the clergy, and their general disregard for religious life and duty. As many of them were non-resident, he invited Lefèvre, Farel, and others, to occupy their pulpits and preach to the people, the bishop preaching in his turn; and the people flocked to hear them. The bishop also distributed the four Gospels gratuitously among the poor, and very soon a copy was to be found in almost every workshop in Meaux. A reformation of manners shortly followed. Blasphemy, drunkenness, and disorder disappeared; and the movement spread far and near.[19]

As in Germany, Hungary, Scotland, England, the Netherlands, and the Scandinavian countries, it was the wide distribution of the Bible that brought depth and momentum to the French reform movement. Roche says:

> Unified around Calvinism, the Huguenot movement [as it soon became known] spread through the young entrepreneurial class of France and grew with it. Propagators of the faith worked with a zeal unknown since the days of the early Christians. From the great mill in Geneva, tons of booklets were smuggled over mountains and down the valleys, on manback and muleback, until every hamlet in France had copies of the Bible—and of Calvin's doctrines.[20]

At first the Catholic Church and French king, Francis I, took little notice of the new Protestants, who, like spring plants growing under the leaves, were spreading the message of biblical authority, or a "Bible revolt"[21] as it was called, throughout France. But as Smiles reported, "they speedily rallied from their stupor."[22] The alarm spread not only among Catholic authorities in France but among Vatican officials in Rome. "At the same time, Rome, roused by her danger, availed herself of all methods for winning back her wandering children, by force if not by persuasion."[23] As early as 1521, the Sorbonne had condemned Martin Luther as "a heretic and a blasphemer."[24] In 1523 Jean Vallière, the first Protestant of the modern Reformation era, was burned at the stake[25] in Paris "through the efforts of the Sorbonne and the [French] Parliament."[26] From that point on the "Death to the Heretics" campaign seemed never-ending.

The first effort by the Catholic Church and the French Crown was to stem the tidal wave of Bibles flowing into France. Bible readers were officially declared to be "heretics."[27] Roche says:

> The death penalty for mere possession of a Bible was quickly instituted. Yet smugglers brought contraband copies to the smallest villages. Within fifty years after the first printing of the Bible in French, half a million copies were circulating in a country where no more than a million people could read them.[28]

As noted earlier, the invention of the Gutenberg press made the difference in the spread of the gospel in country after country of the Great Reformation. In 1867 Samuel Smiles wrote:

> The fears of the priests increased as they saw their flocks becoming more intent upon reading the Scriptures, or hearing them read, than attending mass; and they were especially concerned at the growing disposition of the people to call in question the infallibility of the Church and the sacred character of the priesthood. It was every day becoming clearer to them that if the people were permitted to resort to books, and pray to God direct in their vulgar [native] tongue, instead of through the priests in Latin, the authority of the mass would fall, and the Church itself would be endangered.
>
> . . . One Catholic Vicar declared in a sermon, "We must root out printing, or printing will root out us."[29]

The impact of widespread Bible reading was immediate, especially in the upper entrepreneurial classes, more of whom could read. Roche says:

> Thousands were shaken by the difference between the practice of the Established Church and the doctrines expounded in the New Testament. Under shadow of exposure and death at the stake, they slowly formed a loose family of assemblies. By the 1550's there may have been two thousand such assemblies in France. Literacy and membership in the new [entrepreneurial] class were characteristics that set the Huguenots apart from the people of France as a whole.[30]

According to Smiles, in those early years of the French Reformation, the Bible "was known to be the very charter and title-deed of Christianity—the revelation of God's own will to man; and now, to read it or hear it read was like meeting God face-to-face and listening to His voice speaking directly to them."[31]

The second great effort by Catholic authorities of both church and government was to check the enormous loss of constituents to the newly reformed Calvinist church. Thus began the long torturous war by the Catholic authorities to rid France of its Protestant citizens either by "forced conversions" back to the Catholic Church—or by extermination. A grim slogan during this period was "Dye or be Catholick."[32] It is difficult to imagine, but the attempt to eliminate Protestants from France between 1523 and 1715 rivals or exceeds in brutality the Catholic Crusades to Jerusalem (1096–1270) and Catholicism's Spanish Inquisition (1480–1809), when 35,534 men and women "heretics" were hanged or burned at the stake.[33] As we will see, many more evangelical Christians died in France in the grim tragedy known as the St. Bartholomew's Day Massacre and in the years following than died in the 329-year history of the Spanish Inquisition.

Before we review the events that led to the infamous St. Bartholomew's Day Massacre on August 24, 1572, it is important to study the theological, political, social, and economic issues that contributed to the disaster, referred to by Roche as "the blackest day in their country's history."[34]

THE CONFLUENCE OF ISSUES LEADING TO THE
ST. BARTHOLOMEW'S DAY MASSACRE

First Issue:
Royal Excesses Allowed Catholic Advisors to Control the French Royal Court

The common people of France were increasingly stressed by the heavy taxes that were required to maintain the lavish lifestyle of the French kings. In addition, the French kings were so enamored of the pleasures of their royal court that they often allowed the Catholic Church to make major decisions related to religious matters. This privilege caused serious problems for the Huguenots. Durant says, "The King's pleasures did not allow him much time for government,"[35] and he describes the "King's pleasures" and the expensive operation of his household:

> Twenty lords served as stewards of the King's cuisine, managing a staff of forty-five men and twenty-five cupbearers. Some thirty boys functioned as royal pages . . . and a host of secretaries multiplied the hand and memory of the King. A cardinal was Grand Chaplain of the royal chapel . . . and fifty diocesan [Catholic] bishops were allowed to grace the court and so augment their fame. . . .

> We must not forget seven physicians, seven surgeons, four barbers, seven choristers, eight craftsmen, eight clerks of the kitchen, eight ushers for the audience chamber. Each of the King's sons had his own attendants—stewards, chancellors, tutors, pages, and servants. Each of the two queens at court—Claude and Marguerite—had her retinue of fifteen or ten ladies in waiting, sixteen or eight maids of honor. . . .

> The cost of all this perambulating glory was enormous. The treasury was always near bankruptcy, taxes were forever mounting, the bankers of Lyons were dragooned into risky royal loans. In 1523, perceiving that his expenditures were losing sight of his revenues, the King promised to put a limit on his personal indulgences, "not including, however, the ordinary run of our little necessities and pleasures."[36]

Clearly, the minds of most French kings were not on the fate of their Protestant citizens.

There were numerous smaller massacres of Protestants prior to the St. Bartholomew's Day Massacre. Historian Martyn points out that Cardinal Francois "was the chief instigator of these massacres" and that he "became the confidant and adviser of the king. He was thus enabled to give loose rein to his atrocities."[37] This leads us to the second issue that set the stage for the great massacre of 1572.

Second Issue:
The Power of the Roman Catholic Church over the King

In 1523, in a futile war with Spain, France's King Francis I was captured and imprisoned at Madrid. He gained his own release by leaving his two sons in prison in his place. Charles V, the emperor of the Holy Roman Empire, the last emperor to be crowned by a pope, demanded a ransom of 1,300,000 livre for the release of the king's two sons. The Catholic Church of France paid the full ransom with the stipulation that King Francis take a firmer stand against the French Protestants.[38] Francis received additional pressure from Pope Clement VII. In 1534 the pope and King Francis met at Marseilles in southern France to discuss, among other things, the city of Milan, Italy. Amazingly, the pope agreed to give France control of Milan if he, Francis, would "root out" the French Protestants.[39] In addition to pressure from the pope, King Francis had to pacify a Catholic cardinal and fifty resident bishops at his palace in Paris. As Martyn says:

Figure 2. This is Louis XIV's dining room at the Louvre in Paris. Obviously, electric lights have been added since the days of Louis XIV.

Influenced by and pushed on by the incessant solicitation of the churchmen resident at his court, as well as by the active example of Emperor Charles V, Francis I was persuaded to persecute the reformers, timidly at first, but finally with Titanic energy.[40]

Later, Martyn says of the king:

Francis I, never afterwards paused. The demon of persecution took full possession of him. To the end of his life he continued to slaughter his subjects with an indiscriminate malignity which bordered on frenzy.[41]

THE JESUITS

Another major means of Catholic Church control over French kings and other Western monarchs was the new Catholic order, approved by Pope Paul III in 1540, called the Society of Jesus, or simply the Jesuits. The Jesuit order, founded by Ignatius Loyola, a military man, was Catholicism's principal tool in launching the Counter-Reformation against the Protestants.

The Jesuits clearly established "the new militant stance of Rome."[42] Shelley writes. "More than any others, the Society of Jesus stemmed, and sometimes reversed, the tide of Protestantism in France, the Low Countries, and Central Europe."[43] Protestantism's worst earthly enemy, the Jesuits started in Paris[44] and had an immediate influence on a succession of French kings. It was said, for example, of Colbert, the great French finance minister under Louis XIV, who was conciliatory toward the Huguenots, that "the Jesuits were stronger than he was, and the king was in their hands."[45] Shelley cites a comment in an 1816 letter from John Adams to Thomas Jefferson: "If ever any congregation of men could merit eternal perdition on earth and in hell, it is the company of Loyola."[46]

All the French kings with the exception of the quasi-Protestant King Henry IV were Catholics and needed little outside influence to persecute the Huguenots. Most of them, however, attempted to be conciliatory toward their Protestant subjects. They decreed eight different edicts of toleration, which provided some degree of tolerance, though not complete freedom. But again and again these edicts were ignored or withdrawn because of pressures by the authorities of the Catholic Church. Sutherland says, "Thus there was, on the one hand, the extreme Catholic policy of extermination and, on the other, the royal policy of moderation and civil containment."[47]

Had the Huguenots in France been afforded the same opportunity for development as those in Germany, says Cubberley, "their work would have greatly exceeded the Lutherans in importance and influence on the future history of mankind."[48] However, the evangelical community in France faced a church and state alliance unequaled elsewhere, with the possible exceptions of Spain and Italy. Rothrock says:

> At their coronations French kings were blessed and anointed by the Church; throughout their reigns they drew both revenue and personnel into their service from the [Catholic] Church; generally their enemies were damned by churchmen, who threatened hell's fire for those who would harm a king or resist his legitimate authority; and the continuance of their lineage was guaranteed by the Church, which blessed their marriages and endorsed the legitimacy of their children. Nowhere in Europe had the highest civil authority greater cause to be well pleased with the existing religious settlement, or greater reason to be willing to defend it with all the awesome power of the state.[49]

Third Issue:
A Lack of In-Country Leadership in the Protestant Church of France

John Calvin, Daniel Lucero says, was the "father of French Protestantism."[50] Through no choice of his own, Calvin was an absent father of the French evangelicals. Being a Frenchman and educated at the University of Paris, he undoubtedly would have preferred, like Luther in Germany, to give on-site leadership to the Protestant cause in France. But he, along with William Farel and Jacques Lefèvre, was driven from France on threat of death. Lefèvre was later allowed to return, but his age and retiring personality were handicaps to his becoming a strong Protestant leader.

The lack of in-country leadership surfaced time after time as a major impediment to the stability of the fast-growing evangelical community. If the French Protestants had had forceful resident leaders with the skills of a Luther, a Calvin, or a Knox, the outcome might have been far different from the near annihilation they ultimately experienced.

Calvin, Farel, Lefèvre, and even Luther and Melanchthon provided the French Protestants with considerable external leadership through the distribution of Bibles and other written materials. Calvin was by far the most helpful, providing hundreds of highly trained missionary pastors and Christian school leaders, all of whom were well educated at Geneva Academy in Switzerland. Lindsay writes:

> But what Geneva excelled in was its training for the ministry and other learned professions. Men with the passion of learning in their blood came from all lands—from Italy, Spain, England, Scotland, even from Russia, and, above all, from France. Pastors educated in Geneva, taught by the most distinguished scholars of the day, who had gained the art of ruling others in having learned how to command themselves,

went forth from its schools to become the ministers of the struggling Protestants in the Netherlands, in England, in Scotland, in the Rhine Provinces, and, above all, in France. They were wise, indefatigable, fearless, ready to give their lives for their work, extorting praise from unwilling mouths, as modest, saintly, "with the name of Jesus ever on their lips" and His Spirit in their hearts.[51]

Calvin was in constant correspondence, providing counsel to these Protestant leaders and to French nobles who had become evangelical Christians. What he accomplished as an absentee leader is amazing. However, had he lived in France, it is probable that several unfortunate events would not have taken place.

THE INCIDENT OF THE PLACARDS

Prior to October 17, 1534, King Francis I had been mildly tolerant, at least by Louis XIV standards, of the Vaudois and Calvinist "heretics." All of that changed when Anthony de Marcourt, along with an extreme faction of evangelicals, oblivious of the country's explosive religious and political environment, posted offensive placards in Paris, Orléans, Tours, Blois, and Amboise.[52] Durant explains what happened:

> French reformers posted in the streets of Paris, Orléans, and other cities, and even on the doors of the King's bedchamber at Amboise, placards denouncing the Mass as idolatry, and the Pope and the Catholic clergy as "a brood of vermin . . . apostates, wolves . . . liars, blasphemers, murderers of souls." Enraged, Francis ordered an indiscriminate imprisonment of all suspects; soon the jails were full. Many printers were arrested, and for a time all printing was prohibited. Marguerite, Marot, and many moderate Protestants joined in condemning the placards. The King, his sons, ambassadors, nobles, and clergy marched in solemn silence, bearing lighted candles, to hear an expiatory Mass in Notre Dame. Francis declared that he would behead his own children if he found them harboring these blasphemous heresies. That evening six Protestants were burned to death in Paris by a method judged fit to appease the Deity: they were suspended over a fire, and were repeatedly lowered into it and raised from it so that their agony might be prolonged. Between November 10, 1534, and May 5, 1535, twenty-four Protestants were burned alive in Paris.[53]

Unfortunately, the king's over-reaction set the tone for things to come. The unwise incident of the placards would probably not have happened had there been firm leadership among the Protestants in France. Sutherland says that "the notorious affair of the placards in October, 1534, . . . definitely turned the king against heresy in France."[54]

THE INCIDENT OF THE STATUES

If we were somehow transported back to sixteenth-century France, we would learn that, as Baird puts it, "the age of brotherly love had not yet dawned."[55] It was, in fact, an age of unbelievable cruelty. Thirty thousand Huguenots were killed even before the terrible Bartholomew's Day Massacre.[56] Martyn writes, "France bled at every pore."[57] Laws abounded, like Venus's-flytraps, to snare the unwary Protestant and sometimes non-Protestants as well, for the slightest infraction. Prince William of Orange

Figure 3. Renegade Protestants pulled down religious images in a Catholic Church in Paris, igniting a furious response from the Catholic civil and religious authorities.

said that "no escape was possible, since one had to do no more than look askance at [a Catholic] image to be sentenced to burn at the stake."[58] Roche provides further insight into this grim period:

> Typical of this phase of the Terror was the conviction in Angiers of three pastors and a congregation of forty who had unauthorized psalm books and copies of the Bible in French. They were sent to the stake with their books as fuel. The accounts of the time note hundreds of cases such as "Two rascally heretics" burnt on a pile of fuel consisting of "pestilential books" from Geneva—where John Calvin's bookmill was working overtime. . . . At Meaux, fourteen book readers were caught. The authorities built a giant ring of bonfires and burnt them all at once.[59]

With no in-country leadership to moderate normal human reaction to such atrocities, it is not surprising that "unauthorized" bands of Protestants, ungoverned by principles of nonviolence, broke into Catholic churches, pulled down statues of saints, and destroyed Catholic relics. Lindsay says, "The rising tide of sympathy for the persecuted Protestants was checked by these deeds of violence."[60] Durant describes one incident particularly destructive to the cause of evangelical Christians:

> On May 31, 1528, [King Francis] was dismayed to learn that both the heads on a statue of the Virgin and Child outside a church in the parish of Saint-Germain had been smashed during the night. The people cried out for vengeance. Francis offered a thousand crowns for the discovery of the vandals, and led a somber procession of prelates, state officials, nobles, and populace to repair the broken statues with silver heads.[61]

> Calvin, from distant Geneva, attempted to quell such vandalism, but to no avail. Lindsay says, "Calvin and de Bèze wrote, energetically urging their followers to refrain from attacks on churches, images, and relics. But it was all to no purpose."[62]

THE GREAT ERROR OF A PROTESTANT ARMY

Had Calvin been present in France, it is unlikely the Protestants would have fallen victim to "Protestant" nobles who persuaded the Calvinist church leaders and their constituencies to follow them into battle against the Catholic military forces. Professor Nichols describes the circumstances that led to the formation of the Protestant army:

> About this time the Protestant movement changed its character somewhat. Many of the higher aristocracy had been won for the Reformation. These great nobles, some of them princes of the blood royal, would not meekly submit to persecution, and began to talk of armed revolt. Under their leadership the Protestant movement became not only an endeavor to spread evangelical religion, but also a struggle against the government for liberty to profess such religion. This change was marked by the name "Huguenot," henceforth borne by the French Protestants. War broke out in 1562, the Huguenots under Admiral Coligny and the Prince Condé fighting against the queen regent, Catherine de Medici. This was the first of the eight "Wars of Religion," which covered more than thirty years, and almost ruined France.[63]

Both Calvin and Luther were opposed to the idea of a Christian army and of going to war against enemies of the Protestant community no matter how cruel or unjust they might be. Calvin said that "the kingdom of Christ is strengthened and established more by the blood of martyrs than by force of arms."[64] Ultimately, as we will learn, Calvin's belief was all too clearly affirmed in the history of French Protestantism. The point, however, is that had Calvin or another strong Protestant leader been available to provide strong in-country leadership to the Huguenot believers, it is not likely they would have fallen victim to the politically motivated nobles who persuaded them to become a political party and to take up arms. Durant observes:

> The nobility, shorn of its former political power by the kings, looked with envy at Lutheran princes victorious over Charles V; perhaps a similar feudalism could be restored in France by using widespread popular resentment against abuses in Church and state. Prominent nobles like Gaspard de Coligny, his younger brother François d'Andelot, Prince Louis de Condé, and his brother Antoine de Bourbon, took active part in organizing the Protestant revolt.[65]

Once the Huguenot church leaders signed the "Covenant of Association"[66] with the nobles, they learned quickly that the nobles, who were unaccustomed to democracy, ignored their Calvinistic principles of "rule by consent of the governed." After eight wearisome wars that gained little for the cause of Christ, the Huguenot church leaders reprimanded their military leaders for continually ignoring their counsel and violating their representative democratic ideal of "the common consent of all."[67] They also learned that some of the nobles were less than sincere believers. Samuel Smiles said, "Being no longer available for purposes of faction, many of the nobles, who had been their leaders, fell away from them and rejoined the old church."[68]

The long night of the eight "religious wars" lasted from 1562 to 1629—or sixty-seven years.[69] Professor Hudson says, "In retrospect, it is regrettable that the Reformed [Church] community allowed itself to be weakened by an armed resistance which was not only unwise, but futile."[70]

THE ST. BARTHOLOMEW'S DAY MASSACRE

Few events in history are more grim and chilling than the mass murder of 70,000 Protestants in France,[71] beginning in Paris in the early morning hours of August 24, 1572, the eve of St. Bartholomew's Day, and lasting "for four nights and three days."[72] Nichols describes it:

> In a time of peace many Huguenot nobles were gathered in Paris for the wedding of one of their chiefs, Henry of Navarre [future King Henry IV]. In an attack made by night, at the instigation of Catherine de Medici [mother of young King Charles], several thousand of them,

including Admiral Coligny and most of the other leaders, were killed. Massacres were ordered in other parts of France, and altogether seventy thousand perished. The Pope sent congratulations to Catherine, and both thought they were done with the Huguenots.[73]

Given the condition of the Catholic Church in that day, we should not be surprised that the pope in Rome applauded the deaths of seventy thousand French citizens whose only crime was that they were non-Catholic. Baird says that "the pontiff . . . openly applauded the assassination of Admiral Coligny [the military leader of the Protestants] and the Massacre of St.

Figure 4. Seventy thousand Protestants died throughout France in a killing spree that began in Paris on August 24, 1572, known as "The St. Bartholomew's Day Massacre."

Bartholomew's Day."[74] The nation-wide massacre was ordered by Catherine de Medici, mother of France's underage King Charles, because it was generally suspected that she had arranged the murder of Admiral Coligny and believed a mass extermination of the Huguenots was the only means to prevent Protestant reprisals on the royal family.[75] Lambert says:

The court leaders of this perfidious butchery galloped through the streets on horseback, shouting: "Mort aux Huguenots. Kill! Kill!! By the King's orders!!! Kill every man of them!!!! . . ."

The Huguenots were murdered in their beds or endeavouring to escape, without any regard to age, sex, or condition.[76]

After the massacre, French authorities cleared the streets of Paris of dead bodies by throwing them into the River Seine. Extra workers were hired to unclog the river of 1,900 corpses.[77] This same horrendous scene was repeated in other French cities as the great massacre spread.

The rivers of France were so filled with corpses that for many months no fish were eaten by Frenchmen. In the valley of the Loire, wolves came down from the hills to feed upon the decaying bodies of Huguenots.[78]

The terrifying ripple effect of the massacre flowed throughout the French provinces over a three-month period. Roche describes the massacre in Lyons, in southeastern France:

> But as Paris quieted, the bloody flood inundated the provinces. When news of the massacre in the capital reached Lyons, the [Catholic] clergy there called on the faithful to go and do likewise. Lyons Governor Mandelot tried to hold the mobs back, then ordered all Huguenots into "protective custody"—of the monasteries—and proceeded to confiscate their homes and goods. A Huguenot overflow of about seven hundred persons was placed in less protective custody in the Lyons prisons. Sunday night, August 31, the faithful, fresh from priestly incitement, broke down the prison doors and cut the throats of everyone inside, from the aged to babes in arms. Frightened of consequences, Mandelot ordered his own men to kill all surviving Huguenots so tales of the massacre could not be carried elsewhere.[79]

Martyn characterizes the French atrocities as "excesses of brutality which human nature blushes to record."[80] Among the multitudes of personal tragedies in France was the loss of hundreds of evangelical Christian school educators. Their amazing story is told in the next chapter division.

2. The Huguenots and Their Commitment to Christian School Education

With the possible exception of the first-century Christians, it is doubtful that Christian school educators anywhere ever carried out their mission under circumstances more stressful than those faced by Huguenot teachers in the sixteenth and seventeenth centuries. Before we review their incredible hardships, we would do well to review their amazing achievements.

The greatest growth of Protestantism in France took place during the reign of King Henry IV, or "Henry the Great" as he was called.[81] If not a Protestant at heart, Henry IV was at least sympathetic to the evangelical cause. He began his reign in Paris on March 22, 1594, in a solemn procession from Notre Dame Cathedral to the Louvre, the French palace. From the beginning of his reign in 1594 to its close in 1610,[82] a period of unprecedented prosperity in France brought a welcome period of peace and limited freedom to the evangelical Protestant community. It should be noted that in the famous peasant revolt against the crown in 1789, known to the world as the French Revolution, "the only royal bust not destroyed by the mobs was that of Henry IV."[83]

Figure 5. (right) The gigantic rose window of Notre Dame is classic cathedral art. The distance from Notre Dame to the Louvre (the French palace at the time of Henry IV) is a few blocks. Figure 6. (above) The Louvre as it appears today.

From 1538 when the first Huguenot church was established until Louis XIV's tragic 1685 Revocation of the Edict of Nantes (the famous Protestant Edict of Pacification), [84] the church and school movement of France steadily grew. As early as 1561 there were 2,150 Calvinist churches and schools in France.[85] Every congregation had its own elementary school.[86] Cubberley provides the best description of the Huguenot schools:

> True to the Calvinistic teaching of putting principles into practice, they organized an extensive system of schools, extending from elementary education for all, through secondary schools or colleges, up to eight Huguenot universities. As a people they were thrifty and capable of making great sacrifices to carry out their educational ideals. The education they provided was not only religious but civil; not only intellectual but moral, social, and economic. Education was for all, rich and poor alike. Their synods made liberal appropriations for the universities, while municipalities provided for colleges and elementary education. They emphasized, in the lower schools, the study of the vernacular and arithmetic, and in the colleges Greek and the New Testament. The long list of famous teachers found in their universities reveals the character of their instruction.[87]

Even as Geneva Academy became the jewel of Calvin's ministry in Geneva, so his ideas on Bible-centered Christian school education flourished in France against enormous resistance by Catholic authorities. Calvin's Christian school movement in France was undergirded by the "Christian school missionaries" who streamed across the nearby French border having been trained at Geneva Academy. Others came from Wittenberg University. Baird provides insight into the philosophy of Huguenot education:

> It was no accident that, even amid the fires of persecution, during a period in which the Huguenots were denied . . . rights of conscience . . . when their public exercises of worship were alternately restricted within narrow limits and utterly proscribed, their ministers forbidden the kingdom or made liable to imprisonment and death at the gallows, this devoted people should have pondered long . . . over the general subject of popular education. A creed that exalts the authority of the written word of God and pays little attention to human tradition, that vindicates the right of every Christian to read and judge for himself respecting the truths which the Divine Author intended to convey in the pages of that word . . . [it is not surprising] that the Huguenots of France should make it their first care to provide the people with that primary instruction which the Roman Catholic clergy had failed to furnish to their flocks.[88]

The end result of the Huguenot philosophy of education was nothing short of amazing. It is possible that Christian school education, under the worst political and economic conditions imaginable, reached its zenith in France. Baird continues:

> In the kingdom of the Very Christian King it was as true as throughout the rest of Western Europe, that "popular instruction was the child of Protestantism." Not a city, not a town or village, was conquered by the "new doctrines" but a Protestant school followed closely upon the newly instituted church, and the teacher was esteemed a scarcely less essential officer in the ecclesiastical polity than the preacher of the gospel himself. It was not long before every child

Figure 7. Protestant churches and their Christian schools flourish under the reign of King Henry IV.

Figure 8. A French Christian school in the seventeenth century.

of a Huguenot family was acquiring not only the arts of reading and writing, but the rudiments of religious doctrine as contained in the catechism of John Calvin. The enemies of the Protestants observed, with feelings akin to despair, that, throughout great tracts of country, "the children were learning religion only in the catechism brought from Geneva, and all knew it by heart."[89]

In addition to 2,150 elementary schools, the French Huguenots established 35 colleges [Christian high schools][90] and eight academies or universities which, in reality, were pastor training institutions.[91] It is helpful to review once again the modern equivalency of terms. Hudson offers the following:

The term collège is used throughout when discussing those schools which were roughly equivalent to the modern secondary school, offering instruction in six to eight forms to boys ranging in age from seven or eight to approximately sixteen. Those Protestant institutions which offered in addition lectures in philosophy, Greek, Hebrew, and theology for the training of pastors were called academies.[92]

The impact of the Protestant educational system, especially in southern France, was phenomenal. Buisseret says:

Considering that the Protestants never composed more than a twelfth of the population of France in the sixteenth century their influence on affairs of all kinds was very remarkable. This disproportionate influence was primarily the result of their educational system.[93]

The effectiveness of the Protestant schools of France, plus the growing pressure from prominent Catholic families who "could not help observing the insufferably slow progress of their sons"[94] and the new humanist Renaissance schools,[95] eventually forced the Catholics to offer an alternative educational system. That response took the form of Jesuit-sponsored secondary schools for boys and Ursuline Convent Schools for girls. The rapid development of these schools was a significant part of Catholicism's Counter-Reformation strategy. Buisseret describes the Ursuline Convent Schools:

> The nearest equivalent to the Jesuits among women was the Ursuline order, founded in Italy in the sixteenth century and called to France in 1594. From their first convent at Avignon the Ursulines rapidly spread all over the country, until they eventually ran more than three hundred educational institutions.[96]

It is well documented that the proliferation of these new Catholic schools was a direct response to the Protestant Christian schools. Much more is written in that regard, however, about the Jesuit high schools for boys than the Ursuline convent schools for girls. Buisseret says,

> The establishment of the Jesuit order rapidly led to the growth of academic institutions, from which emerged clerics and laymen fit to take on the trained minds of Geneva.[97] . . . Jesuit colleges were often established in deliberate competition with Protestant institutions.[98]

These high schools became the centerpiece of the Jesuit plan to reclaim the constituency Catholicism had lost to the Great Reformation. The Catholic Church, until then not known for the spread of literacy, suddenly awakened from its medieval slumber. Cubberley says:

> The church as an institution . . . learned from the Protestants the value of education as a means to larger ends, and soon set about using it. . . . For long the [Catholic] Church had had the Inquisition, but, while it had rendered loyal and iniquitous service, the results had been in no way commensurate with the bitter hatred which its work awakened. Excommunication, persecution, imprisonment, the stake, and the sword had been tried extensively, but with only partial success. In education the reformers had shown the [Catholic] Church a new method, which was positive and effective and did not awaken opposition, and from the reformer's zeal for Latin grammar schools to provide an intelligent ministry the [Catholic] Church took its cue of establishing schools

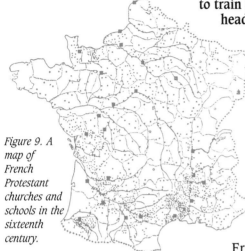

Figure 9. A map of French Protestant churches and schools in the sixteenth century.

to train its future leaders. It was a long-headed and far-sighted plan, and its success was proportionately large.[99]

When reduced to its lowest common denominator, the Catholic Counter Reformation—which spread from France to Belgium, Holland, the German states, Austria, Poland, and Hungary—was in reality a 'war' about education. The trigger for that war was the successful Protestant Christian schools of France. More than any other aspect of the Protestant community, it was the success of the Protestant schools that embarrassed and threatened the Catholic Church.

It must be noted, however, that the Catholic response in the form of Jesuit-run secondary schools was by no means a commitment to educate the masses.[100] Nor was it to promote common literacy to elevate a personal understanding of the Bible. Least of all it was intended to promote one's responsibility to live in harmony with the Scriptures. Sad to say, the only harmony advocated by the collective mind of the Catholic Church in those years was the French slogan "Dye or be Catholick."[101] The difference in the Catholic and Protestant philosophies of education is well stated by Professor Cubberley:

> Under the older religious theory of collective judgment and collective responsibility for salvation—that is, the judgment of the [Catholic] Church rather than that of individuals—it was not important that more than a few be educated. Under the new theory of individual responsibility promulgated by the Protestants, the education of all became a vital necessity. . . . The modern elementary vernacular school then may be said to be essentially a product of the Protestant Reformation.[102]

IGNATIUS LOYOLA, FOUNDER OF THE JESUITS

In his youth Ignatius Loyola (1491–1556) served as a page in the Spanish court of Ferdinand and Isabella.[103] He received his M.A. degree in

1535 at the University of Paris.[104] It is interesting that Ignatius Loyola, founder of the Jesuits, and John Calvin, founder of Calvinism, may have attended classes together at the University of Paris—having been students there at the same time.[105]

As leader of the Jesuits, Loyola was answerable "alone to the Pope."[106] He was aggressive in his campaign against the French Huguenot school system. Benson says, "The Jesuits' most successful method of counteracting Protestantism was their educational work."[107] To counter the impact of the Protestant Christian high schools of France, Loyola and his followers established ninety-two Catholic high schools. It should be noted that the

Figure 10. Ignatius Loyola, founder of the Jesuits.

Jesuits established numerous elementary schools outside of Europe. Cubberley explains:

> With the education of the masses of the people the [Jesuit] Order was not concerned. This is not true of their missions in foreign lands, where the mission priests usually gave elementary instruction. Elementary schools were maintained in the Jesuit missions of North and South America. Thus a mission school was established at Quebec as early as 1635, and one at Newtown, in Catholic Maryland, in 1640. After 1740 elementary parish schools were opened by the Jesuits among the German Catholics in Pennsylvania. From these beginnings Catholic parish schools have been developed in the United States.[108]

Francis Xavier, one of the original six Jesuits, is credited with saying, "Give me the children until they are seven years old, and anyone can take them afterwards."[109]

The Jesuits were serious about rolling back the influence of Protestant schools. Of the 22,589 members of the Jesuit Order in 1773, "about one-half . . . were teachers."[110] From the standpoint of education, there is no question that the Jesuits were good teachers. Durant says, "They became the greatest educators of their time."[111] The underlying purpose of the Jesuit Order, however, was not to advance education but rather to eliminate so-called heresy. It was the Jesuits who said, "The Catholic Church has the right and the duty to kill heretics, because it is by fire and sword that heresy can be extirpated."[112] Largely because of the military background of its founder, Ignatius Loyola, there was a militancy among the Jesuits unknown to other cloistered Catholic orders. Cubberley says:

> [The Jesuit Order] was organized along strictly military lines, all members being responsible to its General, and he in turn alone to the Pope. The quiet life of the cloister was abandoned for a life of open warfare under a military discipline. The purposes of the Order were to combat heresy, to advance the interests of the Church, and to strengthen the authority of the Papacy. Its motto was *Omnia ad Majorem Dei Gloriam* (that is, All for the greater glory of God), and the means to be employed by it to accomplish these ends were the pulpit, the confessional, the mission, and the school. Of these the school was given the place of first importance.[113]

The Jesuits believed in blind obedience to the pope. Loyola told his fellow priests, "We ought always to be ready to believe that what seems to us white is black if the hierarchical church so defines it. . . ." He also said, "we must train ourselves to be unquestioning servants of God, and of God's vicar on earth, the Church."[114] The Catholic "vicar on earth" was, of course, the pope.

The history of Christian school education would have been much different in France, Belgium, Holland, the German states, Austria, Poland, and Hungary, if the Christian schools of these countries had been allowed to flourish alongside the new Catholic schools, which the Protestant schools had inspired. The idea of an "even playing field," however, was impossible within the context of Catholic doctrine. The Catholic Church considered itself divine and "incapable of being at fault in belief."[115] Therefore, as Durant says, "her opponents must be agents of satan, and against these devils perpetual war was a religious obligation to an insulted God."[116] This viewpoint explains why the Jesuits set about "to close the doors of every Protestant school in France"[117] and in all the other Counter-Reformation countries.

3. The Extirpation of All Protestant Schools in France

The word *extirpate* means— "1 a: to destroy completely: WIPE OUT b: to pull up by the root 2: to cut out by surgery."[118] This threefold definition aptly describes the eventual elimination of all Protestant academic institutions in France. Eby and Arrowood say:

> After the revocation of the Edict of Nantes in 1685, France remained Catholic and the Huguenots were well-nigh exterminated. Throughout France, education was in the hands of the Jesuits and of such minor orders as met with their approval.[119]

The rise and fall of the royal Edict of Nantes, the famous edict of toleration of Protestant churches and schools, paralleled the rise and fall of religious freedom in France. The Edict of Nantes included the following assurances for evangelical Christians:

1. Liberty of conscience.
2. Protestant churches, including their elementary schools and theological academies, could legally exist in prescribed areas of France (excluding Paris).
3. The greater nobles could hold Protestant services in their castles.
4. The lesser nobles could do the same, provided the "congregation" did not include more than "thirty persons over and above relations of the family."[120]
5. Military leaders were permitted to hold religious services in their apartments provided the doors were kept shut and "there was no loud singing of Psalms."[121]
6. Protestants were allowed "to meet to discuss political questions, provided they first secured the permission of the King."[122]
7. Protestants were generally granted common civil rights such as the right to marry, own property, inherit property, own businesses, trade freely, and even hold political offices in Protestant communities. Additionally, they were given six seats in the French Parliament.[123]

With these limited freedoms, evangelical churches and schools flourished throughout France. As Durant says:

> Despite the recurrent terror, clandestine "swarms" of Protestants existed in 1530 in Lyons, Bordeaux, Orléans, Reims, Amiens, Poitiers, Bourges, Nîmes, La Rochelle, Châlons, Dijon, Toulouse. Huguenot legions sprang almost out of the ground. [124]

These Protestant freedoms, however, were considered by the Catholic Church and by parliament to be dangerous. It was said:

> The edict [of Nantes] was greatly disliked by the Roman Catholic clergy. . . . The parliament of Paris shared this dislike, but was forced by the king [Henry IV] to register the edict on Feb. 25, 1599.[125]

Because it was still very much a Catholic world in the sixteenth and seventeenth centuries, the fortunes of the new Protestant church and its system of Christian schools rose and fell at the whim of Catholic monarchs, on pronouncements from the pope in Rome, and on "the sleepless activity of the hostile clergy of the established church."[126]

After the death of Henry IV in 1610, life for the Protestant community became progressively worse. The crowning blow came at the hands of King Louis XIV (1638–1715), the grandson of Henry IV. On October 18, 1685, Louis XIV, without a doubt the most vain and cruel of all French monarchs,[127] revoked the Edict of Nantes. Samuel Smiles provides a concise list of the severe limitations imposed on the evangelical believers:

1. The demolition of all the remaining Protestant temples throughout France, and the entire proscription of the Protestant religion;
2. The prohibition of even private worship, under penalty of confiscation of body and property;
3. The banishment of all Protestant pastors from France within fifteen days;
4. The closing of all Protestant schools;
5. The prohibition of parents to instruct their children in the Protestant faith;
6. The injunction, under a penalty of five hundred livres in each case, to have their children baptized by the parish priest, and brought up in the Roman Catholic religion;
7. The confiscation of the property and goods of all Protestant refugees who failed to return to France within four months;
8. The penalty of the galleys [work as oarsmen on a French galley ship] for life to all men, and of imprisonment for life to all women, detected in the act of attempting to escape from France![128]

The Edict of Nantes had been the "Charter of French Protestantism."[129] When Louis XIV revoked it in 1685, the Catholic Church, from Rome to Paris, burst into prolonged celebration. Smiles says:

> GREAT was the rejoicing of the Jesuits on the Revocation of the Edict of Nantes. Rome sprang up with a shout of joy to celebrate the event. *Te Deums* were sung, processions went from shrine to shrine, and the Pope sent a brief to Louis conveying to him the congratulations and praises of the Romish Church. Public thanksgivings were held at Paris, in which the people eagerly took part,—thus making themselves accomplices in the proscription by the King of their fellow-subjects. The provost and sheriffs had a statue of Louis erected at the Hotel de Ville. . . .

> The Roman Catholic clergy were almost beside themselves with joy. The eloquent Bossuet was especially fervent in his praises of the monarch:—"Touched by so many marvels," said he (15 January, 1686), "let us expand our hearts in praise of the piety of the Great Louis. Let our acclamations ascend to heaven, and let us say to this new

Constantine, this new Theodosius, what the six hundred and thirty fathers said in the Council of Chalcédon, 'You have strengthened the faith, you have exterminated the heretics: King of Heaven, preserve the king of earth.'"[130]

At Rome the pope had a medal struck with the likeness of Louis XIV engraved over the words *Heresis Extincta*, to commemorate the revocation of the Edict of Nantes.[131]

There was, of course, no rejoicing among evangelical believers. Jean Claude, pastor of the 14,000-member Protestant church near Paris, was among those pastors forced out of France.[132] In his memoirs, written in 1707 in exile in Holland, he spoke against the French Catholic leaders, particularly the priests, who led armies of French Dragoons, "who have," he said, "depopulated a whole kingdom, and plunder'd above five hundred thousand [Protestant] families." He continued,

> Do we live in an Age wherein Religion is made to consist in having no Fear of God, or must we imagine that the Fear of God, consists in that furious Zeal, which inspires such sorts of Violences? Can any think these Excesses are pleasing to Christ, whom we both profess to own as the Author of our Faith, and that He can ever be willing to have His religion propagated, by such treacherous and wicked Devices? [God] has said indeed, that He will not suffer the Gates of Hell to prevail against His Church; but He has no where said, He will open Hell Gates for the propagating of it. Now if ever anything in the World may be said to carry the Air of the Gates of Hell, certainly it must be this Persecution in France.[133]

Figure 11. King Louis XIV revoked the Edict of Nantes and closed Protestant churches and schools.

There are no substantiated figures documenting the number of Protestants tortured and killed before and after the disastrous Revocation of the Edict of Nantes—Protestants whose only crime was being non-Catholic. The remaining pages of this book could be filled with the heartrending accounts of murder and misery inflicted on the Huguenots by leaders of Roman and French Catholicism over a protracted period of 250 years. Strangely enough, it was the French emperor Napoleon

Bonaparte who put an end to the Spanish Inquisition and restored Protestantism in France as a legal entity.[134]

The following accounts by historians will serve to illustrate the magnitude of the terror suffered by the French Huguenots. They are indeed difficult to read:

Protestants Were Given No Legal Standing

Protestantism was, by a legal fiction, supposed to be entirely extinct, its adherents had no standing in the sight of the law. One could neither be born as a Protestant, nor be baptized as a Protestant, nor be married as a Protestant, nor be buried as a Protestant. With every civil act a profession of Roman Catholicism was closely bound up. There could be no wedlock recognized by the state, unless the marriage was performed by a priest of the Romish church; and to obtain his intervention it was needful both to exhibit the evidence of baptism and to partake of the communion. Without such a ceremony the children that were the off-spring of the union were branded as bastards, and were incapable of succeeding to the property of their parents.[135]

Open Hostility Toward the Bible

Troops were brought against them, who inflicted unspeakable atrocities; but the hatred which was manifested to the Scriptures and good books, the stuffing of the leaves of the Bible into the mouths and wounds of the dying sufferers, the jeers and blasphemies which were addressed to them for calling upon God, and the nature of the insult offered to their mortal remains, all plainly declared that the cause was not political, as Papists alleged.[136]

Christian Schools Closed

Huguenot academies and other schools were subject to measures so repressive that they soon declined as an educational force.[137]

All Protestant schools were closed, and the whole educational organization of the nation was placed in the hands of the Jesuits.[138]

Protestant Children Forced to Attend Catholic Schools

After the revocation of the Edict of Nantes, the persecuting government of Louis XIV, bethought itself of the village schoolmaster as a useful agent in its work of forcible conversion. A royal edict of December 13th, 1698, gave orders to take the children of heretics from their families at five years old, in order to bring them up, by compulsion, in Catholic schools. But these Catholic schools did not yet exist. The edict, therefore, went on to provide that "there should be established, so far as it was possible, schoolmasters and schoolmistresses in every parish which was without them, in order to instruct the children of both sexes in the principal mysteries of the Catholic, Apostolic, and Roman religion.[139]

Hundreds of Thousands of Protestants Escaped[140]

These cruelties were, however, of no avail in checking the emigration. The Huguenots continued to flee out of France in all directions. The Great Louis, still bent on their "conversion," increased his guards along the frontiers. The soldiers were rewarded in proportion to the captures they effected. The aid of the frontier peasantry was also invited, and thousands of them joined the troops in guarding the highways, the bridges, the ferries, and all the avenues leading out of France. . . . In vain!—the emigration continued. . . .

They went in all sorts of disguises; some as pedlars, others as soldiers, huntsmen, valets and beggars. Some, to disarm suspicion, even pretended to sell . . . rosaries. The Huguenots conducted the emigration on a regular system. They had Itineraries prepared and secretly distributed, in which the safest routes and hiding-places were described in detail,—a sort of "underground railroad," such as existed in the United States before the abolition of slavery. Many escaped through the great forest of Ardennes into Luxembourg; others through the Vosges mountains into Germany; and others through the passes of the Jura into Switzerland. Some were shot by the soldiers and peasantry; a still greater number were sent to the galleys; yet many thousands of them nevertheless continued to make their escape.[141]

CONCLUSION

The estimated number of evangelical believers escaping the hostile environment of French Catholicism ranges from 400,000 to 1,000,000. The number of Protestants who remained in France is estimated at 1,000,000.[142] It is not known how many men, women, and children died in France solely because they were non-Catholic, nor do we know the number of Christian school educators who died. In the tradition and training of Calvinist pastors, we know that many pastors also served as schoolmasters, especially among smaller congregations. We can assume, therefore, that Christian school educators were either driven out of France as pastor/schoolmasters or were killed or imprisoned in France.

It must be remembered that it was the success of Christian schools in France and elsewhere that gave rise to the militant Jesuit Order, which was the backbone of Catholicism's Counter-Reformation. With reference to the Jesuits, Cooke says:

[Catholic authorities] proceeded then, in those countries where the advance of Protestantism demanded it, to match school with school and educational advance with educational advance, principally by way of Loyola's Jesuit program.[143]

The rapid success of Protestantism's Christian schools revealed the embarrassing shortcomings of the Catholic Church, not only among the common people of France but also among their adherents in most countries of the Western world. Regretfully, they were not willing to simply "match school with school and education advance with educational advance."[144] They chose to literally eliminate the competition through annihilation. Lewis summarizes it well:

The liquidation of the Huguenots [and their Christian schools] is a story one would gladly leave untold were it possible to do so, a crime which stood preeminent in its vileness for over two hundred and fifty years, until a more advanced civilization produced the gas chamber and the concentration camp.

. . . the Huguenot was, in a sense, the Jew of Louis XIV's kingdom.[145]

Catholicism's Counter-Reformation began in France, spread to Belgium, Holland, Germany, and eastern Europe. In chapter 12 we will see the same courage among believers in those countries that we have seen among the Huguenots of France. The remarkable courage of the French Huguenot educators in the face of unbelievable cruelty is one of the great legacies of modern Christian school education.

Endnotes - Chapter Eleven

[1] Richard Heath, *The Reformation in France* (London: The Religious Tract Society, 1886), pp. 130–131.

[2] Samuel Smiles, *The Huguenots* (New York: Harper and Brothers, Publishers, 1868), p. 27.

[3] O.I.A. Roche, *The Days of the Upright* (New York: Clarkson N. Potter, Inc., 1965), p. 7.

[4] Henry Mortyn Baird, *The Huguenots and the Revocation of the Edict of Nantes,* vol. 2 (New York: Charles Scribner's Sons, 1895), p. 426.

[5] Roche, p. 13.

[6] W. Carlos Martyn, *A History of the Huguenots* (New York: The American Tract Society, 1866), p. 27.

[7] Roche, p. 7.

[8] *"De sorte qu'il est beaucoup plus difficile de vous résister, que de résister aux Empereurs Payens."* Cited by Baird, vol. I, p. 564.

[9] Roche, p. 306.

[10] David Buisseret, *Huguenots and Papists* (London: Ginn and Company, 1972), p. 32.

[11] Martyn, p. 117.

[12] Roche, p. 307.

[13] Martyn, p. 116. Martyn cites: Sismondi, *History of the Albigenses*, p. 129.

14 Smiles, p. 26.

15 Ibid.

16 Will Durant, *The Reformation* (New York: Simon and Schuster, 1957), p. 503.

17 Ibid., p. 502.

18 Ibid., p. 500.

19 Smiles, pp. 26–27.

20 Roche, pp. 12–13.

21 Ibid., 9.

22 Smiles, p. 27.

23 Ibid.

24 Lars P. Qualben, *A History of the Christian Church* (New York: Thomas Nelson and Sons, 1942), p. 308.

25 N.M. Sutherland, *The Huguenot Struggle for Recognition* (New Haven: Yale University Press, 1980), p. 14.

26 Buisseret, p. 26.

27 Roche, p. 9.

28 Ibid., p. 8.

29 Smiles, pp. 19–20. Smiles cited Lord Herbert, *Life of Henry VII*, p. 147.

30 Roche, p. 7.

31 Smiles, p. 20.

32 Jean Claude, *A Short Account of the Complaints and Cruel Persecutions of the Protestants in the Kingdom of France* (London: Printed by W. Redmayne, 1707), p. 109. Note: Jean Claude was the pastor of the largest Protestant church in France—14,000 members—located five miles southeast of Paris. He died in exile in Holland in 1685.

33 *The Barcelona Catholic Banner,* cited by C. Leopold Clark, *The Christian Church and the See of Rome* (London: Protestant Truth Society), p. 180.

34 Roche, p. 143.

35 Durant, p. 494.

36 Ibid., pp. 495–496.

37 Martyn, p. 151.

38 Durant, p. 504.

39 Buisseret, p. 27.

40 Martyn, p. 140

41 Ibid., p. 145

42 Bruce L. Shelley, *Church History in Plain Language* (Dallas: Word Publishing, 1982; updated 1995), p. 277.

43 Ibid.

44 George Lambert, *The Huguenots* (Canterbury: A paper read before the directors of the French Protestant Hospital, July 26, 1884), p. 9.

45 Smiles, p. 141.

46 Shelley, p. 276.

47 Sutherland, p. 4.

48 Ellwood P. Cubberley, *The History of Education* (Boston: Houghton Mifflin, 1920), p. 332.

49 G.A. Rothrock, *The Huguenots: A Biography of a Minority,* Subtitle: "Introduction: Church and State in Medieval France," (Chicago: Nelson-Hall, Inc. Publishers, 1979), pp. XXIV–XXV.

50 Daniel W. Lucero, *Protestantism in France in the 16th and 17th Centuries, The Huguenots* (unpub-

lished paper for Life Bible College, 7 April 1993), p. 2. Note: Lucero is a Fulbright scholar serving as a Foursquare Church missionary in Nancy, France.

51 Thomas M. Lindsay, *A History of the Reformation,* vol. 2 (Edinburgh: T and T Clark, 1908), p. 133.

52 Qualben, p. 309.

53 Durant, pp. 504–505.

54 Sutherland, p. 28.

55 Baird, vol. II, p. 6.

56 Ibid.

57 Martyn, p. 183.

58 Prince William of Orange, "Apoloigie de Guillaume IX, Prince d'Orange contre la Proscription de Philippe II, Roy d'Espagne," in du Mont, vol. 5, part 1, pp. 384–385, 389–390, 392, 395–397, 401–402, 405–406; ed. and trans. by Herbert H. Rowen, *The Low Countries in Early Modern Times* (New York: Harper and Row, 1972), p. 87.

59 Roche, pp. 26–27.

60 Lindsay, vol. 2, p. 192.

61 Durant, *The Reformation,* p. 504.

62 Lindsay, vol. 2, p. 191.

63 Robert Hastings Nichols, *The Growth of the Christian Church* (Revised edition),(Philadelphia: The Westminster Press, 1945), pp. 211-212. Nichols' footnote: *"Huguenot" was at first a nickname applied to the French Protestants by the Roman Catholics. Its origin was this: The Protestants of Tours used to meet by night at the Gate of King Hugo. The people of the town believed that King Hugo's spirit walked by night. So a monk said in a sermon that the Protestants ought to be called Huguenots, meaning kinsmen of Hugo, because like him they went out only at night.*

64 John Calvin, cited by Martyn, p. 195.

65 Durant, *The Reformation*, pp. 520–521.

66 Roche, p. 27.

67 Ibid., p. 169.

68 Smiles, p. 131.

69 *Encyclopaedia Britannica,* vol. 2 (Chicago: William Benton, Publisher, 1961), p. 871.

70 Elizabeth K. Hudson, "The Protestant Struggle for Survival in Early Bourbon France: The Case of the Huguenot Schools" p. 293.

71 Nichols, p. 212. Also see Lindsay, vol. 2, p. 200. Note: Other sources cite lower figures.

72 Lambert, p. 26.

73 Nichols, p. 212.

74 Baird, vol. II, p. 61. Note: Lindsay wrote that Admiral Coligny was "recognized to be the greatest statesman in France."—Lindsay, vol. 2, p. 197.

75 R.E.D. Clark, "Masacure of St. Bartholomew's Day," *New International Dictionary of the Christian Church,* J.D. Douglas, ed. (Grand Rapids: Zondervan, 1974), p. 108.

76 Lambert, p. 25.

77 Roche, p. 142.

78 Ibid., p. 141.

79 Ibid., p. 140.

80 Martyn, p. 193.

81 Claude, p. 172.

82 *Encyclopaedia Britannica*, vol. 2 (Chicago, William Benton, 1961), p. 442.

83 Roche, p. 298.

84 Baird, vol. 2, p. 25.

[85] Cubberley, *The History of Education,* p. 332.

[86] Buisseret, p. 94. Also see: Richard Heath, *The Reformation in France* (London: The Religious Tract Society, 1886), pp. 130–131. Heath cites their "Discipline," which reads, "The churches shall make it a duty to raise schools."

[87] Cubberley, *The History of Education,* p. 333.

[88] Baird, vol. 2, pp. 474–475. Baird's footnote: Villars to the Guises, October, 1560, in *Négociations sous François II,* 671. See *Rise of the Huguenots,* I. 429.

[89] Ibid.

[90] Buisseret, p. 94.

[91] Baird, vol. 2, p. 477.

[92] Hudson, p. 272 (see footnote).

[93] Buisseret, p. 94.

[94] George Ruppert, *Public Schools in Renaissance France* (Urbana: University of Illinois Press, 1984), p. 9.

[95] Hudson, p. 271.

[96] Buisseret, p. 99.

[97] Ibid., p. 46.

[98] Ibid., p. 97.

[99] Cubberley, *The History of Education,* p. 336.

[100] Ibid., p. 337.

[101] Claude, p. 109.

[102] Cubberley, *Public Education in the United States* (Boston: Houghton Mifflin Company, 1919), p. 10.

[103] Benson, p. 90.

[104] Brian G. Armstrong, "Ignatius of Loyola," *The New International Dictionary of the Christian Church,* J.D. Douglas, ed. (Grand Rapids: Zondervan, 1974), p. 499.

[105] Durant, *The Reformation,* p. 459.

[106] Cubberley, *The History of Education,* p. 336.

[107] Benson, p. 93.

[108] Cubberley, *The History of Education,* p. 337.

[109] Benson, pp. 192–193.

[110] Cubberley, *The History of Education,* p. 138.

[111] Durant, *The Reformation,* p. 915.

[112] Frank Hugh O'Donnell, *The Ruin of Education in Ireland* (London: David Nutt, 1902)—opposite title page.

[113] Cubberley, *The History of Education,* pp. 336–337.

[114] Durant, *The Reformation,* p. 909. Durant cites Longride, *The Spiritual Exercises of St. Ignatius Loyola,* p. 119 for the first half of quote.

[115] H.M. Carson, "Roman Catholicism," *The New International Dictionary of the Christian Church* (Grand Rapids: Zondervan, 1974), p. 853.

[116] Durant, *The Reformation,* p. 923. Also see Martyn p. 135. Martyn cited Pope Leo X, who said, ". . . the Pope sitting as God, in the temple of God cannot err."

[117] Baird, vol. 2, p. 477.

[118] *Merriam-Webster's Collegiate Dictionary,* 10th ed. (Springfield, Mass.: Merriam-Webster, Inc., 1995), p. 412.

[119] Frederick Eby and Charles Flinn Arrowood, *The Development of Modern Education* (New York: Prentice-Hall, Inc., 1934), p. 365.

120 Lindsay, vol. 2, p. 222.

121 Ibid.

122 Ibid., p. 223.

123 *Encyclopaedia Britannica,* vol. 16 (Chicago: William Benton Publisher, 1961), p. 71.

124 Durant, *The Reformation*, p. 406.

125 *Encyclopaedia Britannica*, vol. 16 (Chicago: William Benton Publisher, 1961), p. 71.

126 Baird, vol. II, p. 477.

127 John C. Rule, ed., *Louis XIV—Great Lives Observed* (Englewood Cliffs, NJ: Prentice-Hall, Inc., 1974), p. 66. Note: In Paris there are more statues of Louis XIV than of all other French monarchs. With reference to Louis XIV, Baird said, "No man was more selfish and unscrupulous, none could be more inhuman." Baird, vol. 2, p. 13.

128 Smiles, p. 157.

129 Lindsay, vol. 2, p. 221.

130 Smiles, pp. 156–157.

131 Baird, vol. 2 (see cover page and page 426).

132 Claude, Preface, p. viii. Note: Narissee, writer of the foreword to Jean Claude's book *Cruel Persecutions of the Protestants in France,* said, "The Court would not grant [Jean Claude] the fifteen days allowed by the Edict to all the ministers, without distinction, but as soon as this document was published in the Metropolis, Claude was 'commanded to leave Paris within four and twenty hours, and forthwith to depart the Kingdom. For this end they put him into the hands of one of the King's footmen, with orders not to leave him till he was out of his dominions.' He took the coach at Paris, the next day, for Brussels, with his escort, who, it is said, was very civil to him all the way to the frontier, where they separated. The criminal, of whom France was not worthy, had evidently made a very favorable impression upon the royal servant. It is interesting to know that the senior pastor of Charenton, as he journeyed through France, received many marks of kindness, not only from his brethren, but even from some of his enemies."

133 Claude, pp. 203–204.

134 Baird, vol. 1, Preface, page i.

135 Ibid., vol. 2, p. 464.

136 John G. Lorimer, *The Protestant Church of France* (Philadelphia: Presbyterian Board of Education, 1842), p. 23.

137 Eby and Arrowood, p. 349.

138 Smiles, p. 341.

139 Matthew Arnold, *The Popular Education of France* (London: publisher unknown, 1861), p. 19.

140 "Huguenots," Microsoft®,Encarta®,96 Encyclopedia.©,1993-1995 Microsoft Corporation. All rights reserved.©, Funk & Wagnalls Corporation. All rights reserved.

141 Smiles, pp. 162–163.

142 "Huguenots," Microsoft®,Encarta®,96 Encyclopedia.©, 1993-1995 Microsoft Corporation. All rights reserved.©, Funk & Wagnalls Corporation. All rights reserved.

143 Robert L. Cooke, *Philosophy, Education and Certainty* (Grand Rapids: Zondervan, 1960), p. 115.

144 Ibid.

145 Lewis, pp. 104–105.

Illustration Sources

Figure 1 *Map* - Global Mapping International, Colorado Springs, CO.

Figure 2 *Dining room* - Photo by author (PBA).

Figure 3 *Renegade Protestants* - David Buisseret, *Huguenots and Papists* (London: Ginn and Company, 1972), p. 32.

Figure 4   *Massacre* - Samuel Smiles, *The Huguenots* (London: John Murray, 1889), opposite title page.

Figure 7   *Henry IV* - Edward Smedley, *History of the Reformed Religion*, vol. 2 (London: J.G. & F. Rivington, 1834), opposite title page.

Figure 5   *Rose window* - (PBA).

Figure 6   *Louvre* - (PBA).

Figure 8   *Classroom* - Ellwood P. Cubberley, *The History of Education* (Boston: Houghton Mifflin Company, 1920).

Figure 9   *Map of Protestant churches* - S. Mours, *The Reformed Churches in France, Paris*, Protestant Bookshop, Strasbourg, Oberlin Bookshop, 1958, p. 51.

Figure 10   *Loyola* - Ibid, p. 337.

Figure 11   *Louis XIV* - James Henry Robinson and Charles A. Beard, *Outlines of European History* (Boston: Ginn and Company, 1907), p. 59.

Christian Schools and the Counter-Reformation

When Louis XIV died in 1715 at age 77, he assumed he had cleansed France of all of its Protestant churches and schools. "The dying monarch himself supposed the religion of Calvin and Beza to be virtually extinct."[1] France, the birthplace of Catholicism's Counter-Reformation, may have plundered, dragooned, and terrorized its Protestant population to the point of extinction, but in the long run, what had it gained? It gained an exodus of some of its most resourceful citizens and the loss of good will around the world. With reference to the great Huguenot exodus, Samuel Smiles says,

Figure 1. King Louis XIV drove the Protestants and their 2000 Christian schools out of France.

"The loss which it occasioned to France was not far short of a million persons, and those her best and most industrious subjects."[2] W.H. Lewis claims that France's dubious victory over the Protestants provided a net loss of "honor and good faith on the part of the Crown, [and instead] misery, fear, hatred, deflations, bribery, savagery [and] the enmity of all Europe."[3] In modern terms, France lost "political capital" at home and abroad, a loss that culminated in the French Revolution of 1789.

One wonders, then, why the Counter-Reformation gained momentum and spread to Belgium, Holland, Germany, and the eastern European countries. Why were the Pope, the Jesuits, the Holy Roman Emperor Charles V, and his son Philip II so forcefully behind it? It is obvious the motivation was based on ideological fervor and not on practical outcomes. Cooke says, "The [Counter-Reformation] failed in large measure . . . to bring men back to the fold of the Mother Church, and the spread of the Reformation was not seriously checked."[4]

One of the foremost issues of the Counter-Reformation was education, particularly Protestantism's Christian school education. The militant Jesuit educators were the "ecclesiastical shock troops"[5] of the Catholic Counter-Reformation. Their mission was to overcome the embarrassment created by the successful Protestant schools through extirpating Protestants and establishing their own Jesuit high schools throughout Europe and non-European countries including Canada and the American colonies. According to Wilds:

> Realizing that the Protestant leaders were relying upon education as a most effective agency to advance their cause, the Catholic leaders determined to use the same instrument to root out heresy and win the dissenters back to the Catholic fold.[6]

In Austria, for example, Catholic authorities established Catholic schools to counter the proliferation of Protestant Christian schools. With reference to Protestant schools, James Von Horn Melton says:

> Shocked by the spread of Protestantism in their territories, Catholic princes followed suit. . . . In Habsburg Austria, schools became a central battleground in efforts to roll back Protestantism. As Luther's teachings spread rapidly throughout the Habsburg domains, so did Protestant schools. Cardinal Khlesl fretted in 1587 that fifty-seven schools attached to Lutheran parishes had been established in Lower Austria alone, many at the instigation of Protestant nobles.[7]

Chapter 12 will focus on that unique period of history that forged the fundamental characteristics of the modern Christian school movement. The chapter divisions are:

1. *The Political and Ecclesiastical Objectives of the Counter-Reformation*
2. *The Forms of Christian School Education That Flourished in the Counter-Reformation*
3. *Lessons Learned*

To suggest that the Jesuits, in their quest to rid the world of Protestants, were not successful in some areas would be an error. For example, Catholic authorities were as successful in Belgium at eliminating the evangelical Protestants as they were in France. Clarence Benson says, "When the Jesuits entered Belgium in 1542, it was only half Protestant. A century later it was exclusively Roman Catholic."[8]

Other countries where the Counter-Reformation was reasonably successful in forcing a return to Catholicism were Hungary, Poland, Bohemia, and Ireland. It was not nearly as effective in Holland, Germany, Switzerland, England, Scotland, Iceland, or the Scandinavian countries. Mixed in with this long struggle was the Thirty Years' War (1618–1648), which brought devastation to Germany and eastern Europe. Impeding the progress of Protestant Christian schools was at the center of Catholicism's strategy. To better understand the nature of the Christian schools of the Counter-Reformation era, one must have at least a surface knowledge of Europe's political environment between 1521 and 1727.

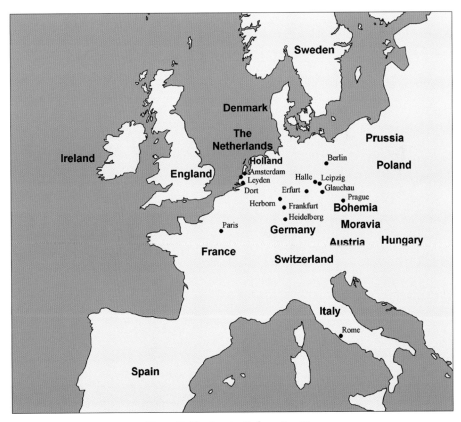

Figure 2. The Counter-Reformation Map

1. The Political and Ecclesiastical Objectives of the Counter-Reformation

Figure 3. Near the end of his life the Holy Roman Emperor, Charles V, said he regretted that he had not rid his Western World empire of Protestants.

In 1558 (the year he died), Emperor Charles V, the last emperor of the Holy Roman Empire to be crowned by a pope, said he regretted that he had not "cut out the root" of heresy. Durant says that "[Charles V] regretted that he had allowed Luther to escape him at Worms."[9] "Cut out the root"[10] of heresy, "Death to heretics,"[11] and "Dye or be Catholicks"[12] express the prevailing sentiment among the Catholic Church and state leaders of the sixteenth and seventeenth centuries.

THE NETHERLANDS

The Netherlands suffered a persecution of churches and schools second only to that of France. Latourette says:

> The Reformed Churches were persecuted, notably in the Netherlands and France. The Netherlands were peopled chiefly by the Dutch in the north, Flemings in the centre, and French-speaking Walloons in the south. Luther's writings early won a wide following, but in the latter half of the sixteenth century Calvinism largely supplanted Lutheranism. In the north Protestants were in the majority whereas the south was predominantly Roman Catholic.[13]

There was a high concentration of Anabaptists in Holland, and they also suffered persecution.

It was the Catholic General Council at Trent in the mountains of Italy—which lasted eighteen years (1545–1563)—that officially set in motion the militant anti-Protestant spirit of the Counter-Reformation. With Protestant churches and schools flourishing, particularly in Holland, it is not surprising that on September 25, 1550, Emperor Charles V issued an edict in the form of placards distributed throughout Holland and the Netherlands. The placards read in part:

> No one shall print, write, copy, keep, conceal, sell, buy, or give, in churches, streets, or other places, any book or writing made by Martin Luther, John Oecolampadius, Ulrich Zwingli, Martin Bucer, John Calvin, or other heretics reprobated by the Holy Church . . . nor break or otherwise injure the images of the Holy Virgin or canonized saints . . . nor hold conventicles, or illegal gatherings, or be present at any such in which the adherents of the above-mentioned heretics teach, baptize, and form conspiracies against the Holy Church and the general welfare. . . . We forbid all lay persons to converse or dispute concerning the Holy Scriptures, openly or secretly . . . or to read, teach, or expound the Scriptures, unless they have duly studied theology, or have been approved by some renowned university . . . or to entertain any of the opinions of the above-mentioned heretics . . . on pain of being . . . punished as follows . . . the men [to be beheaded] with the sword, and the women to be buried alive, if they do not persist in their errors; if they persist in them they are to be executed with fire; all their property in both cases to be confiscated to the Crown.[14]

Figure 4. Philip II, King of Spain and husband of "Bloody Mary" of England, continued in the quest of his father, Charles V, to rid the Western world of evangelical Protestants. He was a major force behind the Counter-Reformation.

Before Charles V died in 1558, he abdicated his title of Emperor of the Holy Roman Empire to his brother Ferdinand and made his son Philip II king of his other dominions. Robinson and Beard explain:

> The chief ally of the Pope and the Jesuits in their efforts to check Protestantism was the son of Charles V, Philip II (1556–1598), who succeeded to the kingdom of Spain and its colonies, Milan, the Two Sicilies, and the Netherlands. Philip was a fanatic, who was willing to sacrifice even his kingdom to put down heretics.[15]

Within the first year of his reign, Philip gave to the Jesuits the task of ridding the Netherlands of Protestants.[16]

With this grim anti-Protestant sentiment hanging over them like a cloud, it is amazing that the Protestants in Holland, like their fellow believers in

France, gave serious attention to establishing elementary and secondary Christian schools. The greatest distractions to the calm environment required for education happened between 1567 and 1609, when Philip II sent two armies to suppress the growing number of Protestants. Clarke says:

> Philip II, of Spain first sent a German Army of 13,000 into the country, and then to inflict more severe punishment, the Duke of Alva with an army of 20,000 European mercenaries, who ravaged the country with fire and sword for the space of six years, committing unspeakable atrocities and practising the most barbarous violence. The Protestants went armed to their Churches, their numbers exceeding 100,000.
>
> A so-called "Council of troubles" set up by this inhuman monster condemned to death in the first three months of its existence no less than 1,800 persons.
>
> The Duke boasted that he had caused 18,600 of the inhabitants to be executed during his rule. This of course leaves uncounted the multitudes who were massacred by the soldiery of whom the historian Motley says: 'Men, women and children, old and young, nobles and paupers, opulent burghers, hospital patients, lunatics, dead bodies, all were indiscriminately made to furnish food for the scaffold and the stake.'
>
> For this performance, Pope Pius V, rewarded him with the distinction for special service to the Church, in the form of a jewelled hat and sword.[17]

THE THIRTY YEARS' WAR IN CENTRAL EUROPE

A similar disruption and distraction hovered over central and eastern Europe with the great tragedy of the Thirty Years' War from 1618 to 1648. However, Christian schools flourished in the midst of that hostile environment as well. Eby and Arrowood provide this description:

> The entire country was more or less devastated, much of it was depopulated, while the inhabitants of Germany decreased one-half. In many places the people were reduced to savagery. In the villages there was often not a wagon nor a draft animal to be seen; many a peasant was forced to harness himself or his wife and dog to the plow. A number of the free cities never recovered their ruined trade and industries. The Moravians who inhabited the central theater of the conflict were exiled and well-nigh exterminated. . . . The people lapsed into barbarity, ignorance, superstition, and crime. Except in the largest centers of population, every trace of the schools passed away. Church and school buildings often were requisitioned as hospitals or barracks for soldiers, or even as stables for their horses.[18]

The central questions of the Thirty Years' War were, 'Who owns the land?' and 'Which religion will prevail?' Prior to the Great Reformation of 1517, the Roman Catholic Church was the world's largest landowner and largest employer, the only 'legal' church, and most important the world's most powerful civil authority. As the Church's monolithic empire began to crumble, wars like the Thirty Years' War were predictable. While the specifics of that war are not germane to our study, this overview is helpful in understanding the spiritual, political, and cultural environments in which these early Christian schools were forged.

2. The Forms of Christian School Education That Flourished in the Counter-Reformation

C.B. Eavey's statement that "everywhere Protestantism went—Christian schools were founded"[19] was nowhere more true than in Holland. The Dutch gained an early start on Christian school education largely through the impact of the Brethren of the Common Life schools, which had their genesis in Holland in the fourteenth century under the leadership of Gerhard Groote. These schools became widely accepted and developed into an unofficial Catholic school system throughout the Netherlands. As the evangelical movement gained momentum, changes took place in the educational institutions. Frederick Eby explains:

> The University of Leyden, established in 1575 . . . became the most progressive center of learning in northern Europe, and the city of Amsterdam became a rendezvous and refuge for learned men from every country. Most of the teachers became Protestant; especially was this true of the Brethren of the Common Life, who had long been inclined toward evangelical faith. Almost every man, woman, and child had learned to read in the pre-Reformation public schools. As the schools were already in the hands of the town authorities, the transfer to the new order was effected without much opposition. With the general acceptance of Protestantism, the city councils forbade the teaching of Catholic prayers and religious practices, and required the substitution of the reformed catechism and doctrines.[20]

The theological and philosophical "fingerprints" of Calvin were everywhere evident in the Dutch churches and schools—for example, a close interdependent relationship among church, home, and school. Cubberley observes, "Interwoven thus with the very life of the church was a school system in which the schoolmaster was an officer in the church, and the curriculum of the school included conscious preparation for participation in the service of public worship."[21]

In 1618 to 1619 the Dutch Calvinists, known as the Dutch Reformed Church, held a synod in Dordrect, south of Amsterdam. The Synod of Dort, as it was called, set forth a bold plan for education that involved the church, home, and school in a closely integrated fashion that would indeed have warmed the heart of Luther and of Calvin. The resolution began with a statement about catechismal instruction:

> In order that the Christian youth may be diligently instructed in the principles of religion, and be trained in piety, three modes of catechising should be employed. I. In the house, by parents. II. In the schools, by schoolmasters. III. In the churches, by ministers, elders and catechists especially appointed for the purpose. That these may diligently employ their trust, the Christian magistrates shall be requested to promote, by their authority, so sacred and necessary a work; and all who have the oversight of churches and schools shall be required to pay special attention to this matter.[22]

Then followed a comprehensive plan that involved the entire nation in Christian school education. It begins with instruction to parents:

> The office of parents is diligently to instruct their children and their whole household in the principles of the Christian religion, in a manner adapted to their respective capacities; earnestly and carefully to admonish them to the cultivation of true piety; to engage their punctual attendance on family worship, and take them with them to the hearing of the Word of God. . . . Parents who profess religion, and are negligent in this work, shall be faithfully admonished by the ministers; and, if the case requires it, they shall be censured by the Consistory, that they may be brought to the discharge of their duty.

> Schools, in which the young shall be properly instructed in the principles of Christian doctrine, shall be instituted not only in cities, but also in towns and country places where heretofore none have existed. The Christian magistracy shall be requested that well-qualified persons may be employed and enabled to devote themselves to the service; and especially that the children of the poor may be gratuitously instructed, and not be excluded from the benefit of the schools. In this office none shall be employed but such as are members of the Reformed Church, having certificates of an upright faith and pious life, and of being well versed in the truths of the Catechism. They are to sign a document, professing their belief in the Confession of Faith and the Heidelberg Catechism, and promising that they will give catechetical instruction to the youth in the principles of

Christian truth according to the same. The schoolmasters shall instruct their scholars according to their age and capacity, at least two days in the week, not only by causing them to commit to memory, but also by instilling into their minds an acquaintance with the truths of the Catechism.[23]

Dutch ministers and church elders were given responsibility for the oversight of Holland's Christian schools:

In order that due knowledge may be obtained of the diligence of the schoolmasters, and the improvement of the youth, it shall be the duty of the ministers, with an elder, and, if necessary, with a magistrate, to visit all the schools, private as well as public, frequently, in order to excite the teachers to earnest diligence, to encourage and counsel them in the duty of catechising, and to furnish an example by questioning them, addressing them in a friendly and affectionate manner, and exciting them to early piety and diligence. If any of the schoolmasters should be found neglectful or perverse, they shall be earnestly admonished by the ministers, and, if necessary, by the Consistory, in relation to their office.[24]

Dutch historian William H. Kilpatrick provides insight into the textbooks used. The following texts were used in the Christian schools in the city of Utrecht in 1650:

The Great and Small ABC Book

The Heidelberg Catechism and the Gospels and Epistles

The Stairway of Youth

The Mirror of Youth (Dutch History)

The History of David

Proverbs and Psalms[25]

There were three levels of Christian education in Holland:

1. Town schools for boys and girls called public schools, "where children of quality as well as of poor families, for a very small sum, could be well and Christianly educated."[26]
2. Latin secondary schools for boys which were prep schools for professions and for the university.
3. The University of Leyden, founded by Prince William II of Orange in 1575. Prince William, the celebrated founder of the Dutch Republic, established religious freedom in Holland.[27]

Figure 5. William II, Prince of Orange (later King William III), was the much beloved founder of the Dutch Republic and the champion of Protestant causes. He was the leader of the rebellion against Spain.

Most of these schools were underwritten by revenues from vast proper-ties (one-fifth of Holland) formerly owned by the Catholic Church but now by the government. Eby explains:

Another great advantage for the Netherlands was the ease with which the revenues and property of the old [Catholic] church were now diverted to the support of the public [Christian] schools. In 1580 the state of Utrecht set apart its ecclesiastical property for the maintenance of schoolmasters. Three years later Zealand passed a similar law, on the ground that education "is the foundation of the commonwealth." In 1603 the revenues of the old church were turned over to the support of common schools in Friesland.[28]

The outcome of the Dutch system of Christian school education can only be described as remarkable. John Motley, foremost historian of the Netherlands, wrote with reference to Holland's Christian schools:

> It was a land where every child went to school, where almost every individual inhabitant could read and write, where even the middle classes were proficient in mathematics and the classics, and could speak two or more modern languages. . . .

> An excellent reason why the people were so well governed, so productive, and so enterprising, was the simple fact that they were an educated people. There was hardly a Netherlander—man, woman, or child—that could not read and write. . . . In the cities, as well as in the rural districts, there were not only common schools but classical schools.

> In the burgher families it was rare to find boys who had not been taught Latin, or girls unacquainted with French. Capacity to write and speak several modern languages was very common, and there were many individuals who had made remarkable progress in science and classical literature.[29]

Italian historian Guicciardini claimed that "even the peasants in Holland could read and write well."[30]

ANABAPTIST AND MENNONITE SCHOOLS

It should be noted that the thousands of Anabaptists, including the Mennonites, living in Holland during this period were the most persecuted among the evangelical believers. Durant says, "In some Dutch towns it was estimated that two-thirds of the population were Anabaptists; in Deventer even the burgomaster was converted to the cause."[31] However, the Catholic authorities were unusually cruel to them. Lindsay records the following:

> The severest persecutions . . . before the rule of Philip II, were reserved for those people who are called the Anabaptists. . . . They had been tortured on the rack, scourged, imprisoned in dungeons, roasted to death

before slow fires, and had seen their women drowned, buried alive, pressed into coffins too small for their bodies till their ribs were broken, others stamped into them by the feet of the executioners. . . . The Government made great exertions to crush the movement. Detachments of soldiers were divided into bands of fifteen or twenty, and patrolled the environs of the cities, making midnight visitations, and hauling men and women to prison until the dungeons were overcrowded with captured Anabaptists.[32]

Because of the severity of the persecution they suffered, the Anabaptists and the Mennonites developed only a few Christian schools. Like the first-century Christians in Rome, Anabaptists and Mennonites taught the young clandestinely in their homes.[33]

THE PIETIST SCHOOLS

Pietistic and rationalistic education appeared together in the seventeenth and eighteenth centuries in central Europe, emerging side by side from the ashes of the devastating Thirty Years' War. It was a harbinger—a canary in the mineshaft—of things to come in both secular and religious education. The newest enemy of true Christian education was no longer ancient paganism from Rome nor medieval Catholicism but a new emphasis on "practical education" independent of church influence—an education based on human reason. This emerging rationalistic education marked the genesis of purely secular education. All previous education had been religious in one form or another. Ernst Helmreich explains:

Whereas pietism stressed inward feeling, faith, meditation, and prayer, rationalism stressed reason, knowledge, and understanding. Pietism was bent on strengthening religion and reawakening the church; rationalism on breaking the control of the church and strengthening and revitalizing the state. One point the two movements had in common . . . was their emphasis on the practical in education, although their concepts as to what was practical were at variance. Both welcomed with somewhat different emphasis more instruction in the vernacular, and in such subjects as arithmetic, history, geography, and nature study—but when it came to religion they differed sharply. While one stressed inner piety and prayer, the other stressed rational inquiry and training in ethics and morality. One wanted a Christian education tied to the catechism and the historic confessional creeds; the other wanted a general religious instruction based on nature and reason.[34]

The Pietist movement in central Europe was a "Reformation of the Reformation." In its spiritual condition the Lutheran "ship of state" was listing badly at the beginning of the Thirty Years' War in 1618, and it grew progressively worse as the war went on. Kenneth Gangel best describes the decline of Germany and the Lutheran Church during the war:

> During the war "lawless armies plundered and devastated northern Europe, and 10 million of Germany's 16 million people were killed. Whole cities were destroyed, and almost none was left unscathed; orphaned children roamed the woods like packs of wild animals." Controversy raged among Protestant church leaders, and many of the clergy were ruled by secular civil authorities. Religious education centered on intellectual development and orthodox doctrine rather than personal purity and holy living. The clergy themselves were poor examples of Biblical teaching. Church services tended toward a formal rigidity which repudiated the dynamic vitality of the New Testament.[35]

Eby says, "Pietism was the reaction against all this cold, deadening, rancorous system."[36] Pietism was a much needed revival within Lutheranism and did much to restore the original vitality of her churches and schools. "The movement was, in fact, very largely in harmony with Luther's early evangelical point of view."[37]

THE INFLUENCE OF COMENIUS AND FRANCKE

The foremost Pietist leaders in Protestant education reform during the Counter-Reformation period were John Amos Comenius (1592–1670) from Moravia and August Hermann Francke (1663–1727) from Prussia (northern Germany). Some historians appear to suffer historical amnesia concerning the spiritual and academic significance of these two men.

COMENIUS

John Amos Comenius was born Jan Amos Komensky on March 28, 1592, in the small community of Nivnice[38] in southeast Moravia, now a part of the Czech Republic. Like other scholars of the period, Comenius latinized his name from Jan Komensky to John Comenius. While known as an education reformer and later called "the first evangelist of modern pedagogy,"[39] he was equally prominent as a church leader, serving as the last bishop of the Czech branch of the Unity of the Brethren,[40] known today as the Moravian Church. The Moravians are among the oldest if not the oldest evangelical church body with an unbroken tradition of Christian school education—dating back to John Huss and the Hussites in fourteenth-century Prague.[41]

Comenius was among the few Unity of the Brethren believers to survive the Thirty Years' War. With reference to the Unity of the Brethren Church, Hamilton and Hamilton write:

> . . . the Thirty Years' War brought the practical annihilation of its congregations throughout the twin lands [Bohemia and Moravia] of its birth. All organic ecclesiastical life other than that of the Roman Catholic Church was suppressed. Evangelical Christians faced the sorrowful choice of renouncing either their faith or their homes and friends and possessions. A significant number preferred exile to the denial of their beliefs and fled across the northern borders of Bohemia and Moravia into Saxony and Silesia.[42]

Durant says, "These 'Moravian Brethren' were almost exterminated in the fury of the Thirty Years' War; they survived through the leadership of John Comenius."[43]

CHRISTIAN SCHOOLS FLOURISHED AFTER THE THIRTY YEAR'S WAR

As the Thirty Years' War subsided, central Europe was ready for spiritual renewal and educational reform. It can be said that Comenius, who believed in "the Christian education of all youth,"[44] became the first Christian school missionary. He shared his vision for education reform in Germany, Holland, England, Poland, Hungary, and Sweden. In addition to the stress of his outlaw status as a Protestant believer, he suffered the grief of losing his wife and children in a plague.[45]

Comenius' own education began at a village elementary school in his homeland.[46] He then journeyed to Nassau in the Netherlands, where he attended a Calvinist secondary school called the College of Herborn.[47] He later studied theology in Germany at the University of Heidelberg.[48] Comenius was an exceptional scholar, and as Mayer says, "Comenius can be called a 'God-intoxicated thinker,' for to him God was the beginning and the end of education." And again, "He was certain that . . . education should have a Christian orientation, otherwise it would be a journey in vanity."[49]

Comenius was something of a utopian visionary, believing strongly in what he called a "Christian Republic in which all were united through knowledge and faith."[50] A prolific writer, he authored more than a hundred books—many of them textbooks.[51] His greatest contribution to educational thought was *The Great Didactic*, a book Eby describes as "the most remarkable treasury of pedagogical wisdom ever written."[52] Its complete title was as follows:

THE GREAT DIDACTIC

**Setting Forth
The Whole Art of Teaching all
Things to all Men**

or

**A certain Inducement to found such Schools in all the Parishes,
Towns and Villages of every Christian Kingdom,
that the entire Youth of both Sexes,
None being excepted, shall,**

Quickly, Pleasantly, Thoroughly

**Become learned in the Sciences, pure in Morals,
Trained in Piety, and in this manner
Instructed in all things necessary
for the present and for the future life.[53]**

It was clearly as much a mission statement as a book title. In *The Great Didactic* Comenius offered the following fundamental educational principles, selected at random:

1. The morning hours are the most suitable for serious study.
2. All the subjects that are to be learned should be arranged so as to suit the age of the students, that nothing which is beyond their comprehension be given them to learn.
3. That the knowledge of things precede the knowledge of their combinations.
4. . . . . that examples come before rules.
5. That, before any special study is introduced, the mind of the student be prepared and made receptive of it.
6. Schools . . . should be organized in such a manner that the scholar shall be occupied with only one object of study at any given time.
7. That all studies should be carefully graded throughout the various classes, in such a way that those that come first may prepare the way for and throw light on those that come after.
8. That he who is sent to school must be kept there until he becomes well informed, virtuous, and pious.

9. That the school must be situated in a quiet spot, far from noise and distractions.
10. That the scholars receive no books but those suitable for their classes.
11. That these books be of such a kind that they can rightly be termed sources of wisdom, virtue, and piety.
12. That neither in the school nor in its vicinity the scholars be allowed to mix with bad companions.

He concludes: "If all these recommendations are observed, it is scarcely possible that schools should fail to attain their object."[54]

In his concept of Christian school education within a Christian Republic, Comenius advocated four levels of instruction:

1. Schola materna—the mother's knee (birth to age 6)—in every home.
2. Schola vernacula—the vernacular school (childhood)—in every hamlet.
3. Schola Latina—the Latin School (boyhood)—in every city.
4. The Christian university and travel (for advanced students only)—in every province.[55]

Comenius was a pioneer in school textbooks, with ideas that were revolutionary for that era. Wilds explains:

Comenius was a firm believer in the value of the textbook as an agency of instruction. Up to his time textbooks were scarce and expensive, and there was a serious lack of uniformity. Most schools were still following the medieval custom of each pupil copying his own text from dictation by the teacher. Comenius wanted each pupil to have his own copy of the text, and all pupils to have the same text covering the entire subject matter of the course. One of his greatest contributions to education was in the writing of many textbooks for use in the schools. He wrote textbooks for his School of the Mother's Knee and the vernacular school, but he was best known for his many Latin textbooks.[56]

Comenius was an aggressive opponent of the pagan classics. He said:

If we wish our schools to be truly Christian schools, the crowd of Pagan writers must be removed from them. . . .

Some one else may object: "They are not all lascivious writers. Cicero, Virgil, Horace, and others are serious and earnest." I answer: None the

less, they are blind pagans, and turn the minds of their readers from the true God to other gods and goddesses.[57]

Comenius, whose counsel on education reform was sought by the government leaders of several countries, believed strongly in a much wider range of school subjects than was common in Europe in his day. These subjects would prepare students for a variety of options. He said:

> They will learn, not for the school, but for life, so that the youths shall go forth energetic, ready for everything, apt, industrious, and worthy of being intrusted with any of the duties of life, and this all the more if they have added to virtue a sweet conversation, and have crowned all with the fear and love of God. They will go forth capable of expression and eloquence.[58]

To the ancient trivium (grammar, rhetoric, dialectic) and quadrivium (arithmetic, geometry, astronomy, music), Comenius added natural science, physics, geography, chronology, history, morals, and religion. He even suggested periods of play and relaxation for students—unheard of in the seventeenth century. Like Luther, Comenius believed that history was particularly important:

> An acquaintance with history is the most important element in a man's education, and is, as it were, the eye of his whole life. This subject, therefore, should be taught in each of the six classes, that our pupils may be ignorant of no event which has happened from ancient times to the present day.[59]

Comenius devoted a chapter in *The Great Didactic* to teaching children about God and Christian living. He believed that "piety" was the supreme purpose of education.

> Our schools, therefore, will then at length be Christian schools when they make us as like to Christ as is possible. How wretched is the teaching that does not lead to virtue and to piety.[60]

Eavey explains Comenius' concept of piety:

> He says that piety is the gift of God given to man by the Holy Spirit. To him, piety is what one has after he has come to know thoroughly the conceptions of faith and of religion, when the heart has learned to seek God everywhere, has found Him, and is following and enjoying Him. The sources of piety, he states, are three: the Bible, which is the Word of God; the world, which is God's handiwork; and man's self, which is inspired by God. Piety is drawn from these sources by meditation, prayer, and examination. Training in piety is to be started as soon as

children begin to talk and use their eyes and feet, for it is early in life that best and most lasting impressions are made. Training is to be intensified as the child grows, with parents watchful lest anything minimizing piety reach the eyes and ears of their children.[61]

It is easy for Christian school educators today to identify with Comenius, who believed that "there is no more certain way under the sun for raising sunken humanity than the proper education of the young."[62] And to him "proper education" was Christian education. Eavey says:

> Comenius was definitely evangelical. . . . To him the Bible was God's inerrant Word. He maintained that his theology was what was written in the Bible. He considered the Bible to be the basic and the most important source of knowledge. . . . To him education was the means for bringing men to the place where they would accept Christ and by accepting become able to fulfill God's purposes for their lives; education is not a direct agent in conversion; it is only a means whereby conversion may be brought about. He believed that the Holy Spirit was sent to draw men to God, to indwell, to teach, and to guide believers, and that He usually works through parents, teachers, and ministers, as natural agents. . . . He said that in every Christian school the Bible should rank above all other books and that every youth should be taught its truths from childhood. It was his contention that the Scriptures are equally suitable to all, that they contain truth comprehensible even to little children.[63]

Comenius was a true Christian school educator. If he were alive today, he would be a welcome guest in Christian school circles anywhere in the evangelical Christian community. This would also be true of Francke of Germany, who thought highly of Comenius.

GERMANY'S GREAT NEED

Within one hundred years of Luther's death, the German Lutheran Church and her Christian schools had lost much of their spiritual momentum, largely because of the stifling control of Germany's civil government under whose auspices they served.[64] Germany's spiritual decline along with the war's massive destruction had left the nation devastated, as Melton describes:

> The Thirty Years War only deepened this sense of failure and decay. Devout Lutherans like Duke Ernst the Pious of Saxony-Gotha attributed the war to divine punishment, retribution for spiritual disobedience, and corruption. At mid-century, contemporaries found it difficult to contest the duke's gloomy diagnosis. A century after the death of Luther, extensive areas of Germany lay ravaged by war. Orphans, widows, and vagabonds roamed its cities and towns. Lutheran princes, far from tend-

ing to the spiritual welfare of their subjects, increasingly indulged a taste for luxury and display in the style of Louis XIV. During the closing decades of the seventeenth century, the siege of Vienna in 1683 and the devastating impact of the wars of Louis XIV seemed to provide further evidence of divine disfavor.[65]

PHILIP SPENER, FOUNDER OF THE PIETIST MOVEMENT

The initial leader of the Pietist movement in Germany was Philip Jacob Spener, a Lutheran pastor and university professor first in Strassburg, then in Frankfurt. Spener became alienated from many Lutheran leaders because of his more conservative theology.[66] The struggle between pietism and the Lutheran Church is well described by Eavey:

> The Lutheran Church was ruled from without by civil authorities. Within it there were a number of theologians, each with his own official clergy, who were as autocratic as the papacy had been. These theologians were at odds with one another; the result was an immense amount of quibbling on questions of doctrine. In the midst of the struggle over doctrine, a religious formalism had developed. . . . For Luther's emphasis on faith they had substituted intellectual reasoning, holding that if knowledge were properly imparted the will would be directed aright as a natural consequence. Instead of placing the Bible above dogma as Luther had done, they reversed the order, with the result that the church neglected the Bible in home and in school. Christian living and the practicing of Christian virtues were at a low ebb because pastors did not teach them.[67]

As previously noted, the Pietistic movement was not an attempt to break away from the Lutheran Church but rather to reform it from within. Of German Pietism, Eavey writes:

> It required the separation of the individual from the world and his avoidance of carnal pleasures. Pietism opposed dancing, attendance at the theater, ostentation in dress, joking, and the reading of literature appealing to the flesh. Pietists combined Luther's emphasis on the study of the Scriptures, prayer, and faith with the Calvinistic stress on puritanical conduct. However, they went further than either of these in insistence upon the experience of the new birth and the work of the Holy Spirit in the life of the Christian.[68]

Philip Spener himself best explains the essence of Pietism:

> We must let his Word penetrate our hearts. It is not enough to partake outwardly of the Eucharist, or to pray only with our lips, or to serve God outwardly in his temple. . . . The individual must serve God from deep within the temple of his very soul.[69]

THE IMPACT OF PIETISM ON THE SCHOOLS

A hallmark characteristic of Pietism was its service to the needs of the poor, especially the thousands of children who were orphaned by the Thirty Years' War. The older German Lutheran schools were available mostly to the upper classes and had become spiritually weak. Professor Spener was openly critical of them. He listed these concerns:

> (1) They provide for secular knowledge, which is of service only in this life, but they do nothing to cultivate the feelings which produce a living Christian faith and the fruits thereof. Teachers must have regard to the godly living of their students as well as to the acquisition of knowledge. (2) Most of the time is devoted to learning Latin, the language of the learned class, and very little time is left for Greek and Hebrew, the languages of the Scriptures. (3) Too little attention is given to the Holy Scriptures, and too much to memorizing dogmatic doctrines. (4) In the course of study the heathen ethics of Aristotle takes the place of practical Christian morals.[70]

FRANCKE

August Hermann Francke, a Pietist Christian school educator, was a major influence in bringing about the "Reformation of the Reformation" in Germany, particularly in its large northern Protestant state of Prussia, after the Thirty Years' War. Eby says of Francke, "He was the noblest example of the practical Christian educator of Germany."[71] The son of a lawyer, Francke had received a good education. In 1677, at age fourteen, Francke enrolled in the University of Erfurt in northern Germany, where Martin Luther had earned his master's degree in 1505. Francke later transferred to the University of Leipzig, where he earned a degree and served on the faculty for two years. It was there he became a Pietist under the influence of Philip Spener. With Spener's recommendation, Francke became a language and theology professor at the new, and more conservative, University of Halle, fifty miles southwest of Wittenberg. He also served as pastor of a nearby village church in Glaucha.[72] Eby says:

> Here, in this dual capacity as university professor and village pastor, Francke found a favorable setting for colossal achievements in philanthropy and education. Here he established an astonishing number of institutions and sent forth an influence which penetrated throughout Germany and had a very definite power in America and elsewhere.[73]

Francke's accomplishments are even more admirable in view of the village where he served, "a seedy slum on the outskirts of Halle"[74] as described by Melton, who adds:

Glaucha was particularly poor adorned by little beyond a few slaugh-terhouses and a remarkable number of alehouses. Beer and schnapps had been the chief products of the town since the fifteenth century. The year Francke arrived in Glaucha, 37 of the 200 houses in the town were taverns. On weekends Glaucha became a raucous center of plebeian entertainment, attracting day laborers, the unemployed, and prosti-tutes in search of amusement and clients.[75]

As pastor of the Glaucha village church, Francke was shocked at the poverty, the ignorance, and the general immorality of not only the adults but the children. He was so moved with compassion that he went without his evening meals and used the money to start a Christian school for poor children.[76] Using himself as an example of sacrifice, he persuaded a host of others to contribute to his tuition-free school. It was an immediate success, and he expanded his program to include a complete system of Christian schools in Halle, with his university students as teachers.[77] In Francke's schools the day began at 7:00 A.M. and concluded at 3:00 P.M. Melton describes the curriculum:

> Early morning was devoted to prayer, the singing of hymns, and the reading of a passage from the Scriptures. This was followed by cate-chism drills, two hours of reading instruction, an hour of writing, and an hour of arithmetic. The schoolmaster also led the pupils on daily walks, which provided physical exercise as well as an opportunity for lessons in natural history. On Sundays, the pupils accompanied the schoolmaster to worship service and Sunday school.[78]

The spiritual and academic reputation of Francke's schools gained momentum, and soon middle- and upper-class parents offered tuition for their children to attend. He then opened a secondary school in Halle called the Pädagogium for "the children of ranke and means,"[79] to prepare them to attend the University of Halle. His system of Christian schools expand-ed, and with it his need for carefully trained teachers. Therefore, in 1705, he founded northern Germany's first specialized teacher training institution called Seminarium Praeceptorium.[80] Francke's staff for his schools ulti-mately reached "over three hundred teachers, workers, and attendants."[81] More than twenty-two hundred pupils attended his Christian schools in Halle and Glaucha.[82] He also founded two orphanages, which stimulated the founding of orphanages throughout Germany.

Francke was an energetic leader with unusual entrepreneurial talents. In addition to fund-raising, he found other ways to generate income for his expanding programs. For example, he established a print shop and bookstore and sold Bibles, tracts, and sermons. He even employed a Christian physician, Friedrich Richter, to organize a pharmacy that sold pharmaceutical remedies to the community. Melton says, "The pharmacy proved so profitable that it was able to subsidize most of the subsequent expansion of Francke's schools."[83]

In 1698 Franke persuaded [the "Great Elector" of Prussia and Prussian King William I] to exempt all supplies purchased for his schools from sales taxes—possibly the first such exemption in history for Christian schools. It is interesting that Cotton Mather, president of America's first college (Harvard), was among the contributors to Francke's work in Halle and placed a number of Francke's books in the Harvard Library. Mather referred to Francke as "the incomparable Dr. Franckius"—using his latinized name.[84]

Francke personally supervised the training of his teachers and wrote pedagogical books that reflected his pietistic theology and educational philosophy, which were inseparable. He wrote to his schoolmasters:

> . . . we are not to be satisfied if the child exhibits an outer show of piety but at heart remains unchanged. . . . The purely external, no matter how fair its appearance, cannot stand before the omniscient eye of God without the power of Christ in one's heart.[85]

In his book *Brief and Simple Treatise on Christian Education,* Francke wrote: "All learning and knowledge is folly if it does not have as its foundation true and pure love toward God and Man."[86] It was supremely important to him that his students experience a spiritual change of heart. Eavey says, "Francke was not content with mere formal inculcation of Christian teachings; he appealed directly to experience, seeking to make spirituality a reality, a genuine personal experience of each pupil."[87] He told his teachers:

> One dram of living faith is more to be valued than one hundred weight of mere historic knowledge; and one drop of true love, than a whole sea of learning in all mysteries.[88]

Like Luther and Comenius, Francke had little regard for humanism and the Greek pagans. Eby says, "The charge has been made, and it was undoubtedly true, that classic Greek was neglected for the reading of the New Testament."[89] Like the other great reformers, Francke was committed to biblical authority, and he aggressively promoted Bible reading among the common people and among the students in his Christian schools. As Melton explains,

Pietists were unrestrained in their advocacy of Bible reading among the laity. During his brief pastoral tenure in Erfurt, for example, Francke distributed over 900 Bibles and New Testaments to his parishioners. In Glaucha he required every household to have a Bible, while his Halle schools provided every pupil with a copy. . . . Once pupils had mastered the catechism and the rudiments of reading, two periods a day were devoted to the reading of Scripture.[90]

The printing press was a vital tool for August Hermann Francke. In his work we see again the power of the printed page in the spread of the Gospel of Christ:

The establishment of a Pietist printing press in Halle was further testimony to the Pietist promotion of lay Bible reading. The press was established by Carl Hildebrand von Canstein, the leader of the Berlin Pietist community. . . . Canstein's press printed not only the textbooks for Francke's schools, but also inexpensive editions of the Bible and New Testament. Within a year of its establishment in 1712, the Canstein Bible House had printed 10,000 inexpensive copies of the New Testament. By 1727, it had become one of the world's leading distribution centers of religious literature. By then, more than 400,000 Bibles and New Testaments had been published. At the end of the century, the total had risen to 2.5 million.[91]

An example of Francke's educational wisdom and sound Christian philosophy is expressed in these words:

In order to educate children so that they preserve true and candid piety up to their old age, teachers as well as parents, yea, all around them, must be conscious of their Christian duty. But, indeed, that requires more than the intelligence of natural man. We need wisdom from above to seek always and everywhere the honor of the Almighty and the glory of His name. Such wisdom does not deviate but goes the way of righteousness shown to us by the Word of God; it tries to understand the great love that He has for the young . . . and it finally knows that man cannot well accomplish such a great work as education out of his own skill and virtue. Rather those endowed with Christian wisdom know that there is no power in him who plants, but the power is in God alone who must bestow His blessing.[92]

Near the end of his life in 1727, when acclaim began to multiply in recognition of his remarkable achievements, Francke humbly wrote:

The world ascribes these works which have gone through my hands to my activity. . . . The foolish world alone gives no honor to God but ascribes everything to the power of man. . . . I have been in all matters always passive, have sat quiet, and have not gone a step farther, than I had the finger of God before me. When I saw what the hand of God had in store, I went at it like a slave and realized it without care or trouble. Accordingly, what has not turned out a success for others with all their intelligence, craft and wisdom, has come about for me without effort.[93]

THE HISTORICAL IMPACT OF FRANCKE'S WORK

There is little doubt that the King of Prussia created a favorable climate for Francke's work. In 1713 Frederick William I became the king of the German state of Prussia, a kingdom that would ultimately extend from Estonia in the east to the Netherlands in the west. It was a Protestant stronghold with Berlin as its capital. Southern Germany remained largely Catholic. King Frederick William I was a strict Calvinist. "His life was simple and puritanical, being founded on the teaching of the Bible."[94] Prussia had become a haven for Protestants when Catholic leaders drove them from Catholic territories such as France and Austria.[95] King Frederick William I was an advocate of Christian school education and a strong supporter of August Hermann Francke. Eby says:

> Frederick William I, King of Prussia, visited The Halle Foundation and became its avowed patron. He later established the Prussian elementary school system on the principles of Francke.[96]

When the king died in 1740, he had established eighteen hundred state-run Christian schools in Prussia.[97]

Payday among Christian school educators often comes in the form of success by their students who go on to lead meaningful lives. Certainly this was true of Francke. His graduates were in demand as pastors, Christian schoolteachers, schoolmasters, orphanage supervisors, and missionaries. The King of Denmark, for example, was interested in evangelical missionary work in India, and "Francke was asked to make the selection of the missionaries from among his students."[98] One of Francke's students, Johann Julius Hecker, distinguished himself as a pastor-educator. Eby describes the impact of Hecker's work in Berlin:

> In 1739, Hecker became pastor of Trinity Church, Berlin, a position which presented an excellent opportunity to engage in educational reform under advantageous circumstances. The King of Prussia [Frederick the Great, son of Frederick William I] followed Hecker's efforts with closest attention, and supported his institutions with royal bounty. Hecker began his reforms by improving the instruction of poor children. In almost every street, well appointed and supervised schools were established.[99]

Figure 6. Frederick the Great served as King of Prussia from 1740 to 1786. In 1763 he commissioned Johann Julius Hecker, a Christian school educator and pastor of Trinity Church in Berlin, to write the general school regulations for his growing empire. His statewide plan was the genesis of the later Prussian public school model that intrigued American public school educators in the 19th century.

Hecker founded a teacher training institute for Christian schools in Berlin patterned after Francke's model in Halle. King Frederick the Great was so impressed with Hecker's teacher training program that he required that "all teachers to be employed in the schools located on his private domains must be educated in this institution."[100]

The zenith of Hecker's influence, however, was his appointment by Frederick the Great to write the kingdom's "General-Land-Schül-Reglement" or General Regulations for Elementary Schools and Teachers in Prussia of 1763."[101] It is amazing that Hecker was chosen to write the regulations because, unlike his father King Frederick I, Frederick the Great was only a nominal Christian believer,[102] if a believer at all, yet he selected a highly respected Christian school educator to formulate a statewide school plan. It is equally amazing that the king did not alter the Bible-centered character of the state school regulations clearly revealed in these words written in the preamble: ". . . we find it necessary and wholesome to have a good foundation laid in the schools by a national and Christian education of the young for the fear of God, and other useful ends."[103]

The strong Christian theme of the Prussian school plan and its close tie with the church community is obvious in the comprehensive course of study, summarized as follows:

Morning:
1st Hour —Singing of a hymn, a different hymn to be learned each month. This followed by a prayer, and this in turn by instruction

in the Catechism. Luther's "Smaller Catechism" for younger children; the larger for the older. Saturday lesson to be preparatory for Sunday, the Epistle for that day being read and written.

2nd Hour —A B C class; reading from Old and New Testament; spelling; finding passages in the Scriptures; and memorizing verses from the Bible and learning Biblical names.

3rd Hour —Reading, writing, spelling; writing in copybooks the rules of reading. School closes with prayer, and reading of psalm. On Saturday children exhorted to behave well on Sunday; to be quiet in church; and to treasure the word of God for their salvation.

Afternoon:

4th Hour —Pupils sing verses, read a psalm, and are taught Biblical history from Rochow's "Manual for the Instruction of Children in Country Schools."

5th Hour—Catechism, after method given in the "Berlin Reader." Pupils commit to memory, reading it with the teacher. Interpretations for the larger children. Children to learn a Bible verse weekly. During second half of hour, larger children to learn to read, middle class to spell; and lower class to learn their letters, as in second hour.

6th Hour—Upper class write and cipher; middle class spell; and lower class study their A B C's.[104]

The Christian school movement led by John Comenius, August Hermann Francke, and Johann Hecker was tied to Europe's Pietistic reform movement called "The Reformation of the Reformation." Regrettably, as Pietism and dependence upon God waned, there emerged a corresponding apathy toward Christian values and to Bible-centered Christian school education. Consequently, the focus of European education shifted to rationalism, a change that left Europe, especially Germany, vulnerable to the likes of Adolf Hitler and the devastation of two tragic wars.

3. Lessons Learned

In the midst of the brutal Counter-Reformation, under the direst of circumstances, we have learned that true Christian school education can flourish:

1. When educators who, like Comenius, Francke, and others, are themselves Bible-centered believers who regard their principal mission to release the power of the Gospel of Christ, as revealed in the Scriptures, into the lives of their students,

2. When there is sufficient political liberty for Christian school education to flourish as exemplified by Holland's Prince William of Orange, Prussia's King Frederick I, and his son Frederick the Great,

3. When the evangelical church community is solidly behind Christian school education,

4. When parents of students support in the home what is taught in the school,

5. When students themselves are convinced that their Christian school education is of supreme value in preparing them for their future service to Christ and the world of opportunity into which they are born.

In these historical studies of Christian school education thus far, beginning with the first-century Christians, continuing with the hidden schools of the persecuted church, the great Christian school leaders like John Huss, Martin Luther, Philip Melanchthon, Johann Bugenhagen, John Sturm, Martin Bucer, Ulrich Zwingli, John Calvin, the courageous Huguenots, the Dutch Calvinists, Comenius, and Francke, the above five principles have been evident in varying degrees usually in direct proportion to their success or failure. The primary lesson from all we have studied is that these fundamental principles do not change. They were as true in the first century as they are today.

We have learned that Christian school education, when allowed to develop, can indeed be a beneficial force for good in society. On the other hand, we have witnessed just how fragile Christian schools are during periods of spiritual and political decline.

We have also learned that Christian school education, like so many things that are of value to society, rises and falls on leadership. Huss, Luther, Calvin, Knox, Comenius, and Francke were all "God-saturated leaders" imbued with a clear vision of what God wanted them to do. Fortunately, they had the courage and the natural gifts to fulfill God's noble purpose for their lives.

Finally, as we have seen, medieval Catholicism's Counter-Reformation succeeded in stamping out the evangelical Christian schools of France and

Belgium. Grim and horrendous as it was, the Counter-Reformation was not successful in the Protestant strongholds of Holland, the Scandinavian countries, and northern Germany. Christian schools not only survived in these countries but flourished, especially in years following the Counter-Reformation. In order to provide a complete historical picture of the Christian schools of this era, we have exceeded the time frame of this volume by 133 years. Our next study will take us to England, where we will measure the impact of the Great Reformation on the church community and on Christian school education.

Endnotes - Chapter Twelve

[1] Henry M. Baird, *The Huguenots and the Revocation of the Edict of Nantes* (New York: Charles Scribner's Sons, 1895), p. 425.

[2] Samuel Smiles, *The Huguenots* (New York: Harper & Brothers, Publishers, 1868), Preface VI.

[3] W.H. Lewis, *The Splendid Century* (London: William Morrow & Co., 1953), p. 112.

[4] Robert L. Cooke, *Philosophy, Education and Certainty* (Grand Rapids: Zondervan, 1960), p. 115.

[5] T.J. Cook, *The History of Education in Europe* (London: Methuen & Co. Ltd., 1974), p. 5.

[6] Elmer Harrison Wilds, *The Foundations of Modern Education* (New York: Rinehart and Company, 1936), p. 299.

[7] James Von Horn Melton, *Absolutism and the Eighteenth-Century Origins of Compulsory Schooling in Prussia and Austria* (Cambridge: Cambridge University Press, 1988), p. 5. Melton cites the following: Grosperin, *Les petites écoles*, pp. 14-16; Mireille Laget, "Petites écoles en Languedoc au XVIIIe siècle," *Annales*, 26 (1971), p. 1417; Furet and Ozouf, *Reading and Writing*, pp. 58-69. Gustav Strakosch-Grassmann, *Geschichte des österreichischen Unterrichtswesens* (Vienna, 1905), p. 44; Helmuth Feigl, *Die niederösterreichische Grundherrschaft* (Vienna, 1964), p. 270; Hubel, "Das Schulwesen Niederösterreichs," pp. 27-38.

[8] Clarence H. Benson, *A Popular History of Christian Education* (Chicago: Moody Press, 1943), p. 97.

[9] Will Durant, *The Reformation* (New York: Simon and Schuster, 1957), p. 642.

[10] Ibid.

[11] O.T.A. Roche, *The Days of the Upright* (New York: Clarkson N. Potter, Inc. 1965), p. 135.

[12] Jean Claude, *A Short Account of the Complaints and Cruel Persecutions of the Protestants in the Kingdom of France* (London: W. Redmayne, 1707), p. 109.

[13] Kenneth Scott Latourette, *Christianity Through the Ages* (New York: Harper Chapel Books-Harper and Row Publishers, 1965), p. 182.

[14] J.L. Motley, *Rise of the Dutch Republic,* vol. 1, p. 101. Quoted by Durant, *The Reformation,* p. 634.

[15] James Harvey Robinson and Charles A. Beard, *Outlines of European History,* Part II (Boston: Ginn and Company, 1907), p. 28.

[16] Lars P. Qualben, *A History of the Christian Church* (New York: Thomas Nelson and Sons, 1933), p. 312.

[17] C. Leopold Clarke, *The Christian Church and the See of Rome* (London: Protestant Truth Society), pp. 182-183.

[18] Frederick Eby and Charles Flinn Arrowood, *The Development of Modern Education* (New York: Prentice-Hall, Inc., 1934), p. 293.

[19] C.B. Eavey, *History of Christian Education* (Chicago: Moody Press, 1964), p. 156.

[20] Frederick Eby, *The Development of Modern Education* (New York: Prentice-Hall, 1934), p. 121.

[21] Ellwood P. Cubberley, *Readings in the History of Education* (Boston: Houghton Mifflin Company, 1920), p. 277.

[22] Henry W. Dunshee, *History of the School of the Collegiate Reformed Dutch Church* (New York: Aldine Press, 1883), pp. 3-4. Cited by Eby and Arrowood, p. 291.

[23] Ibid., pp. 291-292.

[24] Ibid.

[25] William H. Kilpatrick, *The Dutch Schools of New Netherland and Colonial New York* (Washington, DC, 1912), p. 34. Cited by Cubberley, *Readings in the History of Education,* pp. 279-280.

[26] A quote from a letter from Count John of Nassau. Cited by John Lothrop Motley, *History of the United Netherlands,* vol. 3 (New York: Harper and Brothers, 1867), p. 119. Quoted by the noted Dutch historian J.L. Motley, *Rise of the Dutch Republic* and by Eby, *The Development of Modern Education* (second edition), p. 122.

[27] *Encyclopaedia Britannica,* vol. 13 (Chicago: William Benton, Publisher, 1961), p. 989.

[28] Eby, *The Development of Modern Education* (second edition) p. 121.

[29] John Lothrop Motley, *The United Netherlands,* vol. 4 (New York: Harper and Brothers, 1867), p. 432 and pp. 566-567. Quoted by Eby, *The Development of Modern Education* (second edition), pp. 29-30.

[30] C.M. Davies, *History of Holland and the Dutch People,* vol. 1, p. 487. Quoted by Douglas Campbell, *The Puritan in Holland, England, and America,* vol. 2 (New York: Harper and Brothers, 1893), p. 340. Cited by Eby, *The Development of Modern Education* (second edition), p. 29.

[31] Durant, *The Reformation,* p. 633.

[32] Thomas M. Lindsay, *A History of the Reformation,* vol. 2 (Edinburgh: T. and T. Clark, 1908), pp. 236-237.

[33] James E. Reed and Ronnie Prevost, *A History of Christian Education* (Nashville: Broadman & Holman, Publishers, 1993), p. 200.

[34] Ernst Christian Helmreich, *Religious Education in German Schools* (Cambridge, Massachusetts: Harvard University Press, 1959), p. 23.

[35] Kenneth O. Gangel, "August Hermann Francke," *A History of Religious Educators,* Elmer Towns, ed. (Grand Rapids: Baker Book House, 1975), p. 190. Gangel quotes C. Manschreck, *A History of Christianity,* vol. 2 (Englewood Cliffs, NJ: Prentice-Hall, 1964), p. 264.

[36] Eby, *The Development of Modern Education* (second edition), p. 324.

[37] Ibid., p. 325.

[38] Rudolf Rican, *The History of the Unity of the Brethren* (A Protestant Hussite Church in Bohemia and Moravia). Translated by Danie Crews (Winston-Salem, NC: The Moravian Church in America, 1992), p. 335. Note: Other historians refer to Comenius' birthplace as Nivnitz.

[39] Gabrial Compayre, *The History of Pedagogy* (Boston: D.C. Heath and Company, 1885), p. 122.

[40] Mathew Spinka, "Comenius," *The New International Dictionary of the Christian Church* (Grand Rapids: Zondervan, 1974), p. 242.

[41] Latourette, *Christianity Through the Ages,* p. 187.

[42] J. Taylor Hamilton and Kenneth G. Hamilton, *History of the Moravian Church* (Winston-Salem, NC: Interprovincial Board of Christian Education, Moravian Church of America, 1967), p. 13.

[43] Durant, *The Reformation*, p. 172.

[44] Eavey, p. 170.

[45] Spinka, p. 242.

[46] Ricon, p. 335.

[47] Eby, *The Development of Modern Education*, p. 179.

[48] Spinka, p. 242.

[49] Frederick Mayer, *A History of Educational Thought* (Columbus, Ohio: Charles E. Merrill Books, Inc., 1960), pp. 215 and 213.

[50] Ibid., p. 114.

[51] Eavey, p. 169.

[52] Eby, *The Development of Modern Education*, p. 200.

[53] Ibid. Note: The word *didactic* as used here "means a system of moral instruction."

[54] John Amos Comenius, *The Great Didactic,* quoted by Mayer, pp. 216-220.

[55] Eby, *The Development of Modern Education,* p. 184. Eby cites M.W. Keatinge, *The Great Didactic of John Amos Comenius* (London: Adam and Charles Black, 1896), p. 418.

[56] Elmer Harrison Wilds, *The Foundations of Modern Education* (New York: Rinehart and Company, Inc. 1936), pp. 342-343.

[57] Keatinge, pp. 383 and 395. Quoted by Eby, p. 193.

[58] S.S. Laurie, *John Amos Comenius* (Syracuse: C. W. Bardeen, 1892), p. 200. Quoted by Eby, p. 183.

[59] Keatinge, p. 432; Eby, p. 193.

[60] Ibid., p. 226; Eby, p. 183.

[61] Eavey, pp. 176-177.

[62] Keatinge, p. 166; Eby, p. 183.

[63] Eavey, pp. 171-174.

[64] Eby, *The Development of Modern Education* (second edition), p. 236.

[65] Melton, p. 24. Melton cites Gerald Strauss, *Luther's House of Learning* (Baltimore: The Johns Hopkins University Press, 1978), pp. 268-308.

[66] Robert Ulich, *A History of Religious Education* (New York: New York University Press, 1968), p. 183.

[67] Eavey, p. 178.

[68] Ibid., p. 179.

[69] Philip Jacob Spener, *pia Desideria,* Kurt Aland, ed. (Berlin, 1955), p. 151. Quoted by Melton, p. 28.

[70] Eby, *The Development of Modern Education,* p. 247.

[71] Ibid.

[72] Ibid., pp. 247-248.

[73] Ibid., p. 327.

[74] Melton, p. 34.

[75] Ibid. Melton noted: My description of Glaucha is based on Neuss, "Lohnarbeiter in Halle," pp. 116-117, 146-153.

76 Eby, *The Development of Modern Education* (second edition), p. 250.

77 Eavey, p. 184.

78 Melton, pp. 34-35. Melton cites: Francke, *Glauchisches Gedenck-Buchlein, order einfältiger Unterricht für die christliche Gemeinde zu Glaucha an Halle* (Leipzig and Halle, 1693), pp. 122-124, republished in A.H. Francke, *Schriften über Erziehung und Unterricht,* ed., Karl Richter (Berlin, 1871), pp. 218-255.

79 Melton, p. 35.

80 Ulich, p. 183.

81 Qualben, p. 365.

82 Ibid.

83 Melton, p. 36.

84 Ibid., p. 35 (see his footnote 37).

85 Ibid., p. 38. Melton quotes Francke in *Paedagogio zu Glaucha*, p. 94.

86 Gangel, p. 192.

87 Eavey, p. 183.

88 Francke, quoted by Henry Barnard, *German Teachers and Educators* (Hartford: Brown and Gross, 1878), p. 413. Cited by Eby p. 249.

89 Eby, *The Development of Modern Education* (second edition), p. 253.

90 Melton, pp. 39-40. Melton cites: Kurt Aland, "Bibel und Bibeltext bei August Hermann Francke and Johann Albrecht Bengel," in *Pietismus and Bibel* (Witten-Ruhr, 1970), p. 90, Francke, *Glauchisches Gedenck-Buchlein*, p. 137, and *Schriften*, p, 219. Francke, *Kurzer und einfältiger Unterricht, wie die Kinder zur wahren Gottseligkeit und christlicher Klugheit anzufüjtrm domf* (Halle, 1702), p. 22, as republished in Francke, *Pädagogische Schriften*, pp. 13-66, and Oschliess, *Arbeits-und Berufspädagogik*, pp. 30-31.

91 Ibid.

92 Francke, *Brief and Simple Instruction How to Lead Children Toward True Piety and Christian Wisdom* (Chapter 17), quoted by Ulich, p. 186.

93 Francke, quoted by D.G. Dramer, *Francke's Pädagogische Schriften* (Langensalza: H. Beyer & Söhne, 1885), cited by Eby, *Development of Modern Education* (second edition), p. 249.

94 *Encyclopaedia Britannica,* vol. 9 (Chicago: William Benton Publisher, 1961), p. 724.

95 Ibid., vol. 18 (Chicago: William Benton Publisher, 1961), p. 653.

96 Eby, *The Development of Modern Education* (second edition), p. 254.

97 Cubberley, *Readings in the History of Education*, p. 456.

98 Eby, *The Development of Modern Education*, p. 254.

99 Ibid.

100 Ibid., p. 256.

101 Frederick the Great (Preamble), *General Regulations for Elementary Schools and Teachers*, Aug. 12, 1763, quoted by Cubberley, *Readings in the History of Education*, p. 459.

102 *Encyclopaedia Britannica,* vol. 18 (Chicago: William Benton Publisher, 1961), p. 654.

103 Cubberley, *Readings in the History of Education*, p. 459.

104 Ibid., pp. 463-464.

Illustration Sources

Figure 1   *Louis XIV* - Giraudon/Art Resource, NY, Marble by Coysevox, Antoine (1640-1720) Dijon, France.

Figure 2   *Map* - Global Mapping International, Colorado Springs, CO.

Figure 3   *Charles V* - Erich Lessing/Art Resource, NY, Seiseneggor, Jacob (1505-1567).

Figure 4   *Philip II* - Foto Marburg/Art Resource, NY, Portrait by Honthorst, Gerrit van, Mauritshuis, The Hague, The Netherlands.

Figure 5   *William II of Orange* - Scala/Art Resource, NY, Portrait by Honthorst, Gerrit van, Mauritshuis, The Hague, The Netherlands.

Figure 6   *Frederick the Great* - Helen W. Pierson, *History of Germany* (New York: George Routledge & Sons, 1884), p. 183.

English Education During the Reigns of Henry VIII and His Children

To understand England during the Great Reformation period, one must understand King Henry VIII—or at least attempt to understand him. While Henry VIII, who came to power in 1509 at age eighteen,[1] did many things characteristic of a Protestant monarch, he was by no means an evangelical Protestant. Cubberley says, "Henry VIII was no Protestant, in the sense that Luther or Calvin or Zwingli or Knox was."[2] And it wasn't because Henry VIII disliked Martin Luther, nor that Henry had six wives, two of whom he

Figure 1. This symbol of English monarchy in York is a reminder of England's long history of a union between ecclesiastical and civil government.

had beheaded at the Tower of London.[3] King Henry VIII was Protestant only in the sense that he protested the thousand-year tradition of a Roman pope having civil and ecclesiastical authority over England. Thus began a curious reformation—a revolt, if you will, much different from what happened on the continent of Europe. In this chapter we will explore the English "Reformation" and the dramatic impact it had on English education. The three divisions of chapter 13 are:

1. *Four British Royals Who Changed the Course of English History*
2. *The Shifting Educational Pattern of English Schools*
3. *The Menacing Climate of Conformity*

As far back as the despotic and flamboyant King John, who briefly defied Pope Innocent III in the thirteenth century, English monarchs had made Roman popes uneasy.[4] England had always been a maverick subject of the Holy See—much less a Catholic nation at heart than France, Spain, and Italy. Thus it is not surprising, that the Reformation, albeit a hybrid form of the Reformation, found fertile soil in England.

1. Four British Royals Who Changed the Course of English History

The initial reformation in England was far more political and economic than theological and spiritual. It must be understood, however, that in Europe, and especially in England, politics and theology were closely allied. Political issues during this period were never thought of in terms of liberal versus conservative but rather in terms of Catholic versus Protestant. In our study of the fortunes of English education, we need to begin with at least a cursory overview of the Catholic and Protestant politics of the period. Such an overview requires a look at one of England's most treasured institutions—the monarchy.

HENRY VIII (1491–1547)

King Henry VIII began his reign, like his father, as a Catholic king serving England under the authority of the pope in Rome. In 1521 he had received the treasured "golden rose" from the Vatican and was called by Pope Leo X "a defender of the faith."[5] It is not surprising, therefore, that Henry VIII shook the world when in 1534, with Parliament's approval, he became the Supreme Head of the Church of England.[6] As such, he became the first king in modern history to head his nation's schools. The historical significance of these remarkable developments cannot be overestimated.

Henry was physically "a giant of a man," but he was by no means a "spiritual giant" in evangelical terms. Philosophically, he was a student of the Renaissance and "an enthusiastic humanist."[7] His initial motive for wrenching England away from what had been a thousand years of subservience to the Vatican[8] was the pope's refusal to grant him a divorce from his first wife, Catherine of Aragon. Catherine was the youngest daughter of the king and queen of Spain, Ferdinand and Isabella. Henry VIII was disap-

Figure 2. Henry VIII was England's maverick monarch who changed the course of history when he declared himself as the head of the Church of England. He is also remembered as having been the husband of six wives, two of whom he had beheaded at the Tower of London.

pointed with Catherine because she failed to produce a male heir to the throne. Over a period of eight years Catherine gave birth to six children; all but one were stillborn or died in infancy. The one survivor was Mary Tudor, who eventually became Queen of England and, for reasons that will become apparent, is remembered as "Bloody Mary."[9] From Henry's subsequent five marriages only two more children were born, Edward VI and Elizabeth I, both of whom would serve as British monarchs.[10]

It can be safely said that the Church of England established by Henry VIII and Parliament in 1534 was not a true Protestant Church. Cubberley agrees:

> The English National Church [The Church of England] merely took over most of the functions formerly exercised by the Roman Church. In general the same priests remained in charge of the parish churches, and the church doctrines and church practices were not greatly altered by the change in allegiance. The changing of the service from Latin to English was perhaps the most important change. The English Church, in spirit and service, has in consequence retained the greatest resemblance to

the Roman Catholic Church of any Protestant denomination. In particular, the Lutheran idea of personal responsibility for salvation, and hence the need of all being taught to read, made scarcely any impression in England.[11]

The Catholic nature of the newly formed Church of England explains England's long delay in forming schools for children of common people. John Miner says, "England was the last industrialized Western nation to . . . establish a system of national education."[12] This important issue will be studied more further on in this chapter.

England's "under the surface" Catholicism explains that nation's curious policy on heretics. With reference to Henry VIII, Durant writes:

> Since his theology was still Catholic in every respect except the papal power, he made it a principle to persecute impartially Protestant critics of Catholic dogma, and Catholic critics of his ecclesiastical supremacy. Indeed, the prosecution of heresy had continued, and would continue, all through his reign. In 1531, by order of Chancellor More, Thomas Bilney was burned for speaking against religious images, pilgrimages, and prayers for the dead. James Bainham was arrested for holding that Christ was only spiritually present in the Eucharist; he was tortured to draw from him the names of other heretics; he held fast, and was burned at Smithfield in April 1532.[13]

Henry VIII, or "Henry the Terrible" as some called him, the father of the other three monarchs considered here, "was the most absolute monarch that England had ever known."[14] The British House of Commons, with many members hand-picked by Henry himself, yielded to him unprecedented authority to rule England almost as he pleased.[15] Pollard says, "In Henry's reign the English spirit of independence burned low in its socket, and love of freedom grew cold."[16] This is surprising, given the fact that England in 1215, in response to its tyrant monarch, King John, fashioned the famous Magna Carta, with its long list of individual liberties for all English citizens.[17] "The people," said Durant of Henry VIII's reign, "escaped from an infallible pope into the arms of an absolute King . . . only a few men dared withstand him, and they were buried without their heads."[18]

EDWARD VI (1537–1553)

Henry VIII was succeeded as England's monarch by each of his three children but not in order of their birth. Edward, the youngest of the three, became King of England at age nine and reigned only six and a half years. His mother was Jane Seymour, the third of Henry's six wives. Edward VI, the young king and now the Supreme Head of the Church of England, showed a greater propensity toward true Protestantism than his promiscuous father. With the assistance of his adult advisors, called lord protectors, he persuaded Parliament to repeal what was called the "Anti-Lutheran Six Articles."[19] One of these articles had made it illegal in England not to believe in "transubstantiation," or the real body of Christ in the communion bread and the real blood of Christ in the communion cup. Failure to believe in the doctrine of transubstantiation under the reign of Henry VIII meant, "death by burning, without opportunity to abjure, confess and be absolved."[20] During Edward's reign, the Church of England's statement of faith or the Thirty-nine Articles of Anglican Faith, as it was called, was more in line with Lutheran Reformation theology.[21] Young King Edward, regarded as "an ardent Protestant,"[22] allowed the return of many evangelical believers who had escaped Henry's wrath. Durant says:

> English Protestants who had fled from England returned with the pollen of Luther, Zwingli, and Calvin on them; and foreign reformers, scenting the new freedom, brought their diverse gospels to the troubled isle.[23]

In the wake of England's new openness to evangelical Protestants, London witnessed the removal of crucifixes, Catholic paintings, and statues from former Catholic churches.

Figure 3. King Edward VI was the only son of Henry VIII. His six-and-one-half-year reign was characterized by a move toward true Protestantism. John Knox was one of his court chaplains. Edward died at age fifteen.

> Most of the stained glass in the churches was destroyed; most of the statues were crushed; crucifixes were replaced with the royal arms; whitewashed walls and stainless windows took the color out of the religion of England. There was a general scramble in each locality for [Catholic] church silver and gold; and in 1551 the government appropriated what remained.[24]

It would be a mistake to presume, however, that under young King Edward the Church of England had wholeheartedly embraced evangelicalism. On the contrary, as Durant says, the Church of England "retained much Catholic ritual and could be accepted by not too precise a Romanist."[25]

When King Edward VI died in 1553 at age fifteen, Britain's warming toward Protestantism cooled dramatically at the ascension to the throne of Edward's older half sister Mary, known to history as "Bloody Mary."

MARY TUDOR (1516–1558)

The youthful Edward VI had ruled England and Ireland a brief six-and-a-half years but the reign of Queen Mary Tudor was even shorter—a mere five years. Reared a Catholic by her mother, Catherine of Aragon, Queen Mary relentlessly pursued England's full return to papal authority. She persuaded Parliament to rescind most of Edward's Protestant laws. All Protestant preaching was prohibited. Protestants who had flooded England under Edward's reign now rushed back to the continent, and with good reason.[26] Included in the exodus of Protestants was John Knox of Scotland, who had served King Edward as one of his six court chaplains in London.[27] Mary's dislike of Protestants soon became evident. Latourette says:

Figure 4. Mary Tudor, an ardent Catholic, served a mere five years as Queen of England. During her brief reign she became known as "Bloody Mary" for her many public excecutions of Protestants. She died of "ague fever."

The reign of Mary witnessed a number of beheadings and burnings, so much so, indeed, that her critics remembered her as "Bloody Mary." . . . The spirit of the times regarded as normal the execution of the leaders. Moreover, to the Catholic, heresy [being a non-Catholic] was a major crime against God and society. The laws against heresy were revived and under them about three hundred went to the stake. About a third were clergymen and about a fifth women. Two-thirds were in the stronghold of Protestantism, London and the South-east. By Continental standards the number was small, but it was much greater . . . than the number of Catholics who suffered the death penalty in the long reign of Elizabeth. The most famous of the victims were Bishops Latimer, Ridley, and Cranmer, all of them burned at Oxford. The first two suffered together. Latimer is said to have encouraged his comrade at the stake with the words: "Be of good comfort, Master Ridley, we shall this day light such a candle by God's grace in England as, I trust, shall never be put out."[28]

Durant says, "Most of the martyrs were simple workingmen who had learned to read the Bible."[29]

Latimer's prophecy came true. The public reaction to Mary's rampage of public executions during the second half of her short reign soured England on Catholicism.[30] Historians generally agree that Mary Tudor does not deserve the dubious title "Bloody Mary"—that she was the victim of her Catholic advisors, "ecclesiastics who . . . sought revenge."[31]

On November 6, 1558, eleven days before she died of "ague fever" and other complications, Mary sent England's crown jewels to her younger Protestant half sister Elizabeth. Durant says, "It was a gracious act, in which love of the [Catholic] church yielded to her desire to give England an orderly succession." [32]

ELIZABETH I (1533–1603)

Elizabeth I was born to Anne Boleyn, Henry VIII's second wife, whom Henry had beheaded for alleged adultery when Elizabeth was three years old. Elizabeth was twenty-five when she received the crown jewels from Mary Tudor[33] and began her long reign of forty-five years. She remained single throughout her lifetime and, like her other royal siblings, left no heir to the English throne. Elizabeth I was a "Church of England Protestant" with a low level of tolerance for Puritans and Nonconformists, whose numbers were growing daily in most areas of her kingdom. Historian Latourette says of Elizabeth, "She knew much about Christianity but probably had little religious conviction."[34] Clayton agrees, "Elizabeth is rather a daughter of the Renaissance than of the Protestant Reformation."[35] Much of her disdain for Catholicism stemmed from the fact that the Catholic Church had declared her illegitimate and therefore ineligible to be queen.

In 1570, Pope Pius V declared her a heretic, deposed her from her throne, and issued a Bull of Excommunication that absolved her subjects, the people of England, Wales, and Ireland, of their allegiance to her. The papal bull further offered a "reward to anyone who should compass her destruction."[36] As a result, throughout her reign, there were numerous attempts on the queen's life. Cardinal William Allen denounced Elizabeth I as a "heretical usurper."[37] "Thus," as one historian writes, "between 1581 and 1587, a long string of plots against her life found their inspiration in [the Catholic] religion and their hope in Mary Stuart,"[38] who, as a descendant of Henry VIII, was next in line to the British throne.

As mentioned in chapter 9, Mary Stuart or "Mary Queen of Scots" was the Catholic queen of Scotland who was a constant "thorn in the flesh" to

John Knox and Scotland's reformation movement. She was suspected of being an accomplice to the murder of her husband, Lord Darnley, who, as he slept, was sent sailing through the roof of a house in Edinburgh by an enormous blast of gunpowder that had been placed in the floor under his bed. Shortly thereafter, a coalition of Scottish nobles forced Mary Stuart to abdicate her throne.[39]

On the death of Queen Elizabeth in 1605, James became king not only of Scotland, where he was King James VI, but also of England, Wales, and Ireland, where he was King James I. His name became known around the world because he was the King James of the Authorized Version of the Bible, commonly known as the King James Version, first published in 1611.[40] This is important to Christian school educators

Figure 5. Queen Elizabeth I was a "Church of England Protestant" and ruled England for forty-five years. She did much to strengthen England's economy and improve education for the upper classes.

because the King James Version of the Bible was the centerpiece of early American education. How that came about will be explained in more detail in the next chapter.

Elizabeth I ruled during one of the most prosperous periods in English history, a period that had a significant impact on British education. Of Queen Elizabeth's rule, Clarke says:

> England prospered and became "Great" as it espoused and extended the Reformation movement, and correspondingly broke the vaulting ambitions of the Papacy and destroyed its paralysing superstitions. Her success in these movements is attributable under God to the masterly handling of complex difficulties, at home and abroad, and the farseeing diplomacy of the "Virgin" Queen, who outwitted for fifty years the combined statecraft of the courts of Europe, and laid the foundation of British prestige on land and sea—in commerce, art, and war—on a firm basis.[41]

Elizabeth re-established many of the Protestant measures of her half brother Edward VI. In 1559, early in her reign, she persuaded Parliament to reinstate the Act of Supremacy, which had been passed in 1534, and she added the Act of Uniformity, making the Church of England the only legal church. While these acts severed England from the oversight of the pope, they forced conformity of the English population to Anglicanism, a "cousin religion" to Catholicism. As never before, the Anglican Church became the official Church of England. Eby and Arrowood describe the impact of these Acts as follows:

> Elizabeth's church policy rested upon the Act of Supremacy and the Act of Uniformity. The first statute conferred upon the civil government full authority over the church; the second required of all subjects outward conformity to the faith and worship of the Established Church. The ecclesiastical commission and the successive primates, who were the instruments of the government in enforcing uniformity, were empowered to deprive nonconforming clergymen of their benefices. Schoolmasters were required to profess their faith in the doctrinal standards and to attend the services of the Established Church. Catholics and Protestant dissenters alike were forced into an outward show of conformity or were punished for their noncompliance. The vigorous measures taken by the government and the intense national spirit aroused during Elizabeth's reign completed England's transition from Catholicism to Anglicanism.[42]

This climate of conformity or "uniformity," as established by Elizabeth, ultimately led to the exodus of Pilgrims, Puritans, and Huguenots to America. With the required oath of allegiance to Anglicanism, the new conformity had a stifling effect on English education. Cubberley explains:

> The English Church merely succeeded the Roman Church in the control of education, and now licensed the teachers, took their oath of allegiance, supervised prayers, and the instruction, and became very strict as to conformity to the new faith, while the schools, aside from the private tuition and endowed schools, continued to be maintained chiefly from religious sources, charitable funds, and tuition fees. Private tuition schools in time flourished, and the tutor in the home became the rule with families of means. The poorer people largely did without schooling, as they had done for centuries before. As a consequence, the educational results of the change in the headship of the Church relate almost entirely to grammar schools and to the universities, and not to elementary education. The development of anything approaching a system of elementary schools for England was consequently left for the educational awakening of the latter half of the nineteenth century.[43]

This leads us to our next chapter division, which compares English education under Catholicism and under Anglicanism.

2. The Shifting Educational Pattern of English Schools

We begin with an overview of education in Catholic England before Henry VIII, whose curious reformation in 1534, with the help of a majority made up of hand-picked Parliament members, overruled papal authority and established Henry as "Supreme Head" of the newly constituted Church of England and of England's schools. For the most part, Catholic education in England, prior to King Henry's "great usurpation," was more advanced than in any other country in the Western world for two reasons:

(1) The English had felt an ongoing animosity toward the French that stemmed from the Hundred Year's War that began in 1337. They did not want their children to be "rude and crude," as they considered the French. Historian Alexander says:

> . . . the war caused bitter anti-French feelings to develop in England just as a violent hatred of the English took hold among the French. But as an intense dislike of French manners and customs became characteristic of the English people, a more rapid spread of education and literacy occurred.[44]

(2) In addition, in the early years of the sixteenth century, the English upper classes became fascinated with humanism and classical education, which the Catholic Church had not only endorsed but embraced since 1263.[45] Freeman Butts writes:

> The golden age of English humanism dawned with a remarkable succession of scholars preaching the glories of classical learning as they had discovered it in Italy. There had been a long background of scholarly contact between England and Italy, but the upsurge of interest was stimulated by Erasmus, John Colet, Thomas Elyot, Thomas More, and Juan Luis Vives, to name only the most familiar, during the first three decades of the sixteenth century. This was the period when the humanists were campaigning vigorously for the new learning.[46]

Henry VIII and his three descendant monarchs, Edward, Mary, and Elizabeth, were all educated in England's classical learning—or the "new learning" as it was called. When Henry VIII assumed his new role as the head of England's Church, he ignited an educational revolution. Since all education under Catholicism had been controlled by the church, Henry VIII soon found himself the first king in history to be the official head of schools, universities, and all former Catholic Church properties. In England, Catholic Church properties equaled twenty percent of the kingdom.[47]

Regretfully, in his "transfer of ownership" of the vast Catholic properties to the Crown, Henry diverted much of the income to various causes other than education.

Catholic historian Pierre Marique refers to the king's takeover of Catholic property as "plundering" and offers the following assessment of Henry's new role as England's chief educator:

> In England . . . between the years 1536 and 1546, there were suppressed "600 monasteries, 90 colleges [high schools], 2,300 free chapels, and 100 hospitals." Henry VIII thereby secured an annual income of 150,000 pounds. About one-half of the plunder thus secured, Henry spent upon coast defenses and a new navy, and much of the remainder he distributed among his favorites and supporters. Very little of this money was spent for education, higher or secondary, to atone for the wholesale destruction of schools and colleges he had wrought . . . Of the hundreds of schools which had come down from the Middle Ages very few remained open. Contemporary writers bitterly complain of the deterioration in learning and education. Not until the end of the seventeenth century had the secondary schools recovered from the blow they had received in the early sixteenth, and as late as 1865, there was not in England any provision for elementary education comparable to what it had been before the reign of Henry VIII. . . . With this ruthless suppression of colleges and monasteries went the destruction of their libraries. The costliest manuscripts and books were sold to grocers and soap-sellers for a few pence. One merchant bought the contents of two noble libraries for forty shillings.[48]

There is no question that Henry VIII and many of his greedy friends mishandled the royal acquisition of English properties formerly held by the Catholic Church of Rome, and it is true that the level of learning deteriorated after the great "takeover."[49] It must be remembered, however, that Catholic education in England prior to the Reformation was the same as it was in other Western countries—ecclesiastical education whose sole purpose was to advance the cause of the Catholic Church. In his classic work *The Schools of Medieval England*, A.F. Leach, Britain's foremost education historian, makes the following insightful observation about England's Catholic schools:

> In spite, however, of the ample and continually growing supply of schools, the results were disappointing. So long as the monasteries furnished a safe and easy refuge from the struggle for existence, and monasticism enforced celibacy on churchmen, who largely depended

on the patronage of the monasteries for their chances of promotion, education made little impression on society at large. It was in vain for clever boys to be educated and to be promoted to the chief offices in church and state, when they were doomed to die without issue; or worse, produce the "scholars" who filled the papal purse by obtaining the innumerable dispensations from the bar sinister. . . . The advancement of science and learning comes from a cultured middle class. No such class could be formed when the cultured individual established no family to be a centre of culture, and left no sons behind him to inherit his ability and widen the circle of culture, by founding more educated families to hand on the lamp of life. . . . While monasticism prevailed, that source of national energy was cut off. . . . as long as the clergy was sterilized, and yet monopolized a large and ever-increasing proportion of the territory and wealth of the world, progress was checked.[50]

EDUCATION UNDER THE CHURCH OF ENGLAND

Like other areas of English life, the educational patterns under the Church of England were, in most respects, similar or identical to those under their Catholic predecessors. The following chart summarizes the similarities and differences:

Catholic Schools and Anglican Schools Compared		
	Catholic	Anglican
Latin Grammar schools regarded as feeder schools for Oxford and Cambridge Universities.[51]	Yes	Yes
The schools offered elementary education to limited categories of students.[52]	Yes	Yes—in the Elizabethan Period
The schools provided limited education for girls.[53]	Yes	Yes—in the Elizabethan Period
All school personnel were required to sign an oath of allegiance to the church leader.[54]	Yes—an oath of allegiance to the pope	Yes—an oath of allegiance to the English monarch and to the Articles of the Anglican Faith

Required a teaching license from the church for schoolmasters, ushers (assistant schoolmasters), and instructors.[55]	**Yes**	**Yes**
Education was offered in strict conformity to the teachings and practices of the ruling church. All other forms of education were outlawed until the Act of Toleration in 1689.[56]	**Yes**	**Yes**
The focus of education was to provide literacy and learning for all levels of society.[57]	**No**—Upper classes only	**No**—Upper classes only
The wide distribution of the Bible ultimately led to an increase in literacy among the laity.[58]	No	Yes—Primarily during the Elizabethan period

ENGLAND'S "PUBLIC" SCHOOLS

England's public schools today are decidedly different from America's public schools. Americans define public education as an open enrollment system of schools paid for with tax dollars and operating under the auspices of local, state, and federal government agencies. By American standards, England's public schools are private schools.

The English definition of a public school has shifted to some degree in recent years,[59] but during the post-Reformation era it was as follows:

> By and large a "public school" was one which had been chartered or authorized by a public authority. It was constituted as a corporate body with a board of trustees or managers who held the property in trust and to which endowments could be given. The corporate body employed the teachers and gave general supervision in school affairs, using the income for the benefit of the school and not as income or profit for themselves. Such a public school was also theoretically open to all who could meet its standards and pay its fees, although some became known as socially exclusive and others as catering particularly to the "free" students who came on scholarships.[60]

To the American mind, such a school would be a private, independent, lay-board operated school—but not so in England. Surprisingly, England's two oldest schools do not meet the English definition of a "public school." These are The King's School Canterbury, founded in 598, and King's School Rochester, founded in 604.[61] These "schools of privilege" had their ancient beginnings as Catholic cathedral schools under England's first archbishop, Augustine. It should be noted that the Augustine of England in 598, was in no way related to the well-known St. Augustine of Hippo (A.D. 345–430) of North Africa. These venerable schools and several others like them were later refounded by King Henry VIII in 1534 as Anglican schools.[62] They remain Anglican schools today.[63]

The independent public schools in England were more broadbased and independent than the schools owned by the church but were required by law to remain compatible with Anglican theology and loyal to the reigning monarch. Eby offers the following description of England's public schools between 1491 and 1603:

> These institutions were the English equivalent of the schools of the Italian nobles and the Knightly Academies of Germany. Their purpose was to train boys of the higher class to fill the offices of church and state. Boys of the nobility were sent to them as a matter of course; some of the lower class were selected because of special intellectual ability and given an opportunity through the patronage of some person of commanding influence. These schools took the boys of six to eight and prepared them to speak, read, and write Latin so that they were ready to enter one of the colleges of Oxford or Cambridge. These schools were, therefore, the chief preparatory schools of England.[64]

England's foremost public schools today are Winchester, Eton, Westminster, St. Paul's, Merchant Taylors', Shrewsbury, Charterhouse, Rugby, and Harrow—nine that are often referred to as the "Great Public Schools." Three of the nine—Winchester, Eton, and St. Paul's—existed before the Reformation.[65] The following were the student rules at Westminster school during our period of study:

> The boys, on rising in the morning, were to make their beds, say their prayers, and wash themselves before proceeding to church. They were not to carry in their hands bows, sticks or stones, and were not to run, jump, chatter or play any trick on a townsman . . . on the way. In church they were to endeavour to fix their eyes on the altar and to copy the good customs of their elders, and they were neither to laugh nor to giggle if anyone should happen to read or sing indifferently. . . . On holidays the boys were to keep to a definite place assigned beforehand for playing in moderation . . . but should any boy be found with dice in his possession, he must taste a stroke of the rod for each pip of the dice.[66]

The Church of England, like its Catholic predecessors, focused its educational efforts on the society's upper echelons and had little concern for literacy of working class children. The Anglicans were not stirred by the

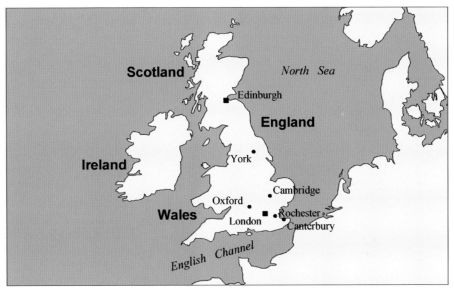

Figure 6. Henry VIII Map.

principles of the "great commission" (Matthew 28:18)—the idea that the message of Christ is for everyone and that the ability to read the Bible should be common among all citizens. According to Freeman Butts,

> . . . while we may say that organized education was becoming increasingly available to the upper 50 percent of the population in England during the early modern period, it is clear that it does not include the lower half of the population comprising the working classes. . . . Probably half of all boys and a vast majority of girls did not attend a formal school at any time during their lives.[67]

Unfortunately, this lamentable neglect of education for the children of the working classes would characterize English education well into the nineteenth century. England's pattern of ignoring the literacy needs of the common people was vastly different from that of the evangelical reformers, Luther and Calvin in Europe, and the English Pilgrims and Puritans who came to America in the early 1600s.

It should be noted, however, that among the upper classes in England the quality of learning improved dramatically, particularly during the latter years of the Elizabethan period. In fact, the upper half of England's population reached "the highest rate of literacy . . . and the greatest proportion of young men attending university-level education in any society in history up to that point."[68]

OTHER FORMS OF ENGLISH EDUCATION

In addition to the elite, heavily endowed boarding schools, England had other forms of education for the children of its middle and upper-class citizens. Some of these were:

1. **Private tutors:** Parents who could afford it taught their children at home with the aid of a private tutor. The tutors reflected the growing prosperity of the English economy.

2. **Petty schools:** The schools that undoubtedly contributed most to the elementary education of England's middle classes were the village petty schools. Butts provides the following description:

Figure 7. Since many common people could not read or write, they hired letter writers like this one, who had stalls along the street.

In this period English elementary schools, commonly called petty schools, spread widely through the rural sections of England, in the villages, as well as in the towns and cities. . . . Typically, the petty school took children (often girls as well as boys) from about the ages of four years to eight years and gave them two or three years of basic instruction in English literacy. They were vernacular [non-Latin] schools concentrating on reading, spelling, and writing of the alphabet and single sentences in English. The instruments were a hornbook, containing the alphabet, syllables, and a prayer, the catechism, a religious primer, and selections from the Bible. . . . The evidence for their availability stems from the conclusion that by 1640 half of the adult males in favored towns and cities and a third in villages were literate.[69]

Many of America's early colonial schools were patterned after these English petty schools. The rapid proliferation of the petty schools in England was the vision not of the monarchy but rather of the entrepreneurial middle classes, who saw the need for basic education. A.F. Leach writes:

. . . it was the middle classes, whether country or town, the younger sons of the nobility, or farmers, the lesser land-holders, the prosperous tradesmen, who created a demand for education, and furnished the occupants of Grammar Schools.[70]

The curriculum in these English elementary schools focused on the fundamentals of reading, writing, and the Anglican catechism. A child's first textbook was the hornbook developed in Europe in the fifteenth century. It was a simple flat board with a handle. Tacked on the board was a sheet of paper covered over with a semi-transparent material called "horn." On the paper was the alphabet in upper and lower case, a list of phonemic letter combinations, a prayer of benediction, and The Lord's Prayer. The small hornbook was usually hung around a child's neck or fastened on a belt at the waist.[71] The other textbooks included an ABC book and a reading text called a "primer."

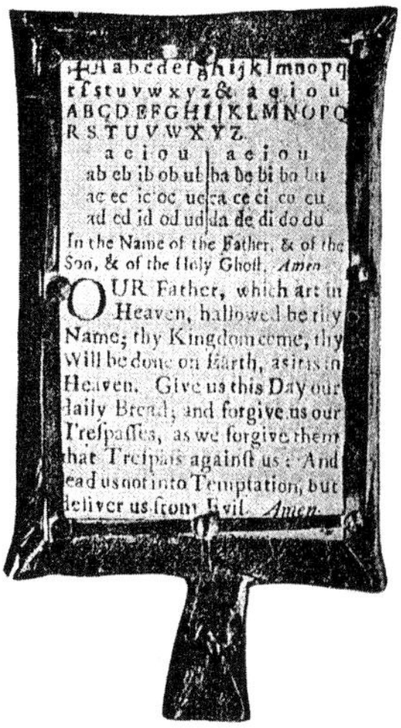

In the English tradition of not wanting to be "rude and crude" as they viewed their French neighbors across the English Channel, the private tutors and elementary instructors in the petty schools made adherence to good manners and morals the centerpiece of their curriculum. The spirit of these early schools was captured by Charles Hoole, who said, "The sweet and orderly behavior of children addeth more credit to a schoole than due and constant teaching. . . . Good manners are indeed a main part of good education."[72] A poem used by these early English schoolmasters and instructors reflects the strong emphasis on manners:

Figure 8. This seventeenth-century English Hornbook was a child's first textbook in English schools. This same "textbook" was used widely among America's colonial schools.

> First, I command thee God to serve,
> Then to thy Parent duty yield;
> Unto all men be courteous,
> And mannerly in Town and Field.[73]

Education beyond the private tutor or the petty school was almost nonexistent for girls.[74] Boys, after "graduating" from elementary tutor instruction or petty school, had three options for what one might broadly define as secondary education: public or private grammar school, private English school, or apprenticeship in the upper or lower trades.[75]

PUBLIC OR PRIVATE LATIN GRAMMAR SCHOOL

We have already described the corporate nature of England's elite public Latin grammar schools. They were, in effect, independent, nonprofit, lay

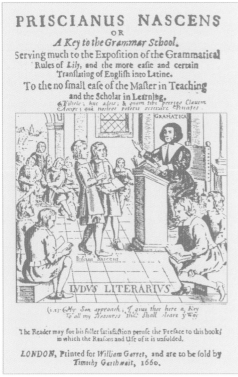

PRISCIANUS NASCENS
OR
A Key to the Grammar School.
Serving much to the Expofition of the Grammatical
Rules of *Lily,* and the more eafie and certain
Tranflating of Englifh into Latine.
To the no fmall eafe of the Mafter in Teaching
and the Scholar in Learning.

Figure 9. The title page of a seventeenth-century Latin grammar school textbook using William Lily's rules. Lily was an Oxford professor who became the schoolmaster at St. Paul's School in London.

corporations whose existence, curriculum, and personnel were approved by the monarchy through the Church of England. A private Latin grammar school, on the other hand, was a far less formidable institution. It consisted of an entrepreneurial independent teacher whose salary was derived from student tuition. These unendowed, one-teacher, private grammar schools were popular throughout England, particularly among the growing middle class. Approximately one-sixth of English boys, ages nine to sixteen, attended either a public or private Latin grammar school.[76] As the name implies, the academic emphasis of these schools was Latin grammar and the classic literature of Greece and Rome. Eby and Arrowood say, "the leading . . . schools [of England] in the 16th century had two characteristics: they were classical schools and they were schools for the ruling class."[77] English educators were not above weeding out slow learners. A.F. Leach writes:

> If any boy turned out remarkably slow and stupid or naturally unfit for learning, he, after long trial, was to be expelled "that he may not like a drone consume the bees' honey," and the conscience of the masters was solemnly charged to use their best diligence to get all the boys on, and not to suffer any of the drones to linger uselessly among the rest.[78]

A popular text for both the public and private grammar schools was Lily's Grammar, written by William Lily, an Oxford professor who became the schoolmaster at St. Paul's school in London. Lily's Grammar "was for centuries the grammar most widely used in England and in North America."[79]

PRIVATE ENGLISH SCHOOLS

There were economic forces at work in England that preempted the traditional Latin education of the upper classes. England's growing economy brought into focus the need for secondary and post-secondary education of a more practical nature. Freeman Butts says:

> . . . it now seems evident that England developed in this period a remarkable network of private English schools that were directly oriented to teaching practical subjects, a formal system of apprenticeship operating under public authorities and involving some emphasis upon literacy education as well as technical skill . . . in organized institutions in the city of London, a development sometimes referred to as England's "Third University.". . .

> One of the most common types of school had to do with teaching the subjects most pertinent to rapidly expanding commerce and trade. These included arithmetic, Italian double-entry bookkeeping, accounts, letter writing, and useful knowledge about currency, exchange, weights and measures, credit, and the like. Such subjects had long been taught in the municipal schools of Italy, Holland, Flanders, and northern Germany. England did not follow their example by setting up municipal schools, but it was widely recognized that Dutch prowess in international commerce was related to their mercantile schools. So private schools appeared in substantial numbers in London and other commercial centers. Merchants, aspiring merchants, and upward-bound craftsmen found such knowledge very practical indeed.[80]

It was professional and business leaders who defined these new private English schools—which taught in the English language and prepared students for a wide range of upper and middle-class livelihoods. It was a revolt, of sorts, against Latin learning and a move toward practical education. It was also a revolt against the Latin language so treasured by England's Latin grammar schools. Richard Mulcaster, "the most astute educational mind of his day" and advocate for the use of English in education, said:

> I love Rome, but London better. I favor Italie, but England more. I honor the Latin, but I worship the English. . . . I do not think that anie language, be it whatsoever, is better able to utter all arguments either with more pith, or great explainnese, than our English tongue is.[81]

In 1563 the British Parliament passed the "Statute of Apprentices" for all trades and industries. S.J. Curtis describes this form of education, which laid the foundation for England's powerful industrial revolution that would be so important. Curtis writes:

The enrolling of an apprentice was a solemn ceremony. The would-be apprentice promised to serve his master faithfully and to keep secret the craft mysteries entrusted to him. He bound himself to good behaviour and to remain single during the period of his apprenticeship. The master swore that he would receive the youth into his own house, feed and clothe him, and teach him the craft. The usual age for apprenticeship was twelve.[82]

Today's child labor laws would not allow this practice, but in Elizabethan England the apprenticeship system was a popular option for many high-school-age young men.

At the college level, only 2.5 percent of boys went on to Oxford or Cambridge.[83] Many others went on to what became known as the "Third University of England," which was simply the city of London with its many options for training professionals and tradesmen. One of the more interesting educational options was the Inns of Court, a series of four "splendid halls" in London devoted to training men for service in the royal court. In addition to being a law school, the Inns of Court were prestigious schools for a general education:

> . . . there were in the 15th and 16th centuries many students of the inns who had no legal ambitions but joined them for the purpose of general education (which was by no means neglected there). Since the universities were still strongly ecclesiastical, the inns were much frequented by the sons of wealthy families who had no intention of becoming lawyers.[84]

The Inns of Court in London were forerunners of the more broad-based post-secondary liberal arts education so characteristic of colleges and universities today.

OXFORD AND CAMBRIDGE

In 1600 William Camden wrote, "Suffice it to say of Oxford what Pomponius Mela says of Athens, 'It is too well known to be pointed out.'"[85] Oxford and Cambridge had their beginning in the Catholic Middle Ages. When Henry VIII, in 1534, confiscated all English assets held by the Roman Church, two of the prize acquisitions were the vast university complexes at Oxford and Cambridge. Both universities were steeped in Catholicism and medieval classical humanism. The transition to the semi-Protestant theology of the new Anglican Church of England was unsettling to say the least. The dramatic "transfer of ownership" meant:

. . . that the vice-chancellors were to be responsible to chancellors who were lay statesmen (rather than clerical) and that public boards of visitors would be inspecting the loyalty of teachers to the crown and to the Church of England. Academically, it meant that the humanistic and Anglican slant to the curriculum would be speeded in the effort to oust or play down the Aristotelian and the medieval curriculum.[86]

Figure 10. The central library at Cambridge University today.

Professors at both universities found themselves in the center of constant theological turmoil.

Some colleges [at Oxford and Cambridge] became Anglican, and others remained Catholic. When Catholics were excluded by Queen Elizabeth in 1575, the contests were then fought between Anglican Protestants and Puritan Protestants. The Puritans went mainly to Cambridge, where endowments had been made favorable to them, especially at St. John's College, Emmanuel College, and Signey Sussex College. These colleges became the avowed centers of a militant Puritanism, eventually training many of the people who went to America in the seventeenth century.[87]

In addition to the theological changes at Oxford and Cambridge, there was a growing pressure in the latter Elizabethan period to introduce more practical courses of study, which became necessary for schools to remain competitive with London—"The Third University." Mark Curtis says, "From having been training grounds for the clergy, they [Oxford and Cambridge] became training schools for the lay professions and public bureaucracies."[88] As the Western world grew more complex, this shift in higher education from training clergymen to training lay professionals was repeated many times, especially in the New World.

3. The Menacing Climate of Conformity

As the Crown became increasingly intolerant of Catholicism on the one hand and of evangelical Protestants on the other, forced conformity became the order of the day. The forty-five-year reign of Elizabeth I was not as grim as those of her father Henry VIII, "The Nero of England,"[89] and her half sister "Bloody Mary." Still, it was grim enough. One hundred eighty-nine Catholics were put to death during Elizabeth's reign, forty more died in prison, and many more were driven from England.

Among the Catholics executed under Elizabeth was Mary Queen of Scots.

After her forced abdication of her Scottish throne to her son James, Mary fled to England only to be imprisoned for eighteen years by Queen Elizabeth. When it was learned that Mary had collaborated with Catholic authorities in a plot to assassinate the English queen to seize her throne, Queen Elizabeth had her beheaded at Fotheringay Castle.[90] Most Catholics who died during Elizabeth's reign were regarded by the Crown as a threat to "state security" or to the Queen's life.[91] It would seem that Anglicanism had become as bloody as Catholicism.

Near the end of her long reign, Elizabeth intensified her demand for conformity to the national religion.

Figure 11. Mary Queen of Scots listens as her death-warrant from Queen Elizabeth is read.

Schoolmasters and ministers who failed to comply with the uniformity laws were imprisoned. Schools that employed nonconforming schoolmasters were fined. Eby and Arrowood write:

> **Acting under directions from the Privy Council, Archbishop Grindal, Archbishop Whitgift, and various bishops during the last part of Elizabeth's reign exercised close supervision over schoolmasters in all matters concerning their conformity to the national religion and their loyalty to the government. Conditions prescribed for licenses to teach were in accordance with the laws of the realm.[92]**

Elizabeth's repressive measures became the forerunner of even more repression under kings James I, Charles I, Charles II, and James II.[93] This dilemma sprang from the fundamental error created by Henry VIII and his marital problems in 1534. Regrettably, Henry VIII, Elizabeth I, and their royal successors down to this day have misinterpreted the intent of the Great Reformation. What should have been a theological shift from an infallible church to the infallible book (the Bible), they redefined to mean a shift from an infallible church to an infallible king.

In the latter years of Elizabeth's reign, the true Protestant reformers began to make their presence felt. Their numbers were substantially augmented by Calvinists pouring across the English Channel to escape France's relentless attempt to purge itself of Protestants. These and other true Protestants were known by names such as Puritans, Separatists, Calvinists, Brownists (Pilgrims), Presbyterians, Moravians, Mennonites, Quakers, Baptists, Anabaptists, and Lutherans. With a few variations, they saw in the Anglican Church many of the same theological errors they saw in the Catholic Church. Some, like the Puritans, wanted to purify the Church of England. Others rightly assumed that theological reform of the church was not likely. It became increasingly clear that Elizabeth's Uniformity Laws were making life in England more and more intolerable, and not the least of their concerns was the education of their children. The Calvinists, by far the majority of the true Protestant community, were committed to Christian school education. Puritan John Winthrop, a graduate of Trinity College at Cambridge, said, in describing English education:

> **The fountaines of Learning and Religion are soe corrupted as . . . most children . . . are perverted, corrupted, and utterlie overthroune by the multitude of evill examples.**[94]

These problems and others will be the focus of the final chapter of this volume. We'll explore the remarkable background of the Pilgrims and Puritans who settled the American colonies, including their strong commitment to Christian school education.

Figure 12.
The Tower of London
in the sixteenth century.

Endnotes - Chapter Thirteen

[1] Kenneth Scott Latourette, *A History of Christianity*, vol. 1 (New York: Harper & Row, Publishers, 1953), p. 799.

[2] Ellwood P. Cubberley, *The History of Education* (Boston, Massachusetts: Houghton Mifflin, 1920), p. 319.

[3] Will Durant, *The Reformation* (New York: Simon and Schuster, 1957), p. 576.

[4] Frederick Eby and Charles Flinn Arrowood, *The Development of Modern Education* (New York: Prentice-Hall, Inc., 1934), p. 139.

[5] Joseph Clayton, *The Protestant Reformation in Great Britain* (Lonson: The Bruce Publishing Company Milwaukee, 1934), p. 39.

[6] Eby and Arrowood, p. 139.

[7] Ibid.

[8] R. Freeman Butts, *The Education of the West* (New York: McGraw-Hill Book Company, 1947), p. 258.

[9] *Encyclopaedia Britannica*, vol. 5 (Chicago: William Benton, Publisher, 1961), p. 39.

[10] Ibid.

[11] Cubberley, *The History of Education*, p. 320.

[12] John N. Miner, *The Grammar Schools of Medieval England: A.F. Leach in Historical Perspective* (Montreal & Kingston: McGill-Queen's University Press, 1990), p. 34.

[13] Durant, *The Reformation*, p. 549.

[14] Ibid., p. 570.

[15] Ibid., p. 571.

[16] A.F. Pollard, *Henry VIII*, London, quoted by Durant, *The Reformation*, p. 571.

[17] Andrew Miller, *Short Papers on Church History*, vol. II, "The Crusades to the Reformation," (London: Pickering and Inglis), p. 442.

[18] Durant, *The Reformation*, p. 577 and 574.

[19] Latourette, *A History of Christianity*, vol. 1, pp. 805-806.

[20] Durant, *The Reformation*, p. 572.

[21] Eby and Arrowood, pp. 140-141.

[22] Durant, *The Reformation*, p. 579.

[23] Ibid, p. 580.

[24] Ibid.

[25] Ibid.

[26] Latourette, *A History of Christianity*, p. 808.

[27] A.M. Renwick, *The Story of the Scottish Reformation* (London: Inter-Varsity Fellowship, 1960), p. 58.

[28] Latourette, *A History of Christianity*, p. 808.

[29] Durant, *The Reformation*, p. 597.

[30] Eby and Arrowood, p. 141.

[31] Durant, *The Reformation*, p. 600.

[32] Ibid.

[33] *Encyclopaedia Britannica*, vol. 8 (Chicago: William Benton, Publisher, 1961), p. 362.

[34] Latourette, *A History of Christianity*, p. 810.

[35] Joseph Clayton, *The Protestant Reformation in Great Britain* (London: The Bruce Publishing Company Milwaukee, 1934), p. 129.

[36] C. Leopold Clarke, *The Christian Church and the See of Rome* (London: Protestant Truth Society), p. 172.

[37] *Encyclopaedia Britannica,* vol. 8 (Chicago: William Benton, Publisher, 1961), p. 363.

[38] Ibid.

[39] Renwick, pp. 150-154.

[40] Henry R. Secton, "James VI (of Scotland) and I of England, *The New International Dictionary of the Christian Church*, J.D. Douglas, ed. (Grand Rapids: Zondervan Publishing House, 1974), p. 523.

[41] Clarke, p. 170. The actual reign of Elizabeth I was forty-five years.

[42] Eby and Arrowood, *The Development of Modern Education*, p. 141.

[43] Cubberley, *The History of Education*, pp. 320-321.

[44] Michael Van Cleave Alexander, *The Growth of English Education 1348-1648: A Social and Cultural History* (University Park, PA: The Pennsylvania State University Press, 1990), p. 31.

[45] S.J. Curtis, *History of Education in Great Britain* (London: University Tutorial Press LTD, 1948), p. 66.

[46] Butts, *The Education of the West* (New York: McGraw-Hill Book Company, 1947), pp. 258-259.

[47] Andrew Miller, *Short Papers on Church History*, vol. II, p. 520.

[48] Pierre J. Marique, *History of Christian Education*, vol. II (New York: Fordham University Press, 1926), p. 103. Marique cites F.A. Gasquet, *Henry VIII and the English Monasteries*, vol. II, pp. 323 and 195.

[49] Cubberley, *The History of Education*, pp. 322-323.

[50] A.F. Leach, *The Schools of Medieval England*, (London: Methuen & Co. Ltd., 1915), p. 331.

[51] Curtis, p. 22.

[52] Cubberley, *The History of Education*, p. 323.

[53] Curtis, pp. 51-52.

[54] Butts, p. 260.

[55] Eby and Arrowood, *The Development of Modern Education*, p. 153.

[56] Cubberley, *The History of Education*, p. 324.

[57] Eby and Arrowood, *The Development of Modern Education*, pp. 142-143 and 156.

[58] Harvey J. Graff, *The Legacies of Literacy* (Bloomington and Indianapolis: Indiana University Press, 1987), p. 151.

[59] Curtis, p. 44.

[60] Butts, p. 268.

[61] Leach, pp. 3-6.

[62] Edward D. Towne, "The History of the School 604-1542," *The History of King's School Rochester* (Rochester: The Old Roffensian Society, 1989), pp. 3-4.

[63] The King's School Canterbury Brochure, "Religion," Canterbury, Kent, 1995.

[64] Eby, *The Development of Modern Education*, second edition, p. 133.

[65] Ibid.

[66] L.E. Tanner, *Westminster School* (Country Life, Ltd., 1934), pp. 1-2. Quoted by S.J. Curtis, *History of Education in Great Britain*, p. 36.

[67] Butts, p. 264.

[68] Ibid., p. 263.

[69] Ibid., pp. 264-265.

[70] A.F. Leach, *English Schools at the Reformation* (Westminster: Archibald Constable and Co., 1896), p. 109.

[71] Encyclopaedia Britannica, vol. 11 (Chicago: William Benton, Publisher, 1961), p. 751.

[72] Charles Hoole, *A New Discovery of the Old Art of Teaching School* (Syracuse: Bardeen, 1912), p. 63. Cited by Eby and Arrowood, *The Development of Modern Education*, p. 150.

[73] *Coote's English Schoolmaster* (1596), quoted by Eby and Arrowood, *The Development of Modern Education*, p. 150.

74 Curtis, pp. 104-105.

75 Butts, p. 267.

76 Ibid, p. 268.

77 Eby and Arrowood, *The Development of Modern Education*, p. 142.

78 A.F. Leach, p. 314.

79 Ibid, p. 148.

80 Butts, pp. 270-271.

81 Richard Mulcaster, *Elementarie*, (Oxford: Oxford University Press, 1582), pp. 269-274. Quoted by Eby, *The Development of Modern Education*, second edition, p. 131.

82 Curtis, pp. 105-106.

83 Butts, p. 269.

84 *Encyclopaedia Britannica*, vol. 12 (Chicago: William Benton, Publisher, 1961), pp. 374-375.

85 The Pitkin Guide to "The University City of Oxford" (Hamshire: Pitkin Pictorials, 1991), p. 1.

86 Butts, p. 262.

87 Ibid., pp. 261-262.

88 Mark H. Curtis, *Oxford and Cambridge in Transition, 1558-1642* (Oxford: Clarendon Press, 1959), quoted by Butts, p. 269.

89 Lars P. Qualben, *A History of the Christian Church* (New York: Thomas Nelson and Sons, 1942), p. 323.

90 Royal School, *The Primary History of England* (London: T. Nelson and Sons, 1895), pp. 149-150.

91 Henry Kamen, *The Rise of Toleration* (New York: McGraw Hill Book Company, 1967), p. 161.

92 Eby and Arrowood, *The Development of Modern Education,* p. 153.

93 J.E.G. DeMontmorency, *State Intervention in English Education* (Cambridge: University Press, 1902), p. 82.

94 John Winthrop, quoted by George Malcolm Stephenson, *The Puritan Heritage* (New York: The Macmillan Company, 1952), p. 30.

Illustration Sources

Figure 1   *Royal Emblem* - Photo by author (PBA).

Figure 2   *Henry VIII* - A reading book in history, *Our Kinds and Queens* (London: Thomas Nelson and Sons, 1893), p. 133.

Figure 3   *Edward VI* - Ibid., p. 141.

Figure 4   *Mary Tudor* - Ibid., p. 145.

Figure 5   *Elizabeth I* - Ibid., p. 149.

Figure 6   *Map* - Global Mapping International, Colorado Springs, CO.

Figure 7   *Public Letter Writer* - James Harvey Robinson and Charles A. Beard, *Outlines of European History*, Part II (Boston: Ginn and Company, 1907 and 1918), p. 126.

Figure 8   *Hornbook* - Frederick Eby, *The Development of Modern Education*, Second Edition (New York: Prentice Hall, Inc., 1934), p. 267.

Figure 9   *Title Page* - Ibid, p. 302.

Figure 10 *Cambridge Library* - (PBA).

Figure 11 *Mary Queen of Scots* - Royal School Series (no designated author). *The Primary History of England* (London: Thomas Nelson and Sons, 1895), p. 121.

Figure 12 *Tower of London* - A reading book in history, *Our Kings and Queens* (London: Thomas Nelson and Sons, 1893), p. 124.

Just Who Were the Pilgrims and Puritans?

If life proved difficult for evangelical Christians under England's four Reformation monarchs—Henry VIII, Edward VI, Mary Tudor, and Elizabeth I—it would become even more difficult under the next four kings—James I, Charles I, Charles II, and James II. King James I and his son, Charles I, reigned during the era of the first Pilgrim and Puritan migrations to America, in 1620 and 1630 respectively. Because our study focuses on the development of Christian schools, this chapter will not include the fascinating account of the revolt of Parliament against Charles I,

Figure 1. King James I (1566-1625) was England's monarch during the exodus of the Pilgrims to Holland and America. He commissioned the translation of the well-known King James version of the Bible.

led by Puritan Oliver Cromwell. Nor will we study England's involvement in the complex religious and political events across the English Channel in mainland Europe. Rather, we will attempt to answer the questions, Just who were the Pilgrims and Puritans? and What forces drove them to leave their homeland and set sail for the New World? The divisions of chapter 14 are:

1. *The Hostile Political and Ecclesiastical Environment Faced by England's Evangelical Believers*
2. *The Puritans and Pilgrims Compared*
3. *The Pilgrims and Puritans—Catalysts for Change*

Figure 2. King Charles I (1600-1649), son of King James, was England's monarch during the exodus of the Puritans to America.

It should be noted at the outset that the historical descriptions of King James I, for the most part negative, in no way reflect on the validity or literary beauty of the translation and publication of the King James version of the Bible. Walter Powell offers the following account of how that important translation came into existence:

However despicable the character of James the First may have been, yet he was a scholarly man for the age in which he lived. To him must be given credit for the King James version of the Bible. Objections had been made by some of the leading Puritans to the translation of the Bible then used. They proposed that a new translation should be made. To this proposition the Archbishop and Prelates of the Established Church objected. King James, notwithstanding their opposition, appointed a commission of fifty-four of the most learned men in England to make a new translation. They completed their work and, in 1611, gave to the world this incomparable version of the Bible.[1]

Pressure exerted by the Puritan pastors caused King James to appoint the commission that gave us the King James Bible. As we will learn, the life of King James I did not reflect a knowledge of the Bible that bears his name.

1. The Hostile Political and Ecclesiastical Environment Faced by England's Evangelical Believers

When Queen Elizabeth I died on March 24, 1603, England's monarchy shifted from the Tudor family line to the Stuart line, and Scotland's King James suddenly became king of all England.

KING JAMES I (1566–1625)

King James had been Scotland's monarch since age one. Upon Elizabeth's death, by virtue of his ancestry, he became king of England, Wales, and Ireland as well as Scotland. In May 1604 at age 37, James traveled 400 miles south from Edinburgh to London to assume his expanded duties. The impression he made on Londoners was less than royal. As Francis Dillon says, "His big head, rickety legs, complete lack of personal dignity, and a thick lazy tongue mouthing the coarsest speech gave Londoners a shock."[2] As a child his body had been frail and seemed out of balance. "He was almost seven years old," says D'aubigné, "before he began to run alone."[3]

The King of France once referred to James as the "wisest fool in Christendom."[4] He wore gaudy clothes and a "glittering array of jewels."[5] James Leynse writes:

> Even more than his personal inadequacies, the people disliked him for being pro-Spain. To James I, the King of Spain [Philip II] was the greatest monarch on earth. In spite of his training in Presbyterian theology, James I was a Roman Catholic at heart. It was difficult to determine if their sovereign was Catholic or Protestant. Nonconformity was considered rebellion, so that many well-established Englishmen became poverty-stricken refugees in free Holland.[6]

King James had an intense dislike for the Puritans. During the conference at Hampton Court at which he authorized the translation of the Bible, he said, "I will make [the Puritans] conform [to the Anglican Book of Common Prayer] or I will harry them out of the land, or else do worse."[7] Rudyard Kipling, British author and poet, wrote of James I in these lines:

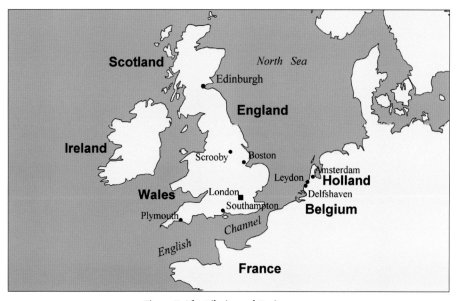

Figure 3. The Pilgrim and Puritan map.

The child of Mary Queen of Scots,
A shifty mother's shiftless son,
Bred up among intrigues and plots,
Learned in all things, wise in none!
Ungainly, babbling, wasteful, weak,
Shrewd, clever, cowardly, pedantic,

. . . .
He wrote that monarchs were divine,
And left a son who proved they weren't!⁸

Years before, when Mary Tudor drove Protestants out of England, many were exiled in Geneva, Frankfort, and Strassburg, where they were influenced by Calvin, Knox, and others. Calvin taught them that "the form of worship should be of the simplest, and that everything that 'savored of Popery' should be eliminated."⁹ On their return during the reign of Elizabeth I, their theology and their styles of worship were incompatible with those of the Church of England, which relished Catholicism's medieval pageantry. The returning Calvinists, on the other hand, referred to the Anglican clerical vestments as "rags of Rome."¹⁰

THE PURITANS OF ENGLAND

England under James I and Charles I inherited the prosperous economy initiated by Queen Elizabeth I. "It was," says Leynse, "an era in which material success was openly pursued."¹¹ Dress among English women became extravagant by most standards and particularly shocking to Puritan minds:

> Costumes were . . . elegant, with slashed sleeves preferred by young women to disclose the silken fabric of their undergarments. They enveloped themselves in a scent of musk, copying the ways of French ladies. They wore a farthingale or hoop to support the back of their dresses, and placed the wire understructure of their farthingales on the floor in a corner of the room before sitting down. Wide ruffs attached to a wire frame around the neck were in fashion, and hair was swept up with artificial wiglets added. . . . Small black beauty patches adorned well-painted faces, and eyes looked out boldly at men through black velvet vizards. Ladies wore high-heeled shoes or heelless Turkish sandals which revealed painted toenails.¹²

Just as shocking to the Puritan mind was the extravagant dress of English men:

> Men of fashion were equally colorful in their attire. A gentleman wore as many as eight rings to match the color scheme of his clothes, and pol-

ished his fingernails pink. Lace jabots decorated his beautifully sewn shirt and a jaunty feather was in his cap. A green plume held by a diamond button was the acme of elegance. The beau used scent bottles which he carried with him, and touched up his curls with an ivory comb. Silken hose covered handsome calves above redheeled shoes. Doublets were brocaded with roses; rosettes decorated silvered shoes.[13]

In contrast, the Puritans were people of common dress. English historian, Lord Macaulay refers to "the ostentatious simplicity of their dress," but concluded that [the Puritans] were "a brave, wise, honest, and useful body."[14] He said, however, that the Puritans were "exposed to the utmost licentiousness of the press and the stage" and "were indeed fair game for the laughers."[15] Professor Stephenson describes their spiritual qualities:

> The Puritan must be born again; he must pray without ceasing; he must refrain from the lusts of the flesh. . . . The Puritan held family devotions, wore plain clothing, and was clean in speech, which was liberally seasoned with scriptural terms. He abhorred the confessional, but kept a diary and daily journal, in which he made dead reckonings of his conduct—an indication of his introspective nature.[16]

In spite of England's royal disdain for the lowly Puritans, their numbers continued to grow, as Nichols describes:

> But Puritanism steadily advanced. This was due partly to general Bible-reading, beginning about 1580 and steadily growing for more than half a century. "England became the people of a book, and that book was the Bible." In that age, when there were no newspapers or magazines, and far fewer books than now, the Bible formed much the larger part of the reading of the people. Because of this, a deep religious and moral earnestness spread in their life. The general spirit of the nation thus became more and more like that of the Puritans.[17]

D'aubigné agrees: "This evangelical spirit possessed great strength among the English people: godly families, lovers of the Bible and of liberty, peopled its cities and its fields."[18]

The Puritans had long been "salt and light" to England in education. Literacy historian Harvey Graff says:

> Puritan strongholds were among the most education-conscious and literate centers in England. In their intense piety and concern about individual access to the Word, Puritans expected their adherents to learn to read. Household and schoolhouse, as well as pulpit and chapel, were centers of schooling. Puritans were for their day a reading people, even if their tastes were often narrow. To an impressive degree, they effected an educational revolution. They also sought to bring their

Word to other corners of the land, and to the colonies they established in North America in the seventeenth century.[19]

The Puritans, like their Protestant counterparts in mainland Europe, created an "educational revolution" in England. Though often persecuted by King James, his son Charles I, and Anglican Archbishop William Laud, they continued to play a significant role in English society, including earning seats in Parliament. And like the Huguenots in France and Holland, their work ethic began to bear fruit in England's business community. Qualben explains:

> The Puritans took a leading part in the economic, industrial, and commercial life of the nation, and eventually amassed great wealth. They became great land-owners, and this admitted them to participation in the affairs of parliament.[20]

Given the positive societal influence of the Puritans, it would appear that the king, the bishop, and the "movers and shakers" of British society should have had, at the very least, a condescending attitude toward them. A closer look, however, at the fundamental beliefs of the English Puritans reveals the underlying source of the crown's animosity:

PURITAN BELIEFS THAT WERE A CONTINUAL SOURCE OF IRRITATION TO THE CROWN

1. Puritans were opposed to the concept of the "divine right of kings" as practiced by the Stuarts in England and by Louis XIV in France.[21] Singer describes the divine right theory:

   > The divine right theory . . . was founded on the belief that the king possessed an absolute grant of authority from God Himself. The king was, therefore, above the law of the land, but at the same time he was directly responsible to God for the welfare of his people, as a father to his family. Thus disobedience to the king was disobedience to God, and therefore sin. This theory of government virtually disappeared in England at the Revolution of 1688–89.[22]

2. In church government, the Puritans opposed the "Act of Supremacy," which established the Anglican Church as the official state church.

3. Puritans believed that Christ, not the king, is the head of the church (the body of Christ).

4. The Puritans believed in a Presbyterian form of church government controlled by a majority vote of representatives at assemblies known as synods.[23] It is understandable, therefore, why Puritans

opposed the Anglican Church government, which included a powerful hierarchy of bishops (including an archbishop and regional bishops) who had at their disposal police and military forces ready to carry out their edicts.[24]

5. Puritans were opposed to such vestiges of Catholicism as continued in the Church of England:

   a. elaborate and costly liturgical garments of the clergy[25] particularly the "surplice," a liturgical scarf regarded by the Puritans as "papistical."[26]

   b. the practice of minimal preaching and much pageantry.

   c. reinstatement of elaborate altars in churches in place of communion tables.[27]

These and other issues greatly concerned those who wanted to "purify" the Church of England.

We shift our focus now to a much smaller segment of the Calvinist community, even more conservative than the main body of Puritans.

THE PILGRIMS

During the reigns of James I and Charles I, the Pilgrims were not known as Pilgrims.[28] They were called Nonconformists, Brownists, Independents, Baptists, Congregationalists, Radicals, and Separatists. More than anything else they were called Separatists—an appropriate name given their stance against the Church of England and their fellow Puritans. We will use the names Pilgrims and Separatists interchangeably. Latourette provides a concise description of the Separatists:

> **Even more radical were the Separatists or Independents. The Puritans wished to remain within the Church of England and to have it cleansed according to their patterns, as the religious wing of the nation's life to which all the queen's subjects would belong. In contrast, the Separatists, or Independents, like the Anabaptists on the Continent, believed in "gathered" churches, not made up of all the inhabitants of a particular area, but only of those who were consciously Christian. They were to be united with one another and with Christ in a covenant. Each congregation so united, with Christ as its head, was a self-governing church which elected its own pastor and other officers after what was believed to be the pattern discernible in the New Testament. No church was to have authority over any other and in each church every member was responsible for the welfare of the whole and of his fellow-members. In theory and to a large extent in practice, such**

churches were pure democracies. They were the spiritual ancestors of the later Congregationalists. They were Separatists in that they withdrew from the Church of England and were Independents in that they believed in the full autonomy of each local church.[29]

Given the political and religious climate in England in the early seventeenth century, and given the beliefs of the Pilgrims, it is not surprising that they found themselves exiled in Holland in 1608.

ROBERT BROWNE (1553–1633)

The new and more conservative strain of Puritanism (the Pilgrims) had its beginning at Cambridge University in the person of Robert Browne, who graduated from Cambridge in 1573. After six years as a teacher, he began preaching in the churches around Cambridge. He claimed that his authority to preach came from independent church congregations and not from the government-sponsored Church of England, represented by the local bishop. His "audacious claim" set in motion the principle of the separation of church and state.[30] It is not known whether his ideas sprang from Anabaptist roots or from Thomas Cartright, a professor at Cambridge University who advocated a similar doctrine. Browne was declared an outlaw by the Anglican Church and escaped to Holland to avoid arrest. While serving as a pastor of an independent church in Holland, he wrote several books that were produced by Dutch printers and sent to England. It was his writings that created the climate for the Separatist movement. Ironically, the Pilgrims disowned Browne because, in his later years, he returned to the Church of England and became a pastor of a parish church.[31] He was called the "Benedict Arnold of ecclesiastical history."[32]

THE SCROOBY CONGREGATION

Three individuals became the spiritual fathers of the Pilgrim Separatist movement: William Brewster, John Robinson, and William Bradford. Brewster and Robinson were "Cambridge University men."[33] Bradford, the son of a wealthy landowner, was a young man during the formative years of the Scrooby congregation in central England. He later became the much beloved governor of the Plymouth Colony in America and authored one of America's most treasured literary documents, *History of the Plimouth Plantation*.[34] As one might suppose, the Separatists were not popular in England. Bradford wrote:

[The Separatists] were hunted and persecuted on every side. . . . For some were taken and clapt up in prison others had their houses besett and watcht night and day, and the most were faine to flie and leave their houses and habitations, and the means of their livelihood.[35]

There were several small Separatist congregations within a ten-mile radius at the confluence of three counties in central England.[36] In 1606, there was a split among these congregations. According to Bradford, "The Separatists in England became 2 distincte bodys or churches, in sundrie townes and vilages, some in Notinghamshire, some of Lincolnshire, and some of Yorkshire."[37] One division of the split, led by Pastor John Smyth, migrated to Amsterdam and formed a new independent church. Many of the Separatists who remained merged with the small congregation at the farming village of Scrooby, located "about half way between London and the Scottish border, approximately in the center of England."[38] Robinson, Brewster, and Bradford became the leaders of the consolidated church,[39] which grew to three hundred members.[40] The congregation met secretly in a large manor house. Built in the fifteenth century by the Catholic Church, the manor house was complete with forty rooms, where "the archbishop and lords of the realm held court on their rare visits ordained by the Papal See."[41] The house was the home of William Brewster by virtue of his position as "Manager of the Post,"[42] or Postmaster, at Scrooby, a position held by his father before him.[43] Thus this former Catholic facility became the birthplace of the Pilgrim church.

Sunday services were held at the Brewster Manor House, "always with a lookout posted to warn of the sheriff's approach."[44] After one year of being terrorized by the bishop's officers, one-third of the Pilgrim congregation voted to leave England and move their families to Holland.[45] William Bradford's description of this momentous decision is amazingly brief: "By a joynte consente they resolved to goe into the low-countries, where they heard was freedome of religion of all men."[46] Edwin Gaustad provides helpful insight into the Pilgrims' dilemma:

> If they stayed in England, they must either compromise their consciences or lose their estates and possibly their lives. If they left England, where could they go?
>
> Holland presented the likeliest option, being only a few miles distant across the English Channel. Also Holland provided a greater measure of religious toleration in the early 1600s than did any other European country.[47]

Bradford points out the hardships the Pilgrims faced once the decision was made:

Figure 4. William Bradford (1589-1657), the youngest of the Pilgrim leaders and second governor of the Plymouth Colony. Bradford wrote the History of Plimouth Plantation, *a historical masterpiece.*

Being now constrained to leave their native soil and country, their lands and livings and all their friends and familiar acquaintances it was much, and thought marvellous by many. But to go into a country they knew not (but by hearsay) where they must learn a new language, and get their living they knew not how, it being a dear place, and subject to the miseries of war it was by many thought an adventure almost desperate, a case intolerable and a misery worse than death. Especially seeing they were not acquainted with trades nor commerce but had only been used to a plain country life and the innocent trade of husbandry.[48]

The Pilgrims assumed that any attempt at a legal emigration would be denied by the authorities. Therefore, late in 1607, they secretly hired a boat to sail from England's Boston harbor to Amsterdam. Unfortunately, the ship's captain betrayed them. Dillon explains:

The ship's captain, like a fair proportion of his fellows in the coastal trade, was a villain, and so too were most of the port petty officials; to them the Pilgrims were mugs it would have been unnatural not to rob. They put them off the ship into small boats and there rifled and ransacked them searching them to their shirts for money. Then, as loyal subjects of the Crown, they turned the wretched people over to the Magistrates, who, Bradford says, used them courteously but kept them imprisoned for a month until they heard from the Privy Council. All but seven, including Brewster, were released and told to go home. The seven were held pending trial, but as no charge was preferred they too were released.[49]

After a winter of being treated as outcasts, they attempted once again to escape to Holland in the spring of 1608. This time they contracted with a Dutch captain. While this attempt ultimately succeeded, their departure suffered nearly as many setbacks as their first venture the previous fall.

AMSTERDAM

The Pilgrim congregation remained only one year in Amsterdam. When they arrived, and not all at the same time, they renewed fellowship with their Separatist friends who, with Pastor John Smyth, had escaped to Amsterdam two years before. The reunion was short-lived, however:

> These Scroobyites did not find their brother Separatists in Amsterdam dwelling in peace and harmony as brothers in Christ. There were contentions and disagreements, not only between the Churches, but between members of the same congregation.[50]

The contentious nature of their Separatist brethren was not the only problem that disturbed the Pilgrims. The city of Amsterdam itself "proved too full of temptations and seductions."[51] In what may be William Bradford's first reference to the Scrooby congregation as "Pilgrims," Bradford wrote, "They knew they were Pilgrims, and looked not much on those things, but lifted up their eyes to heaven, their dearest country, and quieted their spirits."[52]

LEYDEN

In May of 1609 the Pilgrim church moved to Leyden[53] (now Leiden), which lies twenty miles southwest of Amsterdam. Leyden was a smaller city, more suited to the sensitivities of the Pilgrim church. Having come from central England's farming area and being unskilled in the more profitable trades,

> they worked in breweries, brick yards and factories; some became coopers, weavers and dyers. In order to keep the wolf from the door the boys and girls at the earliest age had to be set to work. Bradford says, however, that "at length they came to raise a competente and comfortable living, but with hard and continual labor." Others came to them from England and other places until they had a congregation of about three hundred members.[54]

The Pilgrims remained in Leyden for twelve years. Their hope and prayers were that England would grow tolerant of independent congregations so that they and their families could return to their homeland. Gaustad describes the Pilgrims' longing to return:

> This voluntary exile was assumed to be a temporary one: they would remain in Holland only until England came to its senses, until demands for religious conformity would become less stringent, until England like Holland would grant some measure of toleration to the nonconformist. The Pilgrims waited, then waited some more.[55]

Compared with England and her tyrannical Church of England bishops, Holland had much that appealed to the Pilgrims. The fresh air of religious freedom was exhilarating. In many ways the democratic characteristics of Holland became a model for the democratic institutions carried to New England by the Pilgrims in 1620, and later by waves of exiled Englishmen who migrated from Holland to the colonies. Dillon writes:

> The Dutch Republic was the most solvent state in Europe, and its solid prosperity arose out of the tolerance it had extended to refugees from outside its own frontiers.

> As well as religious toleration the Dutch had established freedom of the press. Most other countries had a strict censorship. Puritan books and pamphlets were burned in England, but freely published in Holland.[56]

While the Pilgrims enjoyed Holland's freedom of religion and liberty of conscience,[57] numerous other aspects of life in the Netherlands caused a growing restlessness among certain members of their congregation. Not the least of their concerns was the negative impact of the Dutch culture on their children. As Clarence Benson observes:

> We err when we say that the Pilgrims came to America seeking religious freedom. To a certain extent they enjoyed that liberty in Holland. It would be more accurate to say that they came to America seeking an opportunity to give to their children the kind of religious education that was impossible either in England or Holland.[58]

William Bradford, in his *History of the Plimouth Plantation*, provided four reasons why the Pilgrims were willing to leave the security of Holland and attempt a voyage to the New World fraught with unbelievable dangers. His list includes:

1. They complained of the hardness of the labor required to earn a living in Holland. He said, "Yea, some preferred and chose the prisons in England rather than this liberty in Holland.[59]
2. Having been in Holland more than a decade, some of the Pilgrims were approaching old age. Bradford wrote: "Old age began to steale on many of them."[60]
3. Clearly, however, the matter that weighed most heavily on them was a concern for their children. Bradford gave as much space to this issue as to the three other issues combined. Under the circumstances there was little opportunity to educate

Pilgrim children, who were required to work long hours in factories to help with family expenses. Bradford said, "their children [were] so oppressed with their hevie labours, that though their minds were free and willing, yet their bodies bowed under the weight of the same, and became becreped in their early youth; the vigor of nature being consumed in the very budd as it were."[61] What was worse, or "more lamentable" as Bradford said, was that the Puritan children were drifting away from their English roots and becoming a part of Dutch society. Powell confirms this:

> They were losing hold upon their children as they grew up. Some married into Dutch families; the boys were becoming soldiers or going to sea; the sports, games, licentiousness and white lights of the Dutch city lured many from the Church.[62]

Any parent, especially a Christian parent, knows the anguish the Pilgrims felt over this distressing problem.

4. Last and "not least,"[63] said Bradford, the Pilgrims were committed to evangelism. Nathaniel Norton, in his *New England Memorial* of 1669, said the Pilgrims had an "inward zeal" for "propagating and advancing the kingdom of Christ."[64] William Bradford, looking ahead somewhat prophetically, referred to the results of their mission to the New World as "stepping-stones, unto others for the performing of so great a work."[65]

An additional motive for the Pilgrims was political. Powell explains:

> Another very serious danger threatened them. In 1609, the Netherlands and Spain, after thirty years of the most bloody and relentless war, agreed upon a truce for twelve years. This truce would expire in 1621, when there was every reason to believe that the war would be renewed, bringing all of its horrors to the people living in Holland. The conditions, therefore, both within and without the Church, were so unsettled, disturbed and dangerous that "those Prudent Governours"—Robinson, Brewster and Bradford, "begane both deeply to apprehend their present dangers, and wisely to foresee [the] future, and think of timely remedy." They concluded therefore, that it was best to remove to some other place.[66]

As Bradford himself said, "[The] Spaniard might prove as cruel as the savages of America, and [the] famine and pestilence as sore here as ther."[67]

On August 1, 1620, thirty-three members of the Pilgrim congregation said farewell to Pastor John Robinson and their fellow church members. They boarded the Speedwell at Delfshaven, a seaport twenty-four miles south of Leyden,[68] for the six-day journey across the English Channel to Southhampton. There, after a series of unfortunate delays, they would board the *Mayflower* for the long journey to the New World.[69]

Ten years later, in March 1630, the Puritans, under the governorship of John Winthrop, set sail from England for New England on board the *Arbella* along with a flotilla of eleven ships and nine hundred passengers, all Puritans. Thus began a new era for Christian school education.

2. The Puritans and Pilgrims Compared

Before we conclude this volume with the coming of the Pilgrims and Puritans to the New World, it will be helpful to draw a brief comparison between these two groups of early Americans. While both were English Calvinists, they were substantially different, as depicted in this chart:

THE PURITANS AND PILGRIMS COMPARED

PURITANS	PILGRIMS
The name *Puritan*, a nickname dating back to the Roman Empire,[70] was widely used as a derogatory term for those within the Church of England who wanted to "purify" England's national church of its Catholic leanings, "and purge the Anglican Church of forms and ceremonies for which there was no warrant in the Bible."[71]	The name *Pilgrim* was not in common use until late in the nineteenth century. We are fortunate to have William Bradford's *History of the Plimouth Plantation*. In that treasured document he referred to the Scrooby congregation as Pilgrims.[72] In their day, the Pilgrims were more likely to be called Separatists and sometimes Brownists. They despised the name Brownists because Robert Browne, one of the early founders of England's independent church congregations, "defected" and returned to the Anglican Church.[73]

PURITANS	PILGRIMS
Among the things the Puritans and the Pilgrims had in common was that Anglican Archbishop William Laud hated both groups. Archbishop Laud, with the assistance of his own police and military forces, had "hanged men and women members of the Puritan and Separatist movement . . . for the crime of choosing their own pastors."[74] He was also known to have clipped the tongues of Calvinist preachers from both groups.[75]	
Puritans were from England's middle and professional classes and were generally well educated. Many Puritan men were graduates of Cambridge University. George Ellis said, "Many of those Puritans were profoundly learned and scholarly men, far surpassing the scholars of our age."[76]	Pilgrims, for the most part, were farmers from central England and were poorly educated with the exception of their leaders, William Brewster and John Robinson, who were "Cambridge men."[77] William Bradford attended evening classes at the university in Leyden and became conversant in Dutch, French, Greek, and Latin. On his own he learned to read the Old Testament in Hebrew.[78]
The Puritans became by far the largest non-Anglican religious group in England.	The Pilgrims, or Separatists, remained "few in number and humble in circumstance."[79]

3. The Pilgrims and Puritans— Catalysts for Change

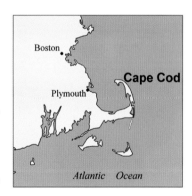

Figure 5. Map of Cape Cod.

When the Pilgrims in 1620 and the Puritans in 1630 left their crowded, sea-battered ships and set foot on the shores of Cape Cod, they had no way of knowing that they were the embodiment of worldwide civil, social, and ecclesiastical change. As their documents attest, they were aware of the essential freedoms so dear to them, but they had no idea that because of them the world would never be the same.

When we left the Pilgrims near the end of the first division of this chapter, they were on board the *Speedwell* en route from the Delfshaven harbor in

Holland to the Southampton harbor in England. As it turned out, the *Speedwell* was improperly named, at least as far as the Pilgrims were concerned. Its hull, "leaky as a sieve,"[80] caused a seven-week delay. Their journey finally got under way, dangerously late, [81] on September 6, 1620. Subsequently, the *Speedwell* had to be abandoned at England's Plymouth harbor and her passengers pressed aboard the already crowded *Mayflower*. Some passengers were left behind for lack of space. It is helpful to observe that the *Mayflower* weighed only slightly more than the steel rudder of England's famous ocean liner, the *Queen Mary*.[82]

Among the hundred and four gallant souls who set out on the historic voyage were the Pilgrims from Holland, several Puritans from London, others who were called "strangers," the ship's crew, and eighteen indentured servants who would work almost as slaves to pay for their passage. Sixty-six days later, on November 11, Captain Jones sailed the *Mayflower* into Cape Cod, one of the great natural harbors on America's east coast.

The arrival of John Winthrop and the first wave of Puritan immigrants to America in 1630 was a much larger and more sophisticated operation than the Plymouth-to-Plymouth voyage of the Pilgrims. As our comparison of the Puritans and the Pilgrims showed, there was a substantial difference in social class, political clout, education, and economic standing between the two

Figure 6. John Winthrop (1588-1649) governor of the Puritans who migrated to the New World.

groups. With reference to the academic superiority of the Puritans in the Massachusetts Bay Colony, Freeman Butts writes:

> The American colonies as a whole may not have been exactly "born free," but the New England colonies were certainly born well educated. . . .
>
> All the evidence seems to point to the fact that the rate of literacy was even higher than in England and the proportion of university graduates was probably higher than in any other society in the world up to that time.[83]

While there were obvious differences between the Puritans and Pilgrims, it is what they had in common that made them "the shining city on a hill" for all the world to see. First and foremost, they loved God, and He was the only sovereign for whom they would die.

Secondly, the Pilgrims, Puritans, and their French counterparts the Huguenots loved freedom and provided the initial stimulus that rendered obsolete the belief that an earthly king has the "divine right" to force subjects to conform to a single religion. The Huguenots laid the foundations for democracy in France. Their struggle culminated in the historic French Revolution that began on July 14, 1787—a revolution that brought about the "complete overthrow of the old order."[84] Across the channel English royalty's worst nightmare was the growing "menace" of the democracy-loving Puritans and Separatists. They advocated a giant shift of power from the monarchy to an elected Parliament. As early as Queen Elizabeth's reign the Separatists advocated "the overthrow of the Church [of England], the suppression of the bishops, and the abolition of the queen's supremacy."[85] At the very time the Pilgrims and Puritans were sailing to the New World, the storm clouds of revolution were gathering in England. It was called "The Great Rebellion" and would lead to the victory of a Puritan-controlled Parliament over the monarchy. The result of that bitter rebellion (1642–52) was a dramatic change of political control and a rapid decline of England's paternalistic government with its system of powerful monarchs, bishops, and nobles. The monarchy continued, its power greatly reduced, as the institution of pageantry and symbolism we see in England today.

Thirdly, the Pilgrims and Puritans were united in their commitment to the spiritual and academic well-being of their children. It can be said that Christian school education, which began with the courageous first-century Christians, continued with the equally courageous founding fathers and mothers of America. Kraushaar says, "Because so many of the colonists had come to these shores in search of religious freedom, schooling devoid of moral and religious content was unthinkable."[86]

CONCLUSION

At the conclusion of this chapter, and of this volume, permit me to answer again the question, Just who were the Pilgrims and Puritans? Their spiritual ancestry is as follows:

1. They were the spiritual descendants of those first-century Christians in Rome who refused to worship an emperor and cared so much for their children that they avoided the local pagan schools

and clandestinely established a system of Christian schools in their homes.

2. The Pilgrims and Puritans were the spiritual descendants of that hardy strain of underground evangelicals who, in their thousand years of existence, were given various names, such as Brethren, Waldensians, Anabaptists, Vaudois, and Walloons. They suffered and often died at the hands of authorities seeking "heretics." They too cherished their children and kept Christian school education alive under circumstances that can only be described as incredible. It was said of them that "the children could read and write, their preachers and leaders possessed portions of the Gospels, and every member received instruction in the Scriptures."87

3 As Englishmen, the Pilgrims and Puritans were indeed spiritual if not ancestral descendants of those two English scholars John Wycliffe and William Tyndale, who became fugitives from Catholic authorities for having translated the Bible into the language of the common people. The Pilgrims and Puritans were indebted to these two men, as we all are, for the King James translation of the Bible—the Bible they carried with them to the New World.

4. The Pilgrims and Puritans were spiritual descendants of no less than John Huss, the Hussites, and later John Comenius and the Pietistic Moravians, who were pioneers and champions of Christian school education throughout eastern Europe.

5. They were, most assuredly, spiritual descendants of Martin Luther, the great reformer from Germany, whose Ninety-five Theses, with their demand for biblical authority, shook the Western world and whose commitment to Christian school education is a legacy to us all.

6. The Pilgrims and Puritans were spiritual descendants of the Lesser Reformers—Philip Melanchthon, Johann Bugenhagen, John Sturm, Martin Bucer, Ulrich Zwingli, and later but not least, August Hermann Francke.

7. As Calvinists, they were most assuredly aware of their spiritual linkage to John Calvin and John Knox, whose patterns of church governance and Christian school organization impacted not only Geneva, Switzerland, and Scotland but also eastern Europe, France, Holland, and through them, the Pilgrims and Puritans, the New World.

This is who the Pilgrims and Puritans were. And the long and rich spiritual ancestry of the Pilgrims and Puritans that began in the first century is the heritage of every true Christian school educator today.

Figure 7. This replica of the Mayflower, *called* Mayflower II, *is anchored in Plymouth, Massachusetts, in sight of Plymouth Rock where the Pilgrims came ashore in 1620.*

Endnotes - Chapter Fourteen

1   Walter A. Powell, *The Pilgrims and Their Religious, Intellectual and Civic Life* (Wilmington, Delaware: Mercantile Printing Company, 1923), p. 33.
2   Francis Dillon, *A Place of Habitation* (London: Hutchinson of London, 1973), p. 80.
3   J.H. Merle D'aubigné, *The Protector: A Vindication* (Edinburgh: Oliver and Boyd, Tweeddale Court, 1847), p. 37.
4   Dillon, p. 80.
5   James P. Leynse, *Preceding the Mayflower* (New York: Fountainhead Publishers, Inc., 1972), p. 39.
6   Ibid., pp. 39-40.
7   Dillon, p. 81.
8   *Rudyard Kipling, A School History of England,* quoted by D. Plooij, *The Pilgrim Fathers* (New York: The New York University Press, 1932), p. 17.
9   Powell, p. 18.
10 Michael Van Cleave Alexander, *The Growth of English Education 1348–1648* (University Park, Pennsylvania: The Pennsylvania State University Press, 1990), p. 161.
11 Leynse, p. 40.
12 Ibid., pp. 40-41.
13 Ibid., p. 41.
14 Thomas Babington Macaulay, "Essay on Milton," *Edinburgh Review* (New York: Doubleday and McClure Co., 1898), pp. 23 and 29.

[15] Ibid., pp. 23-24.

[16] George M. Stephenson, *The Puritan Heritage* (New York: The Macmillan Company, 1952), pp. 15-16.

[17] Robert Hastings Nichols, *The Growth of the Christian Church* (Philadelphia: The Westminster Press, 1945), pp. 227-228.

[18] D'aubigné, p. 31.

[19] Harvey J. Graff, *The Legacies of Literacy* (Bloomington and Indianapolis: Indiana University Press, 1987), pp. 162-163.

[20] Lars P. Qualben, *A History of the Christian Church* (New York: Thomas Nelson and Sons, 1942), p. 326.

[21] Samuel Eliot Morison, *The Intellectual Life of Colonial New England* (Westport, Connecticut: Greenwood Press, Publishers, 1956), p. 22.

[22] C. Greg Singer, "Divine Right of Kings," *The New International Dictionary of the Christian Church* (Grand Rapids: Zondervan Publishing House, 1974), p. 304.

[23] Morison, *The Intellectual Life of Colonial New England,* p. 8.

[24] Leynse, p. 42. Also see Nichols, pp. 266-267.

[25] Ibid.

[26] Alexander, p. 161.

[27] Kenneth Scott Latourette, *A History of Christianity*, vol. 1, (New York: Harper and Row, Publishers, 1953), p. 820.

[28] Leynse, p. 43.

[29] Latourette, p. 815.

[30] Powell, p. 25.

[31] Latourette, p. 816.

[32] Powell, p. 26.

[33] Dillon, p. 82.

[34] *Encyclopaedia Britannica*, vol. 3 (Chicago: William Benton, Publisher, 1961), p. 1003.

[35] William Bradford, *History of Plimouth Plantation: A Condensation* (Boston: compiled by John Wheelwright, 1921), p. 1.

[36] Dillon, p. 85.

[37] Bradford, p. 1.

[38] Leynse, p. 44.

[39] Powell, p. 39.

[40] Leynse, p. 56.

[41] Ibid., p. 44.

[42] Powell, p. 38.

[43] William Deverell, *The Pilgrim and the Anglican Church* (London: Remington & Co. Publishers, 1887), p. 67.

[44] Edwin Scott Gaustad, *A Religious History of America,* revised (New York: Harper Collins Publishers, 1966), p. 52.

[45] Ibid.

[46] Bradford, pp. 1-2.

[47] Graustad, p. 51.

[48] Bradford, quoted by Dillon, p. 89.

[49] Dillon, p. 90.
[50] Powell, pp. 48-49.
[51] Gaustad, p. 52.
[52] Bradford, quoted by Deverell, p. 75.
[53] Dillon, p. 100.
[54] Powell, p. 49.
[55] Gaustad, p. 52.
[56] Dillon, pp. 95-96.
[57] Deverell, p. 77.
[58] Clarence H. Benson, *A Popular History of Christian Education* (Chicago: Moody Press, 1943), p. 100.
[59] Bradford, quoted by Dillon, p. 110.
[60] Bradford, quoted by Wheelwright, p. 7.
[61] Ibid., p. 9.
[62] Powell, p. 53.
[63] Bradford, quoted by Wheelwright, p. 8.
[64] Nathaniel Norton, quoted by Dillon, p. 111.
[65] Bradford, quoted by Wheelwright, p. 8.
[66] Powell, pp. 53-54.
[67] Bradford, quoted by Powell, p. 55.
[68] William Franklin Atwood, *Pilgrim Plymouth Guide* (1921), p. 9.
[69] Powell, p. 66.
[70] Samuel Eliot Morison, *Builders of the Bay Colony* (Boston: Houghton Mifflin Co., 1930), p. 55.
[71] Bradford, quoted by Deverell, p. 75.
[72] Ibid.
[73] Latourette, p. 816.
[74] Leynse, pp. 42-48.
[75] Ibid., p. 42.
[76] George E. Ellis, *Puritan Age and Rule in the Colony of the Massachusetts Bay* (New York: Burt Franklin, 1888), p. 79.
[77] Dillon, p. 82.
[78] Leynse, pp. 197-198.
[79] Lawrence A. Cremin, *American Education: The Colonial Experience 1607–1783* (New York: Harper and Row, Publishers, 1970), p. 151.
[80] William Elliott Griffis, *The Pilgrims in Their Three Homes* (Boston: Houghton Mifflin and Company, 1898), p. 159.
[81] Leynse, p. 246.
[82] Lorraine Sherer and Florence Updegraff, *American Colonial Life,* vol. 1, "Pilgrims and Puritans" (Los Angeles: Los Angeles County Schools, 1937), p. 8.
[83] R. Freeman Butts, *The Education of the West* (New York: McGraw-Hill Book Company, 1947), p. 277.
[84] *Encyclopaedia Britannica,* vol. 9 (Chicago: William Benton, Publisher, 1961), p. 804.
[85] Dillon, p. 75.
[86] Otto F. Kraushaar, "Private Schools: From the Puritans to the Present" (Bloomington, Indiana: The Phi Delta Kappa Educational Foundation, 1976), p. 8.
[87] C.B.Eavey, *History of Christian Education* (Chicago: Moody Press, 1964), p. 115.

Illustration Sources

Figure 1   *James I* - Royal England Readers, *Our Kings and Queens* (London: Thomas Nelson and Sons, 1893), p. 161.

Figure 2   *Charles I* - Ibid., p. 169.

Figure 3   *Map* - Global Mapping International, Colorado Springs, CO.

Figure 4   *William Bradford* - Photo by author (PBA).

Figure 5   *Map of Cape Cod* - Global Mapping International, Colorado Springs, CO.

Figure 6   *John Winthrop* - John Clark Ridpath, *A Popular History of the United States of America* (New York: Nelson and Phillips, 1876), p. 127.

Figure 7   *Mayflower II* - (PBA).

Selected Bibliography

Atkinson, James. "Reform," *Introduction to the History of Christianity*, Tim Dowley, ed. Minneapolis: Fortress Press, 1995.

Babel, Henry. "Ulrich Zwingli," *Men—An Idea: The Reformation.* Geneva: Foundation of Les Clefs de Saint-Pierre, 1985.

Baird, Henry Mortyn. *The Huguenots and the Revocation of the Edict of Nantes*, vol. 2. New York: Charles Scribner's Sons, 1895.

Barnard, Henry. *German Teachers and Educators.* Hartford: Brown and Gross, 1878.

Beard, Charles. *Martin Luther and the Reformation in Germany.* London: K. Paul, Trench, Trübner, & Co., 1889.

Benson, Clarence H. *A Popular History of Christian Education.* Chicago: Moody Press, 1943.

Blackmar, Frank W. *History of Human Society.* New York: Charles Scribner's Sons, 1926.

Boettner, Loraine. *Roman Catholicism.* Philadelphia: The Presbyterian and Reformed Publishing Company, 1962.

Boyd, William and Edmond J. King. *The History of Western Education.* London: Adam and Charles Black, 1921.

Bradford, William. *History of Plimouth Plantation, A Condensation.* Boston: compiled by John Wheelwright, 1921.

Brockett, Linas. *History and Progress of Education from the Earliest Times to the Present.* New York: A.S. Barnes and Burr, 1860.

Buisseret, David. *Huguenots and Papists.* London: Ginn and Company, 1972.

Butts, R. Freeman. *The Education of the West.* New York: McGraw-Hill Book Co., 1947.

Calvin, J. Bonnet. *Letters of John Calvin*, vol. 2. Philadelphia: Presbyterian Board of Publications, 1858.

Campbell, W.E. *Erasmus, Tyndale and More.* London: Eyre and Spottiswoode, 1949.

Clarke, C. Leopold. *The Christian Church and the See of Rome.* London: Protestant Truth Society, n.d.

Claude, Jean. *A Short Account of the Complaints and Cruel Persecutions of the Protestants in the Kingdom of France.* London: printed by W. Redmayne, 1707.

Clayton, Joseph. *The Protestant Reformation in Great Britain.* London: The Bruce Publishing Company, 1934.

Compayré, Gabriel. *The History of Pedagogy.* Boston: D.C. Heath and Company, 1885.

Cook, T.G. *The History of Education in Europe.* London: Methuen & Co. Ltd., 1974.

Cooke, Robert L. *Philosophy, Education and Certainty.* Grand Rapids: Zondervan Publishing House, 1960.

Cremin, Lawrence A. *American Education—The Colonial Experience 1607–1783.* New York: Harper and Row, Publishers, 1970.

Cubberley, Ellwood P. *The History of Education.* Cambridge, Massachusetts: The Riverside Press, 1920.

_____. *Readings in the History of Education.* Boston: The Riverside Press, 1920.

_____. *Public Education in the United States.* Boston: Houghton Mifflin Company, 1919.

Curtis, Mark H. *Oxford and Cambridge in Transition, 1558–1642.* Oxford: Clarendon Press, 1959.

Curtis, S.J. *History of Education in Great Britain.* London: University Tutorial Press Ltd, 1948.

De Felice, G. *History of the Protestants of France.* London: George Routledge & Co., 1853.

DeJong, Peter Y. "Calvin's Contribution to Christian Education," *Calvin's Theological Journal*, vol. 2, no. 1, November 1967.

DeMontmorency, J.E.G. *State Intervention in English Education.* Cambridge: University Press, 1902.

Deverell, William. *The Pilgrim and the Anglican Church.* London: Remington & Co. Publishers, 1887.

Dillon, Francis A. *Place of Habitation.* London: Hutchinson of London, 1973.

Duffield, G.E. *The Work of William Tyndale.* Appleford, Berkshire, England: The Sutton Courtenay Press, 1964.

Dunshee, Henry W. *History of the School of the Collegiate Reformed Dutch Church.* New York: Aldine Press, 1883.

Durance, George M. *From Brethren to Humanists.* Master's Thesis, The University of Calgary, 1978.

Durant, Will. *Caesar and Christ.* New York: Simon and Schuster, 1944.

_____. *The Reformation.* New York: Simon and Schuster, 1947.

Eavey, C.B. *History of Christian Education.* Chicago: Moody Press, 1964.

Eby, Frederick. *Early Protestant Educators.* New York: McGraw-Hill Book Company, Inc., 1931.

Eby, Frederick and Charles Flinn Arrowood. *The History and Philosophy of Education Ancient and Medieval.* New York Prentice-Hall, Inc., 1940.

Ellis, George E. *Puritan Age and Rule in the Colony of the Massachusetts Bay.* New York: Burt Franklin, 1888.

Foxe, John. "Actes and Monumentes," *Foxe's Book of Martyrs.* London: John Daym, 1563.

Gangel, Kenneth O. and Warren S. Benson. *Christian Education: Its History and Philosophy.* Chicago: Moody Press, 1983.

Gaustad, Edwin Scott. *A Religious History of America*, Revised. New York: Harper Collins Publishers, 1966.

Godkin, James. *The Religious History of Ireland.* London: Henry S. King & Co., 1873.

Good, H.G. *A History of Western Education.* New York: The Macmillan Company, 1960.

Graff, Henry J. *The Legacies of Literacy.* Bloomington: Indiana University Press, 1987.

Griffis, William Elliott. *The Pilgrims in Their Three Homes.* Boston: Houghton Mifflin and Company, 1898.

Hamilton, J. Taylor and Kenneth G. Hamilton. *History of the Moravian Church.* Winston-Salem, NC: Interprovincial Board of Christian Education, Moravian Church of America, 1967.

Harnack, Adolf. *The Mission and Expansion of Christianity in the First Three Centuries.* New York: G.P. Putnam and Sons, 1908.

Heath, Richard. *The Reformation in France.* London: The Religious Tract Society, 1886.

Helmreich, Ernst. *Christian Religious Education in German Schools.* Cambridge, MA: Harvard University Press, 1959.

James, E.O. *In the Fullness of Time.* New York: The Macmillan Company, 1935.

Keatinge, M.W. *The Great Didactic of John Amos Comenius.* London: Adam and Charles Black, 1896.

Kirk, J. "Scottish Reformation," *Dictionary of Scottish Church History and Theology.* Edinburgh: T & T Clark, 1993.

Kittelson, James M. "Luther the Educational Reformer," *Luther and Learning*, Marilyn J. Harran, ed., The Wittenberg University Symposium London: Associated University Press, 1985.

Knight, Edgar W. *Twenty Centuries of Education.* Boston: Ginn and Company, 1940.

Knox, John. *The History of the Reformation of Religion in Scotland*, Twentieth Century Edition. London: Andrew Melrose, 1905.

Köstlin, J. "Martin Luther," *Encyclopaedia of Living Divines*, vol. 2, ed. by Philip Schaff. Toronto: Funk and Wagnalls Company, 1891.

Lambert, George. *The Huguenots.* Canterbury: A paper read before the directors of the French Protestant Hospital, July 16, 1884.

Latourette, Kenneth Scott. *A History of Christianity*, vol. 1. New York: Harper and Row, Publishers, 1953.

_____. *Christianity Through the Ages.* New York: Harper Chapel Book. Harper and Row Publishers, 1965.

Leach, Arthur F. *The Schools of Medieval England.* London: Methuen and Co. Ltd. 1916.

_____. *English Schools at the Reformation.* Westminster: Archibald Constable and Co. 1896.

Lewis, W.H. *The Splendid Century* London: William Morrow & Co. 1953.

Leynse, James P. *Preceding the Mayflower.* New York: Fountainhead Publishers, Inc., 1972.

Lindsay, Thomas M. *A History of the Reformation*. Edinburgh, T. and T. Clark, 1906.

Lockerbie, D. Bruce. *A Passion for Learning*. Chicago: Moody Press, 1994.

Lorimer, John G. *The Protestant Church of France*. Philadelphia: Presbyterian Board of Education, 1842.

Luther, Martin. Translated by C.M. Jones, and H.J. Grinn, *Martin Luther's Ninety-five Theses*, Kurt Aland, ed. St. Louis: Concordia Publishing House, 1967.

Lutzer, Erwin W. *Hitler's Cross*. Chicago: Moody Press, 1995.

Macmullen, Ramsay. *Constantine*. London: Groom Helm, 1969.

Marique, Pierre J. *History of Christian Education*, vol. 3. New York: Fordham University Press, 1932.

Marsden, George M. *The Soul of the American University: From Protestant Establishment to Established Nonbelief*. New York: Oxford University Press, 1994.

Martyn, W. Carlos. *A History of the Huguenots*. New York: The American Tract Society, 1866.

Mayer, Frederick. *A History of Educational Thought*. Columbus, Ohio: Charles E. Merrill Books, Inc., 1960.

McGrath, Alister E. *The Life of John Calvin*. Cambridge, MA: Blackwell Publishers Inc. 1990.

Miller, Andrew. *Miller's Church History*, vol. 2. London: Pickering and Inglis, 1924.

_____. *Short Papers on Church History*, vol. 2, "The Crusades to the Reformation." London: Pickering and Inglis, n.d.

Morison, Samuel Eliot. *The Intellectual Life of Colonial New England*. Westport, Connecticut: Greenwood Press, Publishers, 1956.

_____. *Builders of the Bay Colony*. Boston: Houghton Mifflin Co., 1930.

Motley, John Lothrop. *The United Netherlands*, vol. 4. New York: Harper and Brothers, 1867.

Nichols, Robert Hastings. *The Growth of the Christian Church*. Philadelphia: The Westminster Press, 1945.

O'Donnell, F. Hugh. *The Ruin of Education in Ireland*. London: David Nutt, 1902.

Painter, F.V.N. *A History of Education*. New York: D. Appleton and Company, 1905.

Parkyn, Robert. "Reformation Revoked Transubstantiation," *The English Historical Review*, vol. 62. London: Longmans, Green and Co. , 1947.

Plooij, D. *The Pilgrim Fathers*. New York: The New York University Press, 1932.

Powell, Walter A. *The Pilgrims and Their Religious, Intellectual and Civic Life*. Wilmington, Delaware: Mercantile Printing Company, 1923.

Qualben, Lars P. *A History of the Christian Church*. New York: Thomas Nelson and Sons, 1942.

Randell, Keith. *Luther and the German Reformation*. London: Edward Arnold, A Division of Hodder and Stoughton, 1988.

Rashdall, H. *The Universities of Europe in the Middle Ages*, vol. 2, part 1. Oxford: 1895.

Reed, James and Ronnie Prevost. *A History of Christian Education*. Nashville: Broadman and Holman Publishers, 1993.

Renwick, A.M. *The Story of the Scottish Reformation*. London: Inter-Varsity Fellowship, 1960.

Rican, Rudolf. *The History of the Unity of the Brethren*. (A Protestant Hussite Church in Bohemia and Moravia). Trans. by Danie Crews. Winston-Salem, NC: The Moravian Church in America, 1992.

Robinson, James Harvey and Charles A. Beard, *Outlines of European History*, part 2. Boston: Ginn and Company, 1907.

Roche, O.I.A. *The Days of the Upright*. New York: Clarkson N. Potter, Inc. Publisher, 1965.

Royal School Series. *The Primary History of England*. London: T. Nelson and Sons, 1895.

Schaeffer, Francis A. *How Should We Then Live?* Old Tappan, New Jersey: Fleming H. Revell, Company, 1976.

Sencourt, Robert. *The Genius of the Vatican*. London: Jonathan Cape Ltd., 1935.

Sherrill, Lewis Joseph. *The Rise of Christian Education*. New York: The Macmillan Co. 1944.

Smart, James E. *The Teaching Ministry of the Church*. Philadelphia: Westminster Press, 1964.

Smiles, Samuel. *The Huguenots.* New York: Harper and Brothers, Publishers, 1868.

Stephens, W.P. *The Holy Spirit in the Theology of Martin Bucer.* New York: Cambridge University Press, 1970.

Stephenson, George Malcolm. *The Puritan Heritage.* New York: The Macmillan Company, 1952.

Strauss, Gerald. *Luther's House of Learning.* Baltimore: The Johns Hopkins University Press, 1978.

Sutherland, N.M. *The Huguenot Struggle for Recognition.* New Haven: Yale University Press, 1980.

Swindoll, Charles R. *The Finishing Touch.* Dallas: Word Publishing, 1994.

Towns, Elmer. *A History of Religious Educators.* Grand Rapids: Baker Book House, 1975.

Ulich, Robert. *A History of Religious Education.* New York: New York University Press, 1968.

_____. *Three Thousand Years of Educational Wisdom: Selections from Great Documents.* Cambridge, MA: Harvard University Press, 1965.

Ullmann, W. "A Medieval Document on Papal Theories of Government," *The English Historical Review*, vol. 61, 1946.

Vander Walt, J.L. *The Schools That Calvin Established in 1559.* Transvaal, Republic of South Africa: Institute for Reformational Studies, 1984.

Wand, J.W.C. *A History of the Early Church to AD 500.* London: Methuen & Co. LTD, 1937.

West, Andrew Fleming. *Alcuin and the Rise of the Christian Schools.* New York: Charles Scribner's Sons, 1920.

Wilds, Elmer Harrison. *The Foundations of Modern Education.* New York: Rinehart and Co. Inc., 1936, 1971.

Index

Aachen, 62, 70, 77, 87, 88, 127
Abelard, Peter, 98, 99
Academy of Plato, 17
Act of Supremacy, 338, 362
Act of Uniformity, 339
Adrian IV, Pope, 122
Aelfric's "Colloquy," 77
Aesop's fables, 194
"after the darkness, light," 224
Alcuin, 66, 70-72
Alfred the Great, 76
Allen, William, Cardinal, 337
Anabaptists, 79, 143, 205, 302, 309-10, 353, 374
Anglicanism, 339
Anti-Lutheran Six Articles, 335
Arabic numerals, 101
Arbella, 370
Aristotle, 12, 19, 66, 93-95, 104-05, 108, 190, 246
Artemis Orthia, 12
Athens, 13, 77
Attica, 13
Augustine of Canterbury, 64-65
Augustine of Hippo, 4, 24, 92, 105
Augustus, Philip, King of France, 121
Avignon Schism, 126-28

Babylonian exile, 28
"Babylonian Captivity," 126
Baghdad, 101
Baptists, 353, 363
Bardic Literary Societies, 69
bardic schools, 68
Beth Hassepher, 28
Beth-sepher, 29
Beza, Theodore, 220, 223
bilingual education, 25
Black Death, plague of 1349, 85, 90
Bodleian Library, 107
Bonaparte, Napoleon, 289-90
Boniface VII, Pope, 78
Boleyn, Anne, 337
Bradford, William, 364, 366, 369
Brethren, 374

Brethren of the Common Life, 110, 187-89, 199, 219, 305
Brewster, William, 364, 369
Browne, Robert, 364
Brownists, 353, 363
Bucer, Martin, 163, 243, 257, 374
Bugenhagen, Johann, 174-75, 243, 251, 254, 374
Byzantine Empire, 60

Calvin, Gerard, 212
Calvin, John, 96, 211, 223, 225, 230, 243, 273, 305, 360, 374
Calvinism, 212, 353
Calvin's chair, 237
Calvin's Seven Levels of Instruction, 233
Cambridge University, 101, 103, 350-51, 364
canon law, 160
Canstein Bible House, 321
Cape Cod, 371-72
Carlstadt, 165
Cartright, Thomas, 364
Catacombs, 39, 40
catechetical schools, 77
catechisms, 197, 230
cathedral schools, 66, 72, 98, 99
Catherine of Aragon, 333, 336
Catholic high schools, 285
Catholic universities, 85, 92, 107
Cato, Marcus, 22
Celtic Christianity, 69
Charlemagne, 61-62, 70, 72, 76, 87
Charles I, King, 358, 360, 362
Charles V, Holy Roman Emperor, 145, 160, 165, 272, 277, 300, 302-03
Chartres Cathedral, 100
Children's Crusade, 89
chivalric education, 73
Christian Education of Boys (first treatise on Christian school education), 259
Christian high schools, 282
Christian schools, 1, 6, 35, 37, 40-42, 141, 143, 167, 169, 172-74, 177, 185, 218, 220, 230, 281, 290, 299, 300, 304-06, 309-11, 316, 319, 322, 325, 353, 374

Chrysostom, John, 40, 134
Church of England, 333, 342, 344, 364
church-school survey, 173
Cicero, 5, 7, 26, 257
curricular innovations, 189
Claude, Jean, 289
Colbert, 272
Coligny, Admiral, 276
College of Herborn, 312
Colosseum in Rome, 39, 91
Columbus, 106
Comenius, John Amos, 311-12, 325
compulsory school attendance, 176, 229
Condè, Prince, 276
Congregationalists, 363
consensus truth-making, 94, 96
Constance, 128, 139
Constantine, Emperor, 42, 44, 47-49, 51, 61
Constantinople, 35, 44, 47-48, 60, 80
Copernicus, Nicholas, 203
copyists, 72
Council of Constance, 130, 141
Council of Trent, 59, 112, 302
Council of troubles, 304
Council of Valencia, 58
Council of Vienna, 59
Counter-Reformation, 299-302, 305, 324-25
Cromwell, Oliver, 357
crusades, 75, 78, 85-86, 88, 91-92
custos, 22

Dark Ages, 55, 73, 77, 79
"Death to the Heretics" campaign, 268
Debrecen Christian School, 164
Delfshaven, 370
democracy, 10
discipline, Luther on, 196
Disraeli, Benjamin, 199
divine right of kings, 362
"Doctor of the Gospel," 162
Dominicans, 159
dragoons, 289
Druids, 68
Dutch Reformed Church, 306
"Dye or be Catholick," 269, 302

ecclesiastical education, 66, 85, 91, 341
ecclesiastical properties, 171, 309
ecclesiastical wealth, 125
Eck, Johann, 161
Edict of Milan, 42
Edict of Nantes, 280, 286-89
educational reformer, Luther as, 154, 168
Edward VI, King, 217, 333-34, 336, 338, 357
Elagabalus, Emperor, 45
elementary education, 194, 221, 304, 347
Elizabeth I, Queen, 333, 337-38, 351-52, 357, 360, 373
England's crown jewels, 337
England's "Great Public Schools," 344
England's "public" schools, 343
Erasmus, Desiderius, 90, 96, 108, 110-11, 143, 145, 170, 340
Euclid, 19

Farel, Guillaume, 214, 223, 225, 267
Ferdinand, 333
feudalism, 73
"First Blast of the Trumpet...," 229
First Book of Discipline, The, 227, 238
"first general charter on education," 71-72
Francis I, King of France, 272
Francke, August Hermann, 318-20, 325, 374
Francke's Treatise on Christian Education, 320
Frederick the Great, King, 323, 325
Frederick, William I, King, 320-322, 325
French Protestants, 265, 271
French Revolution, 373

Galerius, Emperor, 42
galley slave, 217, 288
Gamala, Joshua ben, 29
Geneva, 214, 273
Geneva Academy, 219-21, 281
German Lutheran schools, 318
Glaucha village, 319
Golden Age of Greece, 13
golden rose, 332
Gospellers (Huguenots), 265
Great Didactic of Comenius, The, 312, 315
Great Schism, 55, 79

great usurpation, 340
Greek alphabet, 9
Gregory, Pope, 41, 51, 55, 63
Groote, Gerhard, 110, 188
guaranteed livings, 169
Gutenberg, Johann, 144, 155
Gutenberg press, 155
gymnastic school, 15

Hadrian, 1,
Hamilton, Patrick, 216
Harvard University, 320
hazzan, 29
Hecker, Johann Julius, 322-24
Heidelberg Catechism, 306
Henry IV, King of France, 277, 281, 287-88
Henry VIII, King, 145, 331-32, 340-41, 344,
    352, 357
heretics, heresy, 56, 78-79, 90, 105, 119, 128,
    132, 133-34, 136, 146, 164, 180, 266, 269,
    274, 285, 303
Hindus, 101
History of the Plimouth Plantation, 364, 368
Hitler, Adolf, 206, 324
Holland's Christian schools, 307
Holy Roman Empire, 61-62, 85-87, 101, 117, 127
Homer, 26
hornbook, 254, 347
Hotel de Ville, 288
Huguenots, 265, 269, 277-78, 280, 286,
    339, 373
humanism, 93, 106, 190, 243, 246, 320,
    340, 350
Hundred Years' War, The, 123
Huss, John, 96, 128-29, 136, 139-40, 243,
    311, 374
Hussites, 79, 142-43, 186, 311, 374
hymn singing, 179

Ignatius, 4
imperial patronage of schooling, 26
incident of the placards, 274
incident of the statues, 275
Index of Forbidden Books, 58, 91, 105
indulgences, 57, 119, 137, 156-57

Innocent III, Pope, 80, 118-20, 122, 132
Inns of Court, 350
Inquisition, 132-34
Inquisitors General, 133
Institutes, The, 214
interdict, by Pope Innocent III, 120
Ireland, 68, 122
Irens, 13
Irish education, 68
Isabella, 333

James I, King, 338, 352, 357-360, 362
Jerome, 5, 56, 71, 109
Jerome of Prague, 239, 141
Jerusalem, 1, 5, 27-28, 66, 75, 77, 85-86, 88-89
Jesuit high schools, 300
Jesuits, 57, 272, 283, 285-86, 288, 300, 303
Jesus, 1, 27, 93, 119
Jewish Temple, 89
Jews, 205-06, 292
John, King, 120, 157, 332
Josephus, 6
"Junker George" (Luther), 163
Jupiter, 1-2
justification by faith, 178
Justinian, Emperor, 35-36

King James Bible, 143, 338, 358, 374
King's School of Canterbury, 65, 343
King's School of Rochester, 65, 343
Kipling, Rudyard, 359
knighthood, 74-75
Knox, John, 171, 211, 215, 223, 225-26, 238,
    336, 360, 374

laconic wit, 12
language study, 200
Lateran Council, 118, 132
Latin, 25, 200, 246, 251
Latin grammar schools, 347-49
Laud, William, Archbishop, 362, 371
lectio devinia, 6
Lefèvre, Jacqües, 266
Leo III, Pope, 61, 77, 87

Leo X, Pope, 157, 160
letters school, 15
Levitical law, 3
Leyden, 367
liberal arts, Aristotle, 66
libraries, 204
Lily's Grammar, 348
Lollards, 79, 138, 141, 143
Lords of the Congregation, 218, 226
Louis XIV, of France, 271, 280, 288-89, 292,
   299, 317, 362
Louvre, 279
Loyola, Ignatius, 284
Luther, Martin, 55, 78, 88, 95-96, 103, 110-11,
   117, 119, 136, 141, 143-45, 152, 159, 185,
   213, 225, 243, 246, 374
Lutherans, 353
Lutherplatz, 191
Luther's broadsides on education, 176
Luther's Works, 230
Lyceum of Aristotle, 17

Macedonians, 20
Magna Carta, 120, 334
Mann, Horace, 174
Marburg Colloquy, 261
Marburg University, 169
Martyr, Justin, 4, 39
martyr's school, 37-38
Mary Stuart, or "Mary Queen of Scots," 338,
   352, 360
Mary Tudor, Queen, "Bloody Mary," 217, 333,
   336, 352, 357
Mayflower, 370, 372, 375
Maximilian, Emperor, 159
medieval castles, 74
Melanchthon, Philip, 174, 179, 187, 194, 205,
   243-45, 374
Menander, 19
Mennonite schools, 309
Mennonites, 142, 310, 353
Mezotur Christian School, 164
Middle Ages, 55, 57-58, 72, 78-79, 85, 106,
   117, 119, 126, 163, 169, 243, 341
Mohammed, 86
monastery, 75, 137
monastic schools, 66, 97, 164

Moravians, 142-43, 304, 311, 353
More, Thomas, 340
"Morning Star of the Reformation, The," 137
Motley, John, 309
music, 196
music school, 15
Muslims, 86, 93
natural science, 203
Nero, Emperor, 37-38
Nicene Creed, 49
Ninety-five Theses, 153, 155-56, 158-59, 374
Noncomformists, 363
Notre Dame, 98-99, 274, 279

Octavian, Emperor, 45
Odoacer, General, 44, 60
Orthodox Churches, 80
Oxford University, 101, 137, 143, 350

pagan education (schools), 35-36
palace schools, 66-67, 76-77
Palestine, 6, 28, 86-87
papal bull, *Exsurge Domine*, 160
papal power, 120
papal tithes and taxes, 124
pardon sellers, 77
parish schools, 99
Parthenon, 14, 20
pedagogue, 14-16
Pentateuch, 29
Pericles, 18
Peter the Hermit, 86, 87
Petronius, 2
petty schools, 346
Philip II, King of France, 121, 123
Philip II, King of Spain, 300, 303-304, 309, 359
Pietism, 311, 317-18, 321, 324
Pietist schools, 310
Pilgrims, 339, 345, 353, 357, 363, 367-68, 370-
   71, 373-74
placards, 274, 303
Plato, 15, 17-18, 95, 101
Plutarch, 11, 12, 13
Plymouth, 372
Plymouth-to-Plymouth, 372
politically correct, 103, 195, 199, 250
Polycarp, 4

Praise of Folly, The, 109
Presbyterians, 353
private English schools, 349
private schools in Rome, 22
private tutors, 22, 346
Protagoras, 15
Protestant army, 276
Prussia, 174
Prussian school plan, 323
public schools, 26-27, 36
purgatory, 137, 140
Puritans, 339, 345, 351, 353, 357, 360, 361-62, 370-71, 373-74

quadrivium, 67, 315
Quakers, 353
Quintilian, Marcus Fabius, 23, 25

rabbinical school, 30-31
Ramus, Peter, 246
rationalistic education, 310
reading and writing schools, 252
Reformation, 85, 95, 111-12, 119, 125, 127, 147, 152, 163, 243
Reformation of the Reformation, 310, 318, 324
Reformers Wall, 223, 226
Renaissance, 23, 95, 98, 104, 243, 250, 333, 337
Republic of Geneva, The, 223
Robinson, John, 364, 369-70
Rome, 77
Romulus, Augustus, Emperor, 44, 60

safe conduct, 140, 161
St Bartholomew's Day Massacre, 270, 277
St Columba, 70
St George School, 199
St Giles Cathedral, Edinburgh, 218-19
St Patrick, 69
St Peter's Basilica, 48, 57, 62, 78, 157
St Peter's Cathedral, 215
St Thomas Aquinas, 56, 90, 93-95, 98, 105
Saxony school plan, 175, 246, 247
scholastic guilds, 75, 100
Scholasticism, 93, 94
school of rhetoric (Rome), 21
School of St George, 190

School Ordinance of Brunswick, 253
schoolmasters, 172, 238, 291, 307, 319, 352
schoolmistresses, 291
Scotland, 70
Scottish school plan, 228
Scrooby, 365
Scrooby congregation, 364
Scroobyites, 367
secondary schools, 100, 187, 199, 282, 284, 304
Separatists, 353, 363, 373
Seven Liberal Arts, 17, 66, 96, 98, 105, 108
Shetach, Simon ben, 28
Sigismund, Emperor, 140
simony, 129, 140
Slave(ry), 10-11, 13, 16, 22, 30, 44
Smyth, John, 365
Socrates, 18, 95, 99
song schools, 65-67
Sparta, 10-11, 17
Spartan conditions, 11
Spartan education, 11
Speedwell, 370-72
Spener, Philip, 317
"state nurse" and "state's child" (Sparta), 11
Staupitz, John, 191
Sturm, Johannes, 187, 219, 243, 255, 374
Sturm's curriculum outline, 255-57
synagogues, 28
Synod of Dort, 306

Talmud, 30
teacher training, 206
Tertullian, 1, 4-5, 38, 79
Tetzel, Johann, 158
textbooks, 314
Theodosius, Emperor, 35-36, 56, 132
Theodosius II, Emperor, 47
"Third University of England," 350-51
Thirty Years' War, 301, 304-05, 310, 312, 316
three popes, 126, 128
"Thundering Scott, The," 226
Titus, 1
Torah, 28
Tower of London, 138
"town and gown conflict," 103
trade schools, 89
transubstantiation, 335

Trinity Church, Berlin, 322
trivium, 67, 315
tuition, 175
Turks, Islamic, 60, 78, 85, 87-88
Twelve Tables, law of the, 21
Tyndale, William, 136-37, 143, 145-46, 243, 374

"underground railroad," of the Huguenots, 291
Unity of the Brethren, 311-12
University of Athens, 36
University of Bologna, 102, 109
University of Erfurt, 190, 192, 318
University of Geneva, 221
University of Halle, 319
University of Leyden, 305, 307
University of Paris, 102-03, 105, 108, 112, 130, 137, 213, 267
University of Prague, 128, 139
University of St. Andrews, 215
University of Salerno, 102
university towns, 106
Urban II, Pope, 87
Ursuline Schools for girls, 283

Vallière, Jean, 268
Vatican, 89, 101, 117, 122
Vaudois, 79, 266, 374
Vergil, 5
Vespasian, 1

Vicar of Christ, 80, 119, 286
Vienna, 129
Viking invasions, 70, 75-76
Virgin Queen, 338
Von Bora, Catherine "Katy," 165, 202
Vulgate Bible, 137, 179

Wales, 337, 358
Waldensians, 58, 78-79, 141-43, 266, 374
Walloons, 302, 374
Wartburg Castle, 162
Warwick Castle, 74
William of Orange, Prince, 307, 325
Winthrop, John, 353, 372
Wishart, George, 216
Wittenberg, 142, 153, 163
Wittenberg, University, 144, 160, 164, 166, 174-75, 192, 244
Worms, 144, 160-61
Wycliffe, John, 96, 136-38, 243, 374

Xavier, Francis, 285

Yahweh, 29
Year of Jubilee, 124
York Cathedral School, 66

Zwingli, Ulrich, 96, 243, 258, 374
Zwingli's *Christian Education of Boys*, 259